James J. Corbett

James J. Corbett

*A Biography of the
Heavyweight Boxing Champion
and Popular Theater Headliner*

ARMOND FIELDS

McFarland & Company, Inc., Publishers
Jefferson, North Carolina, and London

ALSO BY ARMOND FIELDS AND FROM MCFARLAND

Eddie Foy: A Biography of the Early Popular Stage Comedian (1999)

Lillian Russell: A Biography of "America's Beauty" (1999)

Frontispiece: *James J. Corbett, heavyweight boxing champion of the world and actor; at age 30, an entertainment idol (California Historical Society, FN-31469)*

Library of Congress Cataloguing-in-Publication Data

Fields, Armond 1930–
    James J. Corbett: a biography of the heavyweight boxing
champion and popular theater headliner / Armond Fields.
      p.   cm.
    Includes bibliographical references and index.

    ISBN-13: 978-0-7864-0909-9
    (softcover binding : 50# alkaline paper) ☻

    1. Corbett, James J., 1866–1933.   2. Boxers (Sports)—United
States—Biography. I. Title.
GV1132.C7F47   2001
796.83'092—dc21
[B]   00-66452

British Library Cataloguing data are available

On the cover: A popular photographic pose of James J. Corbett, taken immediately after he had won the heavyweight championship in 1892.

Manufactured in the United States of America

McFarland & Company, Inc., Publishers
  Box 611, Jefferson, North Carolina 28640
    www.mcfarlandpub.com

CONTENTS

PREFACE

Throughout the years that James J. Corbett reigned as heavyweight boxing champion and a celebrated vaudeville star, he adamantly refused to allow managers and publicists to employ the nickname "Gentleman Jim." He believed the sobriquet to be demeaning.

When he became a silent film idol, motion picture publicity people unceremoniously advanced the "Gentleman Jim" moniker as the best technique to advertise and promote his pictures. Unfortunately for Corbett, he was unable to restrain them. In 1941, eight years after his death, Warner Bros. released a highly fictionalized account of his rise to boxing fame. Called *Gentleman Jim*, the movie starred Errol Flynn. Today, people know only Gentleman Jim and fail to recognize James J. Corbett. Both the champion and the star would have been greatly insulted.

Countless apocryphal stories have mythologized the life and career of this unusual man who, during his lifetime, attained success beyond all "smart money" estimates, in two vastly different types of popular entertainment. How many people reach such stature? Yet previous accounts center only on Corbett's extraordinary boxing. Until now, his personal life and extensive theatrical career have never been researched or revealed.

Ever since 1892, when Corbett de-feated John L. Sullivan for the world's heavyweight championship, his life has been reported in biased efforts, replete with distortions, errors, and fabrications. To some extent, Corbett himself is to blame for this; in 1925, he wrote an autobiography best labeled revisionist history. But the process of vilifying or deifying James J. Corbett began almost immediately upon his victory over Sullivan and continues unabated to this day. Boxing reportage has focused almost exclusively on a specific contest between Corbett and a particular opponent, paying scant attention to the man himself, critical and influential episodes that affected his life, and the social and commercial environment within which he functioned. It is not surprising, then, that confusion, myths, and inventions surround the man's true life story.

My attempt here is to reveal the real Jim Corbett. I have tried to uncover the man behind the tales and sort out facts from fiction. What stories, anecdotes, and reports I could not verify have been omitted. Nor have I endeavored to elevate him to legendary status, whether as saint or demon. That is left to the decision of the reader.

Corbett was a complex, driven, enigmatic man whose dedicated participation in popular entertainment changed American

1

social values and mores, at the same time
that he invented the notion of national
hero. His story begins on the raucous,
hard-scrabble streets of early San Francisco and ends amid the elegant, sumptu-
ous perquisites of Broadway fame and
prosperity.

Boxing and popular theater were
analogous popular entertainments that
matured almost simultaneously in the late
nineteenth century. Prior to that time,
both types of amusement had existed in
their rudimentary forms. Boxing was prohibited by law in nearly all states, but often
took place in saloons and barns away from
police jurisdiction. While popular theater
was never declared illegal, moral arbiters
of the day proclaimed the pastime "sinful"
and its adherents "subjects of the Devil."
In spite of (or because of) these legal and
moral admonishments, both amusements
attracted large numbers of enthusiasts,
sufficient to make them profitable business
ventures.

Initially, boxing and popular theater
captivated the lower classes—working
men and immigrants—luring to their are-
nas audiences who sought escape from the
daily battle for survival on the streets, in
an increasingly industrialized and deper-
sonalized society. These original patrons
were followed by male members of the
new middle and upper classes, men who
themselves sought entertainment to fill
their newly acquired leisure time. It was
the eventual involvement of these latter
participants that helped to transform both
boxing and popular theater into legitimate, morally acceptable commercial enterprises.

Pugilism—as boxing was referred to
at the turn of the century—had already established itself among the eighteenth century British upper classes as a voyeuristic,
gambling entertainment. It would be another century before the sport made its
way to America. In 1810, Tom Molyneux,

a Negro and ex-slave, gained public attention with his ring exploits. Most
American historians believe that boxing
in the United States began among Southern plantation slaves, their owners having
enjoyed the sport in England as part of
their oligarchic leisure-time adventures.
What better way to promote friendly rivalries and wagering between plantation
owners than to have the strongest of their
slaves battle for physical supremacy?

The first recorded bout in America
featuring two white men, Jacob Hyer and
Tom Beasley, occurred in 1816. It was also
the first bout governed by the English
rules of boxing and open to the public. A
quarter of a century later, Deaf Burke, the
self-proclaimed champion of England,
visited the United States on an exhibition
tour and professed to find no suitable
competition; boxing in the U.S. was still in
its primitive stages.

Thirty-three years after the Hyer-
Beasley bout, the country's first heavyweight championship match took place at
Still Pond Creek, near Baltimore. In 1849,
Tom Hyer (son of Jacob) and "Yankee"
Sullivan were pitted against one another,
with Hyer the winner. In the American
pantheon of he-man, rugged individualist
virtue, this bout authenticated boxing, at
least among the lower classes of society, as
a worthwhile and entertaining sport. This
was the era of bare-knuckle confrontations, which often spawned ring brutality,
even death. Not surprisingly, church and
moral leaders strongly denounced the vi-
olence and criminality of pugilism. The
sport itself was outlawed, and those breaking the laws were arrested, fined, and often
jailed. To the "better" classes of society at
the time, pugilism was anathema, an evil
to be excoriated. The fact that it was generally perceived as a characteristically Irish
domain seemed to give further evidence
for its violent and "low-class" heritage.

It took a titan of the colossal stature

of John L. Sullivan to lay the foundation for boxing's acceptability as popular entertainment. He started as a bare-knuckle bruiser in the 1870s, dominating the American boxing scene with a knockout punch and a bravado that attracted public attention. By the end of his boxing career, in the early 1890s, he had become a glove boxer who adhered to Queensberry rules. Part fighter, part showman, and full-time hedonist, Sullivan created an aura of respect and enjoyment for the profession. His command of the ring drew large and adoring crowds, considerable receipts, and an initial recognition for the entertainment among more "decent" men. (Respectable women were still barred from such sporting activities.)

Early popular theater audiences mirrored those attending boxing bouts: they primarily comprised working class, immigrant men who sought entertainment as an escape from the stresses of daily life and participated in the event as much as they observed it. It was not surprising that one of the stage's most popular performances was the Irish two-act. Dressed in stereotypical costumes, the actors began their routine with friendly banter, singing, and clog-dancing. As the act progressed, the players became increasingly belligerent, their encounter invariably ending in ludicrous physical combat, the more rough-and-tumble the better. Popular theater audiences loved to watch blood being shed.

As popular theater expanded its appeal—moved "uptown" literally and figuratively—it began to attract a better class of audience, one that now included women and children. In turn, its attendance demanded a better class of performance and more graceful performers. As with boxing, the more "decent" people visited theaters, the more legitimate popular theater became.

Around the turn of the century, James J. Corbett combined and legitima-tized the most appealing attributes of both forms of entertainment: boxing and popular theater. He was uniquely instrumental in making both justifiable commercial enterprises, to be enjoyed by all classes of people. Along with these accomplishments, Corbett became America's first national sports hero and went on to help formulate theater's star system.

As heavyweight champion of the world, Corbett transformed boxing from a battle between uncouth louts to a gentleman's "science," thereby laying the foundation for boxing to become one of the most appealing and exciting public entertainments in the early twentieth century. As actor, his contributions to the growth and development of variety, vaudeville, and silent films as vehicles for star power and profitable amusement were duplicated by few performers of his time. Corbett's successes and the manner in which they were obtained provide insight and understanding into the growth and acceptability of entertainment in this country. Moreover, his life and career reveal how an athlete and performer was transformed into a matinee idol, how the dynamics of promotion and merchandising made this possible, and how the notion of celebrity was born. Once performers became celebrities, they, in turn, further legitimatized the entertainment they presented.

Many have contributed their time and expertise to the writing of this book. Boxing historians J.J. Johnston, Nick Beck, Jack Fiske, Herbert Goldman, Steve Lott, and Eddie Foy III kindly offered their knowledge, materials, and insights into the growth and development of boxing and its illustrious exemplars. Richard T. Corbett, a descendant of James J., shared much information and insight about the Corbett family. John Ahouse, curator of the Special Collections Library at the University of Southern California, provided considerable assistance by making

available published information about
boxing, popular theater, and social history.
I am deeply grateful for his continued support. My thanks to Gaio Luong, an intre-
pid researcher. Special thanks go to John
Farrell, editor *par excellence,* whose every
suggestion enhanced the manuscript.

Other organizations who have been
helpful include: University of California
at Los Angeles, Microfilm Division; California Historical Society; Academy of
Motion Picture Arts and Sciences; Mormon Library, Salt Lake City; San Francisco Public Library—History Archive;
Sutro Library, San Francisco; Institute of
the American Musical; Shubert Archive;
The Museum of the City of New York;
New York Public Library for the Performing Arts; Chicago Historical Society;
University of Texas—Harry Ransom Hu-
manities Research Center; Nevada Historical Society; Olympic Club, San Francisco; International Boxing Hall of Fame,
Canastota, New York; Library of Congress.

I offer loving gratitude to my wife,
Sara Fields, who lives with my obsession
with turn-of-the-century heroes and
heroics and continues to support my literary efforts.

Armond Fields
December 2000

1. HARD ROAD TO RESPECTABILITY

In 1856, when twenty-one-year-old Patrick Corbett arrived in San Francisco, he discovered a youthful, turbulent metropolis—exciting, dangerous, and unprincipled, yet full of opportunity. Dazed by this potent panorama of apparently antithetical stimuli, Patrick's deep religious convictions and stern moral upbringing almost turned him back to Ireland. Yet, from the moment he had quit the family farm in County Mayo two years previously, Patrick had committed himself to seek a better life, no matter the obstacles.

For Patrick, as for the many thousands of immigrants who had followed a similar route, the passage to America and San Francisco had been no easy endeavor. Born into a poor farm family in the Irish village of Ballycusheen in 1835, Patrick was the third of four brothers. The Corbett surname had been common in the area for more than 200 years and strongly associated with farming.[1]

In Ireland, during the 1840s and 1850s, more than 750,000 had died of disease and starvation, due to the devastating effects of the great potato famine. In addition, hundreds of thousands more had abandoned the country to escape the ravages of crop failures and economic ruin.

Patrick's father died in 1850, leaving his mother and brothers alone to tend the farm. Like their neighbors and friends, the Corbetts struggled to survive on the meager returns they claimed from farming.

Patrick's older brother, John, had been the first to leave home, journeying to New Orleans. In 1854, eighteen-year-old Patrick sailed for America, buoyed by his brother's reports of plentiful employment, determined to leave the farm to seek a better way of life. For Patrick, survival in a new country had to be better than the future he faced had he remained in Ireland. Strongly attracted by the aggressive promotional tactics of U.S. steamship and landowning companies, further enticed by the offer of a fifty-dollar bonus, Patrick sailed for New Orleans. He was to become one of thousands of workers from Ireland and Germany recruited to labor in Louisiana's burgeoning cotton industry.

At the time of Patrick's arrival in New Orleans, the city had attained a population of more than 100,000 people, to become the fourth largest in the United States. Because of its strong French cultural influence, the city was often referred to as "the Paris of America." New Orleans had also gained, however, the dubious distinction of being the country's most pestilential place. Patrick landed just as New Orleans was recovering from the worst yellow fever epidemic in U.S. history, a plague that had already killed more than 11,000, some ten percent of the entire population. Unfortunately, many of those who died were immigrant workers from Europe, totally unaccustomed to the climate, living conditions, and health hazards of their new environment.

According to historical records of the period, salaries in the cotton fields were reasonably good; but survival was problematic. Those European immigrant workers who did survive were moved to the docks, to help supervise the influx of African laborers. Patrick was lucky enough to find further employment with his brother John, who had entered the hotel business. Still, the experiences of a year in New Orleans did not meet Patrick's expectations, much less his desires, so he decided to move on. John's death from yellow fever hastened Patrick's departure.

The journey from New Orleans to San Francisco would be no easier for Patrick than his Atlantic Ocean crossing. To travel to San Francisco, he had four choices: two by land, either along hazardous, rudimentary trails, or across deserts and mountains as yet uncharted; and two by sea, one route around South America, the other across Panama to the Pacific Ocean. What appeared to be the safest and cheapest route—by boat to Colon, across the 50-mile-wide isthmus to Panama City by coach or wagon, then by another boat to San Francisco—would also take the shortest time, slightly more than a month, depending on the weather. The entire trip cost passengers like Patrick from fifty to seventy-five dollars. What sea and land adventures Patrick actually experienced is unknown, but reports of similar journeys suggest the sort of rigorous and life-threatening events that could

only have made a substantial impact on the survivor.

As a commercial seaport, San Francisco would likely not have existed in the middle 1850s had not gold been discovered nearby in 1849. Franciscan monks had built a mission near Yerba Buena Cove in 1776; and that same year, the Mexican government established a military outpost, called a *presidio*. It wasn't until 1835, however, that the first private dwelling, a canvas tent, was erected on the site by Captain W.A. Richardson, an American mercenary hired by the Mexican government as harbor master. He named the settlement Yerba Buena ("good herb"), the name of a tasteful mint leaf that grew in the area, from which the natives brewed tea.

The name was officially changed to San Francisco in January 1847, after the American flag had been raised there, one of the spoils of victory in the Mexican-American War. According to a census taken in 1848, the population of San Francisco was less than 1,000 inhabitants. The town consisted of 200 buildings, including tents, sheds, and outhouses.[2]

In June 1848, the discovery of gold in California was reported to then Secretary of State (later president) James Buchanan. It took three months for the message to reach him in Washington, D.C. Newspapers in New York, Baltimore, Boston, and Philadelphia rushed to publish stories about the discovery; and by late autumn, many fortune-seekers headed overland for California. The first goldhunters from eastern and southern states, however, were transported by mail steamers and landed in San Francisco in February 1849, settling in a temporary tent-city called Happy Valley by optimistic pioneers. It would be a mere seven years before Patrick Corbett arrived.

In less than a year since the landing of the first '49ers, San Francisco experienced the arrival and rapid departure of close to 50,000 men on their way to the gold fields. The bay was often crowded with useless ships because gold-hungry crews abandoned their stations and took possession of lifeboats, rowing up the Sacramento River toward the mining areas. Many of these ships—rotted away, sunk, or drawn up on the beach—never sailed again.

After the first waves of prospectors, more than half the immigrants who landed in San Francisco chose to remain in town and set up businesses. By 1850, San Francisco boasted a permanent population of 25,000 and had become the foremost American port on the Pacific. The rapid growth of the town caused a confusion of makeshift streets (seldom more than muddy sloughs); shelters, consisting of tents, shanties, and boarding houses (at the exorbitant price of fifteen dollars a night, with no mattress); and stores that sold everything from mining supplies to food, drink, and medicine. Not surprisingly, disease became the inhabitants' biggest problem, as insects, lice, and rats infested the entire town.

By 1852, at the height of the gold rush, San Francisco sustained more than 36,000 permanent residents, of which slightly more than 4,000 were Irish immigrants who had only just begun to reach the town from urban areas such as New York and New Orleans. A town government had taken responsibility for building, sanitation, and transportation and had stabilized the local economy, although it was continually influenced by political intrigue and corruption. Still, streets had been paved, banks opened, hotels and docks built, and businesses established, not only catering to mining companies, but also to the growing industries within the town: grain, beef, fruits, vegetables, and wine. Lumber companies flourished because of the demand from mining and town construction. The demand for trans-portation—freight, steamship, and stagecoach—created jobs for thousands. During the early 1850s, thanks to unprecedented prosperity, banking became the town's leading venture.

In 1855, however, because of a decline in gold production, San Francisco experienced its first depression. Most of the gold near the surface had already been mined. The remaining veins lay deeper and proved much harder to extract, increasing the costs of mining. While inventories in the town continued to build, sales declined, forcing many businesses into bankruptcy. A number of major banks failed. The economic decline affected practically every line of commercial activity for more than a year.

For his part, Patrick Corbett was entirely unaware of the town's financial and labor problems when he landed at the Pacific and Davis Street dock in 1856. His first observations of San Francisco revealed a myriad of sordid and unsavory storefronts along Pacific Street, a disreputable and dangerous thoroughfare, he came quickly to realize, threatening one both physically and morally.

Pacific had been the first street cut through the sand hills. It provided the main road to the western part of town. Yet, as other streets were opened and wharves constructed, Pacific rapidly declined in importance, and soon lost any pretense of respectability, as gambling, drinking, and prostitution quickly followed the miners into town. For more than half a century, the street would be the primary locus of San Francisco vice and crime, later baptized "The Barbary Coast" by the local press, but not until some years after Patrick first walked by its dance halls, melodeons, groggeries, beer dens, and concert saloons, all clearly populated with "finely formed females."[3]

In contrast to eastern U.S. cities, San Francisco offered Patrick and his Irish peers a far warmer welcome. In places like New York and Boston, the reception given the Catholic Irish by native Protestants was far from open-minded. To the eastern establishment, the Irish were feared and despised as the bearers of confusion and distress. Most had come from rural areas and were uneducated. As a consequence, only the poorest-paid jobs were available to them; their housing was at best inadequate; and disease ran rampant among them. Shoved into ghettos, they were made to feel unwanted by the host community, disliked not only for their strangeness, but also for their religion.[4]

By contrast, California, particularly San Francisco, was an area where eastern U.S. social and religious prejudice by natives against European immigrants had never existed. The discovery of gold in 1848–49 produced a fluid, dynamic social structure that tended readily to discard traditional forms and create new ones, in response to unique local conditions and needs. Further, most of these modifications occurred in an incredibly short period of time.

Irish immigrants found few rivalries among whites. (What prejudice did surface centered on the Spanish-speaking Mexicans, displaced to the city from rural areas in the 1860s, and the influx of Chinese in the 1870s and '80s.) By 1860, the Irish represented one-fourth of the city's population. The Irish community was vibrant, and their church ascendant, giving them the opportunity to play an important role in building the city. In addition, relations between various religious organizations, all of them devoted to a common mission against vice, tended to be peaceful and mutually respectful.

Most of the Irish entering San Francisco in the '50s and '60s stayed in the city, settled permanently, and quickly contributed to the development of a business community. Given these opportunities,

the Irish liked living in San Francisco. They were given the occasion to improve their standard of living, obtain a better education for their children, and, above all, own property. All of these factors made allegiance to their new country easy to realize for Western Irish, unlike their Eastern brothers. San Francisco had no past, nor did its new inhabitants feel the need to call on their own histories for psychic support. They both looked toward a future full of opportunity, so they believed.

Most of the incoming Irish initially lived in the neighborhoods south of Market Street and east of Seventh Street, primarily because these areas were close to work. In the 1850s, only horse-drawn omnibuses served the populace, on selected streets. A number of Catholic churches had already been built in the area. Dwellings were shared with businesses, the ground floor devoted to a business enterprise, the upper floors to single rooms.

Upon his arrival, Patrick was likely directed, by the Catholic archdiocese, to St. Patrick's Church, where the Fathers assisted immigrants in finding living quarters and a job. At the time, most of the Irish were male and under forty, most likely uneducated and unskilled. But there was more work than workers, and the opportunity for learning a trade and earning a good living was excellent.

Patrick's first job was as a porter in a hotel on Market Street, his work experience in older brother John's hotel was likely a help in obtaining the position. Luckily, a portion of his salary included room and board at the hotel. The following year, 1858, Patrick was hired as a porter at the prestigious Nucleus Hotel, an obvious improvement in employment. Here, too, he was able to live at the hotel.[5]

In a fortuitous move, Patrick began his own business as a hack driver about the same time that San Francisco was swept into the excitement of the silver

Hotel Nucleus, San Francisco, 1865. Patrick Corbett spent a number of years early in his marriage driving hacks for the Hotel Nucleus. The experience persuaded him to open his own delivery business. (California Historical Society, FN-12550)

rush, a result of the discovery of the Comstock Lode in Virginia City, Nevada. Again, San Francisco became the center for mining companies, miners, and the banks that underwrote their activities. As with the gold rush a decade earlier, the city was launched into another economic frenzy in which prices and wages for all commercial enterprises flourished. Patrick had the benefit of these good times, which would continue for almost a decade. He now lived in a boarding house on Clara Street, near Third Street.

Hack drivers were making about fifteen dollars a week, plus tips, which often doubled the amount usually earned. For Patrick, work would begin before noon and extend into the early hours of the following morning, as most eating and drinking places and theaters remained open late.

The devout Patrick, however, did not work on Sunday, instead attending church in the morning and church socials in the afternoon or evening. At one of these socials, he met twenty-year-old Catherine McDonald, one of a family that had taken the overland route from Philadelphia to San Francisco a few years previously.

In November 1858, Patrick (twenty-four) and Catherine (twenty-one) were married. Thanks to the city's second period of rapid business expansion, Patrick's hack business continued to improve. They lived in a boarding house on Union Street, a considerable distance from her parents and the familiarity of the Irish neighborhood but a good location for his now thriving business. A year later, Frank, the first of ten children, was born.

During the entire decade of the

1860s, San Francisco experienced unprecedented expansion and diversification,
due to the combination of silver receipts,
the Civil War, the grain trade, and population growth. In 1860, the city's population stood at more than 57,000; by the end
of the decade, it would triple. Hotels, theaters, banks, and large general stores lined
the main thoroughfares in the downtown
area. Horse-drawn railways operated on
the main streets and, along with the pro-
liferation of delivery wagons and passenger carriages, often created gridlock. Ferry
boats to and from Oakland mingled with
freight and passenger ships crowding the
bay. The Barbary Coast continued its lucrative business of drinking, gambling,
and available women.

The Irish community prospered, as
well. Enriched by the proceeds from silver
mining, an Irish banking and business elite
was being formed. First-generation Irish
workers moved from blue-collar to white-
collar jobs as their skills increased and jobs
in new industries opened to them. They
moved to better dwellings; and when a
housing society was formed by one of the
leading banks, owned by Irish entrepreneurs, anyone who could convince the
bankers he was a good risk could buy a
home. That alone helped to disperse the
Irish throughout the entire community.

Still, the church remained the inte-
grating force of local Irish society. The
Catholic Archdiocese published its own
daily newspaper. The Church did not
hesitate to get involved in local politics,
and many Irish business leaders obtained
responsible positions in local government. The Church opened an orphanage,
a hospital, an infant shelter, and established St. Vincent de Paul societies to respond to community needs, all supported
by the increasing numbers of prosperous
Irish businessmen. Catholic benevolent
organizations, such as the Knights of
Columbus, supported by the Irish elite,

aided troubled families and wayward
youth.

As first generation Irish married and
had children, they sought the educational
opportunities offered by parochial schools,
secondary academies, and colleges. The
Church's contributions to its own community also augmented the city's prosperity and expansion. By 1880, the Irish made
up one-third of San Francisco's total population and occupied many positions of
power within the community.

During the 1860s, Patrick Corbett
prospered and his family grew. Edward
(Harry), was born in 1862, and Esther in
1865. On September 1, 1866, the Corbetts'
third son arrived and was christened James
John. It seems that, with the addition of
each child, new living quarters were obtained. After Edward's birth, the family
moved to a larger dwelling south of Market Street, a more familiar Irish neighborhood. After Esther's birth, they moved to
24 Perry Street, in a newer part of "Irish
town." With James's birth, the family re-
located yet again to a rented house on
South Brannum. Over the next ten years,
six more children were born: John,
Theresa, Thomas, Joseph, Catherine, and
Mary, and the family moved to four other
locations.

Very little is known of Jim's early
years. He was reported to be a healthy, active child, large for his age. The fact that
he and all of his siblings lived to adulthood suggests the family was affluent
enough to obtain medical attention and
care when it was needed. From all reports,
a stable, loving home also helped. Later
stories told of a continuously close relationship among the siblings as they matured and, as adults, remained amiable.

The 1870 census revealed that the
Corbett property was worth $4,000 and
that an additional $600 was in the bank,
together a moderate estate for the time.
In 1872, Patrick bought a livery stable and

home in the Hayes Valley, a new area on the edge of town, whose streets had recently been surveyed and paved. The house was large, a two-story frame building with Victorian trim along the gabled roof. Patrick's livery stable was on the ground floor, with a wide swinging gate in the center, an office on the side, and a large storage area in the rear for wagons and carriages. The horses were located in comfortable stalls in the center of the building, its warmest section.

The second floor contained the entire living quarters for the family of twelve. At the right front of the building was the parlor; the center contained a family room, with a piano; the dining room was in the left front, containing a long table to accommodate the entire family at meals. There were six bedrooms in the rear and, as a special touch of luxury, two bathrooms. Other buildings on the block were similar in layout, a business on the ground

floor and living quarters above. Within a few years, the Corbett establishment became a local landmark.

When Jim was six, he was enrolled in a nearby parochial school, the fourth Corbett child to attend. While reported to be an avid learner, he was not particularly well-disciplined. His older siblings had all been identified as "good" children by the Sisters; however, Jim apparently did not live up to the family reputation.

By the completion of elementary school, Jim had grown to be a tall (the tallest in the family), strong, athletic youth, reasonably good with his studies, remarkably gregarious on the playground and in the neighborhood. Jim's extracurricular activities were frequently reported to Patrick, who had become quite upset about his son's attitude toward authority, both himself and the Church. "James J. Corbett is an exceptionally friendly boy," an old school record reveals. "However, he

South of Market Street, San Francisco, 1866. The Corbett home, where Jim was born, was located on a side street to the left. He spent his early years playing on these streets, in the city's predominantly Irish neighborhood. (California Historical Society, FN-12550)

is too free with his fists and often involves himself in street fights."

To begin his high school career, Jim was placed in the Jesuit-run St. Ignatius Academy. Founded in 1855, St. Ignatius began as a meeting place for the growing Irish community. A few years later, it opened a school for children who were faced with "the challenges of urban life," a Jesuitical euphemism for children living in impoverished, even destitute families. By the 1870s, St. Ignatius provided a secondary school, a college, and a seminary for clergy in training; its advanced students often helped "delinquent children" in the high school, in a kind of social welfare program.

Near the end of Jim's first year at St. Ignatius, he was expelled from school for fighting on the playground. Almost as a last resort, Patrick had Jim enrolled in Sacred Heart College, a school requiring tuition, known for its strict rules and regulations. At the end of the school year, Jim was again expelled for fighting. This time, the altercation was reported to have been with a teacher who attempted to discipline him. At age 15, Jim had ended his formal education.

Along with the academic turbulence, Jim seems to have had an active extracurricular life, obtaining a further education on the seamier streets of the city. (A section of the Barbary Coast catered specifically to local patrons. Some saloons set aside seats and beer mugs for frequent visitors.) It is likely that Patrick was aware of Jim's activities, but could do little about them.

Some stories had Jim promoting street and saloon fights for money. Others recall his picking fights with larger men simply to show he could best them. While many of these stories may be fiction, Jim was surely, in some way, sharpening his pugilistic abilities. On the more acceptable side, he and his brothers played base-

ball; and Jim seemed talented enough to consider it as a possible career.

Since enrollment at St. Ignatius and Sacred Heart didn't appear to work for Jim, Patrick turned to one of the Irish benevolent societies for assistance. In reality, these societies were social welfare organizations, sponsored by the Church, and underwritten by well-to-do Irish businessmen, to help "delinquent children." One of the contributors to this society was John W. Mackay, an owner of the Nevada Bank. He gave Jim a job as a messenger, accompanied by strict rules regarding his behavior on the job.

Apparently, Jim obeyed the rules well enough that, within three years, he had been promoted to assistant teller, a position strongly perceived by blue-collar families as a significant step toward white-collar respectability. Jim had to dress for the job and he cultivated a well-groomed look, complete with lapel carnation, to attain the requisite bearing. "At the bank," Corbett related, "I had my first look at the good life. I swore that someday those things would be mine, though at the time I had no idea of how I would get them."

"You could always tell where Jim's cage was," a worker at the bank recalled. "It was the one with all the girls crowded around in front." Now a meticulous dresser, Corbett had matured to become a tall, handsome young man with a striking physique, broad shoulders, classic features, and piercing blue eyes that communicated both strength and kindness.

However, Jim's nighttime activities continued, much to the distress of Patrick, who was torn by his son's seemingly inconsistent behavior. On one hand, Patrick was proud that Jim had entered the white-collar business world; on the other, he was dismayed that Jim continued his associations with "malefactors and wickedness." It was reported that Patrick and his son were often not on speaking terms; mother and older brothers Frank and Harry often had to intercede.

An old pal named Lew Harding reminisced about Jim's early pugilistic exploits. Sharing an interest in boxing, they often sparred together. "Jim wasn't a trouble-maker or a wise-guy," Harding said. "Fighting just came natural to him." Nor was this kind of manly behavior atypical of young men frequenting Barbary Coast saloons and concert halls. One could even earn a few extra dollars by engaging in a quickly promoted fight.

One such encounter proved prophetic. Harry Corbett, one of Jim's older brothers, worked as a clerk in City Hall. A colleague, Herbert Choynski, began to argue with him regarding which of them had the better fighter for a brother. The continuing debate ultimately pushed the respective brothers into a physical confrontation, Jim Corbett versus Joe Choynski.

Isador Nathan Choynski, a Jewish gentleman who had become a journalist, publisher, and antiquarian bookseller during the city's gold-rush days, had also gained a local reputation as a muckraker. The family had become well-to-do, with four sons to continue their acquired heritage. Yet, one of Isador's four sons, Joe, had rebelled at the family's insistence on education and entrepreneurial exploits, wanting instead to become a boxer. A strong, tough, muscular young man, a slugger who could also sustain punishment, young Joe used his fists on the streets when ethnic rivalries—like "Jew-baiting"—demanded immediate response.[6]

It was not surprising, then, that the "my brother can beat your brother"

Jim Corbett, age 17, bank employee. Already a well-formed, tall, and handsome young man, Jim was about to begin his athletic career by enrolling in the Olympic Club's boxing program. (Courtesy of the Academy of Motion Picture Arts and Sciences)

argument turned into a confrontation between Jim and Joe, between Irishman and
Jew. In their first meeting, a brief, bare-
knuckle street fight, Jim claimed, "I
knocked him cold." After considerable
baiting between the now adversarial older
brothers, Jim and Joe met again, this time
in a stone quarry outside the city limits,
with only the respective brothers as seconds in attendance.

Patrick heard about the proposed
fight and appealed to Jim not to engage
Joe Choynski because it might jeopardize
his bank job. At first, Jim heeded his father's advice and went to the Choynski
residence to decline the match. There, one
of Joe's brothers berated Jim: "You wait
until this afternoon. You'll see him then,
all right. He'll knock you all over the lot."
Angered, Jim demanded Joe come out and
face him then and there. Jim beat Joe
again, but this time it was a hard, bruising, bloody fight.

They would meet again, five years
later, both of them having become committed, trained, amateur boxers representing rival athletic clubs. What personal ri-
valry had developed at these early meetings
would be resolved in the ring, viewed by
hundreds of cheering spectators, with a
considerable amount of money changing
hands.

Enter again Jim's boss and benefac-
tor John W. Mackay. Among his various
interests, Mackay was an avid sports enthusiast and officer of the prestigious
Olympic Club, an organization that sponsored amateur athletic contests in a variety of sports. Mackay had apparently
heard of Jim's fistic reputation from the
saloon set. Calling Jim into his office one
February day in 1884, the banker said, "I
hear you're interested in boxing." Jim acknowledged that he was, at the same time
fearing that his father's warning was about
to prove true. "Why waste your time
brawling in the gutter for experience?"
Mackay challenged. "I'll take you to the
Olympic Club and introduce you to a professor who can teach you real boxing."

Not yet eighteen years old, Jim Corbett was about to enter the rarefied, if
customarily brutal, arena of organized
pugilism. That this controversial sporting activity had been sponsored and promoted by one of the richest clubs in San
Francisco made the prospect all the more
appealing.

2. Escapades In and Out of the Ring

San Francisco offered three seemingly conflicting pictures of prosperity during the 1870s and 1880s. At the top of scenic Nob Hill stood the lavish, ornate mansions of the merchants Crocker, Hopkins, Huntington, and Stanford, stunning examples of *nouveau riche* excess in a city not yet twenty-five years old. At the bottom of the hill seethed the notorious Barbary Coast, boasting its own forms of decorous entertainment.

Between these two extremes, the city supported a substantial middle class, rapidly expanding by virtue of an increasingly diversified economy based on shipping, fishing, agriculture, and manufacturing. A new means of transportation, cable cars, spread in all directions from the city center, carrying with it this emergent middle class.

'Frisco's downtown had become a haphazard amalgam of multi-storied office buildings, hotels, and factories, adjacent to one another in apparently random fashion, interspersed with restaurants and theaters. Prominent in the midst of these commercial enterprises loomed the omnipresent banks, conveniently located for all of the city's resourceful and progressive entrepreneurs.

Within walking distance of the business district, in the ornate Alcazar Building on Post Street, was San Francisco's most prestigious men's organization, the Olympic Club. It was the oldest athletic club in the nation, having been founded in May, 1860. (The famed New York Athletic Club was established six years later.)[1]

Initially, the club's meetings were held in a hall at Clay and Kearney Streets. Down the street was Frank Wheeler's Gymnasium, a favorite place for both young men and merchants with athletic inclinations to pass an hour of exercise and conviviality. Wheeler, however, was a poor businessman; and when Olympic Club members suggested they unite their respective enterprises, Wheeler heartily agreed to the proposal.

Over the next decade, the club expanded its quarters to include a ballroom and meeting rooms to complement the gymnasium. Rapidly gaining a reputation as the city's preeminent men's organization, the Olympic Club maintained highly selective membership requirements, accepting only those who embodied the best in business acumen, charitable action, and civic responsibility.

The club also became the city's primary sponsor of amateur athletes and athletic events. Sporting activities included track, swimming, wrestling, gymnastics, and boxing. Guided by instructors, aspiring athletes were given the opportunity to train at the club for a nominal monthly fee, as long as they pledged to retain their amateur status and represent the club in its sponsored events and tournaments. Any athlete perceived by the members to have talent could join the club's instructional programs. Such athletes, however, were never considered full-fledged members of the club.

In the early morning of June 20, 1883, a fire broke out at the Olympic Club, not an uncommon event in a downtown where building codes were almost nonexistent and whose fire department remained ill-equipped to handle even minor blazes. The fire destroyed the entire building, including all furniture, paintings (the club was said to own some valuable art work), and athletic apparati. An emergency meeting of members secured a subscription list, and temporary quarters were found nearby. Negotiations with M. H. DeYoung, owner of the *Chronicle,* for the upper floors of the Alcazar Building were completed; and plans for a modern gymnasium were initiated. On May 5, 1885, the Olympic Club was officially reopened. Fifteen hundred of the city's elite attended, escorted through what was considered to be one of the best gymnasiums in the country and then entertained by a promenade concert that ended in an elaborate ball.

The Olympic Club had employed boxing instructors for years, most of them unremarkable. In early 1884, however, with the acquisition of Walter Watson, considered to be one of the most professional instructors of "scientific" boxing, the sport quickly became the club's most popular spectator activity. Though middle-aged, Watson possessed exceptional acumen and extraordinary skills in the ring; he could easily best boxers half his age. He had been persuaded by club executives to give up a good position in England because they believed he had "a genuine ability for imparting knowledge to his pupils and with a keen eye for fighting merit." That he would assist in making the Olympic Club the most fashionable athletic club in town was a decided benefit.

In addition, Watson's philosophy of training proved attractive to club members, who espoused the virtues of manly America. Watson maintained that any young man with a "good head" and "good heart," plus a certain suppleness, could become a good boxer. Practice and hard work were the keys to efficiency and personal success. In his lectures, Watson went on to present his pugilistic philosophy: boxing teaches the lessons of life; for, as the boxer becomes experienced, he appreciates the advantages resulting from caution, as well as the advisability of forbearance. The participant is also brought to the realization that in boxing, as in every progressive act of life, courage and discipline are absolutely essential to success. After all, Watson concluded, there are occasions in the life of every man when he may be called upon to defend himself. Club members heartily applauded his worldly views.

Shortly after Watson assumed his role as boxing instructor, he was introduced to Jim Corbett. Watson observed a handsome, trim young man, a few months shy of nineteen, over six feet in height, weighing in the 160s. He appeared to be friendly, even a little shy. What impressed Watson most about Jim was his careful and refined manner of dress, not to mention his pompadour hairstyle. Watson had also been fully apprised of Jim's past adventures. Jim had just appeared in his first sparring match at the Ariel Rowing Club, facing Billy Welsh, the club's middleweight

The new Olympic Club gymnasium was considered the best equipped in the U.S. Boxing exhibitions were held here monthly, with spectators sitting on temporary bleachers or standing on the balcony overlooking the ring. (California Historical Society, FN-31474)

champion. In a four-round bout, Welsh had easily defeated the untrained youngster for the gold medal.

At their first meeting, Watson suggested they spar a few minutes so "the instructor could better evaluate the pupil." The brief interchange convinced Watson of Jim's potential, but he wasn't sure of his own ability to teach this young man the requisite control and discipline. What gave Corbett a chance, Watson believed, was his keen ambition to learn, to better himself both physically and socially.

Pleased with his acceptance at the Olympic Club, Jim's older brothers gave him the benefit of their admiration.

Patrick, Jim's father, remained dubious, insistent that Jim continue to devote his attention to the bank where he could actually "better himself." When Frank and Harry insisted that they had been knocked "all over the box stall" by Jim, Patrick thought it was a joke.

Moreover, he had his own concerns, more important than his son's boxing lessons. Competition in the livery business had increased substantially in recent years, making it more difficult to pay off a $6,000 mortgage on the stable and home. There also remained twelve people to feed; though Frank, Harry, and Esther were over twenty, none was yet married nor earning a reasonable salary. Jim and his older siblings gave a portion of their earnings to their parents, but it never seemed to be quite enough. Jim later claimed that these experiences convinced him "if I ever got hold of any big sum of money, the first thing I would do would be to pay off that mortgage."[2]

Family concerns and responsibilities did not seem to affect Jim's enjoyment of evening rounds with his friends and the company of young women, like those he met at the bank. His adventures at Barbary Coast saloons, however, seem to have diminished as Jim realized the importance of being seen in more respectable places. He had become a recognized white-collar employee in a responsible business and now had been accepted as an athletic representative by a prestigious men's club. While old chums might deride him as a "dude," he knew the expression was viewed more positively by his new group of friends and colleagues.

Jim's time soon became almost entirely consumed by banking and boxing, working as a teller six days a week, taking lessons from Watson three evenings a week. In addition, Jim sought every opportunity to watch other boxers perform, to learn what he could through observation. Watson expressed pleasure with Jim's progress and, in recognition of his improvement, scheduled Jim to spar two rounds with him at the club's bimonthly boxing night. Club members seemed to enjoy the exhibition, but a caustic newspaper reporter wrote that the sparring exhibition "was devoid of science" and that "he would be glad to meet any of the members with the gloves." When Watson challenged the reporter, he rescinded his comments. For Jim, it was his first public appearance in the Olympic Club ring, as well as his first brush with newspaper commentary. Club members were complimentary, generally agreeing that the young middleweight had talent.

By the end of 1884, Jim had become a featured attraction at Olympic Club sparring exhibitions. Observers could see his development as a boxer: he had gained muscular weight; his movements were quick, responsive, and focused; his ability to endure punishment had greatly improved. At each exhibition, he sparred a few rounds, either with Watson or fellow students, like W.J. Kenealy, Bob McCord, and M.L. Requa. Watson then challenged Billy Welsh to meet Jim in another four-round sparring match. When they met, Welsh was on the floor by the end of the first round. Jim had obviously made extraordinary progress in a relatively short time.[3]

Nevertheless, Jim's growing obsession with boxing had an increasingly negative impact on Patrick. Jim's father tried to persuade him to discontinue taking lessons, at least reduce the time he was spending at the Olympic Club. Patrick's perception of the social class difference between his son and club members may have been a factor in his thinking. Surely, his strong religious beliefs played an important role, as well. Yet when Jim brought home an award he had won at the club, Patrick expressed pride, bragging to friends about his son's accomplishments. It was later discovered that Jim's mother had saved all of his awards and trophies and collected all reports published in local newspapers about her son.

Debates about the legitimacy of professional boxing in San Francisco had recently heated up when a bout between two local bruisers turned into a "bloody brawl." Newspapers decried the manner in which the match had been handled, blaming the referee and seconds for allowing such a "disgrace." Spectators reported being so thoroughly disgusted that many of them claimed they would no longer patronize similar events. The City Council, normally quite passive about boxing in their city, now discussed possible ordinances against what they described as "professional pugilism." There seemed to be an increasing divergence in definition between pugilism and boxing, the former representing the more brutal aspects of the sport, the latter characterizing its new, scientific approach. In fact, San Francisco was one of the very few places in the country where scheduled boxing bouts "to the finish" were legal.

In a move calculated to avoid confrontation with the city's elite, the council deferred action until a court pressed charges against the fighters and their backers. Depending on the outcome of the trial, they would then decide on the imposition of ordinances. But no trial ever took place.

Though politicians seemed unable or unwilling to agree on laws governing the handling of boxing matches, they did express displeasure with "bloody" bouts, that is, professionally staged matches with "fight-to-the-finish" contracts. In contrast, this made amateur exhibitions even more respectable, particularly to the better classes of people who enjoyed them at the city's athletic clubs.

Amateur boxing exhibitions thrived at the Olympic Club and three new competing men's organizations—the California Athletic Club, the Golden Gate Athletic Club, and the Acme Athletic Club in Oakland. What distinguished the Olympic from its competition was the club's standard in the sponsorship of matches: the Olympic promoted amateur bouts only; the other three staged bouts that offered purses, thereby creating some confusion regarding whether participants were professionals or amateurs. These clubs side stepped the debate by offering purses to professionals and trophies to amateurs.

Within a short period of time, the new clubs staked a strong claim for spectators by aggressively promoting matches for financial consideration, along with the opportunity for plenty of side betting. Olympic Club members were outraged, concerned that their own boxers would be lured away. To protect their interests, they made their athletes promise to perform only under the auspices of the club. At this point, however, Jim had no concerns about club loyalty or purses; he continued his ring education under the watchful eye of Professor Watson.

At the end of August, the Olympic Club staged another of its athletic entertainments, which included a sparring match between two famous boxers, Mike Cleary and Jack Dempsey, called the "Nonpareil," not the champion of later decades. Neither received any money for their appearances, but they were heartily feted after the exhibition. In addition, Watson persuaded Dempsey to put on the gloves with his protégé, Jim, "in a friendly set-to." It was the hit of the evening, with Dempsey afterwards declaring that Jim "had a lot of talent." The event gave Jim a good deal of exposure, and local newspapers began to mention his name with increasing frequency, extolling the virtues of this clean-cut, "scientific" boxer.[4]

At about the same time, the City Council finally reached a compromise decision regarding professional boxing in San Francisco, one that certainly revealed the strength of the athletic-club lobby. A law was passed requiring a license fee of $100 for every boxing exhibition held in the city, with the exception of those staged in the "rooms" of an athletic club. Boxing bouts outside the confines of an athletic club almost entirely disappeared from the city, professionals now traveling to other venues to ply their trade.

In November, the Olympic Club continued its entertainments with a sparring tournament, for members and guests. (The gym had space for more than 500 people.) Trophies and medals were tendered the winners of each weight division. Now weighing more than 175 pounds, Jim entered the tournament as a heavyweight. The ever-present *Chronicle* predicted that "Pompadour Jim" would win the heavyweight trophy easily. In three two-round elimination bouts, Jim corroborated their prediction. A full house cheered his triumph, and local newspapers proclaimed him the Olympic Club's new heavyweight champion. Yet, a month later, in a sparring match between Watson and Jim, the instructor demonstrated to the pupil how much he still had to learn by knocking him to the floor several times.

Watson's heralded successes as instructor of the Olympic Club obtained him engagements to give lessons at the university and the Acme Club. He took Jim along to these engagements, to spar with him, "to show what scientific training can do." As Watson's public reputation burgeoned, so did Jim's. This added exposure from the press, detailing Jim's exploits in the ring, motivated some newspapers to attempt matching him against well-known professionals for financial considerations. While Jim turned down these opportunities—Watson and the Olympic Club did not hesitate reminding Jim of their rules—the attention he received did inflate his ego. It was abruptly tested at the club's next exhibition.

Another of Watson's promising pupils, a man named McCarthy, sparred with Jim. Showing a more aggressive approach to the bout, McCarthy surprised Jim to the point that a journalist reported that Corbett had been "bested" and was becoming lazy. Watson seemed amused by the observation, but Jim retorted that the bout was only an exhibition and therefore only a "friendly set-to." In his own defense, Jim stated that he was still champion of the club and was "ready at any time to defend that title."

Newspapers spent the next month baiting Jim with mysterious challengers, the entire effort designed to needle him into saying or doing something newsworthy. Instead, thanks to Watson's guidance, Jim transferred his indignation to his next sparring match, with Australian Dick Mathews. He knocked out Mathews in the second round, with a focused seriousness not previously seen by Watson. The win seemed to relax Jim; it certainly lessened negative newspaper commentary about him, at least for the moment.

Through the summer of 1886, the boxing situation in San Francisco had not changed. In spite of petitions by backers and promoters, some of them supported by politicians, devotees of the sport failed to persuade the mayor and the Council to change their opinion regarding professional boxing. Exhibitions staged at the athletic clubs continued to flourish, particularly those put on by the Olympic Club's competitors. An insightful article written in the *Chronicle* questioned how such matches could be staged in athletic clubs for purses when the same matches would be otherwise outlawed in the city. No one responded to the reporter's query.

It was about this time that Jim was introduced to the world of popular theater. Near the Olympic Club building stood the Bush Street Theater. A young but already veteran comedian, Eddie Foy, was performing farce comedy with the Barry and Fay touring company. One of the skits Foy had devised was to enact the role of a drunken boxer. To observe the characteristic movements of real boxers in action, Foy visited the Olympic Club and, while there, met Jim Corbett. Almost immediately, they became friends.

Fascinated with the theater, Jim was taken to a different theater each night by Foy, exposing him to minstrel shows, melodramas, and variety. Handsome Jim was introduced to performers and stage people wherever they went; some were already familiar with the young man due to his boxing exploits. He attended parties given by local people in honor of visiting actors. His casual yet gentlemanly manners won him quick acceptance from those he met, particularly the young women. One such woman was a pretty college student, Olive Lake, currently attending the State Normal School for teachers. It was a case of instant, mutual attraction. The two quickly became inseparable. Both families, however, opposed the relationship: Olive's father because Jim was pursuing a disreputable and unpredictable career; Patrick because Olive was not Catholic. Naturally, this only strengthened the young couple's resolve to be together.

Near the end of May, the Olympic Club held another of its bimonthly boxing entertainments. On the bill was a sparring exhibition between Jim and McCarthy, the fellow club boxer who had embarrassed Jim a few months earlier. This time, Jim quickly proceeded to let the audience—and the press—know who was the better boxer. He didn't attempt to knock McCarthy out, that would have broken club rules. Yet he had his opponent backpedaling the entire match. Among the club guests was Olive Lake. She and Jim had already begun talking about marriage. But how to arrange it, with their parents vehemently against such a union?

When Watson declared he planned a vacation for the entire month of June, Olive and Jim believed it might be an opportune time for them to get away, as well. Olive had finished school for the year; with Watson away, Jim had no boxing lessons and needed only to obtain time off from the bank. Sometime during the third week of June, Olive and Jim entrained for Salt Lake City to get married.

On June 28, 1886, Jim and Olive were married by a justice of the peace, at Utah House, a Salt Lake City hotel. Because he was underage—Utah law required the man to be twenty-one years of age—Jim changed his last name to Dillon and claimed to be twenty-one. Years later, in his autobiography, Corbett spoke of the marriage as having been annulled and told how, facing a shortage of funds, he had engaged in two boxing matches for purses, to defray the honeymoon expenses. In reality, Olive and Jim remained married for nine years. Jim did appear in one boxing match, against Duncan McDonald, in Butte, Montana, on July 13. It was a professional encounter, in which both the winner and loser received compensation. The bout ended in a six-round draw. To protect his amateur status, Jim fought under his assumed name of Dillon.

When the couple returned to 'Frisco, Jim found his father and mother in bad temper. Not only were they dismayed at Jim's elopement, they were equally angered that Jim had been married by a justice of the peace. And to a Protestant! For Patrick, the marriage was perceived as a personal humiliation, as well as an affront to the Church. There is no evidence to indicate how Olive's father felt about his daughter's actions, though she was not able to continue her college career. To reaffirm their vows (and for Jim to use his proper name), the couple were married again in a Catholic Church in San Francisco on August 21, with their respective parents in attendance.

To further complicate the situation, Jim asked that he and his wife be allowed to stay at the Corbett family home for a short time, until they could afford their own rooms. While the request was granted, relations between Jim and Patrick remained chilly. For Patrick, the entire episode was another reminder of his apparent inability to successfully guide his son along more traditional lines. Seeing the newlyweds each day must have had a

The Corbett family in a typical late-19th-century photographer's pose. From left to right, standing: Mary, Frank, Catherine, James J., John, Harry, Teresa. Sitting: Catherine (mother), Joe, Patrick (father), Tom, Esther.

negative effect on him. At fifty, Patrick had begun to reflect the accumulation of responsibilities brought about by building and maintaining a business and governing a large family. That Jim was his only setback seemed to rankle his sense of personal accomplishment. In retrospect, continual struggles with Jim appear to have exacerbated a gradual decline in Patrick's ability to handle the exigencies of daily life.

Nor did it take long for the 'Frisco press and the Olympic Club to discover Jim's extracurricular exploits. The *Chronicle* labeled Jim a "pug."

> Corbett, late "gentleman" heavyweight of the Olympic Club, has dropped to the lower plane of the professional "pug." He fought a draw with Duncan McDonald last week under the name of Jim Dillon. He is at least entitled to the credit of not having played the "drop" game [throwing the fight].[5]

The Olympic Club Board of Directors were furious that Jim had broken club rules and thereby jeopardized his amateur status. He was almost dismissed from the club, but a handful of members argued successfully to retain him since this was his only transgression. He was, however, forbidden to engage in any club sparring exhibitions for four months and advised to keep a low profile. The event seemed to deflate Jim's ego somewhat; in addition, Watson was instructed to counsel Jim on controlling his zealousness to succeed.

At the Olympic Club's "Paper Carnival," held during the middle of November, Jim was allowed to spar an exhibition with P.T. Goodloe. According to the *Chronicle* reporter, the two "gave a rather pleasing entertainment." Club members allowed that Jim remained their heavyweight favorite. They gave further approbation by assigning him a number of pupils to train. Jim embraced the new assignment with relish.

Watson's connection with the Acme Club in Oakland obtained for Jim a three-round contest with Tom Johnson, "a well-known slugger." Johnson had already expressed a desire to meet Joe McAuliffe for the heavyweight championship of the Pacific Coast. For Johnson, sparring Jim was "practice." For Jim, it garnered additional respect from the press, though the match had no decision. As the *Chronicle* reported the meeting: "Corbett's science asserted itself throughout the bout, and the Acme folks were enthusiastic in their appreciation of the fistic display."

When the *Chronicle* discussed Jim's growing maturity, they pointed to his innovative instruction techniques.

> Jim has a few colts under his care and they are coming on wonderfully. With unmistaking capability, he combines good temper and patience, and does not indulge in any of the rough work so disheartening to those receiving initiatory lessons in the noble art. [6]

Watson seemed increasingly pleased with his pupil's progress, particularly Jim's improved self-control. The Olympic Club Board of Directors expressed pride in their heavyweight representative, but did not hesitate to remind the young boxer about his club responsibilities. The press was not so advisory. They attempted to promote, even provoke, bouts between Corbett and other local favorites. Finally, after reporters chided Jim for not "having greatness thrust upon him," (newspaper-style), Jim responded with a letter to the sports editor of the *Chronicle,* stating his—and the Olympic Club's—position on the issue:

> In the columns of a morning newspaper on Monday last, my name appeared as was used in connection with certain heavyweight boxers of the coast, Tom Johnson, Joe McAuliffe, Con Riordan and Mike Brennan. I wish it to be understood that I have made no arrangements to box any of the above named gentlemen, and I do not thank the sporting editor referred to for his un-warranted use of my name. I do not wish to box anyone, either amateur or professional, for a monetary consideration, and no inducement can make me alter my intention. [7]

Jim was definitely on his best behavior, possibly because rumors of the opening of a number of boxing instructor jobs seemed to provide him an appropriate next step. Rumor became reality when, through Watson's influence, Jim was offered a job to teach two days a week at the Golden Gate Athletic Club. To maintain his job at the bank, Jim taught evenings only. Within a matter of weeks, his classes were oversubscribed, the "young colts" of the city anxious to take lessons from "Pompadour Jim," their blossoming hero.

Not surprisingly, Patrick had a totally different view of his son's ascending boxing career. As he had numerous times before, Patrick attempted to persuade Jim to reduce his boxing activities. Jim was not about to give up his latest opportunities, but did promise his father he would not appear in sparring exhibitions. The Olympic Club, however, had other plans for Jim.

Professional boxer Jack Burke was on his way to Australia, which meant a stop in San Francisco. The club persuaded Burke to train in their rooms and give a sparring exhibition. Members prevailed upon Watson to enlist Jim to meet Burke, for the "good of the organization." In August, the club boastfully announced to the newspapers they had set up an eight-round boxing contest between Jack Burke and Jim, Marquis of Queensberry rules governing the bout, the men using ordinary boxing gloves.

The Corbetts were taken aback by the announcement, and Jim became the target of Patrick's fury. His brothers believed Jim would be badly beaten by the pro and thereby jeopardize his future. His wife was concerned about his handsome face; beaten-up fighters made unattractive bank tellers.

Gleefully, the press heralded the meeting.

Both Corbett and Burke are clever workers on their feet; both have had the advantage of tip-top condition. Although the former has a slight lead in the matter of weight and reach, it is probable that Burke's superior knowledge of ring tactics will balance matters and make it hard to decide who will be the winner. (Although no winner was to be declared.)

The *Chronicle* further fanned the competitive waves by declaring: "There is no doubt that Corbett has been longing for years to stand before a professional of some repute in the pugilistic world, so as to range his own ability."[8]

When Burke arrived in San Francisco, he was met by a brightly uniformed brass band, cheering crowds, and gamblers, already hawking odds favoring Burke, though such wagers were illegal. Nor did it prevent various club members from making side bets on the outcome, and offering out-of-pocket "expense" funds to both boxers. It was publicly reported that Burke would receive a purse for his efforts; Jim would receive nothing, as befit his club association.

Two weeks before the bout, the Olympic Club held a gathering in support of Jim, as well as to sell tickets for the entertainment. Eight hundred tickets, at no less than ten dollars each, were eventually sold. Reporting on the gathering, the *Chronicle* stated: "Corbett will do his level best to uphold the honor of the Olympic Club. It is probable that the attendance in the clubrooms on the evening of the contest will be the largest ever seen there."[9]

On August 28, an overflow crowd of spectators jammed the Olympic Club's gymnasium to see Burke, the professional, meet Corbett, the amateur, in an eight-round match. No referee had been employed, and no decision was to be made on the outcome. Newspapers called the bout "one of the best, from a scientific point of view, to take place in San Francisco."

Observers believed Jim looked pale and overtrained, and his nervousness in the first round was apparent. In his attempts to evade Burke's blows, Jim slipped to his knees a number of times. The press reported rounds two and three even, as Jim recovered his composure. Rounds four, five, and six were in Burke's favor, as he demonstrated the distinction between professional knowledge and inexperience in the ring. Jim gained favor during the last two rounds with his punching and footwork, but it appeared Burke had eased off. At the bout's end, the crowd cheered in admiration for both boxers.

Though the match had been advertised as no more than an exhibition, the event was the talk of the town. The press gave the bout extensive coverage, both before and after the match. Indeed, two newspapers featured the match on their front pages. Discussion of the match permeated athletic clubs and business organizations, as well as the predictable bars and saloons. Suddenly, as if the bout itself had been the catalyst, "scientific" boxing had matured into a proper sport, heavily supported by the city's better classes, sanctioned by the press, and pronounced "the only humane way to display pugilistic endeavors."

That Jim Corbett was party to this redefinition of boxing had not been sheer chance. Desire for improvements in the sport had been mounting for years, as people sought to temper its "blood and thunder" image. Athletic club development of amateur boxing instruction and programs actively advanced the change. The press itself, possibly feeling guilty for promoting ring brawling, called anew for true boxing professionalism. Boxing instructors were hired to teach the new "science."

Enthusiasts of the sport sought out new boxers to represent the growing movement, and Corbett offered all the characteristics to advance it. To many, Jim had become the embodiment of this new form of boxing. Of course, he did not invent it; but he was already its most popular exponent, its unique proponent. Yet, at this point in his career, Jim's public image as a celebrity extended only as far as the Bay area. It would be a few more years before the rest of the country was taken with his model of pugilistic refinement.

At the time, Jim was not really cognizant of the public's feeling about uplifting an otherwise suspect and brutal sport. He was pleased to have lasted eight rounds with Burke, though somewhat disappointed at his performance, as were some members of the press. They had identified his apparent lack of confidence at the bout's inception, and his hesitation to carry the action in the later rounds. Still, they expressed confidence in Jim and complimented him for "maintaining his prestige as the leading amateur of the West Coast."

In contrast to the public's acclaim, Patrick remained unreconciled to his son's appearance in the exhibition. He refused to attend the match, but did follow the press accounts, obviously susceptible to the newspapers' melodramatic reporting of the entire event. Not coincidentally, a week after the bout, Jim announced that he would not engage in any public or private sparring matches in the future, in accordance with "a promise made to his relatives." Some reporters questioned his commitment, pointing out that he had made such promises before. Others manipulated his statement, contriving a challenge to "create" a future confrontation involving another of the city's favorite boxers.

Joe Choynski had recently joined the California Athletic Club and quickly become its resident heavyweight.[10] Choynski had won a number of bouts and was being promoted to take on tougher boxers. He challenged the Olympic Club's W.J. Kenealy to a four-round set-to, a trophy to be awarded the winner. While the meeting was between athletic club amateurs, club members took the bout as an opportunity to place side bets on the outcome, a customary occurrence. Jim assisted Kenealy in his training for the match. He also served as Kenealy's second during the actual meeting. Choynski—or more likely a reporter using Choynski's name—chided Jim for not facing him directly, instead of "hiding" behind Kenealy.

At the end of November, Choynski and Kenealy met in an exhibition of four rounds or "whomever dropped the other man first." Choynski beat Kenealy on points in an exciting bout that lasted the entire four rounds. After the decision, Choynski dramatically pointed his finger at Jim. The press interpreted the gesture as a challenge. Reporters would not give up until they had succeeded in getting Joe and Jim to meet in the ring.

In January, 1888, a number of new Olympic Club board members initiated a debate about continuing or quitting the sponsorship of boxing exhibitions. As the debate progressed, Watson believed he would lose his job as the club's instructor. In a surprise move, early February, Watson announced his resignation from the Olympic Club, though he indicated a continuing alliance with the Acme Athletic Club. In addition, he said he had gone into partnership with another boxer in a saloon venture. (When boxers retired in San Francisco, it seemed they always opened up a saloon.)

Everyone was surprised when the Olympic Club appointed Jim its boxing instructor, as Watson's replacement, at a salary of $150 a month. Club leaders believed Jim's celebrity would prove a great benefit to the organization, enhancing their entire amateur athletic program. The *Chronicle*, however, was dubious of the appointment. "Corbett is undoubtedly a clever young gentleman, but it is doubtful if he will prove the success as a teacher that Watson has."[11]

Despite his father's protestations, Jim quit his position at the bank. The new job both improved his financial position and gained him recognition in his career of choice. He and Olive moved out of the Corbett house (after living there a year and a half) and obtained an apartment at 102 Ellis Street, not far from his new place of work. Patrick expressed dismay at Jim's decision to leave the bank; it was as if Jim had squandered his last chance at respectability. Patrick was further upset that Jim had now openly declared boxing his future career. Though Jim promised his father he would not turn professional, he nevertheless was elated by his new position and "heady" with club members' perception of his being the foremost exemplar of "scientific" boxing.

The club had opined correctly. Within a few months of Jim's appointment, his classes were filled; in fact, they were oversubscribed with young men eager to take lessons from "the professor." A *Chronicle* report extolled Jim's unique drawing power.

> Under the able instruction of Professor Jim Corbett, the popular boxing teacher at the Olympic Club, the boxing class has increased largely during the last few weeks. On each class night there is an average of 20 names on the boxing book, while 35 or 40 are frequently subscribed on several nights throughout the week.[12]

A month later, newspapers reported Jim's classes to be so large that the club planned to hire an assistant to help him.

In fact, boxing classes in general were becoming so popular in San Francisco that a number of new athletic clubs and private instructors (including Watson) opened facilities. It seemed every "young colt" in town desired to emulate Jim Corbett.

During the spring, the California Athletic Club announced sponsorship of a match between Joe McAuliffe and Frank Glover, two well-known professional heavyweights, to take place in club rooms, May 21. The winner would get the gate receipts and title as champion of the Pacific Coast. (Unlike the Olympic Club, the California Athletic Club frequently sponsored "money" bouts among professionals. Other local athletic clubs followed the CAC, but could not offer comparable purses.) Joe McAuliffe asked Jim to assist him in training for the match. As was common at the time, if a boxer won the bout, his seconds would receive a small share of the winnings.

No sooner had Jim agreed to help McAuliffe than some Olympic Club members began to urge that Jim should face the winner of the McAuliffe/Glover bout, in their club rooms. While neither Jim nor the club would likely sanction such a meeting, the press promoted the idea as an interesting challenge. "Corbett's a likely lad, who has increased wonderfully in science and who is quite heavy and clever enough to make it decidedly interesting for either Glover or McAuliffe."[13]

As the date of the McAuliffe/Glover match neared, the press continued their promotion of a meeting between the winner and Jim, claiming that Jim himself was "desirous of a ten-round set-to." Finally, Jim had to publicly announce that he had no intention of boxing the winner. Both the Olympic Club Board of Directors and Patrick were relieved. Instead, in a club sparring exhibition, Jim and Kenealy boxed four rounds, to a full house (ladies included) who cheered the boxers' rendition of "scientific" entertainment.

McAuliffe beat Glover in forty-nine rounds, the bout lasting three hours and fifteen minutes. McAuliffe earned more than $2,000 for his efforts. The press, however, expressed outrage at the length of the bout and its savage result. (Glover's face was a bloody pulp when the fight was stopped.) As had happened before, some local politicians initiated an effort to outlaw professional boxing of this kind. Newspapers, however, used the event as an argument for Jim to meet McAuliffe. Again, Jim and the Olympic Club refused, the club declaring: "He (Jim) is a clever boxer and a very gentlemanly fellow, and he has absolutely nothing to gain by becoming a professional pug. He need do nothing more than he does to maintain his name as a good teacher and good boxer."[14]

In July, at a testimonial for Tom Cleary, a West Coast middleweight, Jim and Frank Glover engaged in a two-round exhibition. Jim clearly demonstrated his ability to match a professional, causing the press to call, even more loudly, for a bout between Jim and McAuliffe. Again, Jim refused.

Throughout the remainder of the year, Jim's classes flourished and his young boxers distinguished themselves in bimonthly club exhibitions. When challenges were made to Jim and the club, they were summarily declined. Whenever Jim appeared in a sparring exhibition, he further enhanced his reputation as a highly competent, strong, fast, and graceful boxer. Thanks to his compelling appearance, the number of women attending these exhibitions increased at each event.

Near the end of the year, the Olympic Club, along with other athletic clubs in the Bay Area, sponsored a track meet. Among the marshals for the sprint events was Jim, whose unlikely assistant was Joe Choynski. Their collaboration was reported to be cordial, and their assigned events were well handled. A week later, when Choynski acted as referee for a match between Billy Mahan and James Leahy, which lasted thirty-three rounds, Jim commended Joe on his control of the bout. Yet some reporters seemed disappointed that the two had not hurled expletives at one another.

The new year, 1889, began with a bidding war among the various San Francisco athletic clubs, each of whom attempted to sponsor the more attractive boxing event. Even the Olympic Club found itself in the position of having to participate if it wanted to maintain its position as the city's most prestigious boxing venue. Bidding for events exceeded $1,000 for a ten-round bout, and contestants had not yet even been selected. Each club strove to be recognized as the best place where boxers could perform for "lucrative" purses. Professional stake contests, in which money was put up by the opponents' backers, meant that many thousands of dollars changed hands, both openly and behind the scenes.

Boxing enthusiasts wondered what had become of amateurism, as their favorites were increasingly enticed into appearing on professional cards. The press seemed to be tacitly approving the situation by suggesting various groups of opponents, not to mention attempting to persuade certain clubs to sponsor specific events. One such proposal was a ten-round bout between Jim and Peter Jackson, a Negro who had just been hired as an instructor at the California Athletic Club, having recently arrived from Australia.

Born in the West Indies in 1861, Peter Jackson began his boxing career in Australia in 1882. He came to California in late 1888 as heavyweight champion of Australia. His intent was to meet the best boxers in the U.S. and make sufficient money to retire. Jackson was a solidly built young man, six-foot, one-inch tall, weighing 200 pounds, who had achieved the reputation of being an intelligent, strong, durable puncher. It wasn't until he reached the States that he realized his color not only prevented him from appearing in parts of the U.S., but elicited statements from potential opponents, such as John L. Sullivan, that they would never face a Negro in the ring. The San Francisco boxing scene, however, presented no such racial barriers; indeed, it welcomed Jackson into the competitive bidding for club supremacy.

The *Chronicle* set the stage for a confrontation between Jim and Jackson. "A general desire has been expressed among the admirers of fistic exercises to see Jim Corbett, the Olympic Club professor, and Peter Jackson, the Australian champion, to come together in a scientific contest."[15]

Jackson had expressed a desire to meet Jim, as long as there was "anything in it" for him. Since each was employed at a rival athletic club, neither sponsor would allow the other to gain the advantage of staging such an event in their own rooms. The press pushed for the bout, even persuading some Olympic Club officials to offer $1,000 to Jackson for a ten-round match in their quarters. The California Athletic Club, Jackson's employer, in turn offered $1,500, the bout to be held in their rooms. Olympic Club members, however, would not be allowed entrance. In spite of the press' efforts, the arrangement was ultimately dropped. Since the two clubs could not agree, it "ended in smoke," according to observers. Nothing is known of Jim's feelings or desires regarding the match, as he seemed to be concentrating his attention on conducting his boxing classes.

At a benefit for Joe McAuliffe, Jim boxed two rounds with Rich McCord, a heavyweight boxing student at the club. At the benefit, Joe Choynski announced

he was going to meet Frank Glover in a fight to the finish, though Choynski was presumably still an amateur. Choynski beat Glover badly, and the newspapers immediately began promoting a contest between Choynski and Jim "for blood," using their supposed animosity as leverage for the argument.

In April, it appeared the press had successfully persuaded both Choynski and Jim to meet. A month-long verbal battle, in which to each boxer was attributed provocative statements against the other, finally created a call for a bout, time and place unspecified. Whether Choynski and Jim had actually made these allegations against one another is doubtful. Both Corbett, in his autobiography, and Choynski, in his interview with *Ring* magazine, later stated that they had been duped into meeting, not only by the press, but also by members of their respective clubs, men intent upon besting their rivals. Corbett claimed that his father, staunchly against the bout in the first place, had persuaded his son not to box for money. Actually, as an employee of the Olympic Club, Jim could not receive direct compensation in any case. Nonetheless, whatever might be obtained from boxing enthusiasts for "training purposes" or "on the side" was generally overlooked, as was common at the time for any match, amateur or professional.

With the match all but imminent, the press suddenly sounded a discordant note of caution, declaring that if the bout took place anywhere except under the auspices of an athletic club, it might cause trouble, not only from the police, but from "young and ardent" admirers of each boxer. At this point, of course, such concerns seemed more a clever ploy to heighten tension about the match.

When a ring is surrounded by two distinct factions composed of hot-blooded youths free of restraints, the contest is not likely to be allowed to proceed with the peaceful hush of a lawn tennis tournament. Under such circumstances, one fight begets money, and nature's weapons moreover are not the only ones used.[16]

Crowds of enthusiasts anxiously awaited the event, and the police were alerted to any eventuality.

Based on a "hot tip," wagonloads of spectators followed the Choynski and Corbett forces to Sausalito on the morning of May 29. From there, they chased the athletes' entourages on the road to Fairfax, "like a Fourth of July procession." Included were politicians by the wagonload; saloonkeepers by the dozen, both on horseback and on foot; thespians, their smart attire soon marred by the dust; along with every other species of ring enthusiast. Before long, half the rural residents of Marin County were well aware that the big city's sporting crowd were transferring their attention to the normally quiet countryside. Vehicles were so hard to find that enterprising drivers charged five dollars to transport spectators, many of them balancing on sideboards, grimly absorbing the shock of roadway ruts.

About two miles short of Fairfax, traveling parties turned through a rustic gateway and pulled up before a large barn, joining an already boisterous congregation of men, horses, and a variety of vehicles that had much in common with the colorful opening of the state fair. Most of those in attendance were uninvited, the powerful seduction of a Corbett-Choynski match having drawn them to this pugilistic presentation.

The press had amply prepared the crowd for the anticipated confrontation: a battle of local heroes who held old grudges; the Olympic Club against the California Athletic Club; labor vs. capital; gentile vs. Jew.

Corbett and Choynski had already arrived and were preparing themselves in shanties near the barn. The ring was situated in the barn loft. A large crowd already filled the barn, threatening by their numbers and weight to bring down the entire structure around them. The event's first dramatic attraction occurred when the invited guests were ushered into the barn to take their rightful ringside seats, evicting interlopers who had been occupying the space. Boos and jeers greeted the monied guests as they made themselves comfortable. A number of strategically placed guards, armed with pistols, guaranteed that the crowd would remain calm.

Jim was first to appear, a grim smile fixed on his handsome face. He wore pink trunks and a green sash (Olympic Club colors), entwined with red, white, and blue. His legs were bare, and he wore his old boxing shoes. Choynski entered the ring covered by a large shirt, his thin legs made to look even more spindly by black tights. When he discarded the shirt, however, the audience was impressed by his imposing physique, thickly-muscled shoulders, and powerful arms.

At 10:45 A.M., bets were still being made when the referee called the boxers to the center of the ring, on the clear, brisk morning of May 30. Corbett weighed 185 pounds; Choynski 165. Both wore lethal, thin leather gloves with almost no padding. When they met with the referee, Corbett offered to bet Choynski $500; but the latter declined. As the men returned to their respective corners, a decorous silence fell over the crowd.

At the gong, both boxers sparred cautiously at long range for a few moments. Jim then took the initiative, displaying dazzling footwork and punching Choynski at will. The entire round consisted of Jim's attempt to confound Choynski, jabbing him frequently from all directions. Choynski, in turn, waited patiently for an opening and shot a left into Jim's ribs, leaving a welt. In the process, both men missed many punches.

The second round was judged to be the best of the short encounter. Jim continued to be the aggressor. He rocked Choynski with a solid left; Choynski responded with a blow to Jim's chin that drew blood. That launched a long exchange of blows, devoid of science, designed simply to knock the other out. Jim's right to the ear made Choynski hold on, and the referee yelled "Break! Break!" They rushed forward again, pummeling one another with punches, shoving, and clinching. Choynski went down, half-struck, half-pushed, but was up immediately. Jim had Choynski on the ropes when time was called.

Their respective seconds warned each boxer to control his temper; so the third round reverted to a simple sparring match, Jim backing his opponent around the ring, Choynski waiting for an opening. Round four was a repetition of the third, no damage done; and spectators began to express their disappointment with the evidently tame encounter.

Just as the fifth round was about to begin, a shout from the roof of the barn warned that the sheriff had been sighted. Immediately, both boxers shed their thin, leather gloves and quickly laced on over-stuffed "pillow" gloves to indicate a friendly set-to was taking place in a picnic atmosphere. By the time the sheriff arrived, the loft had been deserted and the ring stakes taken down. Gentlemen with fishing poles suddenly materialized to inquire if there were any trout streams in the neighborhood. Quietly but firmly, the astute sheriff informed them that they had better pack up and get over the county line if they desired to partake in a prizefight. The boxing parties had been able to charter a train in San Rafael to return to San Francisco. Most others made their way

back to the city the same way they had originally come to the site. Both boxers indicated they planned to meet again in a few days, and the referee consented.

On June 5, the men met again, on a river barge, near the town of Benecia. This time, the bout went twenty-seven rounds, with Jim the ultimate victor. As the *Chronicle* reported: "The Corbett/Choynski prize fight, which had been the absorbing topic in sporting circles for months past, was decided in a manner which settles thoroughly a long disputed question of fistic supremacy that has agitated two athletic clubs."[17]

Information had leaked out the day before that referee Patsy Hogan had ordered the boxers to be ready to resume their battle, this time at a "safe" spot on the Sacramento River, Dillon Point, near the salmon-fishing town of Benecia. For this bout, however, the crowd would be restricted. Those invited were told to board a boat at the Vallejo Street pier at 1:30 A.M., to be transported to the boxing site. By 5:30 A.M., all of the spectators were on the barge. Come six, the ring was ready for the boxers.

At 6:25 A.M., both contenders entered the ring, at which point it was discovered that Choynski had not brought his boxing gloves. After vigorous debate—it reached a point where the match was nearly postponed—Jim agreed to let Choynski wear skin gloves. Jim chose to wear two-ounce gloves because he had injured his right thumb in their previous bout and preferred the protection they afforded him. (Actually, when two-ounce gloves became wet with water or blood, they proved to be as formidable as skin gloves.) This time, Corbett weighed about 180 pounds, and Choynski 172. Both men appeared in fine shape. At about 7:00 A.M., the match began.

Choynski was the aggressor for the first three rounds, with Jim dancing and ducking his opponent's blows. In the third round, a left to the stomach floored Choynski, but he recovered immediately. In the fourth, two jabs to Choynski's mouth drew blood. Corbett won the round, and from there on he took the lead.

In the fifth round, a left to Choynski's nose sent blood coursing down his neck and chest. In the seventh, another left to Choynski's nose flushed yet more blood. Knowing that his chances of victory were rapidly waning, Choynski rushed Jim to attempt a knockout. Instead, a blow to the nose gushed blood down Choynski's chest and onto the floorboards. A hard left to the stomach floored him. So much of Choynski's blood now covered the floor that it became treacherously slick.

Through the fifteenth round—well beyond the limit anyone had imagined the bout would last—the situation remained the same: Jim moved nimbly, punched sharply, and stayed away from his opponent's knockout attempts; though bleeding profusely, Choynski gamely pursued the battle. During the fifteenth and sixteenth rounds, both men looked drained, Jim evidently devoid of strength.

The eighteenth seemed to settle the bout in Jim's favor. A constant rain of blows to Choynski's nose caused an incessant flow of blood, now splattered over ringside spectators. More than once, the quantity of blood in Choynski's mouth nearly choked him. Everyone knew it was only a matter of time before Choynski would have to capitulate. That Choynski endured until the twenty-seventh round amazed the audience. He now seemed able only to stagger around the ring, rushing Jim whenever he could see him.

After a stiff pull at the brandy bottle, Choynski, desperate to bludgeon Jim, rushed him to start the twenty-seventh. A right to the neck dropped Choynski, but he struggled to his feet and rushed Jim again. Crowding Choynski into the ropes,

Jim hit him with a combination left and right to the head, which finally downed his opponent. Choynski rolled over on his back, exhausted and beaten, a bloody, disfigured, and disheartened man.

After the count, the vanquished Choynski managed to struggle to his corner. Jim came over and shook hands with him, moments before he was swept up in a crowd of admirers who had jumped the ropes to congratulate the victor. The bout ended at 8:40 A.M.; by 9:35, the boat was loaded with principles and supporters, on its way back to the city. Attended by a physician, Choynski found that his injuries were more psychological than physical; for almost the entire trip back, he wept bitterly.

Jim displayed few marks from the bout but found that he had fractured his left hand, likely in the fifth round. Since his right hand had already been injured, he had fought almost the entire bout with both hands disabled.

A large crowd awaited the arrival of the boat at the Vallejo Street pier, and the boxers were mobbed as they disembarked. Observing the contestants, the crowd easily discerned who had won, and as the hacks carried the boxers away, they scattered to spread the news throughout the city.

Jim, of course, was euphoric over his victory. He was feted at the Olympic Club and glorified as the foremost exponent of the new boxing science, though the bout had been anything but scientific. It didn't matter. Jim had become the club's hero and defender. No one was surprised that Jim showed "a good-sized head," thanks to all the attention he received, not to mention the numerous financial considerations tendered by ecstatic Olympic Club members.

For its part, the *Chronicle* refused to retire the story. It called the bout "brutal" and continued to portray the contestants as "enemies," all this after having shamelessly promoted the confrontation for months. In its report of the bout's aftermath, the newspaper spent more space commenting on winning and losing bettors than on the boxers themselves. A small note buried in the paper a few days later mentioned that Jim and Joe had met to "settle their differences" and left as friends.

Patrick was not so forgiving. He had refused to attend the bouts in protest of Jim's having broken his word about boxing. Though it was reported that Patrick was pleased by the outcome, he again pleaded with Jim to retire from the ring. A few days later, newspapers reported that Jim had announced his retirement. "Jim Corbett has retired permanently from the ring, and will resume his position of professor of boxing at the Olympic Club, with a largely increased salary."[18]

Jim's monthly salary had indeed been increased to $250, inflating both his pocketbook and his ego. Still, club members believed that Jim, if given the proper incentives, could be persuaded to fight again. They were correct in their assessment, although such efforts took an ironic turn.

A number of Joe Choynski's admirers, among them local boxers, who honored respected losers as well as winners, planned to give Choynski a benefit at Mechanic's Pavilion, a hall frequently used for boxing shows. On July 15, a full house honored the young man for his fighting "pluck." Featured that evening was a four-round exhibition between Joe and Jim. The match was light and friendly, the opponents grinning throughout. At the final call for time, they shook hands and hugged one another, to the cheers of the crowd.

In a discordant note to an otherwise enjoyable evening, the *Chronicle* revealed that Jim had requested payment for his sparring efforts with Choynski.

The Choynski benefit has caused some stir in athletic circles, as Jim Corbett insisted in getting paid for his services in going on to spar four rounds with the beneficiary. Corbett says what is perfectly true, that he made very little out of his battle with Choynski, and as boxing is his business, and his appearance helped equally to swell the gate receipts, he was entitled to some recompense.[19]

One newspaper asked Jim whether he was now a professional or amateur. Another acknowledged his business acumen. Members of the Olympic Club wished Jim would talk less in public. In fact, the *Chronicle* suggested a "muzzle" be put on Jim before he indiscriminately challenged any more "pugs." For a number of months, these admonitions appear to have been successful, as Jim was reported to be working hard with his boxing students, turning down numerous opportunities to himself lace on the gloves in earnest.

Jim appeared in a number of exhibitions at the Olympic Club during the fall, usually with his students, although one, on September 29, was with a professional boxer, John Donaldson. The press, however, continued their relentless campaign to bait Jim with supposed challenges from various boxers, including Joe McAuliffe, who categorically denied the comment. The *Chronicle* went so far as to suggest that Jim "could stand up to John L. Sullivan for six rounds," and, "if Sullivan comes to the Golden Gate on his projected sparring tour he will see that the young professor gets the coveted chance to distinguish himself."[20]

Like many of the press' promotional forays, such challenges quickly disappeared. Nonetheless, they seemed to have had a decided effect on Jim. Observers believed that Jim had become caught up with his own accomplishments, abetted by the accolades received from admirers and supporters. Apparently, Jim believed himself already to be not only an athletic, but also a social success, though only twenty-three years old and from an immigrant workingman's family. Neither family nor friends were able to alter his disposition.

One morning, the Board of Directors of the Olympic Club were shocked to read in the *Chronicle* that their arch-rival, the Golden Gate Athletic Club, in receipt of a telegram from Professor Jim Corbett, announced that he would meet Dominick McCaffrey in their quarters for $4,000, if given the chance. A hastily convened meeting of the Board and Jim confirmed the truth of his offer. While he was admonished for breaking club rules, the Board hesitated banning him from the club in order to protect their own image. Instead, they began a behind-the-scenes search for a replacement for Jim, to be revealed at a more appropriate and less embarrassing time.

Moreover, Jim and his father also had words about Jim's public pronouncements. Only a few months before, Jim had promised Patrick he would not turn professional nor engage in any competitive matches. Both promises were broken when he declared his intention to face McCaffrey. Undoubtedly, Patrick was disturbed by his son's behavior, but Jim did not seem to take the implications of his actions seriously. After all, he had decided to make boxing his career; and there was considerable money to be earned with his acknowledged skills and increasing number of admirers. He had already demonstrated an ability to attract money through "expense ac-

counts" and side bets, along with a coterie of supporters who aggressively promoted Jim at every opportunity.

Even Jim's friends were unable to persuade him that his public appeal was being built by people primarily out for their own financial benefit. Olive, Jim's wife, was equally concerned about her husband's flights of ego. When it was announced that Jim had started a new boxing class for women—the class was quickly filled—she turned to Jim's brothers for help. Members of the press, the same people who had spent two years promoting Jim, now declared that he had "grown too far too fast."

Jim Corbett, age 24. Having undergone four years of vigorous training, including two as the Olympic Club's boxing instructor, Jim was about to embark on a professional career. (Bustout Productions)

On December 21, Jim abruptly re-signed his position as boxing instructor of the Olympic Club, in order to sign for a match against Dave Campbell in Portland, Oregon, for a purse of $500. Simultaneous with this announcement, the Olympic Club revealed they were seeking to hire a new boxing instructor.

Jim's introduction to the ranks of professional boxing could not have begun more inauspiciously, both for his boxing ability and his pride. The meeting with Campbell, a journeyman boxer at best, was for ten rounds, using five-ounce gloves, large for the time. The bout ended in a draw. The *New York Clipper* reported the bout "a farce from beginning to end. Corbett showed the most science, but the display was so tame as to disgust the specta-tors, who numbered about 2,500, so that the principles, and others who had a finger in the pie, fared very well financially."[21]

The *San Francisco Chronicle*, closely following Corbett's new professional role, called the match "purely an exhibition to draw gate money" and definitely not a test for Corbett.

Jim returned to San Francisco embarrassed. The press, previously adulatory, had demeaned his ring performance. He had given up a prestigious job at the Olympic Club. His family and wife were discomfited by his public behavior. Had he made the correct decision? Or had he been carried away by resplendent, mis-leading headlines and persuasive, self-serving admirers?

3. THE ROAD TO SULLIVAN

Jake Kilrain was a heavily muscled bruiser, an exemplar of the old school of ferocious, bullying, bloody pugilism.

Kilrain had been appearing in a sparring olio as part of a theatrical troupe. To secure additional income, he proclaimed an open challenge—and an attractive purse, winner-take-all—to any heavyweight who would face him. His first challenger was a journeyman boxer, Felix Vacquelin. Kilrain easily disposed of him in three rounds, pocketing the prize of $2,000.

Among those applying to meet Kilrain was a relative newcomer to professional boxing, Jim Corbett. Knowing only that Corbett was a young upstart from California, who had been labeled by the San Francisco press "the coming champion of the world," Kilrain agreed to meet him on February 17, 1890, in New Orleans. Fully confident that he had contracted for another easy bout, Kilrain derided the 'Frisco press's adulation of Jim as "a good joke."

Born February 9, 1859, in Greenpoint, Long Island, New York, Kilrain began his boxing career in 1880, a strong young man, five feet, ten and a half inches in height, weighing 195 pounds. In 1884, although losing his three professional bouts, he gained attention by scoring well against Charley Mitchell, Mike Cleary, and Jack Burke, all of them opponents of high repute. Mitchell had recently arrived from England, intent upon demonstrating his abilities in order to challenge John L. Sullivan. Most pugilism observers, however, thought Mitchell harbored delusions of grandeur; his top boxing weight was 157, middleweight by U.S. standards, lighter than Sullivan by fifty pounds. Yet when Mitchell drew with Kilrain in four rounds, many thought Mitchell might at least hold his own against the champion.

The Mitchell/Kilrain meeting had been a bare-knuckle encounter, fought within a twenty-foot-square ring, four posts in each corner, a single rope attached to the top of each post enclosing the ring. The referee was attired in a derby hat and dress clothes. Seconds for each boxer stood inside the ring at their man's corner, often having to scatter when the combatants came their way.

In December, 1887, a now seasoned Kilrain met Jem Smith, bare knuckles, at Isle des Souverain, France, for $5,000 a side and the championship of England. After 106 rounds, the bout ended in a draw, mercifully called on account of darkness. Despite the outcome, Kilrain gained a reputation as a hard puncher with remarkable endurance, both features that appealed to Richard K. Fox, publisher of the *National Police Gazette.* Fox detested Sullivan, and he perceived an opportunity to groom Kilrain to face the champion and bait Sullivan into a match. When Sullivan initially refused to accept Kilrain's (Fox's) challenge, Fox gave the *Police Gazette* heavyweight championship belt to Kilrain. Finally, Sullivan consented to meet Kilrain, partly to retain his title, partly to embarrass Fox.

On July 8, 1889, Kilrain and Sullivan met at Richburg, Mississippi, for $10,000 a side. At the last minute, the match had to be moved from New Orleans because local police warned they would stop the contest. Prior to this meeting, bouts had been fought either bare knuckles or gloved, London Prize Ring rules or the new Marquis of Queensberry rules. With the increasing popularity and use of the

Richard K. Fox, flamboyant editor and publisher of the National Police Gazette. His newspaper's scandalous wood engravings of women and sensationalistic stories made it the top sporting paper in the U.S. for more than fifty years.

Queensberry rules, the Kilrain/Sullivan contest was to be the last bare-knuckles championship bout.

The match was fought in a twenty-four-foot square ring, two ropes extended from post to post, with spectators close enough to the ring to drape their arms casually over the lower ropes. Ostentatiously surrounding the ring stood Mississippi Rangers, rifles in hand. When Sullivan objected to their presence, he was told they were there to "keep the peace." The referee was casually dressed; the seconds located outside the ring, at each boxer's corner. Bat Masterson, once sheriff of Dodge City, later boxing reporter for the *New York Morning Telegraph,* served as the designated timekeeper, sans sidearms.

The match began at midday, under very hot, humid conditions. In spite of the heat and humidity, the spectators, exclusively male, were evidently attired in dress coats, the appropriate garb of the day. Most believed the bout would last but a short time, what with the oppressive heat and Sullivan's vaunted punching power. Yet, comparing the combatants in person, Kilrain seemed equal to Sullivan in size and muscularity. Kilrain's seconds were Mike Donovan, beginning his career as boxing instructor at the New York Athletic Club, and Charley Mitchell, Sullivan's erstwhile opponent.

When Kilrain and Sullivan met with the referee in the center of the ring, each man gave $1,000 for him to hold, as personal side bets. At that very moment, the local sheriff rode up on horseback, dismounted, strode to the ring, climbed through the ropes, and summarily addressed the crowd, declaring that he forbade the bout and warning spectators he would "use every means to restrain the contestants." The crowd laughed and threatened the sheriff to try it. Realizing his predicament, the sheriff quickly departed and the bout began.

To everyone's surprise, the contest lasted seventy-five rounds, both boxers so exhausted at the end they could barely stay on their feet. At that point, the referee gave the decision to Sullivan. Moments before the referee's decision, Mitchell had dispatched a message to the champion's corner, asking if Sullivan would make Kilrain "a present of $2,000" if he gave in. Sullivan agreed; but because the referee ended the bout so quickly, Kilrain lost his "present." In reviewing the contest, Mike Donovan said the fight "was not a punishing affair." Other observers declared the boxers had fought "like old washerwomen." In any case, it surely had been a terrific test of endurance.

Meanwhile, Jim Corbett had returned to San Francisco after his unsatisfactory encounter with Dave Campbell in Portland, Oregon. Chagrined and only a few hundred dollars richer, Jim passed the time by sparring daily at the Golden Gate Athletic Club, sometimes with colleague Joe Choynski. At the same time, he sought work in the ring, preferably a match with a good purse. As for his local contacts, they seemed to be avoiding him since he abandoned his job at the Olympic Club and turned professional. A report indicated that the Olympic Club had made an offer of $5,000 a year to Jack Dempsey to become the club's boxing instructor.

It was at this time that Jim learned of Jake Kilrain's offer, for an announced purse of $3,500, winner-take-all, a very attractive sum of money for a short bout of six rounds. Immediately, Jim cabled a challenge to Kilrain. To his pleasant surprise, Kilrain quickly accepted. The match would be staged in New Orleans, where the Muldoon Combination, a theatrical troupe made up of sparrers and wrestlers (including Kilrain) were appearing. Given the date for the match, February 17, Jim had only two weeks to prepare. Nonetheless, confident that he was already in good condition, Jim believed that some deliberate training would meet the demands of a reputedly formidable opponent. When San Francisco newspapers heard of the planned contest, however, they considered that Jim had taken on more than he could handle. Kilrain had already met the top heavyweights, including his seventy-five-round battle with Sullivan. How could Corbett overcome such experience?

The Corbett/Kilrain encounter was slated as part of a three-event program at the Southern Athletic Club, New Orleans's elite men's club, whose members included the leading cotton plantation owners. In fact, the referee of the bout was a well-known cotton baron by the name of Violette, who declared he would, with objectivity, "decide the contest on its merits." No one objected to the fact that he had never before refereed.

When Jake Kilrain, massive and strong, entered the ring, he stared impassively at Jim. It was announced that Kilrain weighed 201 pounds. Jim had stepped through the ropes smiling. Yet when he stood next to Kilrain, he seemed "a mere boy," according to observers. Jim weighed in at 183 pounds.

At the beginning of the first round, both boxers sprang forward, eager to analyze each other's style, since they had never met before. The first round interchange consisted of Kilrain's launching and missing many blows, while Jim countered with lefts to the head and body. When he shot his vaunted right at Jim, only to find him constantly out of reach, Kilrain seemed flustered. He then took to clinching, using his free hand to slug Jim. The crowd voiced their displeasure with Kilrain's tactics; and when Jim landed with a left to the face, they cheered his counterpunching. By the end of the first, Kilrain looked surprised and somewhat shaken.

The second round opened with Jim

shooting a strong left hook flush to Kilrain's face. Stung, the veteran stared in amazement at his young opponent. Kilrain fought back furiously with a flurry of lefts and rights, any one of which was powerful enough to floor an opponent, if he had been hit; but Jim evaded every punch. When Kilrain finally landed a hard right to Jim's neck, Jim blasted back a left that caught Kilrain over his left eye, opening a cut and drawing blood. The crowd went wild, and Kilrain seemed to lose heart. Suddenly, to almost everyone's astonishment, the outcome seemed decided. Kilrain returned to his corner in a surly mood.

The next three rounds reprised the surprising second, Kilrain throwing hard punches, missing Jim altogether or landing only glancing blows as Jim retreated. Jim countered with lefts to the head and abdomen, forcing Kilrain to clinch. Nevertheless, Kilrain continued his relentless pursuit of Jim and was able to land some blows, particularly as they broke clinches.

When the sixth and final round began, the crowd cheered Jim lustily as he squared off with Kilrain. The seasoned gladiator advanced sullenly, determined that the neophyte not further distinguish himself. Yet when Kilrain landed a left, Jim countered with a left to the stomach. When Kilrain's strong right could only tap Jim's face, Jim caught Kilrain with a right to the nose that made him wince. For the remainder of the round, Kilrain missed blows; Jim countered with concussive shots to the head and chest. Even before the end of the round, the crowd was chanting "Corbett! Corbett! Corbett!"

Jim sat smiling in his corner as the referee awarded him the victory. He acknowledged a sustained ovation and was carried to his dressing room by his seconds and a coterie of new-found admirers. Asked to comment on his surprising triumph, Jim proclaimed, with characteristic modesty, "I am the biggest man in the country now and expect to make a good deal of money off my victory." Was it a boast or a challenge, a boxing enthusiast wanted to know.

Kilrain slumped glumly in his dressing room, first claiming that only five rounds had been fought, then insisting he had not been in top shape due to a cold. He complained of his dissatisfaction with the outcome and suggested he and Corbett meet again, in a ten-round match. Jim responded by saying he would consider Kilrain's challenge but could not promise anything. After all, he was now $3,500 richer.

News of Jim's relatively easy win over Kilrain caused a sensation throughout the boxing world, particularly surprising Eastern promoters and backers. Many still seemed incredulous that Corbett had beaten Kilrain; they suggested that a longer bout with lighter gloves or a fight-to-the-finish would prove Kilrain the better man. When asked for his opinion of the outcome, John L. Sullivan attached little importance to Jim's victory. "I know this man Corbett, and while I am satisfied he is a clever man, I don't think for a moment that he can whip Kilrain Queensberry rules, with smaller gloves."[1]

Yet, the contest brought Jim vividly to the attention of the Eastern boxing establishment. Who is this young man, Corbett? How good are his scientific techniques? Could he beat an Eastern professional? Let's bring him here to see if he is as great as he claims to be, they suggested. So tendered, an invitation to visit New York was extended. Jim was to demonstrate his ring prowess before the country's most discerning boxing critics.

Soon after Jim's victory over Kilrain, seemingly juxtaposed against his win, an amusing anecdote appeared in newspapers nationwide. The *Tucson Daily Citizen* claimed that, when Jim had stopped there on his way to New Orleans, he had been challenged to a match with George Roskruge, the county surveyor, reported to be the town's heavyweight champion. Supposedly, the match had taken place in the card room of the San Xavier Hotel, the press dutifully reporting each round's action in detail. Corbett, it was reported, had been bested by his challenger, even knocked down a number of times. At the conclusion of his victorious battle, Roskruge had been carried through the city streets by the crowd to shouts of "See, the conquering hero comes."

A week later, a reporter for the *Daily Citizen* admitted that the story had been a complete hoax, designed solely as a practical joke upon the county surveyor. The newspaper apologized to Jim, yet just so are myths created among entertainment's star performers.

While Jim was returning to San Francisco, the *Chronicle* reported the story as a hoax and questioned in their usual brassy fashion if there existed any boxer who could beat Jim Corbett, whom they now labeled "the California wonder."

Jim arrived in 'Frisco a hero. Cheered at the ferry dock, he was accompanied by a large crowd to Mechanic's Pavilion, where he was to be feted. When emcee Billy Jorden introduced "the California wonder," Jim was dragged onto the platform, the audience demanding that he speak. Apparently uncomfortable before the cheering throng, Jim modestly acknowledged their acclaim, stating that he had gone down alone to New Orleans and had simply done his best to uphold his reputation, as well as that of California. When he bowed and retired from the stage, the crowd cheered again "to the echo." Following the event, Jim and Olive retired to the Corbett home for a family get-together.

At this same time, Australian Peter Jackson had again arrived in San Francisco with his manager, boxing promoter Parson Davies. He and Davies were now all the more intent on obtaining a match with Jim, due to his win over Kilrain.

Questioned by the *Chronicle,* Jackson replied:

> The results of the Corbett/Kilrain contest surprised me, but I do not think it was a fair test. I had expected that the California Athletic Club would take some steps toward making a match between Corbett and myself, but I have heard nothing to that effect thus far. I've never seen Corbett, but am inclined to believe that he is an exceedingly clever boxer.[2]

Notwithstanding the misgivings of a number of its members, the Olympic Club saw an opportunity to enhance its standing and take advantage of Jim's new status by offering him a return to the club as their boxing instructor, with a year's contract at an increased salary. Jim readily accepted, feeling that the club's gesture recognized both his increased reputation and his boxing abilities, even though he had chosen to become a professional. Before he resumed boxing classes, however, Jim planned to go East, to satisfy the invitation of promoters and athletic club enthusiasts, anxious to see with their own eyes if this young man from California measured up to their standards.

Though Patrick continued to voice his concern about Jim's chosen profession, he nevertheless gave a large reception for his son at the Corbett residence. Friends and colleagues wished Jim good luck and, in recognition of his recent successes, presented him with a diamond pin, a diamond locket, and a gold watch and chain. Jim kindly acknowledged their gratitude and promised "to do my best to render as good an account of myself" in the next performance as in the last. Armed with letters of introduction from the best local people in athletic circles, Jim and Olive left that evening for New York, their first trip to the nation's most advanced and so-phisticated metropolis, as well as its self-proclaimed boxing mecca.

New York newspapers had already begun their buildup, heralding Jim's visit in grandiose terms. "They (the Eastern-ers) are already talking of the young pro-fessor as being the man to beat Sullivan, saying that Corbett is the coming cham-pion of the world and that Sullivan and Kilrain are stale and past their prime."[3]

Veteran Jack Burke, who had previ-ously faced Jim in an exhibition, was asked whom he believed would beat Sullivan. "One of three men," he replied, "Peter Jackson, Frank Slavin, and America's hope is Corbett."

Burke's reference to Jim as "America's hope" was not surprising in light of the way he had been accelerating the changes taking place in boxing. Handsome—re-porters referred to him as an Adonis—clean-cut, well-mannered, an elegant dresser, non-drinker, and non-smoker. Jim was perceived as a "gentleman" of the ring, a marked contrast from the popular image of John L. Sullivan, Jake Kilrain, and their contemporaries.

Among premier boxing professionals of the day, most were imports to the U.S. Those who were not, like Sullivan, repre-sented ethnic, economic, and social groups little respected by middle and upper classes. So far, few native boxers had gained any substantial following or repu-tation. With the advent of scientific box-ing, an English invention appropriated by Americans, Jim had been popularly se-lected as the country's foremost exponent of the innovative method. Scientific box-ing was perceived not only as a greatly im-proved technique, more utilized by intel-ligent (read: American) boxers than by low-class roughnecks (read: foreigners), but also as a means to capture boxing ti-tles by Americans, for Americans.

Boxing's acceptance and appeal, made even more attractive by the adop-tion of the Queensberry rules, had recently become evident among the better classes of society. The entire boxing industry was gaining respectability as more upscale spectators, including an increasing number of women, were attracted to matches. Le-gitimacy of the entertainment helped to promote exhibitions and tours to cities throughout the country, presented at pres-tigious theaters that featured clean, safe matches performed by recognized propo-nents of the sport. That it was also com-ing to be perceived as a business opportu-nity with sizable profit potential made it increasingly appealing to a number of as-tute entrepreneurs and investors.

A hectic round of banquets, tours of athletic club boxing facilities, and confer-ences gave Jim a speedy opportunity to meet and become acquainted with the "movers" of New York's boxing hierarchy. Even before he had stepped into a ring to demonstrate his abilities, it was reported that Jim had become a "welcome guest." An article in the *Chronicle*, repeating a New York story, revealed his triumphs in the East.

> Jim Corbett, in the expressive vernacular of Gotham, "caught on." Jim's plug hat and smooth-fitting, silk-faced Prince Albert coat impressed the New Yorkers at first sight, and his good-natured smile com-pleted the job. He is the athletic lion of New York, and any one who knows the spirit of the metropolis understands what that means.[4]

To everyone's evident pleasure, Jim, responding to a reporter's question about facing Sullivan, stated: "I am willing to meet Sullivan in any business office he may be pleased to name to arrange terms." Newspapers soon turned the offer into an accomplished match. Even the Board of Directors of the Olympic Club tele-grammed Jim "to fight and fight hard," sending him best wishes. Yet, no real arrangements could be made. Sullivan was about to embark on an exhibition tour, and Jim had to return to San Francisco in two weeks. New York's boxing enthusiasts were disappointed, but found their appetites whetted by prospects to match the pair. Prior to Jim's return to California, they got their opportunity to watch his work in the ring.

On April 14, at the Fifth Avenue Casino Theater in Brooklyn, a boxing exhibition was held between Jim and Dominick McCaffrey, a boxer who had already challenged Sullivan and was known in Eastern circles as a strong puncher. The match was considered more than a mere sparring contest because of a recent dispute between the men. It seems that Jim had invited McCaffrey to travel with him on a sparring tour, and the Easterner had initially accepted. But when Jim heard that McCaffrey had boasted he would "best him," Jim refused to have him along. McCaffrey rebutted by declaring that Corbett would not "get the upper hand, if he could prevent it." Whether this contretemps was purely newspaper hype, or had been an actual disagreement is not clear. In any case, although the match had originally been billed as a four-round, scientific contest for points, the audience anticipated a spirited event and hoped for an out-and-out slugfest.

Both the *New York Clipper* and *New York Times* reported spectators disappointed in the contest. Both boxers were faulted: McCaffrey for running away from Corbett; Jim for not knocking out his cowardly opponent. The *Clipper* declared: "Corbett was not able to show to that advantage which he certainly would have done had his adversary stood up manfully before him, but he satisfied everyone present that he is a remarkably clever boxer."[5]

"McCaffrey No Match for Corbett," headlined the *Times*. "Corbett could have knocked McCaffrey into the middle of next week without half trying."[6]

Though the press believed they had not seen enough of Jim to take a position regarding a match against Sullivan, and spectators blamed him for not punishing McCaffrey more, Mike Donovan, the veteran boxer and instructor at the New York Athletic Club, expressed more enthusiasm for Jim. "I regard Corbett as the cleverest big man I ever sparred with, and I have no hesitation in saying that he is the coming champion. Corbett today is the man that Sullivan was ten years ago, and I regard him (Corbett) as the future champion."[7]

In contrast, Kilrain's manager, Frank Stevenson, demeaned Jim's championship aspirations. "Corbett may be a gentleman, but his head has been swelled. Corbett should have been spanked if he didn't worst McCaffrey, for he is a pudding."

Quick to obtain Jim's reaction to Stevenson's opinion, reporters found him feeling good about his bout with McCaffrey; but he did acknowledge, "It was too easy." He spoke highly of his reception in New York and about the hospitality afforded by members of the New York Athletic Club, who had been so kind to him. Before catching the train back to San Francisco, Jim told reporters he "had enjoyed every minute of his stay in the city."

On his way home, Jim telegraphed the *Chronicle* that he planned to reach 'Frisco on Saturday, April 26. Thus alerted to his arrival, his admirers, including many from the Olympic Club, intended to give Jim a "hearty reception."

The *Chronicle* called Jim's tour of the East "triumphal." They reported he returned with so many sparkling mementos that he could open up a jewelry business. Jim's New York souvenirs included a diamond and sapphire ring from well-known horseman and investor, Phil Dwyer (who also offered to back Jim in future contests), a diamond and emerald ring from the New York Athletic Club, a gold locket from *Sporting* magazine editor Billy O'Brien, and various other gems from lesser notables.

Jim's return to the Olympic Club as boxing instructor elicited renewed interest from pupils and spectators alike. "Great crowds assemble on class nights to see Corbett put his colts through their facings and the genial professor seems thoroughly at home teaching the young men how to smite."

In an interview, Jim reaffirmed his agreement with the Olympic Club: instructor for a year and no professional bouts. No sooner had Jim's statement been printed than Frank Slavin posted a 500-pound sterling forfeit at the Sportsman's office in London to meet Jim, whether in England or America, for 1,000 pounds a side. If Jim accepted the challenge, Slavin said he would be ready to fight in six months. Did Slavin really believe he and Corbett would meet, given the obstacles—distance, money, location, and timing—or was Slavin primarily interested in publicity?

In either case, Slavin's challenge was ill-timed. California's new governor asked his attorney general to write a new law forbidding boxing of any kind because it "defames and degrades the soil of our State." In two weeks, the law easily passed the state legislature with little debate. All boxing promoters and backers found themselves out of business, although boxing instruction could continue in sanctioned locations, such as athletic clubs. The California Athletic Club, grievously hurt by the edict, decided to oppose the new law and scheduled a program of sparring matches to force a court case. Contestants included boxers like Joe Choynski, Bob Fitzsimmons, Jimmy Carroll, and Eddie Greany, soon to become a premier referee.

Although police were visibly in attendance, to everyone's surprise, the matches went on uninterrupted, frustrating club directors, who clearly hoped to foment a confrontation. Within a few weeks, however, a court hearing was begun to test the constitutionality of the law. Delays and debates—along with a good deal of political maneuvering from Sacramento—dragged out the trial. Discussion continued through October, boxing enthusiasts waiting impatiently at ringside for a decision. Since the restrictions did not affect amateur athletic organizations like the Olympic Club, they continued to hold bimonthly tournaments, all under the tutelage of Professor Corbett. The club basked in the limelight, not only because Jim was the city's boxing hero, but also because it was the only venue at which the entertainment could be legally displayed.

In spite of the adulation Jim had been receiving, he had become increasingly frustrated with the limitations placed upon him due to his club contract. Admittedly, he enjoyed teaching neophyte boxers, but he chafed at his inability to take advantage of a growing reputation as a professional. In addition, a two-week hospital stay, with an undisclosed illness, as well as family pressures regarding his inability to become "a family man," likely contributed to a surprising outburst.

In an act of inflated egotism, with a seeming disregard for the possible consequences to his career, Jim secretly wrote a letter to Dave Campbell, Oregon's heavyweight champion, challenging him to a match with a purse. By some means or other—rumor suggested Campbell sent a copy of the letter to the *Chronicle*—the letter was published. Response to its publication generated strong negative reactions from local newspapers and Olympic Club members. The *Chronicle* questioned what had ever possessed Jim to write the letter, since it tended to negate all "the good thoughts" people had about him. Olympic

Club directors hastily met to discuss Jim's latest actions. In a highly charged meeting, they had little choice but to agree that Jim's employment be terminated. But how could they do it without embarrassing the club? Patrick and older brothers, Frank and Harry, both currently holding responsible jobs in the public sector, were disconcerted, since Jim's erratic behavior reflected badly on the Corbetts.

No sooner had the newspapers disseminated reports of the contretemps, than Corbett followed with a statement that claimed he had signed a contract with Morrissey and Daily, managers of the American Vaudevilliers, to appear with them for a year, sparring and "giving representation of Grecian and Roman statuary."

"What?!" asked the *Chronicle* tersely.

Less than a week later, Jim submitted to the *Chronicle* a copy of his letter to Frank Slavin, stating that, "if no other pugilist in this country will call down the boastful Melbourne slugger, I will." Again, the *Chronicle* questioned Jim's recent actions, wondering what could possibly have prompted them.

Boxing reporters and followers of Jim's career doubted he could defeat Slavin. It was then revealed by the Olympic Club of New Orleans that Jim had agreed to a contest with Slavin, at their quarters, on or before April 15, 1891, for a purse of $6,000. They further announced that Slavin had agreed, providing Corbett would wager $2,500 as a side bet and forward a deposit of $1,000 as evidence of good faith. Where Jim obtained the funds is unknown; but he wired his acceptance of the terms and the money to New Orleans. In addition, Jim contacted a number of journalists, including the sporting editor of the *New York World*, informing them that he had accepted the provisions of the match and sent the deposit. Jim had apparently forced the issue

and other interested parties quickly entered the scene.

Phil Dwyer requested that Jim meet Slavin at the Pelican Club in New York. The California Athletic Club offered Slavin a purse of $10,000 if he would meet Corbett in their quarters. Dwyer then raised his offer to match that of the CAC and offered an additional incentive—a side stake of $5,000 to the winner. In the meantime, Charles Stenzel, Jim's current manager, secured an offer for Jim at $150 a week, with a $500 bonus, to tour with a group of vaudevillians, to be called Corbett's Congress of Stars.

Pressures on Jim were now strong. He had certainly put himself in hot water, and his hesitation in responding to criticism suggested uncertainty in dealing with the consequences of his actions.

After keeping out of the newspapers for two weeks, Jim announced his resignation as boxing instructor at the Olympic Club. It was reported that members of the club had persuaded him that resignation was the best course to follow, for all concerned.

Next, Jim fired his manager, Stenzel, thus nimbly detaching himself from any vaudeville commitments. Further, Frank Slavin assisted Jim by deciding to remain in England for an extended length of time, thereby making any match in the near future extremely doubtful.

A week later, all eyes were diverted by the announcement of an exciting boxing event: the California Athletic Club—again free to schedule professional contests—had signed Professor James Corbett and the colored Australian boxer, Peter Jackson, to a match in their rooms on May 21, 1891. Compensation was fixed at $10,000, $8,500 for the winner and $1,500 for the loser. The *Chronicle* boasted: "This is unquestionably the greatest match ever made in the heavyweight class, as the two men are known the world over as the most skillful boxers that the ring has ever produced."[8]

However grossly exaggerated, the claim successfully promoted a major contest between ambitious professionals. It also served to deflect any continuing criticism with regard to Jim's previous actions.

At the beginning of 1891, Jim went to New York, without Olive, to appear in a series of sparring matches on the variety stage and determine if his presence attracted good audiences. This was not the first time that boxers had presented sparring exhibitions as part of a variety show. John L. Sullivan had not only appeared in popular theater, challenging anyone to stay with him for four rounds and $100, but was also, at that moment, performing in a boxing-oriented melodrama, "Honest Hearts and Willing Hands," with some success. Audiences didn't seem to care whether Sullivan could act or not; they came in droves to see him demolish local pugs who foolishly volunteered to meet him.

Staged at theaters, such productions gave the general public a chance to see a real champion in action, an opportunity not usually available to them, presented in a safe and predictable environment. Since boxers' finances were problematic, they benefited by participating in these theatrical events. But it remained a question whether the better classes of theatergoers would react similarly to such perceived low-brow entertainment. Parson Davies, Jackson's boxing manager turned theatrical company manager, wanted to find out. What better man to test changing perceptions of boxing as entertainment than a young, trim, handsome, charming, tasteful, and urbane Jim Corbett, whom he generously billed as "the coming champion."

In kindly fashion, the *New York Clipper* introduced Jim to the theatrical community.

Jim Corbett, the San Francisco heavyweight, and Prof. John Donaldson, one of John L. Sullivan's old opponents with the gloves, form a strong pugilistic attraction at the 8th Street Theater, this city, where they will box at each performance during the current week. Corbett created a highly favorable impression at the time of his former visit to the metropolis, and it goes without saying that, with Donaldson as his *vis a vis,* those who visit the theater this week will be treated to a capital set-to, and that the management can count on big business during the stay of the future stars."[9]

The following week, Corbett and Donaldson performed at Hyde and Behman's Theater, Brooklyn, where they were heralded as the "chief features of the bill." Crowds at the 8th Street Theater had been SRO, and audience reaction to the sparring matches went beyond what anyone had imagined. Evidently, customers of high-class variety had, without question, wholeheartedly embraced boxing as an acceptable, fair, and proper entertainment for their amusement. Parson Davies's company had been declared to be an "athletic attraction of good people" and, because of that fact, "will catch on to a large extent." Seated in the audience at one of these shows was William A. Brady, a theatrical manager currently appearing with his "Nero" company at the Standard Theater. Brady had been keenly attracted to Jim's stage presence, and he envisioned opportunities to employ the young boxer's talent in the not-too-distant future.

From New York, the company traveled to Chicago for a two-week engagement, the first week at the Olympic Theater (serving the North Side), the second at the Madison Street Opera House (serving the South Side). Results were similar to those obtained in New York. "Parson Davies's Company drew overflowing houses nightly. The principal feature of an excellent olio and athletic entertainment was, of course, the sparring bouts between James Corbett and Prof. Donaldson."[10]

By the end of February, Jim returned to San Francisco, to begin training for his match with Peter Jackson. His brief theatrical tour had been a great success, and Jim was encouraged by audiences' reception to his performances. It certainly offered considerable financial opportunity, as well.

Demand for seats at the California Athletic Club had been huge, pushing seat prices to the unprecedented level of fifty dollars a ticket. CAC members and boxing enthusiasts alike were launched into near panic, however, when Jackson injured himself in a freak accident. While riding in a cart, he was thrown from his seat and sustained a badly bruised leg. All training had to be stopped. For the next three weeks, newspapers printed daily reports of his condition. On the other hand, Jim was perceived to be, if anything, trained "too fine."

Still trumpeting the immensity of the contest, the *Chronicle* reported: "His (Corbett's) backers are greatly pleased with his condition, and unless he has a great change of luck before the fight comes off, he will be ready to make the battle of his life."[11]

A month before the contest, Jackson found that hot baths helped to heal his leg. Previously, it had been improving so slowly that local boxing patrons worried the match would have to be postponed. Within days, Jackson was reported to be "looking and feeling fine." It now appeared that: "… neither of the principals in the important contest will have the slightest cause for complaint on the score of condition when they meet."

Three weeks before the meeting, supportive delegations visiting the boxers' respective training camps each returned home convinced that their man was a winner. Fervent betting had not yet begun,

but the odds were in favor of Jackson, 100 to 80. Reporters' analyses of the two men's styles suggested the opponents were starkly dissimilar. The "dusky" Jackson was perceived to be a steady, cool, methodical fighter, one who constantly pushed his man, all the time looking for a chance to use both hands, and was fond of crowding him into a corner to deliver body punishment. By contrast, Jim was seen to be of the hit-and-duck-away school, very showy in science and nimble on his feet, more often out of range than in it. Everyone seemed to believe that the contest would be extremely vigorous but of short duration.

A week before the contest, pool selling and betting heated up, begun at brother Harry's just-opened pool hall and betting saloon on Ellis Street. The odds were ranging from 100-90 to 100-70, in favor of Jackson. In spite of the odds in favor of his "colored" adversary, the *Chronicle* reflected support for Jim.

> Some ferocious sports have been offering to bet that Jim would not enter the ring, that his father would stop him at the last moment. Everyone knows the professor feels confident of his determination to make a game fight. His former clubmates are staking all their money on him. Hallowing (councilman) has been putting some coin on Jim at even, so sure is he that the white boy will defeat the colored champion."[12]

At ring time, Jackson weighed 209; Jim 182. In Jackson's corner were Sam Fitzgerald and Young Mitchell. In Jim's corner were John Donaldson, Bill Delaney (who had helped him in New Orleans against Kilrain), and brother Harry.

The bout lasted sixty-one rounds.

Spectators were not entirely surprised at Jim's ring ability in the opening rounds. Though handicapped by almost thirty pounds, his quickness and footwork held off Jackson. Still, Jackson, with his greater strength and experience, looked like a winner. For the first twelve rounds, both boxers contested every challenge, much to the delight of the CAC's packed rooms.

From the thirteenth to the twenty-ninth round, Jim appeared to have gained the edge over Jackson, his cleverness with the gloves driving Jackson back and scoring many points. Jackson proved unable to use his best weapons against Jim; yet Jim seemed to lack the punch to finish Jackson.

In the thirtieth and thirty-first rounds, Jim tried his best to "slug out" his opponent with straight, hard blows; to no avail. It appeared, however, that Jackson had decided he would be lucky to obtain a draw. The Australian seemed to lose all ability to punish, possibly an indication that his strength had waned. For his part, having injured his left hand in an earlier round, Jim determined to keep away from his powerful antagonist. Indeed, Corbett was later admonished by the press for not having pursued Jackson "to the finish," relying on his youth, better condition, and punching ability.

From the thirty-second round to the sixty-first, there was almost no action, spectators calling it "wearisome." One exception was the forty-first, when Jackson connected to Jim's chin, a blow that forced him onto the ropes. For a moment, Jim appeared stunned; but he rallied with a flurry of punches to Jackson's body. Again in the forty-sixth, a blow by Jackson to Jim's jaw staggered him; but nothing more ensued. When Jackson made some feeble leads, the crowd applauded sarcastically. By the sixty-first round, both men were utterly exhausted. They stood in the middle of the ring, staring warily at one another, arms hanging limply at their sides, scarcely able to move hand or foot.

At last, Jackson turned to the referee and proposed a draw. In an unprecedented action, the referee called time, so he could consult with the directors and Jim. Jim objected to the delay and rejected Jackson's offer. Jackson retorted, "Well, go on, and I'll stay with you." The bout resumed. Immediately before the beginning of the sixty-second round, the referee held up his hand. The bout was ended. "It is evident," he announced to the crowd, "this thing can't go on this way and come to a conclusion; and, as it has come to an unsatisfactory conclusion, I declare it no contest."[13]

In response to the referee's declaration, the crowd rose in protest, claiming he had no right to make that decision. Slumped in their corners, both boxers were so spent they didn't have the strength to object. Jim's admirers, however, surrounded him; others climbed on chairs and the ropes to give him three cheers. Jim smiled grimly through his swollen lips. Officially, the match had lasted sixty-one rounds—four hours and four minutes. When the bout ended, it was 1:45 A.M.

In effect, the referee's decision meant that no bout had ever taken place. All bets, then, were off, and neither boxer was entitled to any money. Bettors were outraged. Both Jackson and Jim were indignant, but remained at a loss over what to do. From Mission to Howard, angry crowds filled Ellis Street and New Montgomery Street, blocking all traffic and refusing to disperse. Harry's saloon had been packed, its patrons anxiously awaiting the results of each round by wire. People outside the saloon couldn't hear the bulletins being read, but the news was passed to them "down the line." Cheers and yells greeted nearly every report. When word reached them that the referee had called "no contest," the crowd came close to riot. The *Chronicle* reported its offices had been besieged by "thousands of anxious men" and: "...looking out from an upper window of the Chronicle office, one's glance fell on a writhing, seething, crowding sea of humanity that almost rivaled the great crowds on election nights."[14]

Newspapers called the decision "a pugilistic mistake." All agreed that Jim had been the virtual winner and should be considered the champion of America. Even Peter Jackson admitted his inability to win. Little noticed, however, were the sighs of relief from California Athletic Club members. Since the referee had stopped the bout and declared it "no contest," they had saved themselves thousands of dollars. Soon it started to smell funny. The press demanded an investigation of the bout.

A week later, due to great public pressure, the CAC's Board of Directors met with the boxers. Optimistically, Corbett and Jackson expected to share the $10,000 purse. To their mutual surprise, each was offered only $2,500; and they had little choice but to accept the reduced fee. In joint frustration and anger, both boxers denounced the club and declared they would have nothing more to do with it, nor should anyone else in the boxing community.

It was the beginning of the end for the CAC. An investigation into the finances of the organization disclosed that certain members had been siphoning funds for some time. The reason Corbett and Jackson had received only $2,500 for their Herculean efforts was because the club had little remaining in its equally exhausted treasury. The club closed a few months later, bankrupt. For unknown reasons, no one questioned the referee's decision as a possibly duplicitous act, one intended to protect the club's depleted meager funds.

The last week in May featured another San Francisco pugilistic event, but it did not take place in the ring. The great John L. Sullivan had come to town, appearing at the Bush Street Theater and starring in the melodrama, "Honest Hearts and Willing Hands." Immense crowds filled the seats. Those unlucky spectators sitting on the curbstones were glad to catch a glimpse of the celebrated champion as he jumped from his carriage to the sidewalk in front of the theater. On opening night, as Jim entered the auditorium, he was greeted with a shout from the gallery of "Good boy, Jim;" he was repeatedly obliged to decline giving a speech before the crowd finally abated their ovation so that the play could begin.

In the last scene of the play, James Daly (Sullivan) knocks out a formidable challenger (Joe Lannon, an authentic Eastern heavyweight) to the vociferous applause of the audience. The SRO crowd, however, was really much more interested in a drama other than the action of the play. Both men—John L. and James J.— in the same theater! Wouldn't it be great if they could meet, with gloves on, on the stage?

The next day, as if it had been planned (it was), newspapers proclaimed that John L. and Jim would meet in the ring, at a benefit to be given in Jim's honor, at the Grand Opera House. A truncated version of Sullivan's play would be presented, culminating in the boxing scene. Jim would assume the role of Tug O'Brien, Jim Daly's (Sullivan's) opponent. Instead of a staged knockout, however, the two would spar four rounds. The city was soon electrified at the prospect; the theater would be packed to the walls. "Corbett deserves a benefit," opined the *Chronicle,* "his recent battle with Peter Jackson having netted him only a few hundred dollars after all expenses were paid."

The theater was sold-out days before the performance. Fourteen hundred people paid two dollars each for seats, and the box office could have sold three times as many. Ticket scalpers successfully vended tickets at three dollars, even though the seats they offered were deep in the gallery.

Prior to the performance, the outside of the theater resembled an opera premiere, teeming with throngs of carriages, influential men, and fashionably dressed women, even some without escorts. All the sporting celebrities reserved boxes, anxiously awaiting "the battle of the behemoths." Directors of the Olympic Club looked down on the stage from the Olympian heights of their customary, ornate proscenium box.

The audience sat in distracted silence through the numbers on the variety program. Those bored with the olios strolled into the foyer to examine the dozens of floral tributes. Whenever Sullivan came on stage to enact various scenes—the plot had to be intermittently sketched out so the audience could understand why the boxers were to meet in the ring—the tension emanating from the crowd clearly expressed their mounting suspense.

At last, with an orchestral flourish, the final act began. The curtains opened on an empty ring. Entering from either side of the stage came Jim and John L. To the audience's astonishment, both were fully dressed—and in tuxedos! They acknowledged the crowd with short speeches of thanks, shook hands, and exited the stage as they had entered. The audience cheered and applauded. In characteristic recognition for their greatest theatrical heroes, people in the gallery loudly stamped their feet in unison. All waited for the gladiators to emerge, ready to fight, in ring attire.

When the boxers reentered the stage, with only their coats removed, the crowd endured their first disappointment. Sullivan and Corbett had not even discarded their collars and neckties! "What is this?!" yelled experienced ring-goers. Some hissed; most just gaped in astonishment.

The first round began with the boxers ineffectually patting one another. The *Chronicle's* description of the action was laced with ridicule and sarcasm. "Corbett's right accidentally disarranged John's front spitcurl, and the champion's fist simultaneously put a kink in three hairs of Jim's bristling pompadour."[15]

To allow the champion to collect his wind from the exertion, the referee (manager of the theater) called time. At the beginning of the second round, the contenders rushed at one another, the crowd gasping with anticipated pleasure. Yet their delight quickly turned to hisses, as the boxers seemed to be "aiming blows at the gallery." When Jim, by chance, tweaked Sullivan with a phantom uppercut, time was again called. By this point, the gallery "hissed like a whole barnyard of angry goslings."

As if on cue, the manager strutted to the front of the stage, removed his silk hat, and admonished the audience for their insulting behavior. "These men are friends. They're here to box three friendly rounds. They are," he insisted. "See? Do you want 'em to knock each other out? Eh?" It was an unfortunate question to ask an already dissatisfied audience, who proceeded to overwhelm the stage with a roaring "Yes!" Even before the yelling had subsided, the third round was over; and the "exhausted gladiators" embraced.

Totally disgusted with this battle of noncombatants, the audience, in greatly subdued spirits, filed out of the theater. The only sounds, according to the *Chronicle*, were those of the boxers and their managers counting the loose change in the box office.

One newspaper called the meeting "a love feast." Another reported: "They caressed each other in evening attire and were cheerfully hissed." An old sportsman demanded his money back, declaring indignantly, "I call this a downright dirty swindle and a fake." Many from the audience agreed.

As Sullivan prepared to leave for his

scheduled tour of Australia, he defended his performance to an inquiring scribe, while getting in a "dig" at Jim, as well.

> I want to say something now, and I want you to get it straight. I am sorry the crowd did not like me and Jim's exhibition the other night, just because we did not dress like as if we were fighting. I wanted to show the audience as to how two gentlemen of the ring could meet, and we wore the proper clothes to do it in. It was professional etiquette that I was introducing on stage. Jim was all cut up because the crowd was mad. Pshaw! Jim is a fine boy, but he has a great deal to learn. He is very raw, he is, about etiquette and such things.[16]

The *Chronicle* published a headline: "Gentleman John Met Gentleman Jim," the first time Jim had been so labeled publicly. Nonetheless, back in New York, the enterprising manager William Brady read about the encounter and saw his opportunity to take advantage of Jim's increasing popularity. He wired Jim an offer to appear on stage—in a sparring match—for the attractive sum of $250 a week. Come immediately!

William A. Brady had been born in San Francisco in 1863, in the old Irish section of the city, a neighborhood similar to that of the Corbetts. Brady's father had arrived in 1856, and he soon became an editor of the *San Francisco Monitor,* a newspaper noted for its fiery support of secession before and during the Civil War. A divorce, when Brady was two years old, persuaded his father to kidnap the boy and together they fled to New York. The elder Brady obtained a job in the immigration office at Castle Garden and, when that tried his patience, did free-lance work for local newspapers.[17]

Young Brady's first jobs were selling newspapers and shining shoes on the streets of the Bowery. For young people in that bruising and sorry environment, popular theater was their only means of "clean"

amusement and they embraced the experience enthusiastically. Like children of today, who emulate film stars, youngsters of the 1870s imitated their theater heroes, mimicking the action, playing the roles, and declaiming speeches from the latest melodrama they had been fortunate enough to attend. To make extra money, Brady later claimed he sold over-ripe fruit and vegetables to theater patrons, so they might more directly convey a less than satisfactory response to performances and actors.

At age fifteen, Brady became a steward at the New York Press Club, a position that offered him a first-hand opportunity to meet well-known people and learn the manners and dress of the well-to-do. Thanks to the generosity of some club members, Brady was able to return to San Francisco to launch his career, whatever it might turn out to be.

He began by working as a "peanut

William A. Brady, colorful theater and boxing impresario, guided Jim to the heavyweight championship and a lucrative stage career. Then he dropped Jim for boxers whom he believed promised greater financial returns.

butcher" on a train. Peanut butchers sold a wide variety of food, drink, medicine, papers, hardware, and bedding to passengers, hawking their wares from car to car throughout the trip. A successful salesman had to be loud, confident if not cocky, and expound the benefits of his goods in dramatic, ingenious, and ostentatious fashion. Brady excelled.

Settling in San Francisco in 1882, nineteen-year-old Bill Brady first operated a newsstand. He then obtained a series of jobs in local theaters as a "super," an extra, commonly known as a "spear-carrier," earning fifty cents a night. This led to a minor role in a melodrama, "White Slave," which opened opportunities for him in a variety of shows, doing everything from moving scenery to performing minor acting parts. For the next six years, Brady learned theatrical craft, especially the business and promotional side, and succeeded reasonably well.

In 1888, Brady decided it would be more lucrative to produce plays than to appear in them. He found that the easiest and most profitable way to produce shows was to pirate them, then perform them in places they had not previously been staged. He was able to conduct business in this manner for a time, but the swindle caught up with him. While he was managing a melodrama, "After Dark," its writer, Dion Boucicault, a well-known and respected actor, sued Brady to prevent his use of the play. Boucicault demanded all of Brady's accumulated profits. The suit was pending.

Brady later claimed that he and Jim had been boyhood friends in San Francisco, but there is little evidence to prove it, their early lives apparently having developed in different spheres. Regardless, Brady must have been well acquainted with Jim's increasing celebrity status, as well as his highly publicized bouts, which led to his being promoted as "the coming champion."

Brady surely recognized in Jim a short-term opportunity to increase his own box-office. At the same time, he could now take relatively cheap possession of a potential gold-mine, one sure to pay off handsomely, if Jim did happen to fulfill his boxing potential.

To Brady's surprise, Jim agreed to join the company. Thus began an alliance, more business than personal, in which Brady managed and shaped Jim's immediate career.

"After Dark" (the lawsuit against Brady still had not been decided) opened at Taylor's Opera House, Trenton, New Jersey, on August 13, to "good business. Jim Corbett made his first theatrical appearance, sparring three rounds with Jim Daly. The latter was clever, but is not heavy enough to put up an interesting set-to with the Californian."[18]

At the People's Theater in Philadelphia, Jim became a featured member of the cast, although his sparring match with Daly served solely as an interlude between acts.

> With an audience that packed every portion of the house, "After Dark" was enthusiastically received, Sweeny and Ryland winning flattering applause for their specialties in the concert hall scene. Jim Corbett, who displays his fistic powers, came in for a big ovation. [19]

Brady took advantage of Jim's success in Philadelphia to expand his role from simply an olio act, inserting him and Daly into the concert hall scene, as well. Thanks to increased promotional activity in Boston, "After Dark" was reported to possess "sensational features that would make it famous."

At the same time he was promoting Jim on stage, Brady telegraphed Jackson's and Mitchell's managers to book a match for Jim. Brady presented Jim as initiator of the challenges and had him quoted as daring "the world" to meet him. Though Brady had written the script, Jim was criticized for employing such boasts simply to enhance his engagement with the "After Dark" company. Whatever the reality, Jim does not appear to have interfered in any of Brady's activities. Meanwhile, the press duly noted these challenges and followed their progress as "After Dark" played to full houses throughout the company's New England tour.

During the middle of October, "After Dark" visited the New York area, playing at the Grand Opera House in Brooklyn. Brady had plastered Jim's visage on every wall, kiosk, and pole in the city, with excellent results. Again, Jim was singled out for his sparring performance.

> Melodrama, with strength of scene and mechanical effect, is the attraction offered by Col. Morris and a large audience gave greeting to the opening performance of "After Dark." The music hall scene is enlivened by a friendly set-to between Jim Corbett and Jim Daly. [20]

Successful appearances in Harrisburg, Pittsburgh, and Toledo preceded a run at Chicago's Haymarket Theater. Brady's ads in local papers elevated Jim beyond the production itself.

> W.A. Brady's "After Dark"
> In the concert hall scene: James J. Corbett, the Beau Brummell of the Pugilistic World. William A. Brady plays the part of Old Tom. Jim Corbett, the pugilist, will spar in the concert hall scene, which will impact to the play a classic element otherwise lacking.

The *Tribune* reported the play to have "filled the house at every performance." Similar results were obtained in Cincinnati, Columbus, and St. Louis, where extra performances were staged to accommodate the overwhelming crowds.

Brady persuaded Charley Mitchell, just arrived in the U.S., to face Jim, dangling a $1,000 deposit plus side money to cement a deal. The reluctant Mitchell wanted the contest to take place under the old rules, limited in rounds and fought bare knuckles, since his primary reason for coming to the States again was to obtain a match with Sullivan. With news of the possible match, Jim quickly returned to New York.

Jim and Charley met at the Hoffman House restaurant to discuss their match, greeted each other cordially, and shared a "fizz" together. They agreed to meet at the *Clipper* office to finalize a contract. Mitchell again requested the bout be conducted without gloves, but Jim declined. Finally, after much discussion, the two agreed to meet for six rounds, at Madison Square Garden, with gloves and under Queensberry rules, "to test their fistic skill." Articles were signed and Jim made preparations to begin training for the contest, scheduled to take place February 11, 1892.

At a boxing tournament given by the New York Athletic Club—Jim had last faced Dominick McCaffrey there in an unsatisfactory display—a welcome surprise for spectators was a one-round exhibition, for scientific points, between Jim and Mike Donovan. "Although Donovan is an exceptionally clever man, he was little more than a child in Corbett's hands. Jim showed off to great advantage, and was heartily applauded for his cleverness."[21]

Another member of the club, Bob Center, also sparred a round with Jim, until he saw "more stars in ten seconds than he had ever seen before in ten years."

Brady got "After Dark" booked into the People's Theater in New York, to take advantage of the extensive publicity Jim had been receiving; it turned into a profitable engagement. During the final show, Jim appeared before the audience and told them he was temporarily retiring from the stage to begin training, in Atlantic City, for the match with Charley

Mitchell. Enter Police Superintendent Murray in his zealous quest to uphold the law.

Less than two weeks before the scheduled bout, Murray warned the sporting community "that nothing assimilating to heavy work would be permitted," in effect smothering enthusiasm for the match so that it would be "too insignificant to be worthy of time, trouble and expense," according to the newspapers. Mitchell declared he was no longer interested and left the city to go on a sparring tour. Jim, however, said he would keep his end of the bargain and, in an exhibition to replace the Mitchell bout, would face anyone who volunteered. Jim Daly or Mike Donovan would prove satisfactory replacements. Instead, Brady saw the scheduled event as a unique opportunity to promote Jim and his qualifications to challenge Sullivan.

On February 16, at Madison Square Garden, Jim faced three different boxers, consecutively, in three-round matches, thanks to Brady's negotiations with the backers of the original Corbett/Mitchell contest. Brady advanced the event with typical bravura: "Here is a chance," he exclaimed, "to see Jim Corbett display his skill and strength in his self-imposed task of knocking out three alleged good men without leaving the stage." The crowd paid anywhere from fifty cents to a dollar and a half to watch Jim perform. Afterwards, they filed out of the Garden considerably less than satisfied.

The first two men Jim faced, Bill Spillings and Bob Coffey, turned out to be novices and were KO'd in the first round. The third, a tough, seasoned veteran named Joe Lannon, who had sparred with Sullivan in the latter's melodrama, lasted all three rounds, during which Lannon clearly held his own against Jim, causing him to miss numerous blows. Even Jim's admirers fretted, wondering how their man could stand up against Sullivan if he couldn't "put away Sullivan's plaything." Still, Brady had obtained what he desired, money and publicity for his performer.

Using their recent endeavors as leverage, Brady and Jim next sent challenges to Bob Fitzsimmons and the winner of the proposed Jackson/Slavin bout. Both offers, of course, were mere publicity stunts, since the boxers involved would be unavailable for any such match in the near future. Yet, Brady was able to precipitate newspaper headlines like: "Who Will Box Corbett?" and "Corbett Ahead of His Time," thus positioning Jim as the foremost challenger to Sullivan.

In the meantime, Charley Mitchell and his manager, Paddy Slavin, continued their attempts to entice Sullivan into a match. Sullivan, however, did not believe that Mitchell was really serious about meeting him and he declined the offer. Yet the prospect of a sizable purse remained attractive. Why not himself challenge his own selection of opponents for high stakes? The long-reigning heavyweight champion of the world proceeded to do exactly that. Among the potential opponents that he nominated was Jim Corbett.

4. FIGHT OF THE CENTURY

John L. Sullivan had been subject to stinging criticism due to his reluctance to defend the heavyweight title. Though considered by some in the boxing community to be past his prime—he was thirty-four years old and had appeared in forty-five bouts—Sullivan believed himself sufficiently fit to retain his title. In March, 1892, compelled to action, the champion issued a challenge specifically directed to three likely opponents: Frank Slavin, Charley Mitchell, and James J. Corbett.

> ...I hereby challenge any and all of the bluffers who have been trying to make capital at my expense to fight me either the last week in August this year or the first week in September this year at the Olympic Club, New Orleans, Louisiana, for the purse of $25,000 and an outside bet of $10,000, the winner of the fight to take the entire purse.... I insist upon the bet of $10,000, to show that they mean business.... I give precedence in this challenge to Frank P. Slavin, of Australia, he and his backers having done the greatest amount of bluffing. My second preference is the bombastic sprinter, Charles Mitchell, of England, whom I would rather whip than any man in the world. My third preference is James Corbett, of California, who has achieved his share of bombast.[1]

Displaying his personal prejudices, Sullivan refused to face Negro boxers. Nor did he care for foreigners, boasting that he intended "to keep the championship of the world where it belongs, in the land of the free and the home of the brave." That pretty much excluded Slavin and Mitchell, even if they had agreed to face Sullivan.

Not surprisingly, Slavin refused Sullivan's challenge, giving as an excuse his upcoming match with Peter Jackson. Mitchell, careful not to mar his current sparring tour, agreed to meet Sullivan, but only on his own terms, knowing full well that Sullivan would not consent to them. In marked contrast, Jim verbally agreed to the challenge; and he followed up with an initial deposit of $1,000. Sullivan countered by posting a $2,500 deposit, giving Jim a week to match it. Jim promptly replied, the money coming from Phil Dwyer in New York, Manager Brady, and Jim's sister, Mary. The date of the contest, sponsored by the Olympic Club of New Orleans, was fixed at September 7th. Newspapers immediately labeled the championship contest "the fight of the century."

Back in New York, the reluctant challengers Charley Mitchell and Frank Slavin were scheduled to participate in an exhibition match, as part of a vaudeville program at Miner's Bowery Theater. Jim planned to attend the show, to observe the two boxers and their styles. Both Mitchell and Slavin arrived at the theater drunk and compounded the patrons' disaffection by refusing to appear before a Bowery audience already angry at the men for having ducked Sullivan's challenge, offering what the public considered lame excuses. At the last moment, Jim and his sparring partner, Jim Daly, agreed to perform in place of the disgraced duo. When they met in the theater lobby, Mitchell proceeded to berate Jim, vilely insulting him and his family. Irate, Jim swung wildly at Mitchell, missing with a right hand that fell short. In full retreat, Mitchell bolted from the theater.

When their turn came to perform, Jim and Daly "gave a rattling exhibition of the art of self-defense" for an appreciative audience. The *Clipper* condemned Mitchell as "a full blown blackguard" who deserved "a sound thrashing" by Corbett. Questioned about the incident, Jim vowed he would not forget this slander on his name. Indeed, there would come a time when Jim secured satisfactory retribution for Mitchell's venomous attack.

The encounter, as reported in newspapers across the country, reflected a typically nationalistic criticism of foreign boxers, while demonstrating support for Jim as the best (read: American) man to face John L. Sullivan. The following week, throughout Jim's sparring exhibitions in New England, he was consistently hailed as "America's future champion." When Jim returned to New York to appear in a benefit for Mike Donovan, they put on a three-round scientific contest, to the delight of spectators. According to the *Clipper*, ovations for Jim were so enthusiastic that the house "must have swelled his head and puffed up his chest;" or so it appeared from his response to the adulation.

Early in May, Manager William Brady arrived in San Francisco to announce that Jim planned to appear at the Wigwam Theater on the 14th, to spar with Jim Daly, as a member of a touring vaudeville company. For the previous two weeks, Jim and Daly had been working their way west, performing a series of exhibitions in Milwaukee, Minneapolis, Vancouver, Tacoma, and Portland, to capacity audiences, eager to see first-hand the "coming champion" (Brady's billing) in the ring. Jim was reported to be earning $150 dollars a week for his performances, a considerable sum for fifteen minutes of work. According to his contract with Brady, however, Jim was responsible for his own room, board, and travel expenses, the usual arrangement with performers on tour.

Jim planned to stay in San Francisco for about ten days, then return to New York via sparring exhibitions in Los Angeles, San Diego, Arizona, New Mexico, and Colorado. Except for the single performance at San Francisco's Wigwam, Jim and Olive relaxed and enjoyed the opportunity to visit family and friends.

Upon reviewing Jim's Wigwam Theater exhibition, the *Chronicle* declared coarsely that "he was too fat" and he "left anything but a favorable impression." His hometown newspaper went on to suggest that Jim stood little chance to beat Sullivan. In fact, *Chronicle* critics expressed doubts that he would ever face the champion in the ring, slinging scathing remarks reminiscent of those made about him prior to his bout with Jackson.

As usual, Manager Brady rose to Jim's defense, claiming that he was "in better condition than ever before," indeed "larger and stronger than ever." The city's boxing pundits argued for a week concerning Jim's chances against Sullivan, and the skeptics clearly prevailed.

Before leaving town, Jim agreed to appear at the Olympic Club in a brief exhibition with De Witt Van Court, the club's new boxing instructor. Embraced by his original supporters, Jim was duly feted by a ladies' night crowd. Yet, even some Olympic Club members expressed doubts about Jim's upcoming contest with Sullivan.

The ever-enterprising Brady intended to make money while he and Jim returned to New York. In Canton, Ohio, Jim and Daly sparred during a performance of "Sport McAllister," a play written by Charles T. Vincent, author of previous Brady melodramas. In the play, Jim made his first appearance in a speaking role and, according to the local newspaper, "acquitted himself creditably." On June 6, Jim appeared in "Sport McAllister" at the Bijou Theater, New York, for a week's run, prior to moving to his training quarters in Asbury Park, New Jersey. Confident that Jim would win the championship from Sullivan, Brady had already initiated plans for Jim to star in a new play, to be written by Vincent. An undisguised biography of its headliner, the play was tentatively titled "Gentleman Jim."

Friends persuaded Brady, however, that so obvious a plot and title might detract from the play's success. Not entirely convinced, Brady heeded their advice sufficiently to change the title to "Gentleman Jack" and modify the plot to make the hero a Yale man who becomes a boxer to save his name and win the heroine. The plot would go through other metamorphoses before it reached the stage.

In another of his calculated boasts, Brady declared that Jim "would begin his starring tour on or about November 1." What if Jim lost the bout with Sullivan, asked a reporter; would he still appear in the play? Implying the man's query was preposterous, Brady refused to answer.

Throughout July, assisted by his trainers, Phil Casey and Jack Ashton, John L. Sullivan continued regular and systematic workouts at his training camp at Canoe Place Inn, on Long Island. Casey told reporters he was highly pleased with the progress of "the big fellow on his way to physical perfection." Casey also assured the press that Sullivan was not taking the contest lightly. Although the champion was not fond of such grueling work, Casey noted, he planned to be fit in his encounter with Corbett. At the same time, however, it was revealed that Sullivan himself was studying a role in a new play, to begin the following season, and assisting in the completion of a book about his life and career, to be published in the coming year.

The Corbett camp had its own commitments. Manager Brady did not see the wisdom of paying the entire expenses for Jim's training quarters so he booked a number of sparring exhibitions between Corbett and Daly at Red Bank and Long Branch theaters. Reporters questioned whether this combination of show business and fistic training was "the proper thing" for Jim, to which Brady responded: "It can do Corbett no personal harm, while it may help the treasury not a little." The *Clipper* opined that distracting Jim from the serious work of training diminished public confidence in his ability to stand up to Sullivan.

By early August, Sullivan's trainers reported that the champion's weight was down to 219 pounds, on the way to 210, at which weight he intended to enter the ring. Sullivan expressed confidence that he would accomplish the task he had set for himself. For his part, Jim was reported to be working "systematically and cheerfully," under the watchful eyes of Delaney and Daly, his trainers. Brady talked to reporters almost every day, feeding them tidbits on Jim's own progress toward "perfecting his physical condition."

In New Orleans, according to club managers, work on the Olympic Club arena was near completion. As a precaution against possible disturbances, 100 policemen and 900 club members would be assigned to preserve order. Further, club managers announced that, for the first time, Negroes would be allowed to enter the arena and see the contest; a special gallery was to be set aside for them.

Three weeks before the bout, Sullivan reached his desired weight. He now sought to do little more than maintain his superb physical condition. Sullivan's doctor told reporters the champion had increased his chest measurement by over an inch and a half, added to the size of his biceps, and materially reduced his girth, the last of which came as particularly welcome news to his supporters. Sullivan planned to leave his training quarters on August 27, prior to making his way to New Orleans. Two special train cars had been secured for the champion, his trainers, and backers, one of them fitted with training equipment, so he could work out every day during the trip.

Jim continued training, with plans to leave Asbury Park, September 1, on a special train, with trainers, backers, and intimate friends. For this bout, however, Olive would remain in New York. Meanwhile, the rigors of Jim's training regimen did not dissuade Brady from booking "After Dark" in Trenton for a number of days, during which performances Jim and Jack McVey sparred a few rounds. The *Clipper* noted that such performances "were better omitted" if Corbett hoped to prevail.

In addition to those transporting the combatants and their respective entourages, special trains were scheduled to embark from New York, Philadelphia, Chicago, and San Francisco to carry boxing enthusiasts and bettors to New Orleans. The trains would be luxuriously fitted and serve elegantly prepared meals. To ensure that passengers got a good night's sleep, the trains would halt at dusk and begin the next morning after breakfast had been served. Early odds were 100 to 80, in favor of Sullivan.

From San Francisco came the news that, while the contest was in progress, it would be "illustrated" at the Bijou Theater (at the last minute, the event was moved to the Orpheum Theater to accommodate a larger audience). The Pacific Athletic Club had leased a telegraph wire over which telegrams would be transmitted without interruption from ringside.

> Each lead, counter, parry, dodge, duck and, in fact, every movement of the fighters will be described direct to the theater. At the end of each round, the dispatch will be read aloud and, while waiting the news of the next round, two pugilists, one representing Sullivan and the other Corbett, will illustrate how the previous round was fought. They will follow the movements of Sullivan and Corbett described in the telegram. A ring will be set up on stage and the illustration will be assisted by a referee, seconds and all the accessories of a genuine fight. Provisions will be made for women to witness the exhibition.[2]

This was likely the first time in history that an entertainment would be transmitted to a theater as it was actually taking place.

During the final weekend before Sullivan and Jim were to leave for New Orleans, both "flexed their muscles" in front of New York partisan crowds. At the same time, both made considerable money, since admission was charged at the theaters where they performed. On Monday evening, August 29, at the Claremont Avenue Rink, Brooklyn, and the next day at Madison Square Garden, Sullivan sparred with Jack Ashton. The first event was for men only; the second allowed "the fair sex" to attend.

Four thousand people attended Sullivan's exhibition in Brooklyn; and after critically examining his condition, there were "murmurs of disappointment." At Madison Square Garden, supporters were equally dismayed.

"What was Sullivan's weight when he left his training quarters today?" a reporter called out. "Just 204 pounds, sir," came the reply. "I'd bet it was nearer 240," remarked a spectator who sat nearby.

Newspapers also provided less than glowing reports on the champion's condition. "He looked like anything but a man trained for such a battle as is to take place at New Orleans."

A newspaper advertisement for the Sullivan-Corbett heavyweight title bout, September 7, 1892. Although Sullivan is here portrayed as young and fit, his ring appearance revealed an older, paunchy boxer destined to lose his title.

"When the champion held his head erect, loose folds of fat formed on the back of his head."

"When he leaned forward, his close-fitting belt seemed to cut into his waist. It looked as though one could gather handfuls of fat on his sides and stomach."

"His movements seemed slow and listless."

"Sullivan's only advantage lies in his superior strength. Corbett has on his side youth, agility, and endurance."

The following day, Jim also appeared at Madison Square Garden. In contrast to observations about Sullivan, supporters were "aroused to enthusiastic admiration." "Before the young man had moved a hand it was apparent to the observers that a perfect man from a physical standpoint was before them."[3]

In front of more than 4,000 spectators, Jim went through a complete training regimen. He began by working on pulleys, played handball, and punched the bag. He then retired for lunch. Later, he returned to the pulleys, changed to the medicine ball, and kept his trainers hustling.

By mid afternoon, more than 5,000 people were in attendance, including Olive, who occupied a box and watched her husband perform. When she entered the auditorium, a great cheer of recognition went up and followed her to her seat. Then, John McVey and Jim engaged in some wrestling, albeit with gloves on, to avoid injury. When Jim began punching the bag with lightning-like blows, the crowd rose in unison. Jim completed his workout by running briskly around the track.

After dinner—the crowd had now swelled to more than 6,000 spectators—Jim entered the ring in the outfit he planned to wear in New Orleans: a pair of tight-fitting black trunks, green stockings, and regulation boxing shoes. He and McVey boxed two rounds, the crowd hooting for more dynamic action. When Jim faced Daly, however, patrons soon saw how clever a challenger he really was. When the spectators left Madison Square Garden, they were unanimously convinced that Jim would defeat Sullivan.

A *Herald* reporter summed up public opinion about the upcoming contest. "Comparing the work of the two men, there can be but one conclusion, that Corbett is by far the better man."[4]

On September 3, Jim, accompanied by a military band and 1,000 partisans, left his training quarters at noon to board the Pennsylvania Railroad train. The local station was launched into happy confusion. Thousands of additional spectators had gathered to give Jim a roaring "send off." Crowds besieged him on all sides, to grasp his hand, if they could, and bid him good luck. Jim returned the compliment by shaking hands with everyone he could reach. As the train pulled into the station, Jim, Manager Brady, and the rest of the party boarded the rear car.

They had hardly been seated when superstitious fans in the crowd nearest the car rushed to a window and called out: "For God's sake, Jim, get into another car. This one is 813." Brady bounded down onto the platform to verify their claim, rushed back inside, and escorted Jim into a forward car. As Jim passed into the car, he was showered with rice and old shoes.

As the train gradually crept out of the station, the band played "Yankee Doodle," "Dixie," and, as a finale, "Auld Lang Syne." Olive, standing proudly on the platform, thanked the crowd for their many good wishes for her husband.

The train's first stop was Washington, D.C., where Jim had been scheduled to spar a few rounds at Albaugh's Grand Opera House. When they heard of the proposed exhibition, Jim's New York backers ordered him not to appear, for fear he might be accidentally injured. Brady, however, had already assured the manager of Jim's appearance and he now had to stand before a full house to apologize for the mixup. No sooner had he finished apologizing than Jim, as if on cue, stepped onto the stage. The audience went wild and begged him to spar. Brady stepped forward and explained to the crowd that Jim had to protect against accidents, any of which would jeopardize a contest "worth the substantial sum of $45,000." Jim then moved to the center of the stage to address the audience.

He reiterated Brady's comments, again apologized, and concluded his speech by saying that, while he was about to face the world's most renowned pugilist, "I will do everything in my power to win." As he bowed and retired from the stage, the audience gave him three rousing cheers.

The party's next stop was Charlotte, North Carolina, where they planned to rest a day and give Jim an opportunity to engage in some training. Ironically, both Jim and John L. nearly failed to make it to New Orleans. No one in Jim's party was aware that North Carolina had laws forbidding boxing of any kind. While Jim was sparring with Daly, someone alerted Brady that a sheriff was on his way to arrest Jim for breaking state law. In a burst of fancy footwork, the party quickly boarded their train and left Charlotte to avoid any legal complications.

When John L. and his party were scheduled to pass through Nashville, a constable was waiting to serve an old warrant based on the champion's participation in an allegedly illegal bout with Jake Kilrain. The train stopped in Nashville, but Sullivan's car had been rerouted around the town. It was shifted to the Louisville and Nashville track where, safely tucked among a line of freight cars, the champion and his entourage rolled through Tennessee and Mississippi as quickly as possible—they were afforded right of way—to avoid any other potentially arresting situations.

Jim arrived in New Orleans at 7:45 A.M., September 6. President Campbell, of the Southern Athletic Club, where Jim had been invited to stay, greeted the challenger and escorted the entire party to the organization's elegant Victorian-style clubhouse.

When Jim disembarked from the train, he was elegantly attired in an English tweed suit, white tie, and light brown hat. The crowd cheered Jim as he made his way to the waiting carriage. Though the horses were lashed into a fast trot, hundreds of Negroes ran behind as the vehicle rolled up St. Charles Avenue. Massed before the clubhouse, another crowd had gathered to cheer Jim as he gracefully leaped out of the carriage. In a display of enthusiastic New Orleans *bonhomie,* they bodily carried their hero to the building's entrance.

After taking a bath, Jim was served a large breakfast. He then retired to his bedroom until 3:00 P.M., when he entered the club gym to exercise. At 9:00 P.M., Jim retired for the night, taking gallons of mineral water with him to his rooms; he planned to drink nothing else until after the contest.

Prior to retiring for the evening, Jim sent a confident telegram to Olive: "All's well. With love. It's a cinch."

All fight-day long, Tuesday, September 7, special trains arrived, carrying hundreds of people from California, New York, Minnesota, Texas, and all parts between. Canal Street and St. Charles Street took on the look and vitality of Mardi Gras season. Hotels, saloons, and even more voluptuous resorts were filled with men from all levels of society, mingling freely, drinking everything available. Even sidewalk ice cream and soda water stands plied a profitable trade.

That evening, the streets became increasingly animated. Everyone seemed to recognize the necessity of arriving at the arena early, since it would be packed with more than 10,000 spectators. The pilgrimage began before dark. Hacks were at a premium, and those lucky enough to find one still had to alight several blocks from the arena and push their way through the throng. Hundreds of police were detailed to keep the crowd in order, but soon found they were unable to perform the overwhelming task.

A woman disguised as a man presented a ticket for admission. Her subterfuge was so clever, she got through the gate. When she went to claim her seat, however, a policeman recognized "her sex." Amid the pitiless jeers of those already seated, she was led tearfully away.

About an hour before the scheduled contest, a rainstorm burst upon the city and lasted long enough to fill the gutters. It seemed to deter no spectator, though it did increase their discomfort due to the increasingly humid atmosphere in the arena. The Louisiana summer night was characteristically sultry. Already the sweltering atmosphere was redolent of a bayou swamp. The crowd seemed to be bathing in its own perspiration.

Odds remained in favor of Sullivan, 100 to 80. Betting had been light until the last minute, the majority still for Sullivan. So confident were they of the champion's victory, speculators gave odds in which round Sullivan would end the contest.

Canvas sides of the arena had been raised to facilitate the flow of spectators. The ring itself remained covered by a roof to protect against precipitation. Indeed, a persistent drizzle began bothering the crowd; and when it appeared the rain would intensify, the canvas tarps were rolled down again. Reporters found the suffocating climate particularly annoying, having no choice but to apply slippery pencil to soaked paper. Suddenly, minutes before the contest was to begin, as if preordained, the rain stopped and the stars came out.

At 8:00 P.M., Sullivan was the first to arrive from the St. Charles Hotel. He immediately repaired to his downstairs dressing room. Jim arrived fifteen minutes later and climbed to his upstairs dressing room. At 8:40 P.M., the boxing gloves were brought into the ring. Jim Wakely for Sullivan and Jim Daly for Corbett tossed for choice of corners. Corbett won.

Sullivan was seconded by Jack McAuliffe, Joe Lannon, Phil Casey, and Charlie Johnson. Jim's seconds were Billy Delaney, Jim Daly, Professor John Donaldson, and Mike Donovan. Bat Masterson was Jim's timekeeper.

At 9:00 P.M., to explain club rules, referee John Duffy called the boxers to the center of the ring. Prior to that moment, Jim had been striding around the ring, bouncing to try out the floor and pulling at the ropes to test their durability, evidently entirely oblivious of Sullivan's presence. The procedure was deliberately provocative; and it apparently had its effect on the champion, who seemed puzzled by Jim's actions.

At 9:10 P.M., the gloves were laced and adjusted for each man. A few moments later, they clasped hands and returned to their corners. As they retreated, Sullivan looked over his shoulder at Jim. Upon his return to his corner, Jim's seconds told him of Sullivan's furtive glance. Jim smiled.

At 9:15 P.M., the bell sounded, and the fight of the century began.[5]

Round 1: A ferocious expression on his face, Sullivan rushed Corbett, intent on gaining the offensive immediately. After a number of misses, the champion seemed to lose his temper. A smile on his face, Jim danced and bobbed, weaving his way around the ring, evading each of

Sullivan's lunges. The crowd, however, hissed Jim's tactics. The round ended with Sullivan wearing a look of disgust.

Round 2: Sullivan missed three left-hand leads, Jim easily ducking them. Jim countered with punches to Sullivan's stomach and nose. Sullivan fought back with a left and a right, both of which fell short, but scored to the stomach and shoulder. They clinched; Jim kept away from Sullivan's inside blows to the stomach. Two more rights by Sullivan missed. Just as the bell rang, Jim slammed a left to the stomach that made Sullivan wince.

Round 3: Sullivan came out looking angry, while Jim was smiling. Sullivan's numerous rushes were evaded. When Sullivan landed two rights and attempted to clinch, Jim blasted two quick blows to the stomach. Sullivan missed with two hard attempts, and Jim countered with telling shots to the champion's stomach and jaw. As the crowd cheered the action, Sullivan showed his temper, making a vicious lunge that fell short as the round ended.

Round 4: Jim continued smiling, while Sullivan was now panting. Sullivan's leads and following blows all missed, while Jim got in a left jab to the eye. A series of savage rushes by Sullivan were easily evaded, enraging him all the more. Forcing Jim into a corner, Sullivan furiously strove to knock him out. As Jim danced away, John L. succeeded only in pummeling his challenger's back.

Round 5: Jim became the aggressor. He peppered jabs to Sullivan's face and neck, followed with two hard rights to the jaw. He dodged two heavy hooks by Sullivan, and replied with two more jolting shots to the champion's nose and jaw, sending Sullivan reeling. Sullivan's nose began bleeding, and Jim rushed to attack, landing repeated jabs to the nose, causing blood to flow freely. Sullivan swung wildly, missing Jim completely with roundhouse rights and lefts. At the bell,

Sullivan returned to his corner, apparently weakened.

Round 6: Refreshed, Sullivan came out angry and with renewed determination. He landed a brutal body blow that made Jim wince. Two more blows fell short. Jim countered with a crunching left to the stomach that buckled Sullivan's right leg. Despite the punishment, Sullivan forced the action; yet continued to miss. Jim shot back with jabs to the face. The crowd cheered these energetic exchanges.

Round 7: Jim came out quickly; Sullivan slowly. The champion missed a swing and was punished by a number of straight shots to the jaw, followed by a heavy blow to the stomach that seemed to lift him off his feet. As Sullivan tried to lead again, he was barraged by numerous blows to the face. Jim continued to assail Sullivan's bleeding nose. A blistering right to Sullivan's face staggered him, the bell saving him from further damage.

Round 8: Sullivan tried to take the offensive with a series of tremendous roundhouse swings, most of them missing the mark. Jim returned to the champion's nose and pummeled it with a volley of blows. Sullivan missed a shot to the stomach and was rewarded with more shots to his nose, though he tried to cover up. The round ended with Jim scoring to Sullivan's jaw and stomach, with no retaliation.

Round 9: Sullivan appeared tired, but rushed Jim, believing he had to land convincing blows to stop his challenger. He connected with a few but missed more, Jim absorbing the punches by backing away. Jim countered with sharp jabs to the stomach, face, and damaged nose. They clinched. While in the clinch, Sullivan clobbered Jim on the side of his face, the crowd yelling "foul." By gesture, Jim warned Sullivan not to attempt that again. As Sullivan returned to his corner, he looked distressed.

Round 10: A slow round. Sullivan resorted to sparring, apparently to gather himself. Each rush he made was rebuffed. A stiff blow to Sullivan's neck jarred the champion. Jim caught Sullivan with a left to the mouth that made his head snap back.

Round 11: Jim returned to the offensive, Sullivan backing off. Each time Sullivan led, Jim stopped him, countering with jabs to the champion's now battered face. A hard right to the jaw staggered him; it was followed by a left to the same spot. Confused, Sullivan continued to retreat.

Round 12: Jim appeared strong; Sullivan in distress. Dancing around Sullivan, Jim landed a series of blows to his face and body. Each time Sullivan led, he was punished with counterpunches. Sullivan attempted to rush Jim around the ring, hoping for an opening; yet the challenger dodged all his blows.

Round 13: Little was done in this round. Jim didn't want to let Sullivan get too close, deftly blocking punches and backpedaling. Sullivan grew increasingly frustrated by his inability to connect.

Round 14: Sullivan landed a blow to Jim's body, and sustained a left to the jaw. Toe-to-toe, the combatants exchanged blows. Jim connected sharply to Sullivan's nose, drawing blood again. Sullivan swung hard but missed. He endured a flurry of jabs to the nose. A strong blow to the jaw forced Sullivan to retreat, the crowd cheering Jim's courage and skill.

Round 15: Jim now measured his blows, struck with greater force. When Sullivan got in a number of punches, Jim countered with jabs to the face and nose; Sullivan's lip began to bleed. When the champion led, Jim hit him square on the jaw. A sharp blow to Sullivan's stomach ended the round.

Round 16: Struggling to protect his midsection, Sullivan seemed to be gasping for breath. His blows continued to miss. In response, Jim was able to land punches to Sullivan's stomach and face, almost at will. Another clinch, another glancing blow by Sullivan, another cry of "foul" from the crowd. Toward the end of the round, a lively exchange cheered the patrons.

Round 17: A slow but telling round. A counter to the jaw staggered the champion. Two shots to Sullivan's nose kept the blood flowing. A right hand feint caused Sullivan to retreat. With the champion obviously weakening, the crowd sensed what was taking place.

Round 18: Jim pelted Sullivan's nose and stomach with stinging jabs. The startled champion seemed bewildered. Jim continued to punish his opponent's nose. Sullivan landed a heavy blow to Jim's chest, but Jim responded with fierce rights and lefts to the face and stomach. As the bell sounded, Sullivan smacked Jim with a left; Jim stuck in a right to the face.

Round 19: The round began slowly with Sullivan warily approaching Jim, while the confident challenger danced away, taunting, his gloves dangling insolently at his sides. Near the end of the round, Jim attacked, landing heavy blows to his opponent's stomach, driving him onto the ropes. Another shot to Sullivan's mouth and a left to the stomach punished the champion. Sullivan returned to his corner sorely hurting.

Round 20: A decisive round. A hard shot to Sullivan's nose elicited heavy bleeding. A blow to the jaw caused Sullivan to reel. Jim attacked the champion with savage vigor, his blows to the jaw and stomach backing Sullivan onto the ropes. All but helpless now, Sullivan defended himself as best he could. Jim continued pummeling him. At the end of the round, Sullivan stumbled to his corner dazed. The end was near, and the crowd knew it.

Round 21: With his last remaining strength, Sullivan rushed Jim; to no avail.

In return, he caught a terrific left to the face and was staggered, falling back into his corner. Jim pounced on Sullivan, showering him with blows to the stomach, nose, eyes, and head, jabs, uppercuts, straight rights and lefts. Finally, Sullivan crumpled to the canvas. Still conscious, but so dazed he could not raise his body, the great John L. rolled over face down and was counted out. A new heavyweight champion had been crowned!

When Sullivan finally fell, the crowd erupted, cheering Jim, as he circled the ring, waving, bowing, and throwing kisses to the thousands enthralled by his victory. Admirers jumped the ropes to hug him. Police were unable to control the enthusiasts who rushed the ring. Fearing for their own safety, they quickly gave up.

Sullivan had been carried to his corner, and it was a full four minutes before he recovered himself. Staggering to the ropes, the ex-champion raised his arms in the air to gain the roaring crowd's attention. In a loud, yet choking voice, he proclaimed: "Gentlemen, I have only one thing to say, once for all, and that is this: This was to be, and is, my last battle. I have lost. I stayed once too often with a young man, and to James J. Corbett I pass the championship."[6]

Jim approached the former champion and they embraced, the crowd cheering its appreciation for both men.

The contest between John L. Sullivan and James J. Corbett had become the most important in the history of boxing. The "good old days" of pugilism had given way to a new era. Aside from the incalculable amounts wagered in pool halls and in private, the total of $45,000 in purse and stakes was the largest amount ever tendered in a professional contest. The arena contained the largest number of spectators ever present at a championship bout. Not widely noted at the time, this was also the first time a boxer had moved from amateur ranks to capture a professional championship. Yet it would be many years, more than two decades into the twentieth century, before that feat would be duplicated.

Boxing had also moved onto a new echelon of popular entertainment, as observed by the newspapers. The "tough" element of the sporting fraternity had been altered; it had now captured an audience that "witnessed first-class theatrical amusement."

After telegraphing Olive, Jim went to bed, exhausted but triumphant, having refused the champagne that flowed freely at his victory party. In other clubhouse rooms, Manager Brady, backers, and club members celebrated, repeating *ad nauseum* the round by round accomplishments of their heroic gladiator. Ever the showman, Brady promised the assembled that his play, "After Dark," would be put on the next night at the Opera House and Jim would be there to perform his sparring role.

Jim spent the next day receiving congratulations from friends and reading telegrams from all parts of the country. As he rode about the city in a carriage, he was cheered wherever he appeared. Everyone who saw him noticed that he showed no ill effects from the previous night's battle. Dressed in a light tweed suit, russet shoes, and a brown derby, "Gentleman Jim" (local newspapers were now using the sobriquet freely) visited the *New Orleans Picayune* editorial offices, where he accepted the Olympic Club's check for $25,000. While there, Jim received a telegram from Olive, telling him how much she had enjoyed his victory. With Brady at his side, Jim walked out of the building into a large crowd that had gathered. When they saw their new champion, the public cheered heartily, pushing one another to shake his hand. Many were just happy to have touched him. That evening, as Brady had promised, Jim appeared in his usual role in "After Dark," to a packed theater, with thousands turned away.

In contrast, John L. Sullivan remained secluded in his rooms at the St. Charles Hotel, having his wounds tended. His lips and tongue were swollen, one eye closed, three stitches in his nose, his upper body a mass of bruises. He had fallen into a deep sleep due to excessive drinking after the bout; and his dissolution was quite discernible the next morning. Sullivan was taken to the clubhouse, where he received a rubdown and slept until 5:00 P.M., at which time he was taken back to the hotel to pack. At 7:45 P.M., the Sullivan party took carriages to the train station for their melancholy return to New York.

After Jim won the title, home town San Francisco was called "a city of lunatics" by the *Chronicle*. "If a roof had been placed over San Francisco last night it would have been the largest insane asylum in the world, for it was bedlam turned loose."[7]

In front of 518 Hayes Street, the Corbett home, an immense bonfire raged. Skyrockets shot into the night sky. Five hundred people joined hands, women and children included, capering around in mystic-rite fashion, emitting shrieks of joy. A rotund, gray-haired lady stood on the top step of the house, surrounded by happy young ladies and men. A man broke from the crowd, rushed up the stairs, took the woman in his arms, kissing and hugging her.

"Well, old lady," he exulted, "your boy is champion of the world."

"Yes, dear, I know," she replied. "But are you sure that Jimmy is not hurt?"

Then, the crowd marched downtown, meeting and merging with another procession on Market Street. As they poured down the street, they sang:

Come some other night,
For dar'a gwine to be a fight.

Everybody take their hats off to Jim.
Ta-ra-ra-boom-de-ay.
He's our Jimmy; he licked John.

The wildly uproarious mob approached brother Harry's saloon, which itself had been transformed into a scene of great excitement. Prior to the bout, the pool room had been filled with "local sports" all looking for a bet. Odds had been 10 to 4 in favor of Sullivan. By the seventh round, when Jim was besting the champion, the crowd began to cheer him, even though they might have originally backed Sullivan. By the twelfth round, considerable money had already changed hands because large sums had been wagered that Jim wouldn't last that long. By the twentieth round, all the money was on Jim.

When the telegram containing the account of the last round arrived, the crowd had stilled in anticipation. "Jim lands good right and left; Sullivan groggy; falls upon the floor unable to respond to the call of time."

"Corbett wins!" cried Harry.

"Corbett wins!" echoed the crowd.

For a second, all was quiet. Then there arose a yell that grew into a great roar. Everything in Harry's saloon that was loose—hats, canes, glasses, bottles—was thrown into the air. The plate glass doors were smashed; but no one seemed to care, as the crowd jammed Ellis Street. They soon teamed up with the mass surging from Market Street.

Amidst the tumult, Harry placed Jim's picture over the center of the bar and surrounded it with a wreath of ferns and flowers. Large strings of flowers were hung around the bar and from the ceiling, with the crowd cheering every hammer blow.

Prior to the bout, Patrick, Harry, and Frank had sent Jim telegrams urging him "to bear up and do your best." William Greer Harrison, president of the Olympic

A popular photographic pose of Jim, taken immediately after he had won the heavyweight championship. Signed souvenirs were often passed out to theater audiences attending Jim's play, "Gentleman Jack," his first starring role.

Club, had wired Jim: "Do your best and tomorrow's sun will see you the champion of the world. San Francisco has not acknowledged you yet, but she will be forced to."

The Corbett family made a great deal of money on Jim's victory. Had Jim lost, they all would have been sorrowfully in debt. Harry collected more than $10,000; Mary made $6,000. It was reported that Patrick had placed his last cent on Jim; in all, he had won more than $8,000, enough to pay off any long-term debts. Jim's other sisters and brother Frank also won unknown amounts. Olympic Club members all "cleaned up." In New York, Phil Dwyer, who had put up some of the stake money for Jim, was reported to have won $15,000. Many New York Athletic Club members made in excess of $8,000. In fact, it was estimated that more than $200,000 changed hands in New York betting circles.

Prize fight excitement, which had raged in New Orleans for more than two weeks, ended abruptly as the city returned to its traditional Southern somnolence. The boxers had departed, and so had nearly all the visitors. The arena was already being dismantled. Though Jim had boarded his train at 4:00 A.M., in the rain, a large crowd had gathered to wish him farewell. On each side of his car hung streamers on which was printed "The Champion of the World." The train itself was decorated with flags and bunting.

Late that afternoon, the entourage stopped in Birmingham, Alabama, for the night. Police showed Jim and his party to waiting carriages and escorted them to their hotel. That evening, Jim sparred with Jim Daly at the O'Brien Opera House, completely jammed to SRO, with several hundred more outside, just hoping to catch a glimpse of the champion. Next day, a stop in Atlanta generated a crowd of several thousand gathered at the train station, cheering Jim "to the echo." In fact, at every station, large and small, through Georgia, South Carolina, North Carolina, and Virginia, large crowds came out to honor Jim. When the train arrived in Washington, D.C., at 7:00 A.M., people swarmed around Jim's car and shouted at the top of their lungs for him to appear. Already elegantly dressed, Jim stepped out onto the platform and acknowledged the crowd with a friendly wave and a broad smile.

John L. Sullivan may have been the first American sports celebrity; Jim Corbett, however, had become the country's first sports hero.

Shortly after 1:00 P.M., Jim arrived in New York, to be met at Pennsylvania station by thousands of admirers. Whisked to his carriage, he was escorted by police to the Coleman House, where Olive awaited his return. Manager Brady announced to reporters that Jim would be tendered a testimonial that evening at Madison

Square Garden, complete with a four-round sparring match between the champion and Jim Daly.

A crowd of more than 3,000 attended Jim's testimonial. The *New York Times* noted that the composition of the crowd was entirely different "from the throngs that used to pack the halls to see Sullivan." The orchestra floor was lavish with young men and women dressed as if they were attending the latest opera. In the loge and upper boxes were representatives of New York's boxing establishment, headed by New York Athletic Club members, and local politicians, as well as many members of the theatrical profession, among them, Digby Bell, Charles Frohman, Al Hayman, William Collier, and Jim's old friend and sometime sparring partner, Eddie Foy.

When Manager Brady took the stage to introduce Jim, he announced that the new champion would graciously appear at a benefit for John L. Sullivan the coming Saturday night. With a loud cheer, presumably for both Jim and John L., Jim took the stage, dressed to spar. A storm of applause greeted him, along with countless calls for a speech.

> Ladies and gentlemen. I thank you very kindly for this kind reception. I sincerely hope that Mr. Sullivan will meet success in all his undertakings. I have no ill will. As for myself, I will endeavor to protect the American championship to the best of my ability, and if I succeed half as well as Sullivan did I will feel satisfied.[8]

Earning the championship had been hard work, but fun. Claiming the life of a champion would prove both volatile and elusive.

5. *The Irresolute Champion*

America's newly acclaimed sports hero, James J. Corbett, made his debut as a theatrical star in "Gentleman Jack," October 3, 1892, at the Temple Opera House, Elizabeth, New Jersey.

The auditorium was jammed with patrons, many of whom had come to see the world's champion "in-the-flesh." Manager William A. Brady had strategically scheduled initial performances of the play out of range of New York critics. He remained unsure of Jim's acting ability, not to mention the production's contrived plot, which revolved around his boxing athleticism. He need not have worried as anything Jim did on stage received hearty approval.

Jim played the role of Jack Royden, a bank clerk, Princeton student, and crack athlete. He and the villain, Charles Twitchell (read: Charley Mitchell), played by John Donaldson, fall in love with the same girl. Jack's father, Joseph Royden (William A. Brady), is supposedly dead but reappears as a tramp who secures a menial job at the bank. The villain learns of the relationship between Jack and Joseph and plots to ruin them. He robs the bank and places the safe key where the old man will be suspected. Faced with his father's pending arrest, Jack takes the blame and is discharged from the bank. Soon, he becomes a boxing instructor for the New York Athletic Club. Jack is badgered into a match with Twitchell, but our hero is pressed for funds to bind the agreement. At that moment, his lady love appears and furnishes the necessary funds to finalize the agreement. In the final act, Jack knocks out Twitchell, who admits his crime and is publicly disgraced. Jack and his girl are united.

There were five acts in the play. The first act took place on the Princeton campus. The second act was staged in the office of the banker for whom Jack works while the third portrayed the Madison Square roof garden. The fourth act unfolded at a training site in Asbury Park, and the fifth displayed the Olympic Club ring in New Orleans. Any similarities to Jim's real life were purely intentional.

Following the successful opening of the play, Brady announced his plans for Jim, which covered the entire theater season.

Corbett's tour was almost solidly booked before his fight with John L. Sullivan. He is to tour the East with "Gentleman Jack" until April next, when the champion will start across the continent, playing at San Francisco two weeks during May, and returning to New York in time to sail for Europe, June 15.[1]

A lobby poster for "Gentleman Jack." Jim's name was featured prominently over the play's title, a typical Brady promotional device. (San Francisco History Center, San Francisco Public Library)

Little attention was paid to a challenge Jim received from Joe Goddard, an Australian heavyweight. Goddard backed his challenge with a $1,000 deposit and a side bet of $5,000. Boxing rules required the holder of a title to accept any proper challenge supported with a money deposit, and he was given six months to sign articles of agreement. A champion could not ignore such a challenge, nor did the rules permit him to make a choice of opponent and defer the time of the contest to suit himself. If the champion refused a challenge, he forfeited the title.

When Jim received Goddard's offer—posted with Richard K. Fox, editor of the *National Police Gazette*—he wasn't sure what to do about it, since "Gentleman Jack" had been scheduled to appear in theaters around the country for the next eight months. He and Brady decided to ignore the challenge, at least for the immediate future, until they knew how well the play would be received.

"Gentleman Jack" made brief stops at theaters in New York state, then worked its way through Ohio to a Chicago engagement. Theaters were full, and people were turned away at every performance. A problem in Syracuse, however, revealed continuing disagreement regarding the societal value of boxing. Prior to the production's opening, an injunction was granted against Jim and the company, restraining him from boxing in the play. Instead of closing the play, Brady made a deal with the Syracuse Athletic Club for Jim to appear there, thus sanctioning boxing as an amateur activity. The injunction was withdrawn, and Jim played to a full house.

A week in Chicago was so successful that additional matinees had to be scheduled, and still crowds flocked to see Jim perform. In Cincinnati, Heuck's Theater was "packed to the doors." In each city, local athletic clubs put on dinners honoring Jim's achievements; in return, they were allowed to attend Jim's stage performances as a group.

"Gentleman Jack" arrived in New York in early November, opening at the Grand Opera House. As Brady had feared, in stark contrast to the accolades Jim and the play received on tour, New York critics were not well disposed to the play, nor to Jim's acting ability.

> That Mr. James J. Corbett obscures the play is to his credit. It ought to be obscured, and the public which felt under a certain obligation to Mr. Corbett because of a recent event in New Orleans is still more deeply his debtor. On the stage the pugilist appears to be a modest fellow. He probably does not want to be considered an actor. If he had any such desire its gratifications would be unpleasant to him. He is immensely popular just now, and it is worth going to see such a perfect specimen of the physical human.[2]

In spite of poor reviews, the entire week at the Grand Opera House was SRO.

In Philadelphia, critics similarly disapproved of Jim's "histrionic ability," yet crowds packed the theater. The engagement in Buffalo was sold out before the company arrived in town. A return to New York, this time at the People's Theater in the Bowery, offered another week of crowded houses, as eager patrons availed themselves of "the opportunity to see the conqueror of John L. Sullivan."

While in New York, Jim announced his refusal to accept Joe Goddard's challenge. "Gentleman Jack" had been successful beyond expectations, and the prospect for additional profit was alluring. Why interrupt a highly successful enterprise? However profitable financially, Jim's decision meant that he forfeited the championship, leaving it vacant. Not surprisingly, New York's boxing establishment grew angry, particularly because Jim had

GRAND OPERA HOUSE

Lessee and Manager,.......................Mr. T. H. FRENCH.

RESERVED SEATS (Orchestra Circle and Balcony,) 50 CENTS

COMMENCING

MONDAY, NOV. 7, 1892.

WEDNESDAY—Matinees—SATURDAY

SPECIAL MATINEE, TUESDAY, ELECTION DAY

THE CHAMPION OF THE WORLD,

JAMES J. CORBETT

Presenting CHAS. T. VINCENT and WM. A. BRADY'S New Play,
in Five Acts, entitled

GENTLEMAN JACK

PRODUCED AND MANAGED BY

WM. A. BRADY.

Special Engagement of DAGMAR AND DECELLE, the Famous
Danish Ballad Singers.

—CAST—

JACK ROYDEN, a College Student, better known as "Gentleman
Jack,".................................JAMES J. CORBETT
MR. HALLIDAY, Banker....................Mr. WM. B. MURRAY
GEORGE HALLIDAY, his Son.................Mr. EDWARD WADE
CHARLES TWITCHELL, Champion Boxer of England............
Mr. JOHN DONALDSON
JOSEPH ROYDEN, Jack's Father, under the assumed name of Joe
Blake.................................Mr. J. W. DAVENPORT
SCHUYLER SOUTHGATE, a Tender Young Person.....Mr. JAY WILSON
TOM CHARLTON, Jack's Friend.................Mr. R. M. HALL
PROFESSOR TODD, of Payne College...........Mr. CARL KRAUSS
MAXEY SPLASH, a Fireman and retired Prize Fighter..Mr. C. K. FRENCH
MANAGER SHORT, of the Madison Square Roof Garden..........
Mr. STEVEN MORRIS
SPECIAL OFFICER, of the Roof Garden.....Mr. FRED. M. HARRISON
WAITER at th eRoof Garden..................Mr. W. H. WEBBER
PRESIDENT.........{ Officials of the Olympic {....Mr. DAN KENEALY
CAPTAIN OF POLICE } Club, New Orleans. { .Mr. ANDREW HAYNE
ALICE SAUNDERS, Betrothed to Jack..............Miss LEE LAMAR
MRS. ROYDEN, Jack's Mother.............Mrs. NICK FORRESTER
POLLY GRAHAM, the College Widow..........Miss BELLE LA VERDE
MRS. MORIARITY, an Apple Woman }.......Miss LILLIAN RAMSDEN
TOTTIE SPLASH, a Serio-comic..... }

College Attendants, Bank Clerks, Waiters, Policemen, Visitors to the Roof
Garden, Members of the Olympic Club, Patrons of the Olympic Club,
by numerous auxiliaries.

Mr. William Delaney; who has trained and seconded Mr. Corbett for every
battle he has ever engaged in, will appear in company with the Champion in
the 4th and 5th Acts.

—SYNOPSIS.—

ACT I.—The Campus at Payne College.
ACT II.—The Halliday National Bank, New York.
ACT III.—The Madison Square Roof Garden, New York.
During this Act the following specialties will be introduced:
BELLE LA VERDE, Cloak Dance.
DAGMAR AND DECELLE, Danish Warblers.
LILLIAN RAMSDEN, Songs and Dances.
ACT IV.—Training Quarters at Loch Arbor.
All the Sporting Goods used in this Act furnished by J. P. CROOK & CO.
1191 Broadway, New York.
ACT V.—Olympic Club, New Orleans. This stage setting is an exact
reproduction of the Olympic Club, from instantaneous photographs taken
the night of the Sullivan-Corbett Contest. During this Act Mr. WILLIAM
A. BRADY, will officiate as Referee.

WILLIAM DELANEY..........}..........Business Manager
SAM THALL.................} Representing {..Advance Representative
T. O. MARTYN..............} JAMES J. CORBETT {........Treasurer
C. K. FRENCH..............} and {.........Stage Manager
W. H. WEBBER..............} WILLIAM A. BRADY. {.....Stage Machinist
E. M. HARRISON............}..........Property Master

This was Jim's first appearance at a New York City theater. Brady had originally named the play "Gentleman Jim" but was persuaded to change the title and some aspects of the plot because its promotional intent seemed so blatant.

chosen to pursue a theatrical career rather than defend his title. The local sporting press chastised him.

> He doubtless did know the rules well enough, but it did not suit his purpose to comply with the regulations governing the holding of the championship. The idea of a champion ignoring these rules is simply ridiculous.[3]

The episode initiated a tenuous and contradictory relationship with the New York boxing community. They surely admired his ring abilities; nonetheless, they were discomfited by his disrespect for the rules and upset by his behavior.

Though not directly connected to the apparent disagreement between Jim and the boxing establishment, Jim's $33,000 purchase of six lots in North Manhattan, for the purpose of building a roadhouse, was viewed by some boxing men as less than a champion's commitment to the profession. Jim's reported idea was to "make an attractive resort for the road driver of the metropolis."

These public sentiments came juxtaposed against a number of articles that appeared in New York newspapers discussing recent changes in the business of boxing. Reporters discussed the inflated purses being offered boxers, the greater number of matches being scheduled, and the increased size of crowds. If these trends continued, they reasoned, new venues would have to be built and ticket prices would have to rise. Could the sport of boxing deal with these challenges? As if suddenly aware of boxing's new commercial opportunities, reporters declared the sport to be on the threshold of "a new era" but its direction remained in question. Buried in one such article was an observation about the "new class" of people who were attending matches. No one mentioned the increasing popularity of boxing-related events currently playing in the better theaters around the country.

In Boston, the first evidence of Jim's theatrical appeal and improving dramatic abilities was noted.

> It was the first opportunity offered to his Boston friends to greet Mr. Corbett in a speaking part. That he did very well, considering his inexperience, was evidenced by the applause which followed the few chances his part gave him to be heroic. The star was easy and graceful and, barring an absence of modulation of voice, he rendered his lines with fair effect. There was one occasion, however, when, at the end of act three, he declared that he would defend the championship of America against the world, that the roof of the house was in some degree of being lifted.[4]

The review also noted that Jim had been recalled at the end of each act and floral tributes handed him over the footlights, a sure sign of success.

On its sports page, the *Boston Globe* also noted that Jim had been arrested on an action brought by Joe Lannon—a close friend and second in John L. Sullivan's corner—to recover $5,000 in damages for an alleged breach of contract to spar with Lannon at a benefit. The benefit had been planned at a time when Jim was in the midst of training for the Mitchell match. Jim acknowledged the writ in court and furnished bail. He explained to the judge his reason for being unable to participate in the benefit. The trial was delayed and, months later, dropped.

A brief tour through New England continued to "pack the house." In Lynn, Massachusetts, as in many cities previously visited, Jim was feted by the local athletic club. He was given a grand dinner and elected an honorary member of the club. In return, Jim took club members behind the scenes at the theater that evening.

Engagements in Columbus, Ohio, Grand Rapids, Michigan, and Ft. Wayne, Indiana, preceded a two-week run in Chicago the middle of January, 1893. The stand was divided between two theaters: the Windsor, to attract upscale North Side audiences; and Havlin's, to attract denizens of the gritty South Side. There was then only one bridge over the Chicago River, making travel between the north and south sides of the city difficult, particularly to attend leisure-time activities. Two other bridges were being built in anticipation of the World's Fair, scheduled to open in June.

At the Windsor, "nearly enough people were turned away to have filled the house many times." Havlin's generated SRO audiences throughout the week, their box office receipts "a record breaker."

While in Chicago, Brady negotiated a contract for "Gentleman Jack" to appear at the Haymarket Theater at the beginning of the World's Fair. Jim would be joining such headliners as Tony Pastor, Digby Bell, Weber and Fields, and Lillian Russell, among others, all of whom planned to visit the city to take advantage of the anticipated large fair-going crowds. Both Jim and Brady looked forward to a profitable summer.

Meanwhile, Charley Mitchell had recently been released from prison in England (on charges of attempted murder) and completed arrangements to visit the U.S. In a bold announcement, backed by his manager, Squire Abington (George Baird, a noted and well-heeled British turfman), Mitchell told of his earnest desire to meet Corbett and defeat him. According to newspapers, Jim had his own interest in facing Mitchell—he had not forgotten Mitchell's insults—as long as it did not interfere with his theatrical tour. If they could arrange a meeting, it would give Jim the opportunity to regain his title, or Mitchell a chance to capture it, if he defeated Corbett. Like most such public challenges, Mitchell's call would be subject to extensive press coverage and lengthy negotiation.

Through the winter, Jim continued to play to SRO houses in Milwaukee, St. Paul, Minneapolis, and St. Louis. Back in New York, Brady posted a $10,000 deposit for Jim to face Mitchell. Taken aback by the deposit, Mitchell admitted he didn't have money enough to cover the deposit. Further meetings took place, Mitchell finally agreeing to all of Jim's stipulations for the contest. The most difficult issue they faced would be the venue. Where could the match be held without breaking any laws?

By March, matters had become even more complicated. California's governor had signed a bill prohibiting boxing in the state. A likely city to host the bout, Buffalo, New York, banned the proposed match. Then, Mitchell's manager, Squire Abington, died, leaving the funds set aside for Mitchell's stake in doubt. Mitchell returned to England to attend Abington's funeral and indicated he would not return to the U.S. until September, thus delaying a bout with Corbett indefinitely. Meanwhile, Brady persuaded the Coney Island Athletic Club to sponsor the contest, with an astounding offer for a $40,000 purse. Jim readily agreed to the terms, but what of Mitchell?

"Gentleman Jack" continued to attract large crowds throughout the Midwest and Canada, each engagement a success, as Jim's acting gained increased approval. In early April, however, while the company was appearing in Montreal, a number of cast members retired to honor other summer commitments. This placed a significant burden on Brady to replace them, at a time when most performers had already been booked. Enter Olive and Brady's wife, Marie Rene.

Both had been on tour with their husbands. Having seen the play so many times, both practically knew all the lines. In an innovative move, Brady persuaded both to take part in the play. To everyone's surprise, their opening night appearances met with applause and flowers. For the next two months, they performed above expectations, Jim and Brady pleased with the arrangement and the financial outcome. Brady did promise the women, however, that other performers would take their places when the company reached Chicago.

"Big business" greeted them in Denver, according to the *Clipper*, with added one-night stands in Pueblo and Leadville, where they packed the elegant Tabor Opera House at advanced prices. The company arrived on the West Coast in May, playing brief engagements in Los Angeles, Victoria, B.C., and Tacoma, Washington, before coming to San Francisco for a two-week run. "Corbett Coming to the California Theater," the *Chronicle* proclaimed. "Our Jim, the Actor," headlined the *Examiner*, in anticipation of Jim's arrival.

Judging by the behavior of hordes of San Franciscan well-wishers, it appeared that Jim had won the championship all over again. A delegation of relatives, friends, and admirers took ferries to the 16th Street train station, Oakland, to meet Jim and the Oregon Express. Among those who waited to greet Jim were his mother, brothers and sisters, Olympic Club members, and old friends.

"He's on the last car," several people exclaimed when they saw the decorated coach. Jim and Olive jumped off, hand-in-hand, and ran to greet the crowd. Pulling his mother into his arms, Jim kissed her several times, followed by numerous kisses for his sisters. Olive shared hugs and kisses with the entire family. On the ferry back to San Francisco, Jim devoted himself to reporters. While there had been reports that Jim's condition had deteriorated, he seemed quite fit. "At any rate," a reporter noted, "you don't appear to have consumption."

"Well, I should say not. Never felt much better in my life."

The entire way over on the boat, scores of people stepped up to shake hands with Jim. A large crowd had gathered at the ferry terminal awaiting his arrival. Loud cheers, a fast exit, and Jim and Olive were driven to the Baldwin Hotel.

Early that evening, the hotel lobby was packed with people, including a large contingent of boys and girls, hundreds having come for the sole purpose of getting a glimpse of the heavyweight champion and actor. At the moment, in Jim's suite, a *Chronicle* reporter was interviewing him.

"I'm awfully worried," said Jim. "That speech I'll make is bothering me. I don't really know what to say."

"Just say what your heart prompts," sagely advised showman Brady.

A large contingent of Olympic Club members arrived at the hotel, led by the First Troop Cavalry Band. Streets were completely blocked from the hotel to the theater. Jim had to push his way through the crowd to his hack, shaking hands with everyone who could extend one. The crowd in front of the theater was so large, Jim had to enter through a back door.

Even before the curtain went up, the audience was noisy with whistlers, squawkers, and howlers. The entire Corbett family, proud and happy, were seated in boxes near the stage. When Jim made his entrance, in a white flannel tennis suit and a large straw hat, the din was overwhelming. Olympic Club members cheered their hero with the club yell. It took some minutes for the explosion of esteem and affection to subside but when Jim began to recite his lines, people in the audience shouted for a speech.

"This is the happiest moment in my life," said Jim, and the audience applauded. "I will endeavor and try to prove worthy of this cordial reception," he went on, the audience erupting in cheers yet again.

Finally, Jim was able to continue his acting. Throughout the play, however, frequent applause and cheering made it difficult for the performers to recite their lines. In the final, prize-fight act, while Jim was busy winning the championship, members of the audience kept tossing flowers onto the stage. At the end of the play, when Jack's girlfriend throws herself into his arms, he holds her tightly and exclaims, with a knowing smile to the audience: "Cheer up, darling. Our fortune is made. I'll open a saloon tomorrow."

"Our Jim," as he was affectionately called by Friscoites, had made a decided hit. Though few had come to the theater to evaluate the quality of Jim's dramatic skills, they were pleasantly surprised by his acting ability. "He is the hero of the hour in these parts," exclaimed the *Chronicle*.

Jim spent the next morning meeting friends at the hotel. In the afternoon, he visited the Olympic Club and spent several hours swimming. On Thursday night, a reception was given for Jim at the Corbett residence. The stable had been cleared of horses, carriages, and hay to accommodate a large table, filled with food and drink to provide refreshment during speeches and cheers in Jim's honor. Following the party, Jim asked for, and received, from his hometown fans, some quiet, personal time, except, of course, for what transpired each night at the theater.

Prior to leaving San Francisco for Chicago, and the World's Fair, Jim appeared at the Wigwam Theater, to participate in a vaudeville olio. One of the acts presented was a demonstration of boxing between a kangaroo and its trainer; Jim served as referee for the match. The kangaroo, not used to having another person in the ring, swung his tail and feet as often at Jim as at its trainer. The crowd howled as Jim demonstrated his skill by evading the bestial blows.

The Columbian Exhibition, familiarly

called the Chicago World's Fair, began its run badly. Less than a week after the fair opened, Wall Street markets crashed (later called the Panic of 1893) and the anticipated fair attendance greatly diminished. Coupled with bad weather, the financial collapse caused many of the downtown theaters, whose managers had planned to feature stars for the entire summer, to find themselves with small audiences. Some were forced to shut down entirely; others struggled to survive with reduced box offices.

Gradually, however, thanks to a combination of quick economic recovery, improved weather, and the fair managers' decision to remain open on Sundays and evenings, fair attendance improved and grew throughout the entire summer. Within a few weeks of this turnaround, theaters were again thriving.

"Gentleman Jack" opened on June 18, at the Haymarket Theater, just about the time that theater audiences had begun to increase. The *Tribune* reported: "James J. Corbett, at the Haymarket, brought out a top heavy audience, which used its lungs, feet and hands in proclaiming him a welcome visitor to the West Side."[5]

Success was short-lived, however. Reviewers of the production pointed out that "Gentleman Jack" had already appeared in Chicago earlier in the season. A *Tribune* critic observed that there were, at the time, no less than a dozen boxers "exhibiting themselves through the medium of plays or vaudeville, and in nearly every instance the exhibition is to their disadvantage."

In addition, intense competition from other star performers, in conjunction with large promotional budgets, diminished the likelihood of patronage for the Haymarket Theater, located outside the downtown area. Whatever the combination of factors, "Gentleman Jack" closed in two weeks and Brady had to disband the company. How to utilize Jim's popularity and the fair's crowds to advantage posed an interesting challenge for Brady's showmanship.

In the meantime, Jim and Olive experienced the pleasure of associating with fellow performers and celebrities, such as Lillian Russell, Diamond Jim Brady, Eddie Foy, and Buffalo Bill Cody, at convivial race track excursions, elaborate picnics, and fine restaurants. Newspapers reported on everything these popular headliners did, said, and appeared at, with regularity.

Manager William Brady (the one not sporting diamonds) came through again, promoting a makeshift and temporary engagement, with Jim sparring and some other lesser-known vaudeville acts appearing on the Midway Plaisance in two-a-day performances. The improvised stage and dressing rooms had been purchased from a failed dramatic company, chairs were folding seats, prices low to compete with other Midway attractions. Jim did not care for the arrangement—sparring was harder than acting and much less lucrative—but seemed to go along with Brady.

Spectator reactions to Jim were almost uniformly positive, but when he "beat up" a sparring partner (unidentified), many were shocked. A reporter from the *Evening Post* published a very unkind critique of Jim's ring performance, accusing him of being "a purveyor of blood" who was "in no great danger of growing immensely wealthy on the proceeds of the Midway Plaisance venture." Brady, on behalf of Jim, sued the newspaper for defamation of character and demanded compensation for loss of business. (The suit was filed for $100,000 but later dropped, after Brady and Jim had departed Chicago.)

The newspaper article claimed the attention of fair directors, who, upon reviewing the situation, declared Jim's exhibition "not elevating in character, but rather calculated to demoralize the visitor." The president of the fair ordered Chicago's Director of Works to close the show. When the order was served, both Brady and Jim ignored it. The next day, a restraining order was entered, ousting Jim from the fairgrounds. Brady attempted to obtain an injunction to prevent the ouster, but failed. At the end of July, Jim and Olive returned to their home in New York, Jim considering his Chicago experience a failure. Given the immediate circumstances, boxing seemed to present the better alternative, in the person of Charley Mitchell.

Though Mitchell had not yet signed and sent back the official letter of agreement to meet Jim, he continued to express his desire to beat the ex-champion. In return, Jim presented Mitchell with a final date, August 5, to comply with his challenge. Mitchell then claimed he had not yet heard from Brady regarding final arrangements, but still insisted he wanted to fight. An athletic club in Roby, Indiana, outbid the Coney Island Athletic Club for the match and Jim agreed to meet Mitchell there, though this meant rewriting and again signing, the articles of agreement. If Mitchell did not wish to face Jim, the erstwhile champion expressed a willingness to challenge Peter Jackson, having nothing against facing the Negro boxer again. Witnesses to this alternative challenge were Joe Choynski and Eddie Foy. In fact, when Jim arrived at his Asbury Park training quarters, he did not yet know for sure which man he was going to box.

Final arrangements were apparently settled at the end of September, when Mitchell arrived in the U.S. and promptly signed the letters of agreement to meet Jim for the world's championship. Further, after considerable discussion, all parties agreed to conduct the match at the Coney Island Athletic Club, not in Indiana. The bout would be slated at twenty rounds or more, for a purse of $40,000—the largest ever in the history of boxing—following Marquis of Queensberry rules, glove weight of five ounces. The club had the rights to choose the referee and timekeeper, with each participant able to choose his own assistant timekeepers. The date of the contest was set at sometime between December 5 and December 20, giving the boxers approximately two-and-a-half months to prepare.

At Jim's training camp, improvements were being made. A new business entity, called the James J. Corbett Athletic Club, leased quarters at the Park Opera House Building, in Asbury Park. Besides Jim and Brady, two new members now joined the operation, Joe and Tom Corbett, Jim's younger brothers. Joe planned to spar with his brother; Tom had been designated the equipment manager. Jim began training in earnest, with a strong sense of purpose recapturing the world's championship and punishing Charley Mitchell for his personal insults proved strong motivators.

Even before the local attorney general had an opportunity to denounce the proposed contest, Brooklyn ministers and newspapers came out against the bout. Evidently a number of influential Coney Island Athletic Club members were local politicians, and since the election was only a few weeks away, they decided not to promote the match. Newspapers suggested the contest was only temporarily delayed, until after the election, since neither Corbett nor Mitchell had been officially informed of the club's withdrawal. Indiana was ruled out as an alternative as was New Orleans. So where else could the bout possibly be staged?

Agreement on the date and venue for the match to take place broke down. The

A souvenir card distributed by Haymarket Theater, Chicago, during Jim's performance of "Gentleman Jack." The show played only three weeks and Jim found himself giving two-a-day boxing exhibitions on the Midway Plaisance at the Chicago World's Fair. (Bustout Productions)

Clipper reported the immediate impasse. "...at present writing there is no certainty where the men will meet in the ring, or that they will ever come together."[6]

Already the second week of November, and nothing had yet been settled. Whatever happened, there would be no contest in December. When it was reported that a syndicate of sporting men from Jacksonville, Florida, were interested in sponsoring the match, no one paid attention until they arrived in New York and, in a meeting of principals, offered the same purse as had been tendered by the Coney Island contingent. Serious negotiations began immediately. Regressive forces, however, were at work.

Simultaneously with the announcement that the parties were meeting to finalize an agreement, church leaders in Jacksonville submitted a strongly worded protest to the mayor and city attorney to prevent the bout from taking place. Florida's governor was poised to step in, but no one knew what action he might take.

On November 15, final agreement was, once again, reached on the championship contest. It was to be held in Jacksonville, on January 25, 1894, for a purse of $20,000, winner-take-all. Florida's governor now stepped in and directed the county sheriff to "take all proper precautions to prevent any prize fight in that county." Sponsors of the match sent their lawyers to dispute the ruling, but the governor was adamant. "I do not think the fight will take place in Florida," he declared. In the meantime, Jim and Mitchell continued training, though each camp wondered if it would be in vain.

The state attorney general released a statement presenting Florida's official position on the contest.

Prize fighting is unlawful in this State. Spectators who attend, aid, abet, cheer on and encourage prize fights can be indicted and punished. If the proposed fight occurs in Florida, and parties be arrested, a properly drawn indictment will hold them securely.[7]

Nevertheless, the announcement did not clearly state the contest would be prevented from taking place or interrupted, an encouraging situation if the participants were willing to take a chance against arrest.

A major breakthrough occurred when Jacksonville's city council voted to change the law prohibiting boxing matches; to permit them, as long as they were fought with five ounce gloves. Immediately, plans were put into motion to prepare the boxing venue.

The old fair grounds, about two miles from the center of town (and outside town limits) were purchased. A dilapidated building would be transformed into an amphitheater to accommodate 12,000 people. Streetcars would be routed to the site, on a ten-minute schedule; they would be changed from mule service to electric. Prices for seats would be ten dollars and up, except for boxes, at fifty dollars each. It was an ambitious undertaking with an ambiguous outcome.

Billy Delaney, Jim's trainer, had located training quarters at Mayport, a small town at the mouth of the St. John's River, more than twenty miles east of Jacksonville. Two cottages were leased, and a handball court and ring constructed in preparation for Jim's arrival at the end of December. Jim's traveling party, besides Delaney, consisted of John Donaldson, John McVey, Jack Dempsey, Joe and Tom Corbett, Dan Creedon, Tom Tracey, William Brady, Olive, and her father.

Upon arrival at Mayport, Jim visited the training quarters, declared them pleasant, and returned to Jacksonville, where, that evening, he was feted by sponsors and obliged them by sparring a few rounds with McVey. When interviewed by a local reporter, Jim revealed his feelings about Mitchell.

> The tactics that I shall pursue in the ring depend altogether upon Mitchell's behavior in the ring at the start.... I will be prepared to meet him at every turn.... If Mitchell sees that he can't win the contest fairly, he will use all foul and dirty means that he can devise. I know I can outbox Mitchell; you will see, I think, a short, easy fight.[8]

Charley Mitchell reached Jacksonville on Christmas Day, and retired to Anastasia Island, near St. Augustine, to set up camp. With Mitchell were Jim Hall, Jack Fogarty, Harry Darrin, Pony Moore, Tom Allen, and Steve O'Donnell. Mitchell was welcomed by a crowd of more than a thousand people. In the evening, as Jim had before, Mitchell sparred a few rounds at the local Opera House and seemed to persuade the crowd that he was in top condition.

The legal battle continued, if anything, heated up, as the city council, who agreed to the match, overrode a veto by the mayor. Yet, when the sponsor's attorney made an application to the governor for a charter to hold the event, the governor rejected it. Moreover, he threatened to arrest everyone involved for violating the laws of the state. Still, the threat did not prevent plans for the match from proceeding. Final construction of the amphitheater was undertaken. Special trains were ordered to transport spectators. Tickets sold even faster than mosquito repellent.

Though the governor remained adamant about preventing the match from taking place, sponsors declared their intention to proceed "in defiance of all opposition." They were encouraged when the county recorder of deeds issued a license to hold the contest at the fair grounds, explaining that any interference with the license would be met with a fine and imprisonment, according to city ordinance. For the time being, then, the governor, local sheriff, and militia (who had been put on alert by the governor) could not interfere. When the announcement was made public, evidently assuring sporting men that the contest would definitely take place, additional special trains were scheduled to handle the anticipated demand.

A week before the match, debate still continued whether it would actually occur. In public, sponsors expressed optimism. Governor Mitchell, however, again threatened to send in militia to prevent the bout and he backed up his threat by deploying a battalion to Jacksonville. Betting was slow because there was little money on Mitchell; odds favored Corbett two to one. Still, more than a quarter of a million dollars, a sizable portion coming from New York investors, was available to handle bets.

Sunday, four days before the contest, an expectant quiet seemed to pervade Jacksonville. A court meeting had been planned for Monday, to discuss a proposed injunction to prevent the sheriff from interfering with the bout. Jim and Olive attended church (a Protestant service) in the morning; he played a game of baseball in the afternoon. Mitchell's wife arrived, and he decided to forego training for the day.

Only two days before the championship contest was to take place, Governor Mitchell blocked the use of streetcars to take spectators to any venue outside the city and he again threatened the use of militia. In fact, militia arrived in town that afternoon, marched down the main street in a colorful show of force, and camped at the local armory. As yet, they had received no orders to stop the bout. The sponsors of the match argued about the disposition of the $20,000 check; should it be cashed or not, given the question of whether the contest would actually take place. Jim con-

tinued to train, but expressed doubt the match would "come off." Brady told reporters he would be willing to postpone the match a day or two, but no longer. Conflicting reports thoroughly confused the interested parties.

The day prior to the contest proved a winner for the sponsors. After listening to arguments, a state circuit judge granted the sponsors an injunction restraining the sheriff from any acts of interference. Crowds outside the courtroom were jubilant and marched down the street carrying impromptu signs announcing that the match was on. The governor had not yet been heard from but the militia was ready, if ordered. Well-dressed men hired carts drawn by steers to parade the streets, asking those they passed why their cart was like the fight, and chorusing the answer, "Because the governor isn't in it."

That evening, Charley Mitchell and entourage arrived at the Everett Hotel. Hundreds of people were on the street to greet him but he quickly passed through the crowd, locked himself in his room, and refused admittance to all reporters. Although seemingly in excellent humor and condition—"I've never felt better in my life," he declared—he chafed at not having been served toast and tea when he ordered it.

Jim remained at Mayport, relaxed after a heavy supper, and played a game of whist with Olive before retiring. With a "good-night, sweetheart," he was asleep in ten minutes. The morning of the match, he and Olive walked down to the beach. A barber came to trim Jim's famous pompadour. Jim sent two telegrams: to Mrs. P.J. Corbett—"Now, don't worry a second. I am perfectly well and will win without doubt;" to brother Harry—"Don't bet on the rounds. Play the result at any odds."

An early rain discouraged sponsors, but the weather cleared later in the morning. Unfortunately, the situation at the site was "simply horrible." The ring was only then being built. Lighting was poor. Everything was wet. The seats were poorly arranged, constructed of rough pine boards. A few mule cars, hacks, and wagons constituted available transportation. Newspaper representatives had to pay twenty dollars to enter the arena. Carpenters were still at work at 1:30 P.M., when half of the disappointing crowd of 2,500 had already assembled. There was no attempt to preserve order, and open betting was rampant. The police stood by and did nothing. The militia, with no orders from the governor, remained at the armory.

At 2:00 P.M., all the distinguished guests had gathered around the ring, although not nearly as numerous as they might have been had the contest been a certainty two weeks earlier. Representatives from New York were in the majority. There was little actual betting; Corbett had been installed a three to one favorite, and few people dared to back Mitchell.

A few minutes after two, Billy Madden, the master of ceremonies, entered the ring to introduce the boxers. The noise was so great, no one could hear him; nor did they seem so inclined. When the Corbett cavalcade appeared, the crowd broke loose in earnest. Brady preceded Jim down the aisle; John Donaldson, John McVey, and Jack Dempsey followed Jim into the ring. As he had previously done in the Sullivan affair, Jim inspected the floor and tested the strength of the ropes. After what seemed a long time (actually, ten minutes), Mitchell entered and followed his entire entourage into the ring. As the boxers stood in the center of the ring, their disparity of size caused murmurs to flow through the crowd. Jim stood more than four inches taller, had an obviously longer reach, and outweighed Mitchell by more than twenty pounds.

Referee Kelly called the men together to give them instructions on clinching and breaking away. When they were told to shake hands, Jim refused, and walked back to his corner, a scowl of vengeance contorting his face. "Better hurry up, Kelly," Jim called to the referee. "It's getting cold here." In contrast, Mitchell was talking to his seconds, laughing, and adjusting his gloves. When everything seemed ready, Kelly shouted, "Get together, boys." And the gong rang.

As Jim had predicted, the contest was short, decisive, easy, and profitable.

At the beginning of Round One, Jim sprang from his corner to meet Mitchell, who leisurely walked to the center. Both men cautiously feeling their way, Jim advanced and Mitchell gave ground. Jim worked Mitchell into the ropes, but he escaped the trap. Mitchell's left to the ribs missed, Jim retaliating with a jab to the jaw. They clinched. Mitchell hit Jim in the neck and sustained a left to his nose. Two leads by Mitchell missed; a third reached Jim's neck but Mitchell took a telling smash to his nose. Mitchell struck Jim a light blow to the jaw, but paid for it with a jolting shot to the face. The gong rang.

When the gong sounded to begin the second round, Jim was already in the middle of the ring. Mitchell connected with a left to Jim's mouth and decided to push the action. His blows, however, fell short. Jim took the offensive, maneuvered Mitchell into a corner, and pounded him in the face. In a furious exchange, Jim landed a straight left to Mitchell's head. The blow dropped him. Pouncing on his prey, Jim seemed to lose self-control. Had it not been for referee Kelly's restraining him, he would have lost the bout on a foul. Jim was still struggling with Kelly to get at the fallen Mitchell when the gong sounded.

Between rounds, Kelly warned Jim about fouling, and his seconds begged him to keep his head: "Don't lose the prize that is plainly yours," they warned.

At the start of Round Three, Mitchell came out slowly. Jim sprang at him, obviously angry. Pushing Mitchell into a corner, Jim crushed his nose, drew blood, and connected with a right to the jaw, knocking him down. Mitchell gathered himself through the count while Jim wrestled with Kelly to get at his opponent. Jim's seconds jumped into the ring to push him away. It could have been called a foul, but Kelly knew the end was near for Mitchell.

The moment Mitchell was up, Jim hit him full on the mouth. Mitchell fell heavily, bleeding from both mouth and nose. Relentless, Jim hit Mitchell again, while his outclassed opponent was still in a sitting position. From Mitchell's corner came cries of "foul," and his seconds entered the ring to assist him. Though dazed and defenseless, Mitchell staggered gamely to his feet. Immediately, Jim renewed his savage attack with a terrific blow to Mitchell's jaw. Knocked cold, Mitchell fell on his face.

With a wave of his hand toward Jim's corner, Kelly shouted, "Corbett wins." Mitchell's seconds ran to their man, gathered up his battered body, and carried him to their corner. After repeated ministrations with a bottle of ammonia, Mitchell's eyes finally opened. "You're out," explained his second, Pony Moore; but Mitchell seemed not to comprehend. Baffled, he was led slowly to his dressing room.

Spectators broke loose with shouts and applause. Many crowded into the ring to congratulate Jim. Kelly shook Jim's hand, flourishing the bankroll of $20,000, and told him it was his on demand. Everyone acknowledged that Jim had recaptured the heavyweight crown. After months of controversy, scheming, plotting, and legal entanglements, it took only nine minutes for a decision to be reached.

Soon after the return of Mitchell to

Everett House and Jim to the St. James Hotel, both were arrested on warrants charging them with having committed a fight by agreement. The men were taken to the Court House, where their bail was fixed at $7,500 each, an exorbitant amount. Nonetheless, bonds for their appearance were quickly furnished. Mitchell was scheduled to appear in court the next day; Jim's case was postponed to allow him to keep his engagement at Madison Square Garden. When they appeared in court, much to the surprise of onlookers, they shook hands, exchanged compliments, and parted.

"Good-bye, Charley."

"Good-bye, Jim," said Mitchell cordially, as he grasped his hand.

"I'll see you again, old man," Jim remarked.

"Sure thing," was the reply and they separated.

All of New York's sporting (and betting) men had crowded into hotels that featured tickers: the Hoffman House, the Coleman House, the Sturtevant, the Brunswick and the Gilsey Houses attracted the largest crowds. The result of the bout caused little surprise, although few thought it would end as quickly as it did. Very few large bets had been made. Eddie Foy added $900 to his wallet, thanks to a number of small bets that Mitchell would not last nineteen rounds; a "gift" in Foy's estimation.

Harry Corbett's saloon was a scene of jubilation. The pop of champagne corks was almost as loud as the din of joyful shouts and cheers. Streets adjacent to the San Francisco newspapers were crowded, preventing the passage of streetcars on Market, Kearny, and Geary Streets. When the final result of the contest was announced, the *Chronicle* reported, "it seemed as if half of the city had gone mad."

Harry won more than $5000; other

Corbett siblings made lesser amounts, as did friends of the family and Olympic Club members. Patrick was pleased Jim had won, but there were no reports that he had engaged in any betting.

The day after, Jim and his entire party—Olive, her father, Brady, Delaney, his wife, McVey, and Donaldson—left Jacksonville for New York at 11:20 A.M. on a special train. A large crowd assembled to see Jim off and the train departed amid deafening cheers. At stations along the route to Savannah, groups of country people, including many Negroes, waited for the train and cheered their approval as it passed. No stops had been planned because Jim was scheduled to appear at Madison Square Garden the next evening. The Garden had been rented several weeks earlier, and the winner of the contest—whoever he happened to be—was obliged to appear.

The Corbett train was due at the Pennsylvania Station in Jersey City at 3:30 P.M. More than 5,000 people were already present, along with a brass band, a coach and four horses for Jim and Olive, and additional carriages to carry the remainder of the party. When the train pulled into the station, the crowd let loose with a wild cheer; the band played "Hail to the Chief." Although Jim declined to make a speech, he shook hands with spectators as he and Olive made their way to the waiting carriage.

More than 7,000 people had gathered at the Garden to see Jim and watch a number of sparring exhibitions. Included in the crowd were many women, as well as representatives of New York's social and political elite. Police were there in large numbers, not to break up rowdy behavior, but rather to prevent pickpockets from reaping benefits from the well-to-do gentry.

After a number of preliminary matches, Jim was announced to spar with Dan Creedon. When the crowd yelled for a speech, Jim thanked the crowd "for the kind reception, and I'm glad the championship remained in America," to which the entire auditorium rose in cheers and applause. At the end of the evening, Jim was reported to be $5,000 richer, his share of the charged admissions.

In answer to reporters' questions, Jim declared he was returning to the theater in a few weeks and had scheduled a theatrical tour of European capitals during the summer. With his winnings, he planned to improve his roadhouse and give the remainder to brother Frank to invest. Jim also revealed he had been offered $10,000 to play with the Baltimore baseball team for the season. Theater, however, came first.

A week later, Jim and "Gentleman Jack" opened at the Boston Theater to SRO audiences, his resounding victory over Mitchell providing additional incentive for crowds to see the champion on stage.

> James J. Corbett was welcomed by an audience that filled the house to overflowing. The reception given him was thunderous in its nature and he bowed his thanks tight and left to the cheering masses of humanity before him. The audience was mainly composed of males, yet there was in its composition a very generous sprinkling of the weaker sex.[9]

Simultaneously with Jim's return to the stage, Brady announced the release of two mementos to honor the champion's achievements, to be sold only in theaters at which "Gentleman Jack" played: a large, colored lithograph showing Jim in a sparring attitude, at fifty cents a copy; and a statuette, ten inches high, in ivory finish, showing him in ring costume, to be sold for one dollar. Within two months, they were all sold out.

Engagements in Pittsburgh, Harlem,

Philadelphia, and Washington, D.C., attracted "immense audiences," primarily composed of "the sporting element." While in the nation's capitol, Jim and Olive renewed their acquaintance with Lillian Russell, then playing in her hit, "Princess Nicotine." Together, they attended the race track on a number of afternoons. Joined by Charley Mitchell, Jim and Olive made their way to Jacksonville, where the two boxers were to stand trial for engaging in their prize fight.

It took an entire day to impanel a jury, both attorneys rejecting nearly all candidates. Finally, six men, the number required by Florida law for misdemeanor cases, were secured. When arguments began, the prosecution attempted to prove the contest was brutal and that Corbett and Mitchell had malice toward one another. Then, an attempt was made to bring into evidence the $20,000 check that Corbett had received but witnesses, while acknowledging having seen a piece of paper handed to Corbett, claimed to have been unaware of its character. The defense did not introduce any issues or witnesses. The case was then given to the jurors. After deliberating sixteen minutes, they returned a verdict of "not guilty." That evening, Jim was back on a train headed for Baltimore, "Gentleman Jack's" next engagement.

The play's spring tour included week-long stops in Cincinnati, St. Louis, Newark, and Brooklyn. Reviews for each engagement cited packed houses, primarily due to Jim's popularity as the champion. At the close of "Gentleman Jack's" season, Brady informed the press that Jim would be appearing in a new play the coming season, after returning from his summer tour of the British Isles. Jim, Olive, Brady, a reduced company of performers, and comedian Billy Gaylor prepared to leave for London early in April. Also in the party were Jim's mother and father,

who planned to visit family friends and relatives in County Mayo, their first return since having left Ireland forty years earlier.

Patrick and Catherine arrived in New York about a week before the voyage, during which time Jim and Olive showed them the city and took them to dinner and the theater. Not surprisingly, they were awed by their "big city" experiences, even more so by people's enthusiastic reactions to their celebrated son. As parents of a popular and familiar personality, they too received veneration. It was during this time that Jim first noticed his father's momentary lapses of memory and brief periods of apparent depression. When Jim questioned his mother about the episodes, she denied anything was wrong, although she did admit that Patrick had, on occasion, been verbally abusive toward her. What Jim had been observing were the initial signs of Patrick's gradual mental deterioration.

In addition, Jim had another family dilemma to deal with. Olive's father had decided to move to New York some months before. While Jim trained for the Mitchell contest, the older man had become a frequent visitor to Asbury Park and became a member of the party when they traveled to Jacksonville. His intrusiveness may have bothered Jim because, when the European trip was planned, he was not invited to join the group. Instead of her father, Olive invited a friend, Mrs. Howard, to accompany her. Was something amiss between Jim and Olive?

On April 12, aboard the steamer Fuerst Bismarck, the Corbett party left for Queenstown (later renamed Cork), Ireland, their first stop, where Patrick and Catherine disembarked and headed directly for County Mayo. The steamer then went on to Liverpool, England, where the party entrained for London, to open "Gentleman Jack" in its initial presentation for English audiences.

On April 21, a large crowd received Jim and the company at the Drury Lane Theater. Through a series of interviews with the local press, Brady attempted to portray Jim as a legitimate actor, as well as a boxer.

> I think you will like Corbett when you meet him. If you expect to meet a pugilist of the brutal type, you are quite mistaken. He is a bright, genial fellow, who can hold his own in any society. Our experience in America has been that on a first night we have drawn the sporting fraternity, eager to see their hero. Then it has got round that we are giving a real good show—melodrama, comedy, good acting, a costly production. That draws the regular playgoer in crowds.[10]

Brady had booked the Drury Lane for three weeks, with an option for extending it two more weeks. He hoped it would work out that way.

According to *The Era,* the reception given Jim was "wildly enthusiastic." He was cheered and applauded, with demands for a speech. Everyone seemed delighted with Jim, whom the reviewers portrayed as a handsome, mild-mannered, modest man, "a copious crop of dark-brown hair brushed up perpendicularly from his forehead," and "an extreme gentleman." When Jim was summoned before the curtain after the play, his speech was "a model of brevity and good taste."

Of the play, "Gentleman Jack," reviewers called it "unusually poor stuff," simply a series of scenes in which Corbett appeared and "exploited the fame of a pugilist for theatrical purposes." Successive reviews during the production's three-week engagement were equally negative, although Jim was singled out as a handsome specimen of masculinity. Attendance for "Gentleman Jack" gradually declined.

Probably the most significant event during Jim's London stay was the special dinner given him on May 4 by the National Sporting Club, England's most prestigious athletic organization. "The great American, upon being introduced to the members of the club, was the recipient of an ovation, and his health was drunk with musical honors."[11]

Jim returned thanks for the honor given him and was loudly applauded. No royalty attended the dinner, nor did Jim meet any royalty during his stay in England. Nevertheless, upon their return to the U.S., Brady was not dissuaded from producing a large poster showing Jim shaking hands with the crowned heads of Europe.

From London, "Gentleman Jack" traveled to the Folies Bergere in Paris for one week. French audiences had no idea what to make of the play, but were fascinated by Jim's boxing displays.

The following week, the company returned to England to begin a tour "of the provinces," their first stop, the Grand Theater, Islington. Brady was already worried that they would run out of funds before the tour was completed. Box office results had been good, but expenses were much higher than anticipated. Not only were travel costs considerable, but additional costs at each stop, including payoffs to musical conductors, stage hands, and florists, diminished any profit. Strange routing didn't help either. From Islington, the company traveled to Glasgow, Scotland, then back to Liverpool, Sheffield, Newcastle, Birmingham, and Manchester. Moreover, "Gentleman Jack" was being constantly panned. Still, Jim was recognized for "his athletic exercises," which seemed to elicit much applause. "The piece does not deserve very serious consideration. The pugilist was better than the play, and he was evidently worthy of the honor which could be conferred on him."[12]

From Manchester, the company traveled to Dublin. Jim planned to play there a week and then join his parents in

Ballinrobe, County Mayo, where a number of special events awaited his arrival. Jim's parents had enjoyed their time, renewing acquaintances and visiting old, familiar places. The land remained poor, however, many people still living in thatched-roof huts. Food was at a premium. Compared to their Irish relatives, the Corbetts of San Francisco were perceived as well-to-do business owners, which, indeed, they were.

Jim's engagement in Dublin featured a reception and parade, in which the horses were detached from his carriage, so that he might be drawn down the street by a crowd of people. His theater appearances were most enthusiastically received; few seemed to pay much attention to the play. When Jim and Olive reached the old family neighborhood, they were regaled as hero and heroine. Jim put on a benefit performance for his uncle, the Reverend Thomas Corbett, to aid him in erecting a chapel. That evening, bonfires were lit in town, the streets were arched with flowers, and in windows, candles burned. "It was not much," Jim observed, "but it was all those poor people could do. And it made me feel happier than anything which I met with during my entire trip."

The Corbett entourage sailed from Queenstown for New York, July 20. Jim felt it had been an enjoyable time. For his part, having lost money, Brady was not convinced. Patrick and Catherine returned to San Francisco to repeat stories of their visit to the "old sod" to anyone who would listen. Olive did not seem very happy, but no one paid attention to her.

Brady had already begun negotiations for a match between Jim and Peter Jackson. A purse of $25,000 had been offered by a syndicate of sporting men from Sioux City, Iowa, and both boxers were reported to have expressed a willingness to participate. The mayor of the city, however, as well as the governor of the state, had already come out against staging the contest within their jurisdictions. Though meetings between Brady and Jackson's manager, Tom O'Rourke, continued, it appeared the boxers would not meet.

Meanwhile, apparently never at a loss for commercial opportunities, Brady had made a deal with the Edison Manufacturing Company to have Jim appear in a moving picture featuring an actual boxing contest. The Edison Company had been shooting moving pictures of entertainment and popular culture, in an attempt to record and sell films for commercial purposes, as well as to establish themselves as the premier moving picture company in the country. With the recent introduction of moving pictures into theaters, this new form of entertainment appeared to be a lucrative enterprise.[13]

Edison offered the winner of the staged bout $5,000, the loser $250. Brady was confident Jim would easily beat the challenger, Peter Courtney, an inexperienced boxer from Trenton. Brady also made certain that the deal included film rights, if the moving picture ever appeared in theaters.

Jim was playing at the American Theater, New York City, and would be required to travel to West Orange, New Jersey, to perform before the camera in the "Black Maria," a large, box-like room, the interior painted entirely black, within which the picture would be shot.

Jim beat Courtney in six rounds, precisely the planned length of the film. The entire contest had been staged for the kinetoscope, though the press, as well as Brady, played it as if it had been a serious confrontation.

A *New York Sun* reporter, the referee, Jim, McVey, and Frank Belcher met at the Christopher Street ferry building on the foggy early morning of September 7, 1894. Everyone was worried about the overcast sky, since no pictures could be shot without bright sunlight. The weather report had indicated a fair day, so everyone was encouraged when the morning mist gave way to sun. Once the operators of the kinetograph arrived, the party boarded the ferryboat Secaucus for Hoboken. While on board, Jim discovered that the moving picture people had only recently found Courtney, whom he had met for the first time the previous day. Jim acknowledged that his agreement with the Edison people stipulated he "put the guy out in six rounds," since the machine was so arranged that "a longer fight was undesirable."

The entire trip was conducted in complete secrecy, since New Jersey laws prohibited aiding and abetting a prize fight. Nonetheless, Jim had been recognized by a policeman at the ferry terminal and among passengers on the ferry. Violation of the law would mean arrest and a jail term. As the group took a trolley from Hoboken to West Orange, various members alighted at different stops to divert any suspicion.

Courtney had already arrived at the Edison grounds with his seconds. Reporters observing Courtney believed him a "hard-looking nut to crack."

"I ain't no spring chicken," Courtney said, "and I don't think this here champion will have such a picnic with me as he thinks." Courtney told reporters he was twenty-six years old and had entered the boxing profession about a year and a half before. His primary claim to fame was having lasted four rounds against Bob Fitzsimmons, if he could be believed.

Operators prepared the Black Maria—often referred to as a huge coffin— adjusting the kinetograph and lighting. The ring was fourteen feet square, roped on two sides, the other two being the heavily padded walls of the building. A round was to last a little over a minute, with a rest of up to two minutes, to allow for changing the film cartridges, each loaded with 150 feet of film. Jim was concerned the padded gloves and short rounds would give Courtney plenty of time to recover. Thus, to win the purse, he would have to be vigorous in each round, yet withhold any knockout blow until near the end of the sixth round. Prior to the beginning of the bout, the men were instructed on how they were permitted to clinch. Keep it short and face the camera.

During the first five rounds, Courtney fought gamely and landed some good blows, but Jim's counterpunching and quick left downed the challenger a number of times. At the end of round five, when Jim sat down, he said to McVey: "Now, I'll put him out. I've got to do it quick, though, for there's only a little over a minute."

Jim came out banging. He hit Courtney with a straight left to the jaw that staggered him. A right to the chin knocked Courtney to the floor. Courtney struggled to his feet, then continued to absorb an assortment of blows until, finally, a left and a right to the jaw dropped him for good. He tried to rise to his knees but fell forward on his face. The referee declared Courtney out. End of film.

Immediately, Jim rushed to pick up Courtney and carry him to his corner. When Courtney was revived, Jim shook his hand and congratulated him on his pluck. As he and his party headed for the train station to return to New York, Jim was elated with his success and $5,000 richer. At the station, they were met by more than 2,000 people, all of whom seemed to know there had been a bout at the Edison laboratories. Everyone was pleased that, by jumping on the train and leaving New Jersey on the ferryboat, Jim and his party had eluded the police. Or had they?

A few days later, a New Jersey grand jury opened hearings to examine the match staged before the Edison kinetograph, to determine if any law had been violated. Subpoenas followed, the first of which was handed to Thomas A. Edison himself. Speaking in his own defense, Edison said:

> I don't see how there could be any trouble about that fight.... It was not a prize-fight in any sense of the word.... It was simply a boxing match for a show for which the men were paid, and nothing more.[14]

Edison went on to say that, had he had any inkling that a fight to a finish was to be staged on his property, he would not have permitted it. Who would argue with Edison? The charges were dropped.

The following week, Jim returned to his tour in "Gentleman Jack" with an engagement at Washington, D.C.'s, Grand Opera House.

James J. Corbett appeared for the first time before a Washington audience in his play, Gentleman Jack. The house was full from pit to dome, and the applause and curtain calls were as frequent as they were well-deserved.[15]

One thing, however, was noticeably different from Jim's previous tours and boxing contests; Olive was not accompanying him. It seemed somewhat confusing to his friends, since he had just transferred his roadhouse property to Olive for the sum of one dollar, the deed signed the day before his meeting with Peter Courtney. The transfer, however, had nothing to do with any personal problems. Jim had recently been taxed $10,000 for property ownership and by transferring some items to Olive, he could avoid any further tax-

A poster advertising Thomas A. Edison's 1894 boxing motion pictures of the "Corbett-Courtney battle," the first ever produced. The entire event had been staged, with a knockout planned for the end of the sixth round, when the camera would run out of film. Jim received $5,000 for his part, and another $15,000 in royalties. This showing heralded the beginning of sports motion pictures, and became a decidedly controversial issue among state and city representatives concerned about the morals of their constituents.

ation. Whatever was happening between Olive and Jim remained a mystery, but her absence on his tour was considered an ominous portent.

While "Gentleman Jack" made its way through Massachusetts and New York, Bob Fitzsimmons issued a challenge to face Jim for the heavyweight championship. After some hesitation, Jim agreed to meet Fitzsimmons and had Brady send a $1,000 deposit in preparation for negotiations. If Jim had refused Fitzsimmons's challenge, he would have again forfeited his title, as had happened when he refused Goddard's challenge after the Sullivan match. At an October 11 meeting of the participants and managers, agreements were drawn up, the contest to be sponsored by the Florida Athletic Club, Jacksonville, for a contest on or after July 1, 1895. Agreement appeared to have been reached easily enough. Over the next two and a half years, however, its implementation was destined to entail many adventures and proposed venues.

During the middle of November, "Gentleman Jack" played at Chicago's Haymarket Theater. SROs were common as theater patrons flocked to see, according to the *Tribune,* "the wealthiest sports figure in America." In the audience at a Sunday matinee was a pretty young woman who had expressed a strong desire to meet her champion. When she did, their passionate liaison soon resulted in front page headlines.

6. *Trial and Tribulation*

Jessie Taylor, also known as Vera Stanwood, was born in Omaha, Nebraska, in 1866. Her father worked as a switchman for the newly formed Union Pacific Railroad. At age sixteen, with little formal education to her credit, Jessie became a waitress in a neighborhood cafe, where, it was said, she attracted many admirers. When she was eighteen, Jessie married Alonzo George, a hackman. A baby boy died at age two from an unidentified illness.

George, an alcoholic, abused his wife so severely that she obtained a divorce. In 1893, Jessie moved to Chicago to begin a new life. She soon found a job at the World's Fair. It was later reported that she had often watched Jim sparring in his vaudeville act on the Midway Plaisance. Later, Jessie and a woman friend moved to San Francisco to find work; unfortunately, they discovered little employment available. While there, a violent episode between the two women proved illustrative of her passion for Jim.

On the wall of a saloon the women were visiting, Jessie saw a colored lithograph of Jim in fighting gear. When she kissed it, her friend rebuked her and insulted the object of her obsession. They quarreled. In a rage, Jessie stabbed the woman several times. She fled for Chicago before she could be arraigned in a San Francisco court.

In 1894, while Jim was performing in Chicago, Jessie wrote him, relating the episode and her response to the woman's insult. As was his habit in response to letters from admirers, Jim sent her a ticket to attend his show.

From the moment they met, the two were inseparable. When Jim and the company departed Chicago to continue their road tour, Jessie was his traveling companion.

Court evidence suggests that a member of the company (somewhat sanctimoniously) informed Olive of the coupling. Once the information had been verified, Olive ordered Jim to remove his belongings from their home and demanded temporary compensation to maintain her personal needs. Unhesitatingly, Jim agreed to pay her $100 a week.

Olive then hired the law firm of Howe and Hummel (notorious for pleading high-profile, celebrity divorce suits) to accumulate evidence in preparation for her filing an action of absolute divorce. Their plan was to serve papers to Jim upon his return to New York in June, at the end of the theatrical season, which would have been seven months since the beginning of his liaison with Jessie. When reporters questioned Olive regarding her husband's behavior, she simply declared, "Jim is quite crazy—that is certain." She was emphatically supported by her father, who stated that his daughter had become quite ill, "all because of Jim's indiscretions."

Indeed, it seemed to all those cognizant of the situation that Jim had been completely taken by Jessie, smitten far more powerfully than by any ring opponent. While the real reasons can only be speculated upon, a number of disagreements likely contributed to the breakdown of Jim and Olive's eight-year marriage.

Compatability between Olive and Jim had been deteriorating for some time. Olive had not enjoyed the summer trip to England and Ireland; in fact, evidence suggests she had not wanted to go at all. Her subsequent decision to remain home when Jim began his fall tour in "Gentleman Jack" came as a surprise to everyone, since she had always accompanied him on the road.

Another possible irritant may have been Mr. Lake's insistent presence in the couple's personal life, ever since he moved to New York early in 1894 and rented an apartment a short distance from their home. Mr. Lake's frequent visits to Jim's training site in Asbury Park and his inclusion in the group that went to Jacksonville, Florida, may well have been viewed by Jim as intrusive. When Lake involved himself in speaking for his daughter regarding divorce proceedings, Jim expressed considerable anger at his garrulous father-in-law.

At another level, there remained continuing tension between Jim and his own father. Patrick had shown little evidence of pleasure concerning Jim's achievements, even after his widely admired son had beaten Sullivan and Mitchell. Indeed, Patrick continued his opposition toward Jim's boxing career, with his less than flattering comments often quoted in San Francisco newspapers. Patrick had been noticeably absent during Jim's recent trip to 'Frisco nor had he appeared at the station when Jim departed. Moreover, Patrick's deteriorating mental condition very likely troubled Jim. Perhaps, he worried, the son had, in some way, contributed to the father's problems.

Whatever the specific reasons, Jim seems to have been emotionally fragile at the time he met Jessie, psychologically susceptible, more than ready to accept a beautiful woman who offered him abundant, devoted, unrestricted love. After all, Jim already had a history of responding impressionably to people professing to be interested in him.

Jim and Jessie (Vera) were seen constantly together as the company toured the South and Midwest during the spring of 1895, usually registering as Mr. and Mrs. Corbett at hotels. Though fully aware of the liaison, most of the company said nothing, since such behavior was common among performers on the road for great lengths of time. Personal feelings, romantic or otherwise, toward fellow actors tended to be influenced more by audience reactions to the production. If a play was successful, few paid attention to off-stage escapades; if a play foundered, personal intrigues would likely be cited as the reason for the production's failure. "Gentleman Jack" played to full houses and profitable box offices throughout its entire tour.

A heavy rainstorm in New Orleans did not prevent "crowded houses." A severe blizzard in Milwaukee "did not keep the house from being well-filled." Souvenirs given out during an engagement in Pittsburgh contributed to record-breaking business at the Bijou Theater. Early in May, as the company prepared to conclude its highly profitable tour in St. Louis, Jim announced his intention to take a pleasure trip—with Vera—to California, before returning to New York. Olive interrupted

A **Police Gazette** *wood engraving of Olive Corbett as she sought a divorce from Jim. After nine years of marriage, having actively participated in the development of Jim's career, Olive found herself replaced by Vera Stanhope (Jessie Taylor) as Jim's paramour.*

his plans when she filed for absolute divorce.

Comparison of three contemporary newspapers reveals the publicly selective emotional context of the "notorious" divorce. The *New York World*, a sensationalist tabloid known for its blatant headlines and dubious reporting that often portrayed fiction as fact, shouted "Olive Wants a Divorce" and followed its headline with unsubstantiated quotes from unknown parties. The *New York Times* mentioned a possible divorce in an inconspicuous entry buried at the bottom of the eighth page of an eight-page edition. The *San Francisco Chronicle* devoted the far right-hand column of its front page to the divorce announcement: in larger type, Will Ask For A Divorce; in smaller, Mrs. Corbett Married Life Unhappy; The Cause of the Trouble Is Hidden; Champion Jim and His Wife Cannot Get Along

Together. The *Chronicle* seemed almost apologetic about having to report the story.

Rumors had been circulated to the newspapers—likely by Howe and Hummel—that Olive had definitely filed for divorce. Questioned by reporters, Mr. Lake, speaking on behalf of his daughter, verified the stories. He stated that his daughter had been having "considerable trouble" with her husband and had finally decided she had no choice but to obtain a divorce. "She is too ill to be interviewed," he replied to requests for a statement from the aggrieved party herself, "but, when the time comes, she will tell all."

When William Brady was approached on the issue, he declined to offer an opinion. "If there is trouble between Jim and his wife, I must stay out of it." Actually, however, Brady was completely aware of the situation and increasingly concerned about its effect on Jim's ring and stage careers, not to mention his own wallet.

When Howe and Hummel formally announced Olive's suit against Jim, Mr. Lake again interjected his opinion, showing no hesitation to answer reporters' queries. "My daughter is very ill, and very much worried. He (Jim) has not been himself for some time. This woman has got such a complete mastery over him that he does not know what he is doing."

Two weeks later, Olive's suit for divorce went before Edward Jacobs, whom the judge had named as referee in the case. The co-respondent was said to be a married woman from Chicago, with whom, it was alleged, Corbett had stayed at a hotel for a fortnight. A Chicago report identified the woman as Vera Stanwood.

Testimony in the case began the middle of July. Olive charged Jim with improper conduct in a number of hotels while the "Gentleman Jack" company was on tour. Marie King, a cast member, testified that Vera had been continually seen with Jim. Moreover, she had seen Vera in Jim's dressing room, had witnessed them entering and leaving Jim's room at hotels and on the train, and had verified that they had registered as "J.J. Corbett and wife" at various hotels.

"What was the nature of their conduct toward each other?" Miss King was asked.

"Very affectionate," she replied.

"Did Mr. Corbett make any effort to conceal his relations toward the woman?"

"Not in the slightest," King answered. She further stated that the company had called Vera "Mrs. Corbett" in Jim's presence, and he had never objected.

At the hearing, it was revealed that Olive and the principal witness, Marie King, were longtime friends. Yet neither Jim nor his lawyer made an issue of the women's relationship or challenged King's testimony. Although it was asserted that other women could readily be named in the complaint, Hummel submitted that the evidence against Vera Stanwood, as testified to by Miss King, was alone sufficient to grant the divorce. Hummel also suggested that the articles of separation should include permanent alimony of $100 a week.

A newspaper in Asbury Park reported that, while the trial continued, Jim and Vera were living in a rented cottage near his training quarters. They were seen each evening, walking hand-in-hand.

Prior to the next court hearing, Jim was served final divorce papers and filed answers to the charges. Contained in his response was the promise to deed the 88th Street house to Olive, as well as to continue her $100 a week alimony payments. Although Jim attempted to keep the final arrangements secret, newspapers reported the proceedings in detail. Jim believed that either Olive's lawyers or Mr. Lake were responsible for making the information public, solely to embarrass him.

On July 26, Hummel called additional witnesses to testify to Jim's actions while on tour. In rebuttal, lawyers for Jim called no witnesses but did ask for dismissal of the case, arguing that the allegations of Jim's behavior had not been sufficiently substantiated. The judge, however, pointed to Miss King's testimony as sufficient corroboration. The case was continued.

Next day, the court sustained Olive's request for an absolute divorce. Jim was found to be at fault (he raised no objection); and Olive obtained her decree. Alimony was set at $100 a week, as Jim and Olive had previously agreed. The judge stipulated, however, that alimony would be terminated should Olive choose to remarry. Under the decree, Jim could not remarry in New York state but he was free to do so elsewhere.

Newspapers reported that Jim was angry at Olive and her father for "wanting revenge," their motivation, he reasoned, for exposing his infidelities. For his part, Brady was simply glad the trial was over. To his great relief, it seemed not to have diminished Jim's appeal as plans for the Fitzsimmons bout and a new theatrical production proceeded. In March, 1896, less than eight months after obtaining the divorce, Olive remarried, thereby obviating Jim's alimony payments.

On August 15, two weeks after the final divorce decree had been granted, James J. Corbett and Vera Stanwood were married in Asbury Park, New Jersey. Justice of the Peace John A. Borden presided. It was an event that everyone expected, yet it still created surprise and not a little comment. Jim had shown no more than a passive interest in the divorce proceedings, but few thought his marriage to Vera would come so soon after the divorce from Olive.

The ceremony was to take place at 11:00 A.M. in the Corbett cottage. Amusingly, it proved somewhat delayed because

Justice Borden had, by mistake, brought with him a birth certificate instead of one for marriage. A messenger hastily retrieved the correct document. In attendance were brother Joe; Alice, Jim's favorite cook; and two newspapermen. Brady was conspicuous by his absence; Jim had not alerted him to the event. Jim wore a black broadcloth suit and a black satin scarf. In contrast to the groom's somber attire, Vera wore a lavender silk dress, trimmed with delicate blue ribbon, nicely complemented by her long blond hair.

Vera Corbett reaped the benefits of Jim's popularity and financial acumen. Vera became a strong positive influence on Jim and helped him to maintain his enduring reputation. Traveling together on all tours and trips, she and Jim were inseparable. (Courtesy of the Academy of Motion Picture Arts and Sciences)

The couple joined hands. In less than two minutes, Jim and Vera were married. As the judge uttered the familiar words, "I now pronounce you man and wife," Jim embraced Vera and they kissed twice. The newlyweds left on the afternoon train for a honeymoon trip to Niagara Falls and the Thousand Islands of Lake Ontario. They planned to return early in September, when Jim would begin active training for his match with Fitzsimmons.

Joe Corbett had been keeping the family informed of ongoing events. Patrick was reported to be deeply upset by the trial. He became even more agitated when he and the family learned of Jim's marriage to Vera. In the meantime, Brady was working with the colorful sporting promoter, Dan Stuart, on details of the Fitzsimmons match.

Stuart had been born in Vermont in 1846. A flamboyant and gregarious personality ever since his teens, Stuart soon made a reputation as a gambler who covered wagers on any outcome to which betting could be reasonably attached. In 1872, he moved to Texas and quickly advanced himself as a sporting man and promoter of sporting events.[1]

Some twenty years later, looking the role of a prosperous businessman—Stuart was heavyset, dressed elegantly, sported a bushy mustache, parted his hair carefully in the middle, and observed the world with keen but sympathetic eyes—he boldly announced his intention to stage the Corbett-Fitzsimmons championship contest in Dallas in October. It was proverbial that "all sports are gamblers, but not all gamblers are sports." Stuart was both.

All sides to the bargain seemed eager to conclude a deal but final agreement on the match had to wait while Jim completed divorce proceedings and Fitzsimmons faced a manslaughter charge for his role in the death of a sparring partner, Con Riordan. Though Brady, Martin Julian (Fitzsimmons's manager), and Stuart had been meeting since May, no final agreement had yet been reached.

Undeterred, having enlisted the financial aid of the city's most prestigious businessmen, Stuart had already begun construction of a Dallas arena to house the contest. The religious community in Dallas, however, appealed to the governor to prevent the match from taking place. Though the governor decreed boxing illegal, Stuart continued arena construction and started selling tickets for the event. The governor then stepped in and declared that anyone involved in the proposed contest was "a contemptuous felon." Moreover, he demanded that boxing in Texas be legally prohibited. Though Stuart still believed he could hold the match in Dallas, he began exploring other possible venues, one of which was Mexico. The idea was quickly defeated by Mexican president and "dictator-for-life" Porfirio Díaz, who declared no boxing would take place in his country. (Six months later, presented with a sizable financial incentive, President Díaz found the wisdom to reverse his ill-considered decision.)

Through strong legal and political maneuvering by the Dallas business community, Stuart obtained a court reprieve and an OK to continue building the arena. Jim had resumed training and Fitzsimmons had begun his own after returning from the trial. By mid-September, the intended adversaries had yet to agree on a referee, though the arena was near completion. Ticket orders increased and newspapers stepped up coverage of the impending bout, issuing daily reports from each training camp.

At the end of September, however, an all-out effort by the state's religious community forced the governor to call a special session of the legislature. Fitzsimmons had already arrived in Texas and put on a sparring exhibition in San Antonio. Jim had departed from New York, on his way to Dallas, after giving a sparring exhibition at Madison Square Garden to help defray training expenses. Upon hearing of the governor's decision, the boxers sensed what the outcome would be.

The governor demanded that legislation be passed to conclusively prohibit this "insult to public decency." Two days later, on October 3, a bill was passed, prohibiting boxing in Texas. Dan Stuart was now forced to seek another venue. Hot Springs, Arkansas, seemed a promising alternative but when Jim appeared there, he was arrested, in order to test the law applied to boxing in the state. Repeated court arguments failed to resolve the matter. When it was reported that Fitzsimmons was about to enter Arkansas to take part in an "unlawful fight," he too was threatened with arrest.

On November 2, the Arkansas court declared no championship match could be held in the state. Two days later, Jim appeared with sparring partner Steve O'-Donnell at the Lyceum Theater in Memphis, Tennessee, in an exhibition staged between acts of "The White Squadron." Since the boxing contest was in question, Brady was hard at work preparing Jim's new theatrical production, "A Naval Cadet," hoping to open it within the next few weeks.

"A Naval Cadet" opened at the Lynn Theater, Lynn, Massachusetts, on November 25. The *New York Clipper* reported on Jim's new acting venture.

James J. Corbett is going to attempt a step forward in his production of "A Naval Cadet." Corbett aspires to shine as a light comedian. Manager Brady has surrounded him with a good company, including Annie Blake and McKee Rankin; Mr. Rankin plays the leading role, stages the play, and acts as Mr. Corbett's tutor in the drama.[2]

"A Naval Cadet" was described as a comedy drama in four acts, written by Charles T. Vincent. The first act takes place in the home of Ned Cornell (Jim Corbett), located on the shores of Long Island. The second act contains two scenes: the first in a ballroom; the second in the gymnasium of the U.S. Naval Academy at Annapolis. In the latter scene, Dolly Eaton (Annie Blake), in evening gown, hangs from the swinging rings and engages in an amusing dialogue, before she is rescued. The same scene displays Cornell in an exhibition of bag punching.

It is at the Naval Academy that Cornell has invented a new machine gun, which has been accepted for production by the government. Before it can be patented, however, the plans are stolen by a Frenchman. The third act takes place at sea, with all the key players on the promenade deck of the steamship *St. Louis.* After several intrigues are plotted, the act ends with Cornell being knocked out by one of the schemers. The fourth act, set in Paris, offers a number of exciting episodes, enacted in three scenes: the first in a workingmen's cafe; the second in a street of the Latin Quarter; the third in an underground den of iniquity. In the last of these, Ned, in full evening dress, rescues the heroine after dispatching his abductors with timely, well-placed, devastating blows.

After a week of performances in Massachusetts towns, "A Naval Cadet" came to the Bijou Theater, Brooklyn, ready to be seen by big city critics. To everyone's satisfaction, the show was positively reviewed.

Standing room only, and precious little of that, was the order of things on the opening night. Mr. Corbett has many admirers in this city, and his name alone is sufficient to draw big houses every time he comes here. The play is handsomely mounted, and some of the scenes are very attractive. The piece has many redeeming features in its strong situations. Mr. Corbett was given a great reception, and was liberally applauded, especially in the last act, where there is a rough and tumble fight, in which the champion threw one man out the window and knocked out another, greatly to the delight of the occupants in the gallery.[3]

A week at the Empire Theater, New York City, was equally successful but was overshadowed by a startling public statement from Jim. Even Brady was taken by surprise. In a hastily convened meeting with newspaper reporters, Jim suddenly announced his retirement from the ring and his resignation of the world heavyweight championship. He reasoned that no match could be made with Fitzsimmons, nor were any other contenders available. Brady was reported to be furious with Jim, believing the decision would have an adverse effect, not only on his boxing reputation, but also at the box office. It further signaled an obvious decline in the relationship between Jim and Brady. There was no question in Brady's mind that Jim's interest in boxing had diminished. As a result of Jim's public statement, the heavyweight championship was now open to all challengers. Fitzsimmons moved quickly and signed with Peter Maher for a title contest to be held in February, 1896.

The new year saw "A Naval Cadet" playing to full houses and SRO audiences throughout New England, in Philadelphia, and in Baltimore. Box office receipts exceeded estimates, and Jim acknowledged to reporters he was earning more than $1,000 a week. In February, the company opened a week's stay at the friendly Haymarket Theater, in Chicago. Crowds were "turned away" due to the excitement generated in "pugilistic circles." Along with comments about the full houses, the *Tribune* added a sarcastic footnote, reminding readers that it was little more than a year ago that Jim and Vera had first met in the Windy City.

While in Chicago, Jim met with old friend Eddie Foy, who was currently unemployed due to the failure of a show he had backed and starred in. Jim got Foy and Brady together, and the meeting generated a contract for Foy to play the lead in a Brady production of "The Strange Adventures of Miss Brown." The show was not well received and soon closed, but it gave Foy enough exposure to sign with a New York theatrical organization and gain entry into that market.

Bob Fitzsimmons handily beat Peter Maher for the title that Jim had so cavalierly relinquished. The bout was another Dan Stuart production, staged in Ciudad Juarez, Mexico, across the border from El Paso, Texas. It was really no contest, Fitzsimmons knocking out Maher in one minute and thirty-five seconds of the first round, the fastest championship match in history. Immediately following the report of Fitzsimmons's victory, Jim wired him, to issue a formal challenge for the title, a dramatic reversal from the position he had taken only six weeks previously. When asked by reporters why he had suddenly changed his mind, Jim declared that he had not intended for the title to go to a foreigner and that he wished to reclaim it. Examining Jim's conflicting comments about the championship and his feelings toward Fitzsimmons, the *Clipper* counseled that Brady keep Jim "under wraps," if he could. "It suggests the necessity for securing for Pompadour Jim a keeper who will be able either to bridle his tongue or teach him how to use it in a sensible way."[4]

"I will not pay any attention to him" was Fitzsimmons's response to Jim's chal-

lenge. "Corbett held me off a long time when I wanted to fight him, and then had it fixed when there was a prospect of our meeting so that I could not get to where he was."

According to rules then governing all boxing championships, every titleholder was compelled to accept any proper challenge or else relinquish his title. If Fitzsimmons now chose not to face Corbett, the title would revert back to Jim. Boxing community experts believed that Fitzsimmons could beat Corbett, noting that the Anglo-Irishman was, at the time, "master of any pugilist of the present day." In fact, Jim was being publicly blamed for the fiascoes in Texas and Arkansas, though he had had little to do with them, all negotiations having been handled by Brady. Sensing another great promotional opportunity, Dan Stuart initiated a new campaign to sign the adversaries and find a location to stage the event. It would take him another year of schemes, intrigues, political machinations, and backroom negotiations to cement a deal.

In the meantime, Jim's spring tour through the Midwest continued to attract full houses and excellent box office receipts. In Cincinnati, he received high praise for his improved acting.

> James J. Corbett was given a most cordial reception. The audiences were large and enthusiastic. Curtain calls were numerous. "A Naval Cadet" proved a decidedly better creation than the boxing actor's first play. It was the general opinion that Corbett had greatly improved since his last appearance.[5]

An April return to Chicago, rewarded by "big houses," preceded final season stops in St. Louis and Kansas City. The St. Louis engagement was enhanced by additional performances, in which Jim sparred with Mike Conley. At their opening appearance, however, Jim and Mike were both arrested for violating the state law against boxing exhibitions. Brady appeared in court the next morning and skillfully persuaded the judge that it would be impossible to secure a conviction of so widely popular a performer; thus, the costs of staging a trial would be wasted. That evening, Jim and Mike sparred again, to the delight of the audience.

At the conclusion of the season, Jim and Vera traveled to Hot Springs, Arkansas, for a brief vacation. Their festive sojourn was enhanced by an announcement from a New York court that Jim and William Brady had won a judgment against the Kinetoscope Exhibiting Company for $7,200, comprising the unpaid royalties due them for the Corbett-Courtney moving picture. They also received an additional judgment on an unpaid note for $2,000, signed by Samuel Tilden, the Kinetoscope president. The *Times* reported that Jim had already received more than $15,000 in royalties for the boxing film.

Dan Stuart was pressuring Brady and Julian to agree to terms for their respective boxers to meet in November, at a site not yet chosen. For that matter, not yet found. Brady signed for Jim and posted the necessary deposit but Julian demurred, stating that Fitzsimmons would not consider a match with Corbett until he had defeated another contender. If Fitzsimmons declined Jim's challenge, he gave up the title. Stuart relished the publicity, if only he could persuade Fitzsimmons to fight. The boxer answered Stuart by saying that he planned to leave for an extended stay in England, the end of June.

Simultaneous to Julian's statement that his boxer would not consider a match with Corbett, Brady announced that Jim had signed to meet Tom Sharkey in a four-round contest, to be held in San Francisco on June 24. Jim would receive fifty percent of the receipts, estimated to exceed $25,000. Immediately, reporters questioned Jim's ability to get in shape for such a bout, given only a single month for training. The *Chronicle* revealed that Jim regarded the bout as insignificant, a fact that, according to the reporter, would likely get him into trouble against this opponent, a boxer of great muscular strength, endurance, and ability to withstand punishment. Initial betting favored Sharkey.

Jim and Vera arrived in San Francisco late in May, and he immediately began training at the Olympic Club. Many observers believed that Jim was not taking the match seriously, citing his light exercise regimen as evidence. On Sunday, four days before the bout, Jim took off the entire day and announced his plans to do little work during the remaining days. In contrast, Sharkey was conducting four-round sparring exhibitions every day, in conjunction with vigorous bag punching and road work. Sharkey's proponents claimed that he was in "the finest condition possible and never so fit in his life."

Even Brother Harry seemed worried about Jim's performance. Betting was favoring Sharkey ten to seven. The pool tickets Harry was selling read simply "Corbett stops Sharkey" or "Corbett does not stop Sharkey." What did "stop" mean? It surely meant something less than "knockout." Two days before the bout, betting remained light, most people believing that a four-round match offered neither boxer a good opportunity to knock out the other. Careful bettors wagered that Sharkey would stay the four rounds with Corbett. If, however, he foundered, they suggested that he take the defensive, so as to save their money.

On the day of the bout, the city was typically abuzz. The *Chronicle* predicted that "more money will be taken in than at any similar event held in the state." They estimated that Jim would earn nearly $500 for every minute he boxed, assuming that the contest lasted four rounds. Jim spent the afternoon strolling through the downtown area. Sharkey spent the afternoon at the gym. Both were scheduled to leave their hotels for Mechanic's Pavilion at about 9:00 P.M. and be dressed for the ring by 9:30.

Ten thousand excited spectators saw Sharkey and Corbett give and take heavy blows for four rounds—twelve minutes. At the end, the referee declared the match a draw, even though Jim, weak and panting, was hanging from his opponent's neck and leaning against the ropes to keep himself from slumping to the canvas. Most in the audience believed that, had the bout lasted a few more rounds, a new world's champion would have been crowned.

Jim had entered the ring smiling and apparently confident. He left it trembling and crestfallen. Not only had he failed to stop Sharkey, he himself had narrowly escaped defeat. When, after the match, Sharkey challenged him to a finish contest, Jim had no choice but to accept.

The match itself had proven something of a disappointment, more pushing, shoving, and clinching than boxing. Sharkey had twice wrestled Jim to the floor. Frequent cries of "foul" arose from the spectators. It was in the last round that Sharkey showed his strength. He burst from his corner to the center of the ring and launched a vicious combination to Jim's body and face, raising welts on his opponent's flesh. Jim sought to recover the offensive with smashes to Sharkey's nose and jaw, but still the challenger advanced. Jim then held on, getting his arms around Sharkey's neck but when they had to break, Jim was staggered again. When the men clinched a second time, the referee followed them closely around the ring in an attempt to separate them. Shaking off both referee and Jim, Sharkey tossed the two of them to the floor. Scarcely had Jim regained his feet when Sharkey pounced on him again.

With but seconds left in the bout, the referee called for police assistance. Sharkey was forced to his corner. There he struggled with police to get at Jim, barely standing in the opposite corner of the ring, holding onto the ropes for support. Some spectators cried "Foul! Foul!" Others yelled "Let them fight!" In the midst of the tumult, the referee announced the contest a draw. That said, all bets were off. The crowd tumbled madly over chairs, shouted, cheered, cursed, and hissed. Reporters believed Sharkey should have won. "Men said it should have been Sharkey's fight. I am not a judge, but Corbett looked sadly the worse for wear, and it seemed to me that an idol had fallen—a hero in the dust."[6]

Visibly shaken, Jim made his way through the crowd and hurried into a waiting carriage. Crowds trailed after him until he entered his hotel. As he passed through the reception hall, people politely applauded and Jim humbly tipped his hat in acknowledgment of their support. Waiting to receive him were Vera, his mother and sisters, and a few friends. He embraced each one in turn, clearly relieved that the ordeal was over. A few minutes later, he walked to another room, where the managers were counting receipts and allocating purses. After satisfying himself that he had indeed obtained what he expected, a little over $7,000, Jim returned to his rooms and his family.

Missing from the contest was William Brady. While few ring observers questioned his absence, most were aware of the tension between Jim and Brady. The unsatisfactory outcome of the Sharkey bout could only contribute to the strain. Though Jim publicly claimed he had been in good shape for the match, Brady and Jim's trainers knew otherwise. They believed he had lost his desire to win. To them, this suggested future ring disasters. Even Jim's mother believed that the life of an actor had changed her son.

The next day, with Jim representing himself, he, Sharkey, Sharkey's managers, and newspapermen gathered to discuss arrangements for a return match. While both boxers agreed to terms for the proposed championship contest, questions remained regarding where the match could be held without everyone's risking jail. Tom Sharkey's reputation had skyrocketed overnight. By contrast, many of Jim's admirers still could not believe or understand their hero's poor performance. The following day, Jim and Vera left for New York. To their relief, brief stops for sparring exhibitions in Denver, Kansas City, and Chicago demonstrated no diminution of Jim's popularity.

In New York, Brady and Jim met to discuss their future business arrangement. Shortly thereafter, newspapers revealed that Brady and Jim had separated, though only for boxing, not theater. Brady rightly calculated his client's limited career in boxing, yet he desired to take full advantage of Jim's continued appeal on the stage. Under questioning from reporters, Jim declared only that their new arrangement had been amiably agreed upon; nothing more. Brady's public statement seemed to satisfy the interested parties. "I have twenty-four shows on the road and can't afford to look out for Jim's interests. We are still friends, and Corbett and I are still partners in a few shows in which we are interested."[7]

In reality, Brady now saw little of Jim, even though he had contracted for another year in "A Naval Cadet." New York reporters mused as to the reasons for the separation. One suggested that Jim had tired of being Brady's "money-man." In an expansive moment, Brady had once admitted that Jim's shows helped finance Brady's other enterprises. Another speculated on Vera's influence over her husband's business affairs. Still another observed what seemed quite obvious: Jim

wanted out of boxing to pursue a solely theatrical career and Brady had no interest in such an arrangement. A few years later, in an ironic twist, Jim would face a former sparring partner for the heavyweight championship, an opponent who just happened to be managed by William Brady.

The second contest with Sharkey became even more important when it was announced that Fitzsimmons had forfeited his title by not accepting Jim's challenge, thereby returning the title to Corbett. When, in September, Fitzsimmons's manager, Martin Julian, held a banquet at New York's Hotel Bartholdi, Jim was invited to attend. He refused the invitation. At the banquet, Julian made a speech challenging Jim to meet his boxer. Standing next to Julian was Dan Stuart. He had a good notion where the contest could be held.

Jim promptly accepted the challenge. All parties met on September 12 to finalize the articles of agreement. The championship contest was to take place on St. Patrick's Day, March 17, 1897.

Stuart decided that Nevada had to be the location for the bout, even though boxing remained "a great moral issue" there, indeed, had been outlawed by the legislature. He enlisted the aid of Charles A. Jones, an influential Carson City attorney, to help him draft a law making boxing legal in the state. Behind-the-scenes negotiations with Nevada's governor and other state officials allowed the proposed bill to be introduced into the legislature. Two factors seemed to favor the law's possible passage: first, Nevada was in the midst of a severe economic decline and thus seeking money-making opportunities; second, Nevada had already demonstrated a liberal attitude toward social mores by permitting gambling and the sale of liquor. Boosters in Reno and Carson City flooded the legislature with pro-boxing petitions, and local newspapers' editorials recommended overturning the old law. Though the religious community endeavored to influence state legislators, the bill was easily approved on January 28, 1897. The governor signed it into law a few days later. Stuart was ecstatic. He immediately put together plans for an amphitheater, to be built in Carson City, seating 17,000 people.

On October 17, at the Glen Falls, New York, theater, "A Naval Cadet" opened its second season. A week later, in Montreal, Jim started his fall and winter tour. "A Naval Cadet played to tremendous big business. Mr. Corbett created a very favorable impression. The show is a good one, the characters being in capable hands."[8]

Engagements in Toronto, Boston, Philadelphia, and Providence captured crowded houses and boasted profitable box offices. Any negative public reaction to Jim brought on by the Sharkey debacle seems never to have existed among Eastern audiences. In each of these cities, Jim was invited to local athletic clubs to spar and attend banquets in his honor. In early December, the show played the Grand Opera House in New York "to crowded houses all week." Critics discussed Jim's improvement as an actor and suggested he consider acting over pugilism. After all, they opined, theater paid much better and offered steadier employment.

The boxing community was seriously shaken when, on December 2, Tom Sharkey defeated Bob Fitzsimmons on a foul in the eighth round. The referee, the celebrated former sheriff of Dodge City, Kansas, and Tombstone, Arizona, Wyatt Earp, called the foul just as Fitzsimmons knocked down Sharkey. Indeed, Earp awarded the bout to Sharkey as he lay on the floor. The crowd was decidedly not in agreement. Many were about to enter the ring in protest when Earp drew his gun.

The commotion quickly subsided, and the crowd returned to their seats.

Fitzsimmons claimed he had been robbed. A member of Sharkey's own camp suggested that Earp had been hired to award the bout to Sharkey at the first sign of a reasonably alleged low blow. Immediately, a hearing was held but the case was thrown out on a legal technicality. Sharkey kept the winner's purse and claimed the championship, but no one else in the boxing community recognized him as champion. For a wronged and frustrated Fitzsimmons, anger gave way to searingly focused, dogged determination as he began preparation for his title match against Jim.

Though many boxing experts believed that such a schedule offered him little time for training, Jim planned to tour till early February. Stops in Cleveland, Detroit, St. Louis, and Kansas City attracted large audiences, enthused all the more by the upcoming contest. Yet company members noticed an edginess breaking through Jim's usually cool demeanor. Was he showing some anxiety about the title bout? A number of reported altercations with stage hands and theater managers seemed to underscore Jim's apparent apprehension.

Jim and Vera headed for San Francisco after the company had closed its tour in Kansas City. Along the way, he stopped in Denver and Salt Lake City for money-making sparring exhibitions. Billy Delaney and Joe Corbett went to Reno to arrange for Jim's training quarters. Fitzsimmons planned to leave New York for Carson City in a few days. Work on Stuart's arena was already underway. Although not large enough to protect spectators, a canopy over the ring was designed to protect the boxers in case of inclement weather, a distinct possibility for Nevada in March.

Before leaving San Francisco for training camp, Jim gave two exhibitions before large crowds, sparring with Connie McVey. While some spectators observed a little rustiness in his ring activity, Jim reassured the audience: "My friends need not hesitate putting their money on me, as I am prepared to put up the best battle of my career."

On February 15, via the Virginia and Truckee Railroad, Jim traveled to Shaw's Springs, Nevada, the site of his camp, just outside Carson City. Awaiting reporters observed that Jim seemed nervous and older than his thirty years. More important to the press, however, was the announcement that Dan Stuart had been granted the first license ever issued in Nevada for a boxing contest.

By late February, both boxers were ensconced at their training quarters. Due to a severe snow storm, training was conducted indoors for the first few days. In fact, because of the storm, Fitzsimmons had to walk three miles to reach his quarters at Cook's ranch. Parties in New York, Chicago, Cincinnati, New Orleans, and St. Louis were arranging special trains to Carson City. Final financial agreement stipulated that the winner was to receive $15,000, plus the proceeds of a side bet of $10,000. The loser would receive $9,000.

Reporters from newspapers across the country sent out daily bulletins from both training camps. Fitzsimmons and Corbett each released his own daily statement, both having signed with rival newspaper organizations to provide exclusive dispatches. George Siler, the designated referee, also wrote a daily column, although in the face of criticism from observers who believed he should not express his opinions, since it was his responsibility to remain neutral and objective.

A little more than two weeks before the bout, the Hearst representative (W.W. Naughton) stated that Jim had been suffering from undiagnosed stomach problems, a report denied by the Corbett camp.

Naughton went on to note that Jim seemed to be displaying less vitality. Naughton cited an exchange of punches between Jim and a newcomer to the Corbett camp, sparring partner Jim Jeffries. Normally, Jim did not allow the men with whom he sparred to score off him. In a number of skirmishes, however, Jeffries had landed a variety of blows, to which Jim had quickly retaliated. Nonetheless, the fact that Jeffries got them in at all was carefully noted by observers. Naughton concluded his article with a prophetic summary of Jim's current status, at once specifying the probable cause of the champion's apparent agitation.

> Corbett can't be champion any more unless he goes in and punches Fitzsimmons, for that gentleman, unpunched, can stay in the ring just as long as Corbett. Also Corbett cannot punch without going into Fitzsimmons's range, and when he is there he may receive a blow that will end his career.[9]

Betting on the contest now became heavy, evidently exceeding anything ever before wagered on a boxing match. In New York alone, nearly a quarter of a million dollars in wagers had already been made. Odds still favored Jim, 100 to 70.

With a "can-do" spirit exceeded only by their gift for self-promotion, Carson City's town fathers boasted they were prepared for the onslaught. They claimed the five Carson hotels could feed 2,000 a day; restaurants could feed 300 more; meals for another 1,000 would be available at the county fairgrounds. A barbecue on Main Street would provide food for 3,000. Available hotel rooms numbered 2,000; 4,000 cots in public buildings would also be made ready; private families could accommodate 3,000 more. Pullman cars would also be called into service. For those with no intention of slogging their way to the arena, hacks, wagons, and carts could be had for a price. Hacks were already transporting spectators daily to and from the combatants training camps. Many residents who had initially opposed the match now changed their minds as economic opportunities became apparent. It was optimistically estimated that as many as 30,000 people would appear for the contest.

Ten days before the match, due to continuing newspaper reports, Jim felt it necessary to comment on the rumors regarding his physical condition. "I was never in better condition than I am at the present moment, and I never was in as good health since I made my first appearance in the ring."[10]

Nevertheless, reporters who observed Jim's daily workouts remarked at his irritability and almost obsessive need for training. He seemed to be overworked rather than underworked.

In contrast, newspapermen freely joshed with Fitzsimmons about his refusal to reveal details of his training regimen, since he was preparing published articles himself. "Why should I give you fellows for nothing what I could sell for a good price? Do you suppose Patti sings for nothing and Paderewski plays for fun? Of course not they do it because they are paid."

Dan Stuart, for his part, had been in bed, very ill with fever, subject to daily injections of quinine and morphine. Finally, after two weeks, though still gaunt and haggard, he was allowed out. Given the opportunity, he visited the arena site, rode out to the training camps, strolled through the city center, and supervised the construction of the ring, components for which had just arrived from San Francisco. He quelled local reports that "big city swells" would be engaging in all sorts of extortions and charging exorbitant prices for everything. Stuart recruited and organized a citizens' committee to tour hotels, restaurants, and private homes to ensure

that prices remained reasonable. No one seemed to pay attention, however, to the quantity of homes and stores being transformed into cheap eating facilities.

A week before the bout, a brisk war of words and exchange of threats was occasioned by a chance meeting of the boxers and the episode was gleefully reported by the press. While out jogging, Fitzsimmons and his cohort noticed Jim and his own entourage a few hundred yards ahead. Fitzsimmons decided to catch up with the Corbett party and engage in conversation. When Jim noticed the group running to catch up, he sprinted ahead, forcing Fitzsimmons to increase his pace. Finally, their dogs' snarling encounter caused both boxers to stop running and tend to the canine confrontation. By the time they untangled their dogs, Jim and Bob were shoulder to shoulder.

"Good morning, Jim," Fitz breezily greeted.

"Good morning," Jim responded, his tone intimating no little displeasure with the meeting and Fitzsimmons's doubtful cordiality.

In a friendly gesture, Fitzsimmons extended his hand to shake Jim's. Jim refused. Fitzsimmons turned away.

"Oh, no," said a surly Jim. "I'll shake hands with you if you lick me over there on the seventeenth, not before."

Jim's trainers sensed trouble and prepared themselves for a possible confrontation. Fitz stopped in his tracks.

"What was that?" he asked Jim.

"I said I'd shake hands with you if you lick me on the seventeenth," Jim repeated testily.

Fitz seemed ready to answer with fists rather than words. He and Jim were now toe-to-toe. One of Jim's trainers pulled him away, at once warning and soothing: "Jim."

The danger passed. But Fitzsimmons was not done. In a voice loud enough for

Jim to hear, he threatened, "There'll be a live one there on the seventeenth."

Jim walked away, his trainers frankly surprised at their man's behavior.

In his daily newspaper column, Fitzsimmons related the story of their meeting and took the opportunity to hurl a renewed challenge to Jim.

> I have not forgotten the insults he has heaped upon me through the public press and to my friends. When we stand up before each other on the 17th, I will fight a square fight, but there shall be no mercy, no quarter, no tenderness. I will fight him to the bitter end and conclude this issue and wipe out his insults.[11]

Corbett admirers were surprised when, in his own newspaper column, Jim made no mention of the meeting or Fitzsimmons's statements. Instead, he seemed only to intensify his training efforts, even though his trainers clearly disapproved. They reported Jim to be already sharp at this point. He should be tapering off now and pacing himself for the bout. A widely published, independent report from an eminent physician, Dr. Gibbs, evaluated both boxers' states of health and conditioning. Gibbs believed Fitzsimmons to be in better shape than Jim, who, he observed, appeared more tense.

> The difference between Corbett and Fitzsimmons is simply this—one is a marvelous boxer, and the other a marvelous fighter. Excitement weakens one and strengthens the other. Fitzsimmons should win the fight.[12]

As the day of the contest approached, rumors circulated that federal authorities would prevent the match. Other rumors suggested gangs of toughs had been procured by both camps to break up the bout if their boxer was seen to be losing. To avoid any such confrontations and gener-

ally preserve order, Stuart hired Bat Masterson, fifty Pinkerton men, and scores of deputy sheriffs.

Yet Stuart was most concerned about the weather. Snow had fallen on Carson City the day before the contest, and it had been stormy for more than two weeks. On the morning of the event, however, the sun came out and Stuart anticipated a pleasant day. For the kinetoscope operators, clear weather was definitely good news. They had set up their cameras in a shed near ringside ready to record the first moving picture of a title bout. Cloudy weather would have ruined their plans.

While trains deposited boxing enthusiasts from all over the country, far fewer showed up than had been expected. A disappointing number of people filed into Dan Stuart's arena; no more than 7,000 paying spectators. The match was turning into a financial setback for the promoter, as well as disenchanted town fathers, who had envisioned a highly lucrative return from their sponsorship of the contest.

At ten minutes to noon, Fitzsimmons strode briskly down the aisle from his dressing room, followed by Julian and his trainers. Before entering the ring, he kissed his wife. As he slipped through the ropes, the challenger exuded confidence.

Jim came in a few minutes later, accompanied by his group. He walked the perimeter of the ring and nodded to his friends, while Fitzsimmons stood with his hands on the ropes. Tight-lipped, agitated, pale, Jim looked decidedly nervous. When Martin Julian walked over to him to discuss ring etiquette, Jim ignored him.

Billy Madden, master of ceremonies, announced to the crowd the conditions of the bout and the names of the officials: George Siler, referee; William Muldoon, official timekeeper; James Colville, timekeeper for Corbett; Lou Houseman, timekeeper for Fitzsimmons. Jim's seconds

A film clip from the Kinetoscope moving picture of the Corbett-Fitzsimmons championship bout in Carson City, Nevada, March 17, 1897. Both men wore heavier than usual robes because of the chill air. Jim appeared to be looking over the crowd confidently.

were Delaney, McVey, Donaldson, Charley White, Billy Woods, and Jim Jeffries. Fitzsimmons's seconds were Julian, Jack Stelzner, Ernest Roeber, and Dan Hickey.

After Siler was introduced, Madden retired from the ring. Delaney then examined Fitzsimmons's gloves while Julian examined Jim's. The men shed their robes. Fitzsimmons had on black shoes and stockings, dark blue trunks, and an American flag belt. Jim wore black shoes and gray stockings, red trunks, and his customary belt, the Stars and Stripes intertwined with an Irish-green sash.

Jim crossed over to Fitzsimmons to offer his hand, but Julian stepped in. "No handshake," he directed. Fitz also shook his head, evidently a response to Jim's treatment of him at their meeting on the road. Jim returned to his corner smiling.

At 12:05 P.M., the gong sounded and the championship battle began.

For the first five rounds, the boxers exchanged solid punches and mixed it up well, to the delight of the spectators. Jim's "science" seemed to have the better of Fitzsimmons's slugging, and it appeared to the crowd that Jim had won the early rounds. In the fifth, decidedly in Jim's favor, his left hooks split Fitzsimmons's lip and bloodied his nose.

The sixth round was crucial for Fitzsimmons. A right to the chin and a jolting left uppercut sent Fitz's head snapping back. Another shot to the nose sprayed blood over the men. In clear distress, Fitzsimmons clinched. From the Corbett corner, his seconds shouted advice: "Take your time, Jim." A series of crushing rights and lefts devastated Fitz, leaving him powerless. A smash to the face floored him, and he didn't get up until the count of nine. Another onslaught of blows made the challenger hold on until the end of the round. As Fitzsimmons slumped on the stool in his corner, he looked all but beaten. Jim eagerly awaited the sound of the gong.

Though Fitzsimmons returned few blows and clinched often during succeeding rounds, he nonetheless showed remarkable recuperative powers and defended himself effectively against Jim's constant hammering. Instead of pressing his advantage, however, following the advice of his seconds, Jim backed away to pick his spots and observe his opponent's condition. The strategy, normally sound, gave the sturdy Fitzsimmons time to recover.

Through round ten, Fitzsimmons bled profusely. His shoulders were hunched, and he dragged his legs. Still, Jim's seconds warned him not to carry the fight to his opponent: "Look out for him, Jim, he's faking there. He isn't as bad off as he looks." Yet, by now, Jim himself was beginning to feel the effects of his vigorous effort to end the bout earlier. In fact, panting for breath, he looked increasingly tired. Momentarily, a blow under the heart seemed to hurt him.

In the eleventh round, both men looked spent. They swung short and clinched at every opportunity. Late in the round, Fitzsimmons got in some strong shots to Jim's chin. Jim retaliated with a series of lefts, but they had little steam.

Fitzsimmons came out quickly, launched some ferocious blows, and had a strong twelfth round. For the most part, Jim stayed out of his way, but he still absorbed solid punches to the head, chin, and chest. They clinched often. Jim struck back with a series of hard smashes, tagging Fitzsimmons with ease. Surprisingly, however, the challenger seemed to be gaining strength.

Round thirteen began with both boxers dancing around the ring, Jim with his guard down, a plodding Fitzsimmons stalking him. Fitz's face remained a study in caked and flowing crimson, but he continued the aggressor. Near the end of the round, he landed a hard left to the body, a blow that staggered Jim. Fitz followed quickly with jabs to the face and head. Jim was in pain.

Up to the fourteenth round, according to observers, Jim had the better of the fight, having hit Fitzsimmons whenever and wherever he pleased. He was tiring rapidly, however, and seemed to lack the stamina Fitzsimmons showed. Though Fitzsimmons had been punished during all the preceding rounds, he still displayed strength and determination.

At the start of the fourteenth round, after a brief exchange, Fitz connected with a terrific left to the body. The blow sent Jim reeling backward several feet and hurt him badly. Fitz followed with a right to Jim's face, again causing him to stagger. Jim attempted to respond, but sustained a hard right to the head. Worn out, Jim clinched.

After Referee Siler separated the boxers, Fitz landed a hard right and left to the jaw and the men clinched again. Jim connected to Fitz's jaw but received a forceful right to his own in return. The blow made Jim lean backwards, and he turned his body slightly. He raised his guard, but Fitz exploded a hard left hand to the body, thudding just below the heart.

Jim went white. His arms dropped to his sides, his eyes clenched in pain, and he fell toward the ropes, catching them with his glove. His face was etched with agony. He tried to rise, but Fitz struck him with a right to the chin. Though not knocked out—not unconscious—Jim suffered pain so intense that it flushed all his remaining strength. He clearly had no sense of what he was doing. Desperately, he struggled to rise, but proved unable to do so. Jim Corbett was counted out. Bob Fitzsimmons had become the new heavyweight champion of the world.

Moments after Siler declared Fitzsimmons the winner, Jim rushed wildly at the victor, still unable to grasp the fact that

Jim had just been knocked out by Bob Fitzsimmons in their championship bout in Reno, Nevada, March 17, 1897. This drawing was made by a **San Francisco Chronicle** *artist. Dispatched to the paper, it appeared in the next day's edition, likely the clearest picture of the acclaimed knockdown.*

he had lost. With great difficulty, his seconds managed to restrain him. They had to wrestle him back to his corner. When Jim regained his senses, he walked across the ring to congratulate the new champion. As the two shook hands, Jim demanded that he be granted a chance to win back the title. Fitzsimmons informed Jim that, for the sake of his family, he intended to retire.

What scribes later called the most famous single punch in the history of boxing—the left hook below Jim's heart—became the public's apotheosis of the Corbett-Fitzsimmons contest. Some labeled it the birth of the solar plexus punch, but such blows had been commonly used by boxers for ages. The blow devastated Jim, already spent, as others to the same spot had hurt him in the previous round. By no means was it a lucky punch. Rather, it was the culmination of a series of powerful smashes to the face and body that Jim sustained, from the hands of a very hard puncher, one who had greater endurance and an extraordinary ability to himself absorb severe punishment.

Within seconds of Fitzsimmons's victory, the ring was packed with people. Fitz was long and loudly cheered by the crowd. Police attempted to clear the ring, but failed. Jim and his seconds had to push their way through to the dressing room. Both Harry and Joe supported Jim as they entered a soon-to-be pitiful scene. The dethroned champion sank exhausted in a chair.

"I can't realize, boys," Jim lamented. "I don't know how it happened. I had him almost out … could have whipped him if I'd followed it up."

There was a moment's silence; then Jim leaned against Harry and wept.

"I can't believe it," he sobbed. "I can't believe it, Harry. How can it be, old man? … I'm defeated."

Billy Woods sat in a corner, a cap over his face to hide the tears. White and McVey, themselves heart broken, tried to comfort Jim. Billy Delaney fanned his fighter with a towel to conceal his raw emotions. Harry gruffly ordered everyone to "brace up." Joe sank to his knees beside his brother. "It's all right, Jim," he soothed. "It's all right. Everyone knows it was a chance blow, and that you're the best man yet."

Jim pressed his hand below his heart. "How my heart hurts me. I thought I'd die when I went down. I cannot realize I was being knocked out. The pain was awful. Awful." He paused to catch his breath. "It may kill me yet. And what's the difference if it does?"

Their gear packed up, Jim and his party returned to San Francisco that evening. A planned exhibition at a theater had to be canceled. Deep gloom and silence pervaded the Corbett household on Hayes Street. All the siblings, cousins, and aunts, along with Vera and Jim's mother, had gathered to await news of the contest over a special wire from Harry's poolroom. Their faces were swollen with weeping. Vera was almost unrecognizable. "He's the same old Jim to me," she said bravely. "Nothing can change that."

Jim's mother offered another perspective. "He thought he was in fine condition, but he had a very hard man to fight and I think his theatrical life unfitted him for his work."

Knowledgeable men who had observed Jim's training regimen, such as referee Siler and timekeeper Muldoon, openly criticized him for not properly preparing for the contest. Not only had he not employed the type of sparring partners who could emulate Fitzsimmons's style, but he had pushed himself too far too fast. "Corbett had no one to blame but himself," Muldoon wrote in his newspaper article.

The next day, Jim visited his brother's poolroom and watched hundreds of men being rewarded for having bet on Fitzsimmons. It was not a particularly pleasant experience for Jim, but he affected a cheerful smile and offered cordial greetings to all he met.

Rumors suggested that Jim and the Corbett family had lost their entire property and savings. In reality, Jim had bet little on himself; Patrick had bet nothing; Harry and the other siblings had together lost only a few thousand dollars. Jim had actually fared reasonably well. He obtained $9,000 as loser of the bout, $5,000 for his newspaper articles, and $1,400 for his public sparring sessions prior to the championship match. After paying expenses for training and trainers, more than a few thousand dollars remained in his pocket. It was his heart that had been damaged, both physically and spiritually.

That evening, Jim and Vera attended a performance at the Orpheum Theater, where a hearty cheer of good will greeted Jim as soon as they entered the auditorium. In response to clamorous demands for a speech, Jim mounted the stage and said:

> Ladies and gentlemen: I thank you for this greeting. I can assure you nobody knows how badly I feel tonight. Mr. Fitzsimmons is a wonderful pugilist and whipped me fairly and squarely. All I ask of the American people is to let me have one more chance at Fitzsimmons.[13]

As Jim left the stage, the crowd

cheered long and vociferously. Obviously, the audience still loved and adored him. Yet following this appearance, he remained largely in seclusion for three weeks, coming out of his hotel afternoons only to exercise at the Olympic Club. Through the press, Jim announced that he would challenge Fitzsimmons with a $5,000 deposit, and that he would shortly embark on a theatrical tour. Newspapers reported that Jim was "greatly cast down" but had made up his mind to devote all his energies, at least for the time being, to the stage.

Less than three weeks after the bout, the Academy of Music, in New York, presented the moving picture of the contest. Projected onto a canvas stretched across the stage, the figures appeared life size. A full house, including many women, watched with fascination an extended moving picture, seventy minutes in length, the longest film ever shown in a theater to that date. A few weeks later, the film was cut to twenty minutes, to allow for more showings in vaudeville theaters.

The Lubin Company had acquired exclusive rights from Stuart, a deal that would prove a financial bonanza for the cash-strapped promoter. Stuart, who had lost a great deal of money on the championship contest itself, made it all back on royalties from the film. The first of its kind, "Corbett vs. Fitzsimmons" was a revelation in moving picture making and its appeal swept the country. Many boxing movies followed, but none caused the same sensation. Unfortunately, since neither boxer had included moving picture royalties in his contract, Jim and Fitz received nothing.

Also appearing at the Academy of Music, along with the fight film, was "A Naval Cadet," starring Jim. The *Clipper* stated:

James J. Corbett's reception amounted to an ovation, and the ex-champion pugilist

seemed to be more popular than ever. He received a welcome that proved he still has many friends here.[14]

SROs followed in Harlem, Philadelphia, and Boston, where "the admirers filled the theaters at every performance." Boston was Jim's theater season finale, and he and the company returned to New York pleased with the results. Jim looked forward to a quiet summer, away from the crowds. Vera confided to newspapers that her husband still had not fully recovered from his defeat.

Nonetheless, Jim's drawing power remained strong. When he was asked to appear in a series of baseball games to raise money for the Western Association baseball circuit, he gladly volunteered to play first base for various teams during August and September. Though the games were identified as benefits, Jim received a percentage of the receipts. At the end of games in which he played, as an added attraction, he sparred a few rounds, always to the delight of spectators.

To initiate the new theater season, "A Naval Cadet" opened at the Columbus Theater, New York, October 4. The production was still under Brady's management. As before, Jim continued to star.

James J. Corbett began his season to a crowded house and his reception was of the warmest nature. He surrounded himself with a capable company, and the play gave general satisfaction, curtain calls being given without number.[15]

At the end of the engagement, the *Clipper* reported that "the SRO sign was brought into requisition nearly every night." The same scenario followed Jim into Brooklyn. "When the curtain rang up on James J. Corbett's 'A Naval Cadet,' there wasn't a vacant seat in the house."[16]

While Jim played to full houses on the tour through New England, Montreal,

Toronto, and back to Cincinnati, efforts continued to challenge Fitzsimmons to a rematch, but with little success. Jim seemed so disappointed with the negotiations, he seriously entertained the idea of retiring from boxing. Both Vera and Patrick campaigned for Jim to give up his ring career, but the ex-champion still believed he could win back the title, refusing to acknowledge that he might have lost the zeal to do so. At this moment, it remained an unresolved issue.

Jim's stage career seemed to have won out again when it was announced he had begun rehearsals for a new play, to be called "The Adventurers," slated to open in Peoria, Illinois, at the end of January 1898. Henry Gray Carlton, the author and director of the play, joined the company to supervise rehearsals while "A Naval Cadet" continued to be performed in St. Louis and Chicago. Prior to Jim's taking the stage with this new production, he confided to reporters: "If I make the success of this play that I think I will, nothing can induce me to take up pugilism again."

"What about Fitzsimmons?" a reporter asked.

"There is only one man I care to fight and that is Fitzsimmons, and now I am tired of trying to arrange another mill with him," Jim declared. "I have always been ambitious to become an actor, and my friends assure me that I am getting along well."

"So what will it be, Jim?"

Jim smiled, but he didn't answer the question.

"The Adventurers" consisted of four acts, the first two set on a farm, the latter two in New York City. Jim played Jack King, a young man returning to his old home town after making a fortune in South Africa. He returns in time to assist an old widow whose farm is coveted by two mine owners who have discovered a rich vein of coal on the widow's property. King has just rescued Eleanor Mobray, a ward of one of the mine owners, from an accident. Naturally, he falls in love with her. Because he trusts Eleanor's guardian, he agrees to turn over the widow's property.

In New York, the stock market has fallen and the mine owners are near bankruptcy. Meanwhile, King has discovered the secret of the coal vein. The mine owners hire "Red Mike," a notorious local thug, to get rid of King. Eleanor rushes to King to warn him. They hear "Red Mike" mounting the stairs. King places a terrified Eleanor in a closet and readies himself to face the villain. King is shot, but manfully perseveres. He attacks "Red Mike," and a battle ensues. King knocks out the heavy and is about to deck Eleanor's guardian, too, when she steps between them. The villains leave hastily, and Eleanor throws herself into King's arms as the curtain falls.

Advance publicity indicated that Jim would no longer be exploited as a boxer; his performance would be exclusively as an actor. No suggestion of a prize-fight ring would be injected into the play. The audience would witness a full-blown comedy-drama filled with "exciting elements of action." In anticipation, the theater was full.

Unfortunately, the play received a mediocre response from the audience and poor reviews from critics. "The Adventurers is absolutely devoid of melodrama or exaggerated incidents."[17]

On the other hand, Jim was favorably recognized for his "light comedy display" and "creditable performance."

However the play might be promoted, audiences everywhere wanted to see Jim spar a few rounds and were disappointed when a display of his boxing skill was not included in the program. A reluctant Carleton was immediately instructed to make changes in the plot. Moreover, he was to remain with the company "perfecting the play," a clear signal to reviewers that the production was in trouble.

For Jim, "The Adventurers" was a deep disappointment. He had viewed the play as an opportunity to display both his comedic and dramatic skills. Instead, audiences said they still wanted to see him spar. The play flopped, and it closed in a week. "A Naval Cadet" was reprised, to continue the tour. Apparently, Jim was unable to extricate himself from boxing, even as an actor—a predicament not very promising for a future in theater.

The spring tour took Jim and the company through a series of one-night stands, in secondary theaters, through Minnesota, North Dakota, Montana, Idaho, on to Seattle. All stops produced SRO business. A week in San Francisco was next, Jim's first return since his loss to Fitzsimmons. How would the crowd respond? The *Chronicle* suggested the kind of reaction he was likely to receive.

> James J. Corbett is to reappear tomorrow night at the Columbia Theater in "A Naval Cadet," in which he has been making money in the East. It is written for him and fitted to his style of acting, with some chance of legitimate display of his specialty. Advance sales are good.[18]

Audiences packed the theater for the entire week, and the *Chronicle* commented:

> James J. Corbett received much applause and many flowers at the Columbia Theater, and showed that whether or not he is as good a pugilist as of old, he is a better actor than he was. The house was full, and when he appeared, he was given a vociferous welcome.[19]

While Jim was very gratified by the reception he received from San Francisco admirers—obviously, they still idolized him—he was deeply disturbed about his father's mental condition. Patrick's depressive states had become so severe that he had been forced to retire from running the livery business. These days, he sat at home, or aimlessly wandered the streets. He communicated little with family members and was reported to have been abusive to his wife, irrationally accusing her of seeing other men. Apparently, little could be done to aid Patrick, a concern for the entire family. When he left San Francisco, Jim was saddened and distressed. It was to be the last time he would see his father and mother alive.

The final leg of the spring tour took the company to Los Angeles, Pueblo, Leadville, and Denver, playing to good houses at all performances. The final performance of "A Naval Cadet" took place at the Tabor Grand Opera House in Denver, the theater filled with flowers and tears. The production had been on tour for two years, playing 393 performances in eighty-seven cities, a very profitable venture for both Jim and William Brady.

In July, much to the surprise of the boxing community, Jim and Kid McCoy were matched to fight twenty rounds for a purse of $20,000 ... and the heavyweight championship of the world. True to his pledge, Fitzsimmons had retired and forfeited his title. To fill the vacant throne, the two were to meet at the Hawthorne Athletic Club, near Buffalo, New York, on September 10. Jim's new manager, George F. Considine, a real estate mogul and promoter, had negotiated the contest, whose articles of agreement were signed at his posh New York hotel. Jim had already gone to Asbury Park to begin training for the bout. Finally, the newspapers declared, Jim had the opportunity to regain the title and redeem himself as a national hero.

On August 16, however, a shocking dispatch from San Francisco all but obliterated Jim. Harry telegraphed Jim to report that their father had just shot his wife, then killed himself. At first, Jim refused to believe the news. When it was verified, he collapsed, utterly devastated by the tragic, seemingly senseless, and violent loss of both his parents.

7. ON THE EDGE

The grandfather clock at the head of the second floor stairs had just struck 5:00 A.M. Patrick Corbett ever so quietly slipped out of bed so as not to disturb his sleeping wife. After meticulously dressing in his Sunday best, Patrick walked to his chest of drawers. There, under a row of neatly stacked clothes, he found and took in hand a revolver. Softly returning to the bed, he leaned over his slumbering wife, took careful aim, and shot her twice in the head. Then, evidently without hesitation, he placed the revolver in his mouth and pulled the trigger again. Awakened by the sound of gun shots, family members rushed into the senior Corbett's bedroom. There they discovered Catherine under the already blood-soaked covers and Patrick fallen on top of her, both of them dead.

More than four years before, when Jim had visited San Francisco on one of his theatrical tours, he noticed, on a number of occasions, some inconsistencies in Patrick's behavior. They became even more obvious to Jim when his parents accompanied him and Olive to Ireland. At the time, the family believed Patrick's age and life of hard, physical labor were responsible for his occasionally irrational behavior.

During the next year, Patrick's health continued to deteriorate. Dysfunctional behavioral traits became clearly evident. At times, he would be deeply depressed, showing no interest in his surroundings. When these episodes occurred, the family thought it best to leave him alone.

About two years before the shooting, Patrick had been taken ill with what was diagnosed as acute gastritis. After his recovery, however, he became even more morose, with little energy. Gradually, his condition declined to the point that he could no longer operate the livery business.

When Jim visited home in February 1897, as he prepared to meet Bob Fitzsimmons, Patrick responded little to Jim's attempts at conversation. When he did respond, his contribution consisted of angry outbursts.

Patrick and Catherine had recently spent a few days vacationing in Bartlett Springs, California, when a melancholy episode precipitated their return home. The hope was that familiar surroundings would prove beneficial to Patrick's recovery.

The next day, after lunch, Patrick went out. His first stop was at the general store, whose clerk refused to sell him poison, supposedly to deal with rats in the stable. The second was at a drug store, where he purchased half an ounce of arsenic, offering the same reason as before. He then visited a gun store, where he told the clerk he wished to purchase a revolver to protect himself from burglars who infested the neighborhood. The clerk showed him a hammerless revolver, explained its action, and, at Patrick's request, loaded the gun for him. Patrick told the clerk that, since he wanted the weapon only for an emergency, he needed no more cartridges.

Patrick's son-in-law, Charles King, and his wife, Mary, along with Esther and Katie (Patrick's unmarried daughters), reported that their father had retired at about 9:30 P.M., after chatting amiably with the family. He appeared to be in good spirits, said King. At about four in the morning, the King baby awoke, crying. Catherine rose to tend to the baby's needs and, after calming the child, returned to bed.

Immediately following the shooting, King called for a physician and a priest. After ascertaining that both parents were dead, he called for the deputy coroner to take charge of the bodies. The family requested that the bodies not be taken to the morgue but rather laid out on the bed where they had died, at least for the time being.

When King was interviewed by the press, he tried to identify the reasons for Patrick's actions, but expressed shock more than anything else.

> I think he was crazy. He had been acting queerly for weeks, and had not been well for two years. He ate sparingly, and was sullen and cross. We all knew and spoke of these peculiarities, but laid them in a measure, to old age. He owned this building, and other property, and was well-to-do. He had no creditors, no other annoyances, was not jealous, and did not drink.[1]

The Corbetts' doctor told reporters that Patrick had been suffering "mental aberrations" for the past two years, due primarily to the effects of nephritis (kidney disease) and cirrhosis of the liver. The doctor also revealed that Patrick had recently told him he thought his time "was not long on this earth." A rumor circulated that a suicide note had been found, but the family denied it. Later, when the estate was probated, it was found that Patrick had made final decisions about dispensing his property less than a month before the episode.

While Jim was sparring with one of his trainers at Asbury Park, in preparation for his bout with Kid McCoy, Vera received Harry's dispatch. She ran to the training quarters and, as she handed the message to Jim, fainted in his arms. Jim read the message, turned pale, and was unable to speak. Clearly on the verge of collapse, he clutched the ropes tightly, as he had when Fitzsimmons disabled him.

A doctor was called, and gave Jim a sedative. When Jim recovered from the initial shock, he, Vera, and Tom boarded a late train. It was a five-day trip to San Francisco, during which time Jim quietly mourned his loss.

Upon their arrival in San Francisco, a simple funeral was held at the Church of the Sacred Heart. Though Catholic doctrine normally forbade burial in sacred ground for those who committed suicide, the Church waived its usual proscription, since Patrick was judged to have been suffering from a mental disorder. Family and close friends were present at interment in the Corbett plot at Holy Cross Cemetery. Among all who attended, Jim appeared the most disconsolate.

Ever since he had been an adolescent, Jim's relationship with his father had been one of conflict, confrontation, and compromise. Both had been stubborn in their beliefs and behavior, to the point that family members—notably brothers Harry

A pose taken at Jim's training camp at Asbury Park, New Jersey. Jim was preparing for a bout with Kid McCoy when word came of his parents' deaths. From left to right: Kid Levine, Tom Lansing, Jim, Connie McVey, Tom Corbett, Billy Leving. (San Francisco History Center, San Francisco Public Library)

and Joe—often had to intercede and mediate. Unlike his siblings, Jim had always been a rebel, disputing his father's authority and that of the Church. Indeed, Jim's quest for independence might seem to have been directed against Patrick: choosing a boxing career, resigning from his job at the bank, marriage and divorce outside the Church.

Other less obvious factors surely must have affected Jim, among them, his own inability to have children and become a father, as well as his seeming lack of attention to Patrick's increasingly failing mental condition. Fear also may have played a role in their relationship, Jim's fear that he himself would become a victim of mental illness. (It was admitted that other family members had suffered similar problems in the past.)

For Jim, the immediate result of his father's death were strong feelings of guilt and fear. Ample evidence, based on reported behavior and conversations, indicates that Jim had long harbored contradictory feelings toward his father. Though

such feelings tend to be common between an adolescent boy and his father, for Jim, they continued long into adulthood. Psychologists label such behavior love-hate relationships. For all his successes, all the public adulation he received, there is no question that Jim still craved approval from his father for his myriad accomplishments, a validation rarely forthcoming. Instead, Patrick continued to remind his son of his displeasure regarding Jim's decision to pursue a boxing career. Now that Patrick was dead, Jim had no hope of ever obtaining his father's respect or esteem. Depression often sets in when one loses a parent or must give up a dream, and Jim surely manifested this behavioral pattern.

The results of this episode significantly upset Jim's emotional balance. He frequently wept, openly and unexpectedly. He slumped over when he walked, and dragged his feet. He spoke infrequently and when he did his speech was monosyllabic. Only Vera seemed to offer some solace. Jim could no longer remain in San

Francisco, so he and Vera left a few days after the funeral. She hoped that leaving town would somewhat soothe his turbulent emotions.

Waiting back East was a match with Norman Selby, a.k.a. "Kid McCoy," originally scheduled for September 10, in Buffalo, New York. When McCoy and his manager were apprised of the deaths, they agreed to delay the bout until October 1, with no forfeit of money. At the same time, however, Buffalo's sheriff, under sustained pressure from a committee of ministers, determined to prohibit the match. "I assured the ministers I would stop it," he explained. "This fight will not be pulled off." Managers Considine (for Corbett) and Gray (for McCoy) met to discuss what to do; two weeks of negotiations resolved nothing.

Jim had returned to Asbury Park to resume training, though he displayed little interest or desire to do so. He went through the usual exercises, yet with no apparent passion or commitment. Everyone feared that, if the bout took place in October, Jim would undoubtedly be beaten. Nor had Jim's overall demeanor improved. He rarely smiled or laughed, but neither did he openly express anger.

Finally, after weeks of fruitless meetings, the Corbett-McCoy match had to be called off. Still, George Considine announced that Jim was ready to meet anybody; to prove his sincerity, he increased the deposit. Rumors suggested a match with Tom Sharkey or Jim Jeffries was probable. Observers wondered, however, whether Jim could be ready, whomever he faced.

Two weeks later, Considine announced that Jim would meet Tom Sharkey in a twenty-round bout, on November 22, for a purse of $20,000. Seventy-five percent of the purse would go to the winner, twenty-five percent to the loser. The Lenox Athletic Club of New York City would sponsor the contest. No referee had yet been chosen. Since the bout was only a month away, Jim began a strict training regimen. Nonetheless, his usual desire was still noticeably absent.

Surprisingly, the betting favored Jim, 100 to 80, though sporting men were quite aware of Jim's current mental state. Reports from each camp provided favorable news, and that seemed to cause a spurt of interest in the bout. Newspapers predicted "a great fight, full of fast, clever work on Corbett's part and nervy, bull-like rushes on the part of Sharkey." While Jim remained the favorite right up to the time of the bout, there remained a wide divergence of opinion as to the probable outcome.

One group argued that Jim's height, reach, skill, and speed were in his favor. A rival group pointed to Sharkey's endurance and punching, which would wear Corbett down as had Fitzsimmons. In addition, they argued, strength and conditioning would prevail over "scientific" boxing. If Sharkey could stay ten rounds, his opportunity to win would be great.

Jim had his training site shifted to New York City, McVey and White believing that a change of scenery might prove helpful to their man. Jim worked out at the Lenox Athletic Club and ran in Central Park. While his physical condition seemed sound, his emotional condition remained problematic. "No fire in his eyes," observed McVey.

Unlike the Corbett-Fitzsimmons contest, little commentary emanated from training camps or the boxers themselves. Both managers believed that other promotional devices were sufficient to generate controversy and excitement for the bout, and they were correct. Newspapers published statements and episodes every day, in great detail. They framed the big question: How good was Corbett at the moment? In his usual trim, Corbett could likely whip Sharkey. But without his characteristic vitality, what were his chances?

An enormous crowd of the sporting element from all over the country gathered at the Lenox Athletic Club to see the ex-champion of the world, James J. Corbett meet the battling sailor from Dundalk, Ireland, Tom Sharkey. Reserved seats near the ring went for twenty dollars apiece, and every seat in the auditorium had been sold. At 10:20 P.M., after two dull preliminaries, Tom Sharkey pushed his way through the crowd, on his way to the ring. He was accompanied by his manager, Tom O'Rourke, and his seconds, John Dougherty, George Dixon, Bob Armstrong, and Jack Reid. Sharkey weighed 178 pounds and appeared confident as he stepped into the ring. Jimmy De Forest was Sharkey's timekeeper.

Jim entered the auditorium fully fifteen minutes later, the crowd already anxious for him to appear. A wild cheer arose when he reached the ring, where he stopped for a moment to shake hands with friends, before springing through the ropes. Jim wore a dark olive green dressing gown. His seconds were Charley White, Connie McVey, George Considine, and John Considine, the latter being Jim's timekeeper. The referee called the two men together to give them their final instructions.

The contest turned into a fiasco, stopped in the ninth round by the referee because, for unknown reasons, Connie McVey, one of Jim's seconds, jumped into the ring. Because of the foul, Sharkey was awarded the victory. But, since the referee sensed some "preconceived plan," he dramatically called off all bets, to the crowd's— and bettors'—great dismay.

McVey's conduct was remarkable, since there was nothing that appeared to demand his presence in the ring. Being an old pro, he assuredly knew that his action would cost Jim the bout. Initially, McVey claimed he thought the round was over, that Sharkey had fouled Jim, and he was only protecting his man. Later, McVey changed his story; he stated that he had been reacting to a series of low blows Jim had received, particularly when the two men separated after clinching. Since the referee had not responded to his calls, claimed McVey, he had stepped into the ring. "I guess I lost my head. I could not stand seeing Jim get fouled without making a protest." Sporting men considered McVey's excuses feeble.

When the referee made his decision in favor of Sharkey, Jim rushed McVey and, apparently furious with his second, tried to slug him. Police intervened. McVey was removed from the ring, followed by Jim, who continued to call him names. There was mixed opinion among reporters whether Jim had been seriously angry at McVey or merely acting "in a theatrical manner."

Many reasons were offered for McVey's behavior, most of them suggesting he had been paid to "save" Jim the embarrassment of a loss. With increasing fear in Jim's corner that he was about to be beaten, by breaking the rules in this manner, he could lose without bringing discredit to his record. There was no doubt that, by the eighth round, Sharkey displayed more strength and was decidedly more aggressive than Jim. In fact, observers felt that Jim, having hit Sharkey with his hardest punches without hurting him, had exhausted his stamina at the end of the round.

To this point in the match, Jim had done an excellent job of scientific boxing, showing impressive foot work, dodging, side-stepping, and blocking Sharkey's blows. When it came to solid punching, however, Jim appeared at a disadvantage. Unlike previous bouts, Jim did very little leading, nor did he carry the action to Sharkey, seemingly content to counterpunch and meet him with left hooks.

In the second round, Sharkey had pushed Jim into a corner and, after a series of blows, Jim fell to the floor. Yet, he popped up so quickly, it appeared to be a slip, rather than a knockdown. In the following rounds, Jim hit Sharkey often, evidently, whenever he wanted, but he had no power in his blows and no apparent effect on his opponent. Nor did Jim look as good as he had in previous bouts. According to observers, his body lacked muscle tone, his face was drawn, and his legs were thinner.

Considering the extraordinary circumstances, the crowd remained relatively orderly and no trouble erupted as people left the auditorium. Prevailing opinion in the press held that the contest was "a fake," that McVey's interference had been prearranged. In addition, some cited the referee's decision on bets to be as much a violation of the rules as McVey's action.

Each side to the controversy had its own explanations and opinions. Strong charges were made against Corbett and McVey, but they were mild compared to those directed against the referee for calling off all bets. Major bettors across the country claimed the referee had made an illegal decision and the money should have gone to Sharkey. Charley White, one of Jim's seconds, backed Jim but also agreed that the money belonged to Sharkey. The New York sporting community blamed Jim for the "fake" bout. Others claimed McVey had been bought by Sharkey. Those supporting Jim said that he could never have been party to such a "bungled mess." An unsubstantiated rumor suggested that Jim had wired his brother to hedge his bet, as a supposed "plan" had misfired. Yet nothing was proven. No solid information surfaced, nor did anyone step forward to clarify the issue. Jim contin-

ued to express anger at McVey, whose whereabouts were now unknown.

Five days later, Lenox Club directors announced that a formal investigation would take place, to "find those responsible for the actions of the contest." At the same time, Jim, Tom Sharkey, Charley White, and Tom O'Rourke produced affidavits, declaring under oath that they knew of no deals in connection with the bout. Under questioning by reporters, the Lenox Club admitted that an actual purse did not exist, that the boxers had agreed to receive a percentage of the gate, instead. (This actually worked to the boxers' advantage. Both boxers made a bit more than if an actual purse of $20,000 had been distributed. Sharkey made $16,845 and Jim made $6,845.) McVey was reported to be out of town and unable to attend the inquiry.

At the investigation, Referee Kelly repeated his statements that he had declared all bets off because he believed McVey's entry into the ring had been "prearranged." George Considine, Jim's manager, stated he had bet every dollar he wagered on Corbett and knew nothing of any deal to stop the contest. Charley White was unable to offer any explanations for McVey's actions. Tom O'Rourke said he was dumbfounded when he saw McVey jump into the ring. O'Rourke also denied knowledge of any collusion.

In his testimony, Tom Sharkey said he believed the bout was "on the level" and was convinced that, had the bout gone another round, he would have knocked out Corbett. When Jim spoke, he claimed that, at the time of McVey's untoward intervention, he had been leading on points. Sharkey crisply interrupted, "You didn't have a dead man's chance."

Jim reacted indignantly. "I never faked in my life!"

"Neither did I," retorted Sharkey heatedly.

When both men assumed menacing attitudes and it looked for a moment there would be a brawl; State Senator Sullivan, officiating the inquiry, stepped between the boxers and held them apart. When tensions eased, Jim went on to say that he believed McVey was impelled only by honest motives and that no man could make him believe otherwise.

Final results of the investigation indicated that no "crooked work" could be found. McVey was judged solely responsible for his own actions.

Two weeks after the bout, the Kinetoscope company released moving pictures of the contest to theaters. A report in the *New York Times* quoted a Kinetoscope employee, who insisted on anonymity, that, through a mixup, they had had on hand only enough film to photograph nine rounds, which just happened to be the exact length of the contest when the bout was stopped. A week later, Jim fired McVey from his staff.

The story disappeared from front pages as fast as it had appeared. Jim, however, was feeling no better than he had before the bout; probably worse. The controversial loss could only have added additional burdens to his already dispirited state of mind.

During the next several months, Jim was rarely seen by his boxing and theatrical colleagues. In one rare excursion, Jim attended the Sharkey-McCoy match in early 1899. When he entered his box, he was scarcely recognized by spectators and those few who spotted him hissed feebly. When Jim did emerge, observers noted his wan and distant look, and the slump of his usually straight back. It was obvious to everyone that he was not keeping himself in top physical condition. What Jim was doing for money during this time is not known, but he had earned a good deal in months prior to the Sharkey bout.

In the summer of 1899, almost ten months after his parents' deaths, the *Times* reported that Jim and his business manager's brother, John Considine, had formed a partnership in a saloon, to be opened on Thirty-fourth Street and Broadway. A large electric sign, almost as tall as the building itself, illuminated "Corbett's Bar and Poolroom." A long, ornately carved, dark oak bar spanned the length of the ground floor. Opposite the bar were tables and chairs for patrons who wished snacks with their drinks. Pool tables were on the second floor. Tellingly, no boxing paraphernalia were displayed on either floor.

From its opening, Jim spent each day greeting customers and tending bar. To observers, working seemed to raise his spirits and regenerate some of the self-confidence he had lost. One of his first customers was old friend Eddie Foy, currently performing in New York. Foy stopped by each evening for a beer before going to the theater. Within a few months, sporting men and local politicians found Corbett's a comfortable and congenial place to meet and exchange gossip.

It was during this time that William Brady reentered boxing by assuming the management of Jim Jeffries, Jim's former sparring partner. Jeffries had become a leading contender and was considered to have an excellent opportunity to capture the heavyweight title. Though he had claimed to be no longer interested in the boxing game when he and Jim parted company, Brady now recognized another substantial money-making venture. Shortly after assuming the management of Jeffries, Brady negotiated a Jeffries-Fitzsimmons contest. In June, Jeffries knocked out Fitzsimmons in eleven rounds, for a purse of $20,000 and the championship. Immediately after the bout, Brady began a campaign to match Corbett and Jeffries but Jim expressed little interest. The inimitable Brady, however, was relentless.

Jim Corbett's Saloon at 34th Street and Broadway, not the first boxer's tavern in Manhattan but decidedly the best. It became a White Rats hangout and a meeting place where theatrical and political people could share gossip and a drink. Ultimately, Jim had to give up ownership because his extensive vaudeville touring kept him away from the business.

In the fall of 1899, Jim showed a renewed desire to return to the stage, but the majority of bookings and tours had already been made for the season. Coincidentally, Brady had recently obtained management of Koster & Bial's Theater in New York City and was preparing a production to play there prior to touring. Called "Round New York in Eighty Minutes," the entire show was made up of comic skits and burlesques of various happenings in the city. Brady contacted Jim to appear in one of the skits, to which he readily agreed.

In contrast, Vera was strongly opposed to Jim's appearing in any Brady production, no matter how much it might alleviate his malaise. Had not Brady dropped Jim when the manager believed him no longer a money-maker? Moreover, contrary to what Brady told the press about leaving the boxing business, had he not arranged to become Jeffries's manager, once he saw the young boxer's potential? To make matters worse, in Vera's estimation, Jim would become Brady's employee, playing in the same company with Jeffries and equally exploited.

Yet Jim refused to listen to Vera. Here was his chance to return to the stage. Rehearsals seemed to invigorate Jim. His smile returned and he began to exercise again.

"Round New York in Eighty Minutes" was a polyglot of old jokes, songs, and dancing, presented in typical variety fashion, with no overarching plot or theme. Each performer did his or her specialty and improvised routines, which changed almost daily. The only requisite for the show was that each skit must satirize an actual event that had recently occurred, or a serious production presented in the city. (Brady's idea was likely stolen from Weber and Fields's music hall productions, mounted only a few blocks away.) Though initial reviews were universally poor, audiences seemed to enjoy the loose, improvisational nature of the performance, plus the opportunity to see well-known actors doing their specialties.

The *New York Clipper* reported that:

> ...the entertainment failed to elicit more than a fainthearted response. Some parts of it dragged painfully and lacked both point and interest. The band is crude and the jokes almost invariably resurrect some products of comic opera librettists.[2]

Another manager, faced with such a review, would have abandoned the show, but not Brady. He sensed a money-maker and quickly made changes in skits, music, scenery, and costumes, all of which required additional investment. By the end of the production's second week, the *Clipper* noted:

> Big business now rules here, achieving capacity almost every night. The burlesque has been considerably shortened, new business and skits have been introduced, and as a laughmaker it bids fair to be popular for some time.[3]

During the first week, Jim performed in one of the skits as a straight man to comic-dialect veteran Gus Bruno, the first time he had assumed such a role. During the second week, Brady brought in Jeffries and Sharkey to appear with Jim. Jeffries sparred with his brother, while Jim served as referee; Sharkey had a non-boxing cameo. Others on the bill included Dick Bernard, a German comedian; Bobby Gaylor, a droll, Irish song-and-dance man (Gaylor had appeared with Jim on his trip to England and Ireland in 1894); and a pretty singer, recently recognized for her voice and acting ability, Marguerite Sylva.

The sparring skit had to be dropped when the Jeffries brothers were arrested for violating laws against boxing. Brady was threatened with the closing of his show if he persisted in allowing the performance. He argued his own case before the judge, claiming the bout was part of the production, not an actual sporting event, but the judge ruled against him. In a related event, however, Brady apparently convinced Jeffries to face Jim in some future match, instead of Fitzsimmons or Sharkey.

During the third week of "Round New York," the featured burlesque was a satire of William Gillette in his celebrated role as Sherlock Holmes. Entitled "The Remarkable Pipe Dream of Mr. Sherlock Holmes," the skit starred Jim as the famous detective. Apparently, he played his role in such outrageous fashion as to be considered exceptionally amusing. The *Clipper* reported that the skit—and Jim— "proved one of the brightest bits of the kind yet seen on the local stage this season." Both reviewer and audience response to the performance gave Jim renewed confidence.

Within a matter of days, Brady persuaded Jim and Jeffries to agree to a match, to take place in September, 1900. (Brady did not want any bouts to interfere with the theatrical season, nor potentially profitable tours.) When Vera discovered that Brady was attempting to inveigle Jim into meeting Jeffries, she became irate. Not for the first time, she accused Brady of "using" Jim's name and reputation for his own financial gain. Moreover, she believed that Jim was too naive to recognize it. Vera pointed out her husband's age—thirty-three—compared to Jeffries's twenty-five, and she used the argument to imply that Brady saw an easy victory for his man over the aging ex-champion.

Jim, however, didn't agree with his wife. He saw Brady's offer as a unique opportunity to return to the ring, maybe even recapture the title. The argument became so heated that it temporarily ruptured their relationship, and Vera ordered Jim out of the house until he came to his senses. Saddened, Jim left. At the same time, however, he remained enthused about his boxing future.

The bout was to be for twenty-five rounds, the winner receiving seventy-five percent of the gate receipts, the loser twenty-five percent, with an additional agreement that each party would receive an equal share from all "privileges," such as moving pictures and souvenirs. The latter stipulation was the first time such an agreement had been formalized and it initiated new financial opportunities for boxers in future contractual arrangements. Richard Fox, editor of the *National Police Gazette*, also agreed to give the publication's diamond-studded belt to the winner.

The timing of the announcement pushed "Round New York" to SRO houses and extended the production's run to its sixth week. Jim continued in his role as Sherlock Holmes with great success. The presentation of an ex-boxing champion playing the Gillette-inspired role was in itself a humorous exposition. For the female lead in Jim's skit, Brady hired an English music hall actress, Margaret Corneille. Within days of Jim's departure from the Corbett household, he and Margaret were seen together socially. They remained so until Brady's production closed, Corneille going on the road with a touring vaudeville company, Jim beginning his training for the contest with Jeffries.

Again, Brady demonstrated his showman's abilities. When the revue concluded its sixth week, and elicited signs of wearing out, Brady relinquished his management of the theater; bought the play, scenery, and costumes; and assumed full responsibility for the production. After playing one more week in New York, he put the show on the road, starting with a week in Harlem. Stops during January and February, 1900, in Buffalo, Boston, and Philadelphia proved successful. Jim continued to play Holmes; Jeffries returned to spar with his brother. Brady wanted Jim and Jeffries to continue as theatrical colleagues; it helped to promote their upcoming clash.

In late February, at the end of "Round New York's" road season, Brady publicly announced that Jeffries and Corbett would officially meet for the heavyweight championship on May 11, at the Seaside Athletic Club, on Coney Island. Both men departed for their respective training sites to prepare for the epic battle which, according to newspapers, would represent "the finest in scientific boxing ever seen in the ring."

No sooner had the press, boxing community, and enthusiasts of the sport hailed the coming contest, than Governor Theodore Roosevelt signed the Lewis bill, prohibiting public boxing in the state of New York. Showing some political sensitivity to boxing's entrepreneurs and financial backers, Roosevelt agreed to delay the law's initiation until September 1. That lent the Jeffries-Corbett bout even greater importance, making it possibly the last title bout to be held in the state.

Throughout his entire training, Jim sought to maintain a low public profile. He worked hard to reach top condition, knowing full well his opponent's abilities. Considine, Jim's manager, handled all press reports and offered little information, saying only that Jim was intent on recapturing the championship. In contrast, the Jeffries camp, headed by the ubiquitous Brady, put out daily reports, releasing Jeffries's attributed comments about his old friend, now detested competitor.

I am going to make the pace from the start. I am going right at him, just as I have always done and propose to win just as quickly as I can. Jim's only chance is to win within six rounds, for, with all due respect to him, that is about as far as he can go.[4]

A few days before the contest, Jeffries (or Brady) boasted: "I am going to outbox Jim at his own particular game of footwork and feinting, and I am going to make the pace and get him before the fight goes very far."[5]

Both the press and boxing establishment agreed with Jeffries: Corbett did not stand a chance and would be quickly beaten. A *New York World* report stated: "Jeffries, as champion, is expected to win, of course, and the question of his fitness for the struggle is not doubted." Betting odds were 2 to 1 in favor of Jeffries. Because of this, betting prior to the match itself was light.

On the day before the contest, it was announced that Charley White had been selected as referee. White had been a second to Corbett and was a personal friend of both men. The selection seemed to make people feel more confident that he would be an impartial judge, a person who really "knew" the boxing game. Both boxers were reported to be in excellent condition, Jeffries optimistic about the outcome, Jim eager for the opportunity to regain the title. Nearly all seats at the athletic club had been sold, although betting continued to be light.

The outcome stunned everyone. The contest lasted twenty-three rounds. Although finally knocked out, Jim was ceremoniously recrowned as the public's favorite and a national sports hero. While headlines stated simply "Jeffries Still Champion," a flood of articles bestowed monumental credit upon Jim's courageous performance. "Victor Outclassed as a Scientific Fighter." "Former Champ Lacked Only Strength to Gain the Laurel." "Jeffries Outclassed as Boxer." "Corbett Carries the Crowd With Him Throughout."

Newspapers also remarked that, compared to previous championship matches, this bout had been an "orderly affair."

Though there had been little betting on the outcome of the contest, with Jeffries the clear favorite, those bettors who wagered that Jim would last ten rounds realized a good deal of money. The arena was filled with 7,000 spectators, all of whom had cheered the men with passionate and demonstrative clamor.

In the opening rounds, Jim showed to advantage. He was quick on his feet and darted in and out with grace and speed. He whipped his left into Jeffries face continually and eluded almost all of the champion's punches. Jeffries kept wading in but seemed awkward in doing so. Corbett won the first two rounds on points, but Jeffries's telling blows won him the next two. As the gong sounded to end the fourth, Corbett seemed to have tired.

Jeffries kept making the pace, but Jim slipped away from him. During the next few rounds, spectators began to applaud and cheer Jim's exhibition, as he outboxed Jeffries and seemed to plant his left constantly in the champion's face. Still, Jim had a hard time landing a heavy blow on Jeffries and when he did so, Jeffries seemed unfazed. Jeffries was fighting in his crouching stance, which had proven difficult for Fitzsimmons to solve.

As the bout approached the tenth round, Jeffries displayed more of his strength against Jim, particularly in the clinches. When Jim appeared eager and able at the beginning of the eleventh, many bettors exclaimed their pleasure at having made money; others seemed surprised and encouraged that Jim had been holding his own. Jeffries was well aware that, at this stage of the bout, he was being outpointed. His best chance was to push Jim hard, mix it up, and slug it out. The champion appeared grim and resolute.

For the next few rounds, Jim measured his own attack and avoided the powerful Jeffries. The crowd became increasingly aware of Jim's exceptional performance.

Spectators now rose as one to cheer his every punch and elegant evasion. It was as if they had suddenly comprehended that they were privileged witnesses to an awesome spectacle, a classic battle, one pitting youth and strength against a gallant, scientific mastery of the sport. The pace had been ferocious, and only men extraordinarily fit and well prepared could have endured this long.

By the seventeenth round, Jeffries, concerned that his reputation was in jeopardy, began rushing Jim and landing heavy blows. Jim remained fast on his feet, but his own counter-punches lacked force. He seemed content with avoiding punishment. How long could Corbett keep this game up?

At the twentieth round, spectators began to sense that Jim would go the limit. If he did, he would surely be awarded victory. Although Jim had skillfully avoided injury from Jeffries's furious onslaughts, the champion, still strong, continued to hammer away.

Only three rounds to go. Then, with suddenness, the end came in the twenty-third.

The men had exchanged two quick rallies, followed by some long range sparring. As they came together for another series of solid exchanges, Jim took a hard left to the face, snapping his head back. Jeffries followed quickly with a stiff right to the jaw that floored Jim. The back of his head struck the floor sharply. He rolled over in a valiant struggle to rise. In vain. When his seconds carried him to his corner, Jim was so dazed as to remain unaware.

Jeffries retained his championship, but the crowd cheered Jim instead, in homage to his bravery and his efforts. Someone called for cheers for Jeffries, but the crowd refused to give them. When the question was called on behalf of Jim, thousands echoed their approval. In the ring, there were more people solicitous to Jim than there were congratulating the man who had defeated him. As the *Chronicle* reporter declared of the crowd at the bout's conclusion: "Corbett's skill had made it the best fight they had ever seen and their hopes had been with him from the moment the battle shaped itself."[6]

Newspapers across the country uniformly proclaimed "Corbett the Real Hero," and his courageous challenge made him "the idol of sports." Overnight, Jim's reputation had been resurrected, ironically, due to his having *lost* a championship contest. Public reaction to Jim's performance resurfaced the feelings of adoration they harbored for him, and the event gave them the opportunity to openly reaffirm their allegiance. Though having lost, Jim had overcome heavy odds and "showed up" the champion. That was all the public needed to voice, once again, hearty approval for their idol.

A special *Times* dispatch summed up the public's praise for Jim.

> Although vanquished in defeat that was decisive as it was sudden, Jim Corbett is the real hero. He is again enthroned in popular favor, and for the second time an idol in that world which pays its money for displays of brawn and muscle and pugilistic science.[7]

Even Jeffries admitted to having been surprised. "Corbett is a wonderful fighter, and I give him credit for troubling me more than any man I ever met. It was a surprise, too, I can tell you."

Jim was in a celebratory mood, as well. Yes, he admitted, he wanted to win the title. Yes, he had worked hard to achieve it. Yes, he had had to overcome a personal malaise that could easily have eroded his efforts. By rousing the public, however, Jim had also successfully recaptured his self-esteem.

Jim, Vera (in public, they continued

to appear together), and their friends spent the next day at Sheepshead Bay. Upon returning to the city the next afternoon, Jim was feted wherever he went. Crowds blocked the way of his carriage, and he was kept bowing in acknowledgment to the cheers. Arriving at his saloon, he could not enter because of the throng. Reporters surrounded him for a statement and, in characteristic Corbett fashion, Jim pleasantly complied.

> I cannot say just now what my future plans are. I am not going to retire, I can assure you. I know now that I have still a number of fights in me, and, although I was defeated, I have not been disgraced.[8]

The crowd vociferously agreed. In a graceful gesture of thanks to his faithful admirers, Jim added: "My friends are more loyal to me than ever, and that alone is worth to me more than any purse money."

Jim later revealed he had won a large sum of money on the number of rounds the contest would go. He estimated his earnings to exceed $12,000. Harry had also made a good deal of money, with similar wagering. San Francisco's sporting men were ecstatic, echoing Jim as "the local hero of the hour." After having been defeated by Fitzsimmons and showing poorly against Sharkey, they had believed that Jim, at age 33, was "washed up." Further, they felt that Jim had made a grave mistake in entering the ring with Jeffries. Many had predicted that he would be quickly and summarily dispatched. For once, they were happy to have been proven wrong. The *Chronicle* reported a "general rejoicing among thousands of admirers" and recognized Jim as "the greatest exponent of Marquis of Queensberry rules in the world."

Looking to take advantage of the accolades for his boxer, George Considine announced that Jim would meet Kid McCoy in a twenty-five round match, for a purse of $25,000. Since the contest would take place in New York, it had to be held before September 1, the date the new prohibition on boxing was to take effect. The bout was scheduled for August 31.

During the summer of 1900, activity in New York boxing circles bordered on the frenetic and the results were unexpected. In July, Gus Ruhlin defeated Tom Sharkey in an upset, knocking him cold in the fifteenth, after downing him six times in the round. Jim had seconded Ruhlin. In early August, Bob Fitzsimmons knocked out Ruhlin; Jim again seconded him.

Prior to his bout with Jim, Kid McCoy had fought four times in 1900, winning all four by knockouts: Peter Maher, in five rounds; Joe Choynski, in three; Dan Creedon, in six; and Jay Bonner, in thirteen. McCoy seemed more than ready to take on Corbett. For his part, Jim continued his heavy regimen of training, determined to repeat his excellent showing against Jeffries. In Jim's favor was the fact that Jeffries was stronger than McCoy.

During Jim's training, Margaret Corneille returned to New York. Instead of leaving immediately for England—she had an engagement in London in September—she was seen with Jim. Vera was aware of the situation but she did or said nothing, likely assuming the actress would soon leave the States.

Rumors swirled before the match, no doubt influenced by the sporting community's hectic dealings in the weeks before boxing's prohibition was to take effect. Some people argued that McCoy had not trained properly and expected to lose the bout. Others claimed that the entire match was a setup sponsored by bettors wanting to make a final "killing," and Corbett would win. Still others believed that, based on Jim's showing against Jeffries, McCoy would be totally outclassed.

Crowds jammed the streets around Madison Square Garden on the night of August 31. Sidewalks were blocked by street vendors, selling hot sausages, peanuts, and sandwiches. Hawkers peddling pictures of Corbett and McCoy accosted every passerby. Waiting for a chance to rush past the ticket takers, men and boys minus the price of admission added to the commotion. A police force of 250 men could barely preserve order.

Fully 8,000 people attended the contest sponsored by the Twentieth Century Athletic Club, the largest crowd ever assembled for a boxing match in New York City. Gate receipts were estimated to be more than $50,000. Bettors had selected Jim the favorite, 100 to 80, over McCoy. Backers for McCoy were few, even though gamblers offered them 3 to 1 odds at the last minute, just to obtain more money. By agreement, Corbett and McCoy were each to get half the total gross receipts.

Before the featured contest, two preliminary bouts were staged by local boxers, whom the crowd regarded more as humorous than exemplars of pugilistic skill. Thousands patiently endured the heat and retained their good natures waiting for the main event to begin.

McCoy was the first man in the ring. His weight was announced at 170 pounds. Four minutes later, Jim entered and took the northwest corner of the square, the same choice he had made in the bout with Jeffries. Both men were quickly surrounded by their seconds to prepare them for the battle, and a battle was definitely anticipated. After they were formally introduced to the crowd, referee Charley White gave the men last minute instructions and directed them to their corners to await the gong.

Contrary to spectator expectation, the bout began cautiously. The crowd looked forward to a battle royal, since it had been advertised that both men disliked one another. McCoy promptly took the offensive, crowding in on Jim, who backed away, dancing lightly on his feet. Backing and circling, Jim kept away. Neither man threw any real punches. The entire first round was taken up with posturing, feinting, shifting, and dancing, with McCoy getting in a few light blows. The crowd hissed its displeasure.

The same tactics began the second round, McCoy continuing to lead. Both men displayed good examples of scientific boxing as they blocked and side-stepped each other's blows. The crowd, however, yelled for more action. At the end of the round, two stinging shots by Jim to his opponent's neck and mouth hurt McCoy.

In the third, Jim rushed McCoy from the moment the gong sounded. While a number of blows missed their mark, Jim wore McCoy down as he struggled to evade the onslaught. Each blow Jim struck, McCoy attempted to counter, but with little impact. Forced into a corner, McCoy tried to slip away. Jim leapt in front of him and staggered McCoy with a breath-taking blow to the stomach. He followed quickly with a powerful left to the side of the head and a series of sharp lefts and rights that forced McCoy to clinch and hold on at round's end. The crowd cheered wildly in approval of the action.

The fourth round opened with Jim immediately crowding McCoy, stalking him around the ring. McCoy tried to evade Jim's assault by striking back, but his feeble swings were wild. Jim got past McCoy's defense, smashing a hard right to the mouth and a left to the stomach, causing McCoy to clinch again. At this point, the crowd knew that McCoy was beaten. The boxer himself seemed to realize it, as he repeatedly clinched to save himself from further punishment. The round ended with McCoy weak and dazed.

Sensing victory and encouraged by his seconds, Jim began the fifth by rushing to finish McCoy. McCoy momentar-

ily seemed refreshed, and he landed a hard blow to Jim's chest. Jim retaliated with a strong left to the ribs and a right to the midsection. As McCoy backed away, Jim unleashed a storm of blows that staggered him. McCoy tried to evade Jim but was caught in a corner, which allowed Jim to pummel him at will. McCoy clinched and, when the men were separated, clinched again. Separated, McCoy seemed dazed. He tried to duck away, but again was cut off by Jim. A series of rights and lefts to McCoy's stomach and heart (reminiscent of the blow Jim had sustained from Fitzsimmons) caused him to double over. Half stooped, McCoy endured a number of thudding uppercuts. Finally, he fell.

Gamely, McCoy struggled to his knees but could raise himself no further. The referee counted him out. When McCoy was picked up and carried to his corner, Jim went over to shake his hand, but McCoy refused him.

The crowd had expected a vigorous encounter, but no one was prepared for the ferocious battle that actually took place. They had anticipated a craftily contested bout, with skillful hand-and footwork by two recognized exponents of scientific boxing. What they witnessed was a modicum of scientific boxing that soon evolved into a merciless exchange of heavy blows, with Jim's furious, two-fisted attacks setting a new standard for ring domination.

To celebrate victory, Jim, Vera, Considine, and friends visited Rector's restaurant, whose patrons seemed more than pleased to be dining in proximity to the admirable ex-champion. Bob Fitzsimmons, accompanied by Weber & Fields, dropped in to congratulate Jim. Giving Jim a hearty handshake, Fitz said, "You're the cleverest man in the world." Jim, somewhat taken aback by the kind reception, proved equally cordial. "And you," he responded, "are the hardest-hitting fellow in the world." Several bottles of wine were opened, and Jim and Fitz "vowed eternal fellowship."

Before the match, wild rumors had run rampant through the boxing community. Though such rumors—usually manipulated by gamblers—almost always surfaced prior to an important contest, the fact that this match was the last before the law prohibiting boxing was to take effect seemed to release particular hostility from those who supported the new law. Predictably, they used the claim of "fix" as rationale for their position. "No longer will pugilism be crooked," exclaimed members of the religious community.

Knowledgeable sporting men knew most of these accusations to hold little weight. McCoy had been working hard to earn a shot at Fitzsimmons, and a good showing against Corbett would garner him the right to challenge Fitz. McCoy had already won four bouts during the year, a decidedly successful prelude to facing Jim. For his part, Jim was looking for another chance to meet Jeffries and he had to prove that his abilities had not been eroded by age, not to mention the grueling life of a professional actor. Both boxers had trained vigorously for the match, touted as a clash between the two most scientific men of the profession. The *New York Times* countered their sensationalistic competitors by verifying the equal-share financial agreement and declared that betting had been minimal because Jim had been established as a two-to-one favorite.

Nonetheless, immediately following the contest, McCoy's wife blew the entire issue beyond control. She publicly stated that she was filing for divorce and, while alleging extreme cruelty by her husband, also declared that the McCoy-Corbett bout had been fixed. That was all the tabloids needed to brandish headlines of "fix," "deception," and "greed" for the next several days. What these newspapers failed to reveal was that McCoy himself

had filed divorce papers against his wife several weeks before the bout, claiming that she had not legally divorced her first husband. Apparently, she had used the allegations of "fix" to retaliate against her husband and put him on the defensive, not to mention into an apparently untenable and compromising position. (It was suggested that her lawyers, the ever-resourceful Howe & Hummel, had initiated the idea.) Apropos the McCoy controversy, the *Times* opined, "hell hath no fury like a woman scorned." For those already convinced that the bout had been fixed, the accusations only served to solidify their already existing beliefs.

In the meantime, although Jim and Vera were often seen together in public, they actually had been separated for more than eight months. Indeed, Jim was continuing his relationship with Margaret Corneille. To this point in time, Vera had made little effort to reclaim Jim or dispute his liaison with the actress. Yet, not surprisingly, when Vera discovered that Jim had been having her followed for months by a detective agency and was planning to travel to England with Corneille, she exploded.

Fully aware of Mrs. McCoy's sensational declaration that the fight had been fixed, Vera now captured headlines by denouncing Jim, confirming Mrs. McCoy's accusation, and adding a few spicy anecdotes of her own to the bubbling stew. She said she too was going to file for divorce, on the grounds of extreme cruelty. (Had Vera consulted with Mrs. McCoy and her lawyers?) Those knowing Vera's nature and volatile temper believed she would do anything to humble Jim, bring him back, and protect her own interests.

Much to Vera's surprise, Jim did in fact leave New York for London, on the steamship *Catania*, with his manager George Considine; Margaret Corneille sailed on the same ship, accompanied by her mother. It was reported that the couple had registered as Mr. & Mrs. Martin, although they slept in separate cabins. Rumor had it that Jim had left a note for Vera, intimating that he would never return. Another rumor confided that Jim had sold his saloon and withdrawn all his money from the bank. When Jim's lawyer, in response, revealed his client's estate holdings, none of these rumors was found to be true.

Now, with the open assistance of Howe & Hummel, Vera filed papers to support her allegations of extreme cruelty. Sporting men generally discredited them as the attempt of a woman to secure revenge. Jim's lawyer, Emanuel Friend, declared in an interview:

> It is not true that Corbett went away to evade service. Any time that I cable him that his presence is necessary here, he will return. I want to say too that Mrs. Corbett does not need to wait until her husband returns to bring suit, if she really intends to bring it at all. I will accept any service for him that she may bring.[9]

Generally, most sporting men discounted the revelations coming from Vera and Mrs. McCoy, suggesting they were merely the "rantings of angry women." Mrs. McCoy went on to make further accusations of what was headlined by the tabloids as "pugilistic crookedness," but her charges now seemed even more outrageous than before and were summarily rejected. When Vera, as if to outdo her sisterly colleague in the proceedings, claimed that the Corbett-Sharkey bout had also been fixed, anti-boxing groups used these new "revelations" to once again "verify" their own position. Vera also declared that Jim was still "out of his mind" due to his parents' deaths and that Mr. Considine, his manager, was leading him astray, as had William Brady. Considine, she claimed, had been primarily responsible

for the "fixing" of both bouts.

Kid McCoy came out briskly denying all charges. He accused both his wife and Vera of trying to grab his and Jim's property and money. In fact, McCoy insisted, he had lost money on the bout. Moreover, to counter his wife's complaint that he was hiding money from her, he claimed he had had to borrow $1,000 for training purposes.

Upon landing at Queenstown, Ireland, Jim, too, denied all charges that the contest had been fixed.

> It is ridiculous to say that my fights with Sharkey and McCoy were fake. They are just lying statements put forward by New Yorkers who have sore heads and lost money on the battle.[10]

When Jim arrived in London, he and Corneille were observed to go their separate ways, he to the Hotel Cecil with Considine, she and her mother to a private hotel in the West End. It was reported that they never saw one another again.

Precipitated by Vera's accusations regarding Considine's managerial decisions, an argument between Jim and Considine ensued. When Considine made derogatory remarks about Vera, Jim fired him and ordered his ex-manager to leave the hotel. Intent now on reconciliation with Vera, he cabled her: "The stories about the woman are false. Come over here quick, darling. I will prove it. I love you only."[11]

Vera's public response showed little sympathy for her husband. She said she had only contempt for Jim and would never forgive him. Further, she expressed confidence in her divorce suit against him. But she had not yet served papers on Jim. When she vowed she would block any property transfers, Jim's lawyer replied by stating calmly that no such transfers had or would take place.

In a surprising, conciliatory move, McCoy dropped the divorce suit against his wife and said he would welcome her back. He also revealed to the press that Jim was returning to the U.S. in ten days to refute the fixing charges and win back Vera. When the patrons of Jim's saloon heard the news, loud cheers echoed on the street.

A cable dispatch from London indicated that Jim was returning by the first available steamer, which happened to be the *Catania*. Jim accused unspecified friends of poisoning Vera's mind against him. He said he pardoned Vera for her accusations about fight-fixing, and he claimed that everyone knew he had not seen Margaret Corneille since arriving in London. Jim's former manager, George Considine, remained in London. As he himself left the city, Jim explained:

> Mr. Considine spoke slightingly of my wife and I am done with him. My principle object in returning to New York in hot haste is to bring action against the newspapers that have published the statements about me, and to vindicate my name.[12]

However, Jim had no cause to seek vindication. The fight-fixing debate had already gone the way of previous such episodes. New York state officials declared that, after an investigation, the allegations were deemed to be unfounded, and official proceedings demonstrated absolutely no collusion between the boxers. The boxing charges quickly disappeared, but the divorce suits continued to generate headlines.

When Jim arrived in New York, no one was waiting to serve him papers. He was spirited away to the Cadillac Hotel and went into seclusion. Meanwhile, Jim's lawyer had been urging Vera to meet with her husband.

That evening, at Rector's restaurant, which conveniently adjoined the hotel, reporters found Jim and Vera together again. Seated with friends, the loving couple were all smiles.

"We have made up," were Jim's first words. "She is all the world to me. I have got my wife back, and I am very happy."

In the interview, Jim acknowledged having had a "spat" with Vera, and also admitted his error in having been seen with—what's her name?—Mademoiselle Corneille. "She (Vera) might have said a lot of things about me, which were uttered in a fit of anger," he went on. "But I am happy now. Let the world say what it may. I came back for one purpose, and that was to rejoin my wife."

When Vera finally met with Jim, she flung herself into his arms and declared that she still loved him. She now apologized for all the charges she had made.

"I don't deny that I made those ugly charges against Jim," she told the press. "I was excited and insanely jealous. I am sorry for what I have done."

Jim and Vera embraced warmly.

As to his victory over McCoy, Jim said: "I will leave that question of the battle being a fake to any one who saw the mill. It was a legitimate fight. I trained hard and won on my merits."

"I don't need to fight," he continued. "I have plenty of money, and made it by honest fighting."

Jim would soon need every penny of it. His boxing reputation may have been restored, indeed enhanced; but his theatrical career was about to be dramatically curtailed.

8. KNOCK DOWN, KNOCK OUT

The year 1900 appeared to be a very good one for the country.

The United States had handily defeated Spain and thereby gained control over the Philippines, Puerto Rico, and Guam. Business was booming. Americans showed increasing interest in new technologies—automobiles, telephones, phonographs, subways, and moving pictures—although they were still considered novelties. Less than 8,000 horseless carriages existed in the entire country and not yet ten miles of concrete roads. One hundred taxi cabs solicited business on New York City streets. There was one telephone for every sixty-six people. Prices were low. One could buy a suit for ten dollars; a sofa for fifteen; a turtleneck sweater for eight cents. For a penny, using a hand crank, one could watch moving pictures in kinetoscope studios. The public seemed upbeat about the nation's future, happy and excited about their personal prospects. Indeed, the dawn of a new century appeared bright and encouraging ... but not for actors and actresses.

"Are you a Rat?"

"No."

"All right, then, come in."

That was the common dialogue of the stage in the fall of 1900. The Theatrical Syndicate had given stern orders that all performers known as "White Rats" and their sympathizers should be excluded from work in the theater.

Syndicate managers sent out notes directed to all actors and actresses who had failed to appear for their scheduled performances the previous evening, when the White Rats union had gone on strike. "You will please call at the theater," the notes read, "and get your baggage."

The strikers were no less adamant and equally occupied. Besides their regular clubrooms, at 114 West Third Street, the White Rats had rented the top floor of the Bon-Ton Music Hall on Twenty-third Street. There they assembled in force. Among the first to arrive were George Fuller Golden, president of the White Rats of America, Fred Stone and Henry Dixey, prime movers of the strike, and James J. Corbett, an active member of two White Rat strike committees. Together, they discussed strategy to be employed against the Syndicate, as well as programming for a large benefit performance to be held the next day.[1]

In June, 1900, E.A. Albee, partner and business manager of the Keith-Albee organization, owners and operators of more than 100 theaters throughout the U.S., had assembled the leading vaudeville managers for a series of meetings in

Boston. These included F.F. Proctor, Hyde & Behman, Kohl and Castle, J.D. Hopkins, Tony Pastor, Weber & Fields, and the new Orpheum company, run by Morris Meyerfield and Martin Beck. Together, these men controlled more than 160 first-class vaudeville houses throughout the country. They now sought to gain control of the entire booking business.

Albee persuaded the managers—except Tony Pastor and Weber & Fields, who were suspicious of Albee's intent—that a centralized theater and booking agency was essential for the continued growth of vaudeville. Of course, actors would no longer need agents, nor would they be allowed to negotiate booking by forcing managers to bid for their services.

Implications for performers were ominous. In order to obtain bookings, they had to join the Association of Vaudeville Managers (A.V.M.), the managers' new organization. In addition, performers would be required to pay a five percent fee for each booking they obtained. If performers chose not to sign up with the A.V.M., they had painfully few other venues to play.

In July, performers woke up to read in the newspapers that a new trust, the A.V.M., would now dictate what theaters they could play in, when they could play them, and at what salary. Suddenly, actors and actresses realized that they needed protection, a defense of their livelihood and independence.

George Fuller Golden, an American actor working in England, had fallen on hard times and was stranded in London. A group of London music hall actors, calling themselves the Water Rats, helped him and his wife return to America. Golden arrived in New York just as the A.V.M. announced their agenda. He wondered why actors in the U.S. could not organize a protective and benevolent society like the British Water Rats.

A month later, eight men met to form what was to become the first U.S. actors' union, the White Rats of America. They included, besides Golden, the famous comedy duo of Dave Montgomery and Fred Stone, Sam Ryan, Tom Lewis, Sam Morton, Mark Murphy, and James F. Dolan. At their second meeting, sixteen actors attended, one of whom was Jim Corbett.

By the third meeting, fifty had joined the group. In three months, more than 400 actors had become members, among them some of the top stage headliners, Nat Wills, George M. Cohan, George Evans, Eddie Foy, Bobby Gaylor, Fred Niblo, John Kernall, Pat Rooney, Billy Van, Gus Williams, and Weber & Fields. The new organization's primary objectives were to protect the actors from managers' avarice and lust for power, preserve their salaries, and build respect for performers in the face of the Syndicate's assault on traditional professional standards and practices.

When the White Rats took a public stand against the A.V.M.—a large ad in the *New York Clipper*—Jim's name was prominent among the list of protesters. In response to this ad, the A.V.M. threatened that no member of the White Rats would obtain a booking from them for the season. The Rats' public challenge became a blacklist sent to every theater manager belonging to the A.V.M.

Like most of the other actors on the list, Jim found himself unable to obtain any kind of a job. His only stage appearance through the remainder of 1900 was at a White Rats benefit at the New York Theater in October. Along with donating $100 to the organization, Jim entertained the crowd with a humorous monologue that included caustic remarks about the Syndicate. Among White Rat members, Jim was one of the few actually earning money at the time, from the operation of his saloon.

As the A.V.M. applied increasing pressure on actors to comply with their demands, conflict with the White Rats accelerated. In early 1901, the Rats began formulating a plan to strike at the heart of the A.V.M., its box office receipts.

Albee and his colleagues wanted to prevent such action, since a strike would mean sizable financial losses for their theaters. They met with Golden and the Rat Board and promised to rescind the five percent commission at their next scheduled meeting. But no date was set for that meeting, nor did the A.V.M. move toward setting one up.

In February, 1901, to demonstrate their collective displeasure with A.V.M. tactics, the White Rats struck, refusing to appear for a Thursday matinee at Keith theaters in all major Eastern cities. The result was chaos in these theaters, which prompted the A.V.M. to fire those actors participating in the strike and to refuse them entry to the theaters, except to pick up their belongings.

To support White Rat members and provide compensation for their actions, a spectacular benefit—the entire performance ran from noon to midnight—was staged at the Academy of Music in New York City, on Sunday, February 25. Participants included De Wolf Hopper, Ezra Kendall, Jim Corbett (in a minstrel skit), Weber & Fields, Maurice Barrymore, and a host of other well-known performers. The benefit proved a rousing success, garnering more than $10,000, as well as sizable support from sympathetic audiences. To schedule future benefits, the Rats leased the Academy of Music for the next ten Sundays, along with theaters in Brooklyn and Philadelphia. To observers, it seemed clear that a major war was erupting between the Syndicate and the White Rats.

The following Sunday, a benefit was held at Koster & Bial's Theater, whose manager then proceeded to turn the theater over to the Rats for an entire week. Jim, Barrymore, Golden, and Gaylor headed the cast of a typical vaudeville show. Quickly, the A.V.M. met with the Rat Board and worked out a truce, promising that the five percent commission would be abolished immediately. Believing they had won their battle over the A.V.M., the White Rats were jubilant.

A *New York Times* headline proclaimed that the "White Rats Strike Ended," but in the fine print it was revealed that, while the commission had indeed been rescinded, the A.V.M. had refused to acknowledge the legitimacy of actors' association. The war continued, relegated now to behind-the-scenes action.

To continue fundraising on behalf of its out-of-work members, the Rats decided to organize a vaudeville company to play in Eastern cities. After much debate, Jim volunteered to head the group. Their first engagement was at the Columbia Theater in Washington, D.C., the only house in the city not under A.V.M. control. The *Clipper*, which seemed to favor the Rats' action, gave a positive review of the show. "The White Rats did not have even standing room left at the Columbia last week."[2]

The following week's engagement in Baltimore was again favorably reported. "The White Rats Vaudeville Co. gave one of the best bills of the season to big business."[3]

When the company returned to New York, they settled in at Koster & Bial's for a five-week run, to early May. Box office returns were outstanding. Not only was the press positively disposed to the actors' situation, but audiences also seemed wholeheartedly in agreement. Naively, the Rats believed they had won a major victory over A.V.M. forces. Yet most of them on the blacklist were still blocked from securing bookings.

Secretly, the five percent commission was not abolished. While the Rats celebrated, the A.V.M. approached individual members of the Rats, those appearing to be the most vulnerable, and offered them long-term contracts to book through the Syndicate. At the same time, the A.V.M. manipulated audiences, stirring up resentment toward the White Rats for denying the public their accustomed entertainments.

At the conclusion of the Koster & Bial's engagement, Jim announced he was going to Europe for the summer, but he later had to cancel the trip when he found he could not obtain any bookings for the fall season. Instead, he stayed in New York to help out the Rats, donating a percentage of his saloon proceeds each month, and when Rats members visited Corbett's, they could count on being treated to free drinks and snacks.

By the middle of 1901, the A.V.M. had reduced the White Rats to token opposition. White Rat activity was now reduced to infrequent benefits and social gatherings. Nor did fund-raising efforts collect enough to maintain all of their out-of-work members. Jim proposed to organize a baseball team to play "the big cities," competing against the best local team in the afternoon and presenting a vaudeville show at night. The idea was never implemented because members could not agree whether the ball game ought to be played straight or burlesque, in stage costume.

Benefits held in August and September were designed to help unemployed actors, but it had become obvious to the Rat Board that their membership was rapidly declining. Nor were the benefits raising much money, as audiences seemed to be tiring of the actors' plight. Indeed, it would take more than seven years before the White Rats gained renewed respect from audiences.

Throughout the remainder of 1901, Jim continued to participate in benefits, though now infrequent, for the White Rats. He also spent a good deal of time at his saloon, working hard to improve the business. While other former well-known boxer's saloons had failed—John L. Sullivan's a few blocks away and Peter Maher's near Union Square—Corbett's seemed to manifest magnetic attraction for both the theatrical and boxing crowds. At the same time, Jim renewed his ring training by working out at the new gymnasium run by Professor Walter Watson—the coach who had originally taught Jim at the Olympic Club fifteen years previously—and by assisting heavyweight Gus Ruhlin prepare for his match against Jim Jeffries in November. Jim not only gave Ruhlin counsel on how to box Jeffries, but also sparred with him frequently. The Ruhlin-Jeffries bout was to take place November 15, at the Mechanic's Pavilion in San Francisco, and would be Jim's first visit home since his parents' death.

Upon landing at San Francisco's downtown dock, Jim and Vera were met by a crowd of admirers and escorted to the Baldwin Hotel. Cheers greeted their entrance to the hotel and were echoed every time they appeared in the dining room. A visit to the Corbett home on Hayes Street found family members in good health. The unmarried daughters had moved back home; Joe and Tom were running the livery business; and Harry was still very much involved in the local boxing community, at the same time continuing to operate his poolhall and betting establishment. But Jim felt a hush, a kind of reserve, that seemed to have enveloped the once-vibrant Corbett household. It affected him too; he visited the house only once more while in town.

Jim remained busy with Ruhlin's training regimen, visiting the boxer's camp almost daily and sparring with him on occasion. Ruhlin appeared as ready as he could be to meet Jeffries, but most observers questioned whether that would be enough for him to last ten rounds against the champion. In an interview, Jim dutifully stated his belief that Ruhlin had a chance to beat Jeffries, but his comments were discounted as mere wishful thinking. Bettors favored Jeffries two to one.

The match attracted more than 7,000 people. There were two preliminary bouts: bantamweights Joe Fields and "Spider" Welsh fought a grueling battle, Welsh knocking out Fields in the sixth round, the audience loudly cheering the action. The second bout was a dull affair, spectators shouting and joking as the boxers traded little more than diffident feints. When the contest was called a draw, no one disputed the decision; instead, they hissed the hapless boxers out of the ring.

Before the main event, a crew of carpenters stretched taut a new canvas across the ring, while moving picture people set up lights to prepare for filming the bout. Many ringside spectators complained when the light stands were placed directly in front of their seats. Announcements to refrain from smoking, so as to clear the air enough for the camera to record the action in the ring, were greeted with belligerent boos.

Then the auditorium lights were extinguished, and only those lights surrounding the ring illuminated the site. Under cover of darkness, two women, heavily veiled, the only representatives of the "fairer sex" allowed in the house, slipped unnoticed into ringside seats.

A moment later, Jeffries vaulted into the ring. Wearing a small cap to shade his eyes from the intense lights, he stood casually against the ropes chewing gum and chatting with friends in box seats. Then, Jeffries's seconds entered the ring, followed by Ruhlin and his seconds, who received only a faint echo of the greeting afforded the champion. The boxers were introduced, shed their robes, and retreated to their corners, ready for the gong.

At the end of the fifth round, the toss of a sponge into the ring ended the one-sided contest. Ruhlin had given up.

From the opening of round one, Ruhlin continually backed away in a fruitless attempt to avoid Jeffries's blows. There was no question the champion was bigger and stronger; he stalked Ruhlin "like a big bus." Before the end of the first round, Jeffries had landed innumerable punishing blows. Already the crowd knew Ruhlin was a beaten man.

In the fourth, Jeffries got serious, intent on finishing Ruhlin. The press described the scene as "a fight between a bear and a mastiff." Staggered and tottering, Ruhlin was helpless. The crowd yelled for Jeffries to knock him out.

The fifth round began with Ruhlin desperate to evade Jeffries's powerful blows. But the champion staggered him again. Ruhlin fell to the canvas, got up, clinched, was felled again, yet saved by the bell. Lurching pathetically to his corner, the erstwhile challenger collapsed into the arms of his seconds. Someone threw a sponge into the ring. Quickly, the referee stepped to the center and declared Jeffries the winner. There were few cheers for him, the crowd disgusted by the entire contest. Next day, the *Chronicle* summed up the crowd's beliefs.

> People had come from all over the country for the sake of seeing a fight, and they were rewarded by seeing Jim Jeffries in action, a sight that they could see for prices from $1 to $1.50 by attending one of his theatrical performances.[4]

Jeffries made spectators feel even worse about the contest when he stated: "I suppose some of the people were a bit disappointed in the fight but, candidly, Gus was no match for me."

While Ruhlin and his followers spoke in awe of Jeffries's power, Jim just shook his head in knowledgeable tribute to the man whom he had skillfully fought off for twenty-three rounds.

Upon Jim's return to New York, he visited Watson's gym, where old friend Joe Choynski was in training. Like theatrical audiences enjoying one of Jim's compelling monologues, everyone at the gym halted their workouts to listen intently as he recounted the details of the Ruhlin-Jeffries slaughter.

By the beginning of 1902, the White Rat confrontation with the A.V.M. had deteriorated to where most members had resigned because they badly needed employment. Confident they had repressed the Rats' revolt, the A.V.M. pressed even harder to gain total control over booking, and were easily succeeding in reaching their goal. Nonetheless, along with the core of original protesters, Jim continued to stage benefits to obtain funds for the organization, even though its cause now seemed hopeless. Realistically, Jim knew that the more he campaigned on behalf of the White Rats, the less likely he would be to secure bookings. Yet, never one to quit a fight, he went down swinging.

The final Rats benefit was a sorry affair, the theater less than half full, the applause half-hearted. Everyone realized that the curtain was falling on the actors' revolt against the Syndicate ... and the actors had lost.

Two fund-raising events for the newly organized Actors Home of America, a group whose purpose was to assist aged, infirm, and indigent actors, again found Jim devotedly aiding his theatrical colleagues. William Brady and De Wolf Hopper had arranged the benefits, but it was Hopper who asked Jim to participate, by presenting one of his new monologues.

Monologue formats on the popular stage were not new, having been employed successfully by medicine showmen, carnival barkers, and minstrels in the middle nineteenth century. The monologue was an act complete in itself, built around a theme or story line, flexible enough to modify depending on audience makeup, separate enough to be presented easily and compatibly in either variety or vaudeville format. Monologues usually featured dialect speeches (as in minstrelsy), parodies of orators, or a patter of jokes, usually presented in a bizarre fashion to exaggerate the outrageousness of the act. As the technique became more sophisticated, presented by increasingly experienced vaudevillians, the method grew more polished, the topics more personal and timely, and the pace of the performance more designed to capture and hold an audience. Many of the best monologues really amounted to dialogues between the adept performer and an absent, imagined participant, with the performer playing multiple roles. The technique held great appeal for better-class vaudeville audiences, who could easily relate to this method of story-telling.

Jim could call upon two excellent sources of material: his boxing career and his experiences in the theater, both of which were found to be highly compelling and entertaining subjects. He included enough humor—a good deal of it self-effacing—and "inside exposes" to hold audiences' attention and create a sense of camaraderie with them. Jim's resonant voice, easy-going manner, and relaxed self-assurance invariably won over any audience. Compared to ensemble performances, such one-on-one "conversations" helped to increase identity with and intimacy between the performer and the audience. Even with absent vaudeville bookings, in a short period of time, Jim became recognized as one of the top monologists on the popular stage. And, judging from press coverage, there was no doubt that his long-standing reputation as a sport's hero ably contributed to his success.

Very likely due to Jim's activities on behalf of the White Rat cause, De Wolf Hopper, then head of the Lambs' Club, an exclusive group of celebrated theatrical professionals, nominated Jim for membership. Accompanied by a loud "hip-hip-hooray," Jim was voted in unanimously. A week later, he appeared in the first of many annual Lambs' Gambols, presenting a monologue on the ultimate dramatic challenge, performing to an empty theater. It would prove to be his final stage appearance for three months.

The summer of 1902 was a quiet one for the Corbetts. Jim spent most weekdays at the saloon, sharing the latest jokes and gossip with his customers. He and Vera also devoted time to entertaining destitute children in Bayside, Jim frequently taking the kids to baseball games. An old friend, now manager of the Morrison Theater in Rockaway Beach, persuaded Jim to head a vaudeville cast for two weeks in July. Jim jumped at the opportunity to perfect his monologues before a paying audience. The *Clipper* reported that Jim was cordially received.

On July 25, in San Francisco, Jim Jeffries knocked out Bob Fitzsimmons in eight rounds, before an enthusiastic crowd cheering one of their two hometown boxing heroes. With the loss, Fitzsimmons forfeited his last claim upon the heavyweight championship. Unlike previous big-fight crowds, this one behaved in an orderly fashion. The Bay Area bench and bar were well represented, and visitors from other parts of California displayed by their attire they too represented the better classes. Many heavily-veiled women were seated in the boxes; but their presence was passed over, without the usual demonstrations of disapproval. Illumination from fourteen arc lamps suspended about the ring provided sufficient light for the boxers, as well as for the audience. These were the only lights in the house.

As the contestants were being announced to the crowd, Harry Corbett passed a note to the referee. Having glanced at it, he turned to the crowd and loudly proclaimed, "Jim Corbett has sent a challenge to fight the winner." The audience applauded in approval.

Jim had wired Harry to make the dramatic challenge. Reluctantly, Harry agreed, but he attempted to discourage Jim about his ability to beat either man these days. Jim seemed fully aware of the odds against his winning, but he knew this was likely his last chance to regain the title.

When both boxers shed their robes in the ring, the crowd murmured its admiration of Jeffries's physique. He appeared to have gained weight, yet his muscles flexed firm. A recent tan enhanced the brawn of his appearance. From the opening bell, Jeffries seized the offensive, stalking his opponent in his characteristic crouch, launching a barrage of punches. Relegated to counterpunching, Fitzsimmons was forced to back away.

In the eighth round, two fast, powerful blows floored Fitzsimmons as he was retreating and off balance. The crowd cheered Jeffries's victory, but their casual demeanor suggested that they had assumed that he would best Fitzsimmons. Most bettors had proven even more certain, giving odds of 10 to 4 in Jeffries's favor.

Immediately after the match, Jeffries told Harry that he was not entirely sure he wanted to meet Jim. Brady, however, had no such hesitation. No doubt sensing another box-office bonanza, Brady told Harry that he was interested in setting up a match as quickly as they could. And why not stage the contest right there in San Francisco, both men's hometown?

In the meantime, Jim's friends at the

Lambs' Club were intent on getting him a job during the coming season. His leading role in the struggle against the Syndicate had been duly noted, and his tireless efforts to raise funds for the White Rats should be rewarded. Jules Delmar, manager of a vaudeville company and foe of Klaw & Erlanger, was in the process of hiring a company of independent performers, many of whom had been blacklisted by the Syndicate. Obtaining Jim's services as headliner would go a long way toward making the company a very attractive crowd-pleaser. Delmar and Jim met at the Lambs' clubhouse, and Jim signed a contract for the entire 1902-03 season. He was offered $20,000, plus travel expenses for himself and Vera. Jim also won his brother Tom a job with the company as "stage manager," although Tom had no experience in the theater.

To say that Jim was excited about his new assignment would be to understate his absolute delight at the turnaround in his career. Within days of the signing, he and Vera bought a home in Bayside, Long Island, and moved their entire household there before departing on the tour.

Called "The Empire Show," the production comprised familiar acts of acrobats, singers, comedians, trained dogs, jugglers, exotic dancers, and Jim, in the headliner spot, performing his monologues. The company exemplified those found in high-class vaudeville, their members united by having been banned by the Syndicate. This common misfortune lent a "bounce" to their performance as they toured, since the press frequently emphasized their opposition to the "autocratic forces in theater." Of course, such companies could play only available, independent houses, the managers of which themselves exploited the disagreement to box-office advantage.

With James J. Corbett as the star attraction, the season opened in Milwaukee,

at the Davidson Theater, on September 28. "Jim made his vaudeville debut," the Milwaukee newspaper reported, "and the usual happy condition of affairs ruled at this box office." Encouraged by this reception, the company was booked into Chicago for two weeks, the first at the Olympic Theater, the second at the Haymarket, both still owned by Jim's old friend from World's Fair days, Will Davis. The *Tribune* noted Jim's contributions to "big houses. James J. Corbett caught popular fancy last week with his interesting anecdotes. The bill as a whole was received with favor."[5]

While in Chicago, at a dinner given in his honor by local sportsmen, Jim announced to the attentive audience:

> I am to meet Jeffries in May next year and, although you will not believe it—for even my brother does not—I confidently feel that I can whip the present champion. I am in almost perfect condition at present, having trained all summer, and on my theatrical trip I shall continue to train.[6]

And Jim went on to say, possibly trying to convince himself more than his listeners: "I believe in my heart that I can defeat him and shall not think otherwise until I have been counted out for the second time in the ring with the present champion."

He was loudly cheered. Yet a reporter covering the dinner wondered whether Jim had just tendered a prophetic commentary on his waning boxing career.

Jim's monologues consisted of personal experiences in boxing and theater, as well as anecdotes concerning stage celebrities. As Jim continued to perfect his delivery and stage presence, the topics were increasingly well-received. Two bits offer examples of his repartee.[7]

> After my return from Europe my manager got out a big poster; and on this poster was

an exact likeness of all the crowned heads of Europe in their royal costumes. There were the Czar of Russia, the late Queen of England, and all the other crowned heads standing in a group … and a picture of me, standing in the center of this group, shaking hands with Gladstone. My manager's object, of course, was to indicate that I had met all of these people over there, which I hadn't. I was looking at this poster one day in a little town; and two farmers came along, stopped, and looked at this picture, and one of them said: "By Gosh, that fellow Corbett must be a great actor as well as a great fighter." "What makes you think so?" said the other one. "See what a big company he carries."

In the little towns, some of the rubes didn't even know what the word "vaudeville" meant. I heard two fellows talking one day. One said: "Going to the Opry House tonight?" The other answered, "What's the play?" "Vaudeville." The other rube said: "No, I don't think I'll go. I read the book."

Throughout the remainder of 1902, the tour routed "The Empire Show" to all major cities in the Midwest, as far west as St. Louis, then traveled East for the Christmas holidays. Box-office receipts were good, and the company received excellent reviews at each engagement. An added feature of the show was the unexpected appearance of other well-known performers, like juggler W.C.

CHICAGO OPERA HOUSE.
CONTINUOUS VAUDEVILLE.
WEEK OF MAY 30.

JAMES J. CORBETT
In Amusing Anecdotes of His Interesting Career.
RUSSELL BROTHERS & CO.
Presenting "A Romance of New Jersey."
HOWARD & EMERSON
Comic and Melodic Burlesques on Popular Operas.
HARRIET AVERY STRAKOSCH
Famous Grand Opera Prima Donna Soprano.
GARVIE & THOMPSON
In the Screaming Farce, "Wanted, a Partner."
JOE J. SULLIVAN & CO.
Introducing "The Coal Man," a Roaring Comedy.
PHIL & NETTIE PETERS
Clever Musical and Talking Comedians.
ROBERT CARTER & CO.
Making Merry With "The Wire Mr. Conn."
PIERCE & MAIZIE
Beautifully Costumed Singing and Dancing Act.
LIZZIE WILSON
Delightfully Entertaining Dialect Comedienne.
3—THE CAMPBELLS—3
Musical Specialties and Comedy Bits.
LUCY BYRON
In a Dazzling Dancing Act.
FISHER AND JOHNSON
Comedy Cycle Experts.
BARNEY FIRST
Hebrew Humorist and Impersonator.
THE KINODROME
Sensational Moving Pictures.

Prices, 15 - 25 - 35 - 50 - 75 Cents
Order by Telephone. Main 3380.

A typical vaudeville bill for Corbett's traveling company and an excellent example of the makeup of a vaudeville troupe in 1903. Continuous vaudeville amounted to three appearances a day for all performers, starting in the early afternoon and continuing until late in the evening.

Fields in Cincinnati and, in Indianapolis, singer Nora Bayes. By this time, advertising and promotion for the company featured Jim as the undisputed star of the show. When they visited Eastern cities in early 1903, business had reached and sustained SRO proportions. In Albany, for example: "The Empire Show, headed by James J. Corbett, gave the strongest show of the season, to capacity business at every performance."[8]

In Toronto, "big business ruled." In Philadelphia, the company was acknowledged as "one of the strongest vaudeville organizations on the road," with Jim heralded as "the contributor" to excellent business. The season closed in early April at Hurtig & Seamon's Musical Hall, in Harlem, to enthusiastic, SRO audiences. The *Clipper* reported:

> Bills of compelling attractiveness obtain the desired results at this house, the one offered this week being especially so. It is headed by James J. Corbett, and boasts a strong cast. [9]

On the last evening of the company's surprising and highly gratifying season, Jim held a party at his saloon. Cheers and sobs filled the house until the early hours, as participants recalled the triumphs, funny episodes, and numerous improvisations that had made what would otherwise have been a long, desultory tour, instead, interesting and richly rewarding. In closing, Reynard the ventriloquist, speaking through his wooden-headed family, reminded company members of their victory over the Syndicate blacklist that had, not long before, threatened their careers.

In a move that surprised everyone, Jim decided to sell his saloon. It had indeed helped him while his life was unsettled, but now that he had returned to full-time employment, a headliner who commanded top billing and top salary, he had no time to devote to the business. Since he had spent more than seven months on the road, the saloon had definitely suffered. It seemed clear that, without his presence, business could not be sustained. The prospect of many profitable years touring the country also helped Jim to decide.

"Corbett Looks Better Than When He Went Away," headlined the *Chronicle* upon Jim's arrival in San Francisco. When Jim alighted from the overland train, every one of his old friends remarked at his "younger" appearance. Confidently, Jim exclaimed to the awaiting press, "I feel just as well as I look!" And I will surprise you still more," he boasted, "when I am stripped for work in the gymnasium." Still, one reporter noting the deep lines in his face, reminded readers that Jim was now thirty-six years old, an age well beyond that of champion Jeffries.

Representatives of the Olympic Club met Jim at the train to extend him an invitation to use their rooms for training. Jim readily accepted, although he planned to move to a real training site in a few weeks, after fulfilling theater engagements in San Francisco and Los Angeles.

For two weeks, Jim presented his monologues at San Francisco's Orpheum Theater, heading a vaudeville bill that filled the house every night. At the close of his engagement, in answer to questions about his chances against Jeffries, he told the crowd:

> Every time I stepped into the ring I have been confident of winning, but not so much as I am now. I cannot figure how I am going to lose, unless, of course, Jeff manages to land one of those swings on a vital point. He may do that in the first round, and it may come in the last, but I know better what to expect than I did before. I really believe that I will knock Jeffries out unless he is a lot better than he was when we clashed before.[10]

The audience cheered his speech heartily, but there remained no little doubt regarding his more boastful statements.

When Jim returned from his Los Angeles engagement at the end of May, he and Vera, along with Jim's training entourage, settled in at Croll's Ranch, Alameda, to begin intensive workouts for the upcoming encounter. A few days later, Jeffries and Jim met to sign the articles of agreement for the contest. Jeffries had Billy Delaney (Jim's old trainer) and Joe Egan to back him up, while Jim spoke for himself, with brother Tom assisting on disputed points. James Coffroth, from the Yosemite Club, sponsors of the bout, stood ready to arbitrate any deep disagreements, but none surfaced. The meeting was held in Harry Corbett's back room. Some observers at Harry's hoping for a "lively tilt" between the boxers, were disappointed by the amiable meeting.

The men agreed to split the purse: seventy-five percent for the winner, twenty-five percent for the loser or share in the same proportion, seventy percent of the gross receipts, whichever amount proved larger. The Yosemite Club agreed to furnish a twenty-four-foot ring, as Marquis of Queensberry rules dictated, although most contests in San Francisco in recent years had been staged in smaller rings. A jocular debate concluded the meeting when a question arose about who should pay the referee. Coffroth said he was willing to make the payment if he could select the referee. Both Jeffries and Corbett refused the offer, suggesting the referee's salary should be deducted directly from the gross receipts. Evidently satisfied with the results of the meeting, the attendees dispersed.

Through June and July, both men worked hard at their training quarters. Reporters were allowed to visit a number of times each week, but few comments were made by the boxers, so as to avoid any press manipulation of information and "attributed" comments. Both men agreed to keep such opportunities to a minimum,

having often been the victims of falsely sensational "headlines" in the past. Each Sunday, open houses were held for visitors who wished to observe sparring matches and cheer their favorites.

Jim was training hard, running twelve miles in the morning, exercising and sparring in the afternoon, resting in the evening. He maintained a special diet, supplemented by his usual twelve glasses of spring water every day. By comparison, Jeffries, under Delaney's direction, maintained an easier regimen, exercising in the morning, resting during the heat of the day, and sparring later. Delaney believed that his boxer needed neither long runs in the mountains nor special diets, since he was "a model gladiator, without the physical culture others needed." Having served as Jim's trainer some years earlier, Delaney was preparing Jeffries to meet his opponent's likely challenges.

Only two weeks before the contest, the boxing community was startled to read in the local newspaper that Jim was rehearsing to play the role of Charles, the wrestler, in Shakespeare's "As You Like It," to be presented in an open-air performance, August 1 and 2, at San Francisco's Sutro Park. Nance O'Neill, a nationally-known legitimate actress, was to play Rosalind, opposite Jim. The role demanded considerable rehearsal, noted the press. Meanwhile, what was Jim doing to meet a tough fighter like Jeffries? A reporter suggested that Jim seemed more committed to theater than to boxing. No one came forward to dispute his observation.

During the last week before the bout, Jim abandoned his runs and heavy sparring, choosing to concentrate on strengthening his stomach muscles (no doubt recalling Fitzsimmons) and increasing his speed (his advantage in the previous Jeffries match). Jim weighed 186 pounds and expected to weigh the same at match time.

People watching him train believed he had a good chance to beat Jeffries, at least give him a strong fight. Two-and-a-half to one odds in favor of Jeffries held steady, however, supplemented by an increasing number of bets on how long Jim could stay with Jeffries, as in their earlier bout. Then it was reported that Jim had contracted a slight cold from performing "As You Like It;" and the odds changed, strongly in favor of Jeffries. In another announcement that disheartened Corbett admirers, his trainers idly mentioned that they were tending to a swelling between the fingers of Jim's right hand. Jim himself discounted any problems, flatly stating he was more than ready to meet Jeffries.

Odds continued to run strongly in favor of Jeffries, although there was little actual wagering. Corbett money was short, since most people conceded him no chance of winning. Further, Corbett devotees were somewhat shaken when they heard Jim admit he was not gambling on his own chances. "The glory of winning will compensate me," he was reported to have said. A comment that did little to diminish their concerns.

Seat sales opened a week before the match. All of the ten dollar seats were sold quickly, and buyers were forced to take whatever they could get. Coffroth predicted the amount of money collected would come close to the most ever for a championship contest. Moreover, the number of persons attending would likely be the largest in the history of boxing. Veteran Ed Graney was selected referee. Jeffries's forces worried that, if the match went the limit, Graney would give the victory to Jim, since they were longtime friends. Jeffries indicated he had no such concerns about the outcome.

On the day before the bout, both boxers arrived in Oakland. When Jeffries swung off the train, he danced a few steps and was immediately surrounded by a crowd of friends who came to welcome him. The champion looked healthy, strong, and happy. He claimed to weigh 225 pounds.

"People will see me faster than I have been for a couple of years," Jeffries said. "I walked after Corbett at New York. This time I will be on the run after him."

In contrast, Jim traveled to Oakland in secrecy, with no one aware he had arrived until he and Vera were seen checking into their hotel. As was his pre-fight habit, Jim went to bed early. Jeffries attended the theater, chatted with friends over a midnight snack, and did not get to bed until after 1:00 A.M. Jim arose at dawn on match day; Jeffries did not wake until 10:00 A.M. and enjoyed the company of many admirers. Jim spent the day quietly and in seclusion, with brothers Joe, Frank, Tom, and Harry. Joe had borrowed a month's salary ($500) from his Los Angeles baseball team to put on Jim. Frank had obtained a vacation from his position at City Hall to attend the match. Tom and Harry showed their devotion by claiming "an abiding faith in Jim's ability to beat the champion." All four planned to be at ringside to cheer for Jim.

Newspaper reports on the day of the contest claimed "both fighters feel sure of success," but astute observers believed Jeffries would win easily. Jeffries boasted "I do not expect to have much trouble with him." In reply, Jim stated, "Why should I worry? I have everything to win and nothing to lose."

According to enthusiasts, no sharper contrast in styles had ever been presented in the ring. Jeffries was a "brute" fighter, with a tremendous physique and overwhelming strength. He was stolid and taciturn; nor had any man ever knocked him out. Jim was a highly skillful boxer, a dancer in and out, his arms and legs in constant motion, able to evade hard punches. Their conclusion: Jeffries might win in any round, with a single blow enough to end the affair; Corbett could hope to do no more than gain a decision at the end of twenty rounds, if he lasted that long. Muscle would overcome science.

The largest crowd that ever witnessed a boxing match in San Francisco were poised for what they believed would be "the battle of the best." Railroad magnates sat next to bank tellers, who had forfeited a month's salary to sit close to the ring. Though the audience was filled with Jeffries admirers, it was Jim who received the majority of their applause and for whom the crowd rooted from beginning to end.

Jeffries arrived in the ring first, stripped off his robe, and patiently waited in his corner. Jim slipped through the ropes, wearing a robe that resembled an ulster. A *Chronicle* reporter described the scene.

> Jim, who was known as a "massive" champion in the days when he held the title, looked like a stripling beside Jeffries. His chest looked weak and puny next to the champion. His legs resembled birch saplings next to weather-beaten oak.[11]

As the men met in the center of the ring, a hush fell over the crowd.

The bell sounded, the men advanced, glove smacked glove, and the battle was on. It seemed as if the crowd was holding its collective breath in anticipation of what was about to take place.

In the end, however, Jim simply could not make it. No one really believed that he would, but, disappointingly, he ended farther from the mark than anyone had expected. For nine rounds, a younger man, stronger, "built like a cruiser," beat down and ultimately crushed an older, more slender contender. In the tenth, the immense youth caught the older veteran with one of the most terrific clouts the latter had ever received in the ring. The *Chronicle*, describing Jim's boxing demise, said:

It was a great spectacle, and a great fight in everything but evenness. The Jeffries that toed the scratch last night was a better, faster, more scientific Jeffries. The Corbett who faced him was a Corbett worn out, past his time. The old motions were there—the advance and retreat, the will-o-the-wisp dance around the ring, but the speed, the lithe, easy motion was gone. And once more youth was served.[12]

Two things were apparent from the first: Corbett was nervous; and Jeffries was going to play no waiting game, going after Jim "like a locomotive." Each jab Jim threw into Jeffries's face, the crowd shouted encouragement. But instead of showing his superior speed, Jim seemed to be relying on strength rather than cleverness, coming at Jeffries, hitting and holding his ground rather than slipping away. In response, Jeffries only shook his head, smiled, and came on again.

In the fourth round, Jeffries landed a hard right into Jim's body. He went down, rolled over, recovered, and came up at the count of nine, calling on all his cleverness and savvy to last out the round. In truth, he seemed a beaten man. In the sixth, Jim tried to bore in as before, but a stiff punch to the jaw floored him again for a nine count.

Yet, just when the hopes of Jim's admirers seemed futile, he came back with characteristic brilliance, the final, expiring flicker of his courageous artistry. It was hit and get away, duck and dance—the inimitable Corbett of old, his style designed to wear down the opponent. Jim hit Jeffries two and three blows to the head and body, each time escaping all of Jeffries's swings. Still, while Jim was carrying the action, his blows themselves were weak and Jeffries continued to rush. The crowd was shrieking and howling its approval, seeing once again Jim's old, familiar moves. What would Jeffries do, they wondered, to retaliate?

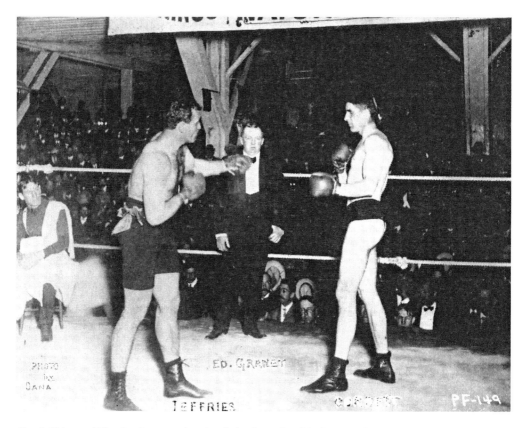

Jim Jeffries and Jim Corbett meeting for their championship bout on August 14, 1903, in San Fran-
cisco. Jeffries was at his peak, Jim a shadow of his former self. Jim was badly beaten and retired from
the ring. Although decisively defeated, Jim gracefully maintained his status as a public hero. (San
Francisco History Center, San Francisco Public Library)

The actual end of the bout came at the close of the ninth round, just as the gong sounded. Jeffries got in a sharp blow to Jim's body and he staggered to his corner. When the tenth round began, Jim came out flat and listless; he seemed to have no steam remaining. In another rush, Jeffries connected with a smashing left over Jim's heart, and he went down. Surprisingly, Jim staggered up again, only to be met by a terrific right to the jaw. It was over, and many minutes before Jim regained his senses.

The house was on its feet with a loud combination of cheering and groaning. Jeffries returned to his corner and stood there taciturn, a proud professional who had done a good day's work. On the floor,

the shining star of the fistic world, who had changed the sport forever at New Orleans, eleven years before, had set for good. The cleverest man the ring had ever seen had fought his final battle. While Jim had made a courageous attempt, he sustained a merciless beating. No matter how hard he had trained, Jim proved unable to inject sufficient vitality into a nearly thirty-seven-year-old body. It was apparent to the crowd from the first that the bout was only a question of how long, never a question of which man would win. When the referee proclaimed Jeffries still champion, the crowd let out no more than a mild, perfunctory cheer. To the crowd, the wrong man had won. And the end was too pitiful to allow for much enthusiasm.

Gross receipts amounted to over $62,000, the third largest in history. The boxers received seventy percent, more than $43,000. Jeffries earned $32,800; Jim got $10,900. Both also earned some royalty money from the sale of souvenirs.

Seated at ringside, Joe and Frank were stunned by the result; Harry and Tom were seen in tears. Vera, listening in the Corbett's hotel room to round-by-round reports of the bout, sat quietly and sadly as it became increasingly apparent that her husband was beaten.

Later, in his dressing room, Jim was in physical anguish. A hot bath and steam-room did nothing to reduce the pain of the body blows he had endured. Three times he attempted to dress himself. Finally succeeding, he went with Harry to a restaurant. When Jim arrived at the hotel, Vera had already gone to sleep. Totally exhausted, mentally and physically, Jim fell asleep in an easy chair.

Those who saw Jim the next morning reported that "he had aged ten years." The lines in his face were accentuated by pain and disappointment. His swollen eyes and mouth gave him a grotesque expression. Deep grief could be read in his eyes, and he still seemed dazed by his loss. His sorrowful talk brought tears to his intimates.

"I made a game fight, didn't I?" he queried each friend who came by with a word of sympathy. And when they grasped his hand, he said, "I fought all there was in me, but it was no use. When I was knocked down, I simply had to get up for the sake of my friends and my good name." At the end of each conversation, he repeated the hesitant question, "And I did make a game fight, didn't I?"

Throughout the days following the contest, Jim maintained his belief that, while he had been defeated, he had not been disgraced. "I staked my all on what I believed I could do, and I was wrong," he admitted sadly. Newspapers seemed to agree. Jeffries himself acknowledged that he had shared the pity of the audience when it became apparent that Jim had no chance to gain the verdict. "I would rather not have thrown that right into the stomach to finish the affair, but I was there to win." Jeffries further declared that he had had no lust for inflicting punishment on an old friend and mentor.

A week after the bout, Jim and Vera left for the East; and Jim appeared quite upbeat about returning to the stage. "My popularity does not seem to have waned on account of my loss to Jeffries. My booking agent wired me to the effect that my season was practically filled at the same houses I played last year, and at advanced prices." In a moment of self-deprecating Irish humor, he added, "A fellow is entitled to some credit for going into the ring with that monster."

On August 31, Jim renewed his theatrical season, to SRO audiences, at the Highlands Theater, in St. Louis, offering them some amusing and revealing stories about his loss to Jeffries. At every performance, audiences gave him standing ovations.

9. TOUR DE FORCE

In the early 1890s, when vaudeville performers toured extensively across the country, they were often confronted by boardinghouse signs that emphatically declared: No dogs or actors allowed!

"Jumps," usually a train trip to the next engagement, were wearisome, tedious, and suspenseful; actors often wondered whether they would get to the next town in time. Travel from Baltimore to Washington, D.C., a journey of forty-three miles, took two hours; Pittsburgh to Cincinnati required seventeen, if the train was on time.

During those years, more than 4,000 actors and actresses crawled across the states and territories, providing entertainment to even the smallest towns. Plain wooden-slat seats or, for added comfort, seats covered with prickly velour, provided only minimal opportunity for rest or relaxation. It was an era of "junctions," which contributed to broken-sleep train changes and long waits in dim, cold, dull waiting rooms.

An actor chose a hotel or boardinghouse nearest the station; these were usually cheaper and eliminated the expense of hiring a hack. Boardinghouses tended to offer more comfort, when actors were allowed entrance and, most importantly, provided meals. Accommodations were simple: bed, dresser with mirror, one ceiling light bulb to illuminate the room, a frayed area rug, a porcelain pitcher and wash pan. Since reputable hostelries did not accept actors, most performers spent their touring lives in faded, worn, often dirty rooms, disgraced with sagging, and lumpy beds, few closets, and no bath.

Food was always problematic; actors had to quickly cultivate an iron-clad digestive system. They ate whatever they could get, whenever they could get it. Nor could an actor afford to fall sick. In those days, no play meant no pay. Even when they were ill, actors continued to perform, for fear the doctor or prescribed medication would make the ailment worse.

Arriving at the next engagement, an actor immediately went to the theater, to get acquainted with the particular stage and any problems it might pose for the act. At the same time, handy emergency exits were located, to protect against the fearsome, ever-present possibility of fire.

Dressing rooms were usually found in the basement. It was best to take a room near the boiler, at least, one would be warm in winter, though sweltering in costume during the summer. Performers washed up in communal troughs, one for each sex, if running water was available. The usual naked bulb hung from the ceiling, making it difficult to apply makeup in front of the pock-marked mirror. There were never enough nails upon which to hang clothes, so, when two or more shared a room, clothing was piled on every available surface. Often, accumulated rubbish from the previous company still littered the floors. More often than not, these less than salutary conditions existed in even the better vaudeville houses. Yet, however bad their latest circumstances, actors had likely experienced worse.

Cleanliness was very important and very hard to maintain. An actor had to present a good appearance, both on and off the stage, to minimize the prejudices people held against the profession. Sundays were wash days. Performers usually carried a bag of fuller's earth with them; rubbed over clothing, the absorbent clay extracted grease and other soil from clothing, giving it a clean-looking, if misleading, sheen.

Because they were considered "odd" or different, actors rarely had contact with local citizens. Townspeople were often surprised to find that actors did not resemble the characters they played on stage. For a few, fleeting hours, performers became the best-known people in town, but they were also the loneliest. Actors found socialization easier than did actresses. The men, at least, could visit after-show saloons and enjoy the company of locals.

An actor's life in the late 19th century was demanding, grueling, punishing, and often frightening. One's own survival was paramount; it signified the opportunity to sign-up for the following season. If an actor could "troupe"—showcase his or her talents, help the show, support colleagues, and lift the spirits of audiences—he or she might court success.

The odds against it, however, were formidable.

When Jim began his theatrical career in William Brady's melodrama, "After Dark," he knew little of what theater life was like. It took him only a few weeks to find out, and he seriously considered quitting the stage to return to the relatively safe and secure confines of the gymnasium and prize-fight ring. Yet, never one to back down from a challenge, he persevered.

In 1904, a decade later, Jim, now a national sport's hero and vaudeville headliner, was preparing to begin a new season's tour. The world of popular theater had changed, vaudeville having evolved to become one of the most popular and prevalent entertainments throughout the country, featured everywhere from big-city palaces to small-town community halls. New audiences were comprised of the middle and upper classes, in stark contrast to the old stag crowds. Vaudeville now catered to women and children, the symbols of decency in the theater. These patrons were not only more receptive to performers, they also attended the theater with a good deal more respect. Performers, in turn, thoroughly enjoyed playing before such enthusiastic, increasingly sophisticated crowds. The old boardinghouse signs had slowly been taken down; they now offered actors "a home away from home."

With the acceptance and prosperity of vaudeville came better hotel accommodations, comfortable dressing rooms, improved costuming and props, Pullman car train sleepers, and good salaries. Improved rail service and schedules helped a great deal, with railroads now traveling to more towns faster and with greater comfort. Tours now traversed the entire country; St. Louis was no longer the western terminus. People in every town and village now had a first-hand opportunity to see and hear the most popular stage celebrities.

For headliners, this exposure and familiarity made previously local or regional stars into national attractions, thus laying the foundation for the star system. A celebrated individual's name carried a show, drawing SRO audiences, to performances widely promoted in newspapers and magazines. The images of star performers graced sheet music covers, even as the stars themselves became well-rewarded spokespersons for commercial products. In a profitable exchange of commerce, newspapers eager to sell advertising space to theaters launched columns featuring entertainment "news" and "celebrity profiles."

Jim had succeeded from boxing olios intended merely to fill an intermission, through melodrama and farce comedy, to vaudeville appearances as an engaging storyteller with a sincere delivery, one who paid careful attention to his audiences' enjoyment. His stories were amusing, his humor self-effacing, his bearing casual and familiar, his facial expressions and mirrored emotions open for everyone to see. His act resembled an uncle's sharing a tale with the family. The tale achieved even more relevance when people believed they were privileged to be so intimately connected to a larger-than-life hero. Few performers had been able to command that kind of rapport with audiences. Further, Jim's professional demeanor also made him popular with colleagues who shared the stage with him.

During the past few years of career ups-and-downs, Jim had learned a number of important survival techniques. First-hand conflicts with the Syndicate persuaded him to shun any involvement with that organization. In fact, throughout his entire career, Jim never played in a Klaw and Erlanger theater. Jim found his best friends among fellow performers, people with whom he could gossip and share experiences, from whom he could gain helpful hints on theaters and audiences to be found along the road.

Jim also decided to take charge of his own bookings by hiring an independent agent who would follow his strategy and look after his singular interests. It was a higher-risk undertaking than booking through well-established agencies or brokers, but Jim believed that, in this way, he gained more control over his career and greater flexibility in negotiating contracts. Stage defeats would come with stage victories, but that was an ongoing part of the theatrical profession. At least, he could determine his own destiny. Nor was he hesitant to extend and expand his repertoire to fulfill new audience desires. Acutely aware of the rapid development of new entertainment media, Jim vowed to make use of them, given the opportunity.

Through the entire 1903-1904 season, Jim headed a vaudeville company comprised of friends and veterans from the Syndicate wars. All exceptional in their specialties, they presented professional entertainment to which audiences responded appreciatively and by which theater managers, counting their box-office receipts, were no less gratified. They played in more than twenty-five large cities over seven months, always at first-class theaters, including three engagements in New York and two in both Boston and Chicago. The results padded everyone's pocketbook. Jim himself earned close to $1,000 a week, plus a percentage from souvenirs sold in theater lobbies.

In addition to meeting his theater responsibilities, Jim was frequently feted by athletic clubs in the cities he visited. There, his speech-making abilities and amusing boxing stories served to enhance his stage reputation. The company ended its season in late April, in Fall River, Massachusetts, to an enthusiastic audience. To commemorate the event, the theater manager passed out souvenir photos of the performers. The result was that large crowds of people surrounded the performers at the end of the show, all of them clamoring for autographs, to which request the delighted actors complied.

No sooner had Jim and Vera returned home than he was asked to make a short Midwestern trip—Chicago, St. Louis, and Kansas City—to appear in a mixed vaudeville troupe, for the attractive sum of $1,500 a week. In Chicago, theater managers had been searching for first-class acts to attract customers back to their theaters. Five months earlier, a disastrous fire at the newly opened, supposedly fireproof, Iroquois Theater had killed more than 600 people, most of them women and children. All Chicago theaters had been closed for more than a month, subject to thorough inspection before being reopened. Months later, theaters had not yet been able to attract a satisfactory number of patrons.

In St. Louis, theater managers offered the enticement of full houses, thanks to the 1904 World's Fair playing in their city. While Jim appeared there, he visited the Fair a number of times, always with some difficulty; each visit ended with crowds wanting to shake his hand and talk about his boxing exploits. A poignant note: while walking through the exhibits, Jim chanced upon an old, wrinkled-faced Indian, in full ceremonial dress, seated at a plain table, hawking photos. The Indian was Geronimo, one-time Apache chieftain and U.S. Army nemesis, selling autographed pictures of himself, entitled "The Last Warrior."

The Corbett summer in Bayside was restful if not entirely quiet. Jim enjoyed a White Rats outing and dinner, where the most combative action consisted of a baseball game. He and Vera attended Fred Stone's marriage to Allene Crater, both of them members of the "Wizard of Oz" company. Playing the role of the Scarecrow, Stone had gained immediate success for his dancing and imaginative costume. (Thirty-four years later, with Stone's aid,

Ray Bolger reprised his dance routines and costumes for the Wizard of Oz movie, which featured a young Judy Garland and veteran vaudevillians Jack Haley and Bert Lahr.)

Exhausted after a long year of vaudeville touring, Jim sought out scripts for the development of a comic drama in which he might star. John B. McKensie, a New York script broker, brought "Pals" to Jim's attention, believing that the story of a sport's hero turned detective would fit his interests. Jim agreed.

The production went immediately into rehearsals. For the first time, Jim also agreed to invest in a show, convinced his reputation would help put it over. Just to be safe, however, he and McKensie decided not to play in New York until the end of the season, if the show lasted that long. Supporting Jim in the cast were a number of highly-regarded actors, including William A. Quirk, Fred Hearn, William Powell, Sr., Hal Davis, and Florence Hamilton. Having learned from his years with Brady the result of staging low-priced productions, Jim was willing to spend money to secure seasoned performers.

"Pals" opened at the State Street Theater in Trenton, New Jersey, September 26, with Jim playing the role of Jim Graham, former sportsman, now an enterprising detective. Originally a vaudeville sketch, the play had now been elaborated into a four-act drama. Unfortunately, the script no longer exists.

A *Clipper* reporter, assigned to cover the opening, wrote:

> James J. Corbett appeared Sept. 26, in "Pals," an original dramatic comedy, in four acts, by Edmund Day. It was well written and staged and proved to be one of the best popular priced attractions ever offered at this house.[1]

Whether or not the review should be

Fred Stone persuaded Jim to play center field for the Stone baseball team in a league made up of other theatrical companies. Jim (back row, fifth from left, dark suit) was the only member of the team not affiliated with the "Wizard of Oz" production.

considered praise for the production, Jim was not sure. No mention of acting or the actors, nor did the theater enjoy a reputation for high-class entertainment. Still, the show played to three days of full houses and garnered numerous curtain calls. A jump to Rochester netted the same results. When the company reached Montreal, the production seemed to jell. Audiences now cheered the performers, and reviews singled out Jim's acting as "surprisingly good." The downside of being an athlete-turned-actor was critics' perennial surprise that Jim could perform creditably on stage.

After engagements in Toronto and Detroit, "Pals" came to Chicago to play at the Great Northern Theater, one of the best in the city. The results here cleared the way for a successful tour. The *Tribune* reported: "During the past week, James J. Corbett, with Hal Davis and Inez Mc-

Cauley in chief support, presented 'Pals' to immense business. The play and star won great favor."[2]

A common experience for an independently produced show, booking problems, forced the company to stop in Peoria, Illinois, and Burlington, Iowa, before going to Milwaukee; still, box-office receipts in both towns were excellent. Engagements in St. Paul and Minneapolis preceded a return to Chicago for the Christmas holiday season. Even though the city observed temporary mourning on the first anniversary of the Iroquois Theater catastrophe and "Pals" had been staged in Chicago only a month before, its success was repeated. "An excellent company which won a hit for them at another theater a few weeks ago, profited well," said the *Tribune*. "James J. Corbett was the drawing card."

Engagements through early 1905 took the company to Midwestern cities, and they gradually jumped their way back East. A review in Cincinnati was particularly gratifying to Jim.

> James J. Corbett appeared in Edmund Day's comedy of "Pals," with Hal Davis and Inez McCauley in leading roles. Business ruled big. The climax was as great a novelty as ever seen out this way, and the verdict was that Corbett is growing as an actor and is decidedly clever.[3]

Much to Jim's pleasure, the company had successfully played all their dates and made it back to New York. Reviews from previous triumphs appeared on advertising posters and in newspapers, an excellent way to be introduced to both audiences and critics. First stop was in Brooklyn, at the Grand Opera House, where they "proved to be a winning card, the patrons crowding the house at each performance." When they moved to the American Theater the following week, "Pals did a fine business."

Newspaper ads for the American engagement hailed "the talented actor and world's famous athlete, Mr. James J. Corbett, in "Pals," a story of heart interest, lightened by delicious comedy." Apparently, the play's theme had changed from that of a detective story to one featuring a love interest. The *New York Times* described the play as:

> ...a love affair of Jim Graham and Grace Winston, which part of the time did not run smoothly because of one Brumley. But in the last act Graham settles everything in a way that results in a permanent effect, and much to the discomfiture of the rival.[4]

While in New York, Jim proudly announced to reporters that he had purchased the rights to George Bernard Shaw's book, "Cashel Byron's Profession." Written in 1901, the story concerns an English prizefighter making his way in high society. Critics viewed Jim's decision a very dubious venture. Playing Brady's prizefighter was one thing, they said; playing Shaw's would be a formidable undertaking for the pugilist-actor. Yet Jim backed up his investment even further, declaring he planned to underwrite the entire production. Rehearsals for the show were to begin in August.

A week in Boston and a return to Oscar Hammerstein's Victoria Theater closed the season for "Pals," climaxing a continually successful thirty-week run. Indeed, the money Jim had earned would be more than sufficient to invest in the Shaw play. Still, he continued to perform, taking the opportunity to appear on a vaudeville bill that followed "Pals" at the Victoria.

> James J. Corbett, the actor-pugilist, holds the black-type position in the billing. He was accorded a hearty reception, and his stories of his personal experiences created a deal of laughter.[5]

Also featured on the prototypical vaudeville bill were: Moore and Littlefield, in a skit called "Change Your Act"; Mme. Herman, contortionist; Patree, juggler; Ward & Curran, comedians; the Three Diamonds, acrobats; Taylor Twin Sisters, song and dance; and a vitagraph one-reeler, "The Globe of Death."

Jim then retired for the summer, except for an Actors' Home benefit, the Lambs' Club annual Gambol, and a charity baseball game against the Black Rats, an actors' group, comprising Bert Williams, a well-known Negro entertainer, and his company. The Black Rats won the game, which, to the delight of spectators, turned into a burlesque on baseball and its fans. Jim also made brief appearances in Chicago and Brighton Beach as part of a vaudeville olio. Most of his time, however, was spent on developing and adapting the Shaw play.

Unfortunately, the production never did "come together." Jim did not care for the adaptation by Stanislaus Stange, an old hack at Americanizing European plays. Nor could he find actors to fill essential roles. In one scene, Shaw called for Zulu warriors to confront the hero. Since Negroes were not allowed to appear on stage in white theaters, Jim had to have the entire scene rewritten. When "Indians" replaced Zulus in the plot, the play began taking on the character of a farce comedy. There was no way the production could be ready to open in September.

By October, the delay forced Jim to perform in vaudeville to cover the play's rising costs. In spite of its problems, Jim remained committed to the play. As a result, Jim's appearances would delay the opening even later than he now hoped, unless he could book all his appearances in the New York area. It did not work out that way.

An engagement in Newark opened Jim's fall season. He then traveled to Albany, Manchester, New Hampshire, and Portland, Maine, before returning to New York. Further, engagements in Brooklyn and New York theaters diverted his attention so that he was unable to dedicate time to the play until early November.

Totally unnoticed, a major breakthrough in vaudeville theater occurred on November 6, 1905, at Proctor's Fifty-eighth Street Theater. Jim and Lillian Russell headlined a bill that also featured veteran Gus Williams in a blackface comedy routine. Following Williams on the bill came a group of Negro singers (who were also required to black up), the first time in New York that Negro and white actors had shared the same stage. Both Jim and Lillian not only agreed to have them on the bill (as stars, their consent was required); they also strongly applauded the singers' appearance, as did the all-white, yet highly approving audience.

Finally, after months of delay and at substantial cost, Jim announced to the press that "Cashel Byron's Profession" would open early in January. Henry B. Harris, a savvy producer, had reworked Stange's adaptation. Opposite Jim, Margaret Wycherly played the heroine. The play would first open out-of-town to work out the predictable plot and scenic problems.

The story relates the love of Lydia Carew, a young woman of good family and possessed of ultra-modern ideas, for Cashel Byron, a "fighting man," the champion of England and Australia. In the first act, Cashel meets Lydia, who gains the impression that he is a professional of physical, not fistic, science, recuperating at Wilstoken Park from the strain of his work, which she imagines to be of a scholastic nature.

In the second act, Cashel's patron, Lord Worthington, plans to play a joke at the expense of Mrs. Hoskyns, a society doyenne. He brings Cashel to one of her Sunday "at homes," in response to her request that he invite a celebrity to grace the occasion. Cashel's actual identity is disclosed, which embarrasses Mrs. Hoskyns and climaxes in Lydia's rejection of Cashel's love due to his unseemly profession.

The third act finds Lydia occupying the lodge at Wilstoken formerly used by Cashel as his training quarters. The act opens on the eve of what Cashel has decided will be his last fight. We are introduced to Cashel's mother and foster-mother, two contrasting types, both of whom play important parts in the ultimately happy consummation of Cashel's and Lydia's love.

The play had its initial opening at the Hyperion Theater, New Haven, Connecticut, on January 1, 1906. After a few performances for "repair" work, the play reopened at the Court Square Theater in

Jim Corbett as Cashel Byron, in George Bernard Shaw's "Cashel Byron's Profession," the story of a gentleman prize fighter who invades English high society. Reports of the play said "Jim came up smiling, but Mr. Shaw was down and out." The play lasted five weeks.

Springfield, Massachusetts. On January 8, Jim bravely brought the production to New York, presenting it at the venerable Daly's Theater.

Critics excoriated the play. "James J. Corbett had a go at George Bernard Shaw last evening. When the final bell rang, Mr. Corbett came up smiling. By that time, however, Mr. Shaw was down and out."[6]

Reviewers went on the deride the Stange/Harris adaptation as "ordinary and undramatic." Nor did they believe that Shaw's original book did anything but display the author's "brightness and pleading."

Jim was commended for his "boyishness of demeanor," "freedom from affectation," and "good-humored naturalness." Yet his mechanics, movements and gestures judged to be artificial, "lost the illu-

sion" of the play. What Jim gained in comedy lines was apparently lost when the dramatic demand was for sympathy and sentiment.

The reviews signaled a quick demise for the show, but Jim's presence kept it alive for two weeks at Daly's, plus another two weeks at the Majestic. When the company moved to Philadelphia, several changes in personnel made the play even more ragged. Jim worked hard to keep the company cohesive, but he had never faced such problems and seemed unable to deal with them. At the end of its Philadelphia run, having performed before small and not very appreciative audiences, the play ignominiously closed. The show had lasted a mere five weeks, after having been delayed four months. Jim not only lost a good deal of money in his first managing venture, he was also shaken by critics' views regarding his acting ability.

When he returned to New York, Jim was decidedly more interested in seeking some sort of gainful employment. Still, having enjoyed the satisfaction of appearing in full-length plays, he was reluctant to return to the vaudeville ranks. In discussions with theater owner F.F. Proctor, the two agreed to have Jim appear in a one-act sketch, in this instance, a condensed version of "Pals."

As part of a vaudeville bill, presented on March 5, at Proctor's Fifty-eighth Street Theater, Jim and three other actors appeared in a twenty-minute skit entitled "A Thief in the Night." According to the *Clipper,* "the audience seemed to appreciate the efforts of the ex-pugilist." Also appearing on the bill were Dave Lewis, an ethnic comedian, and the Three Keatons, featuring eleven-year-old Buster, already a vaudeville veteran, as well as a monkey act and moving pictures.

In fact, response was so favorable Proctor asked Jim to develop another skit, so he could play continuous weeks at each of the four Proctor theaters in the New York area. "Mr. Smooth," a condensation of two scenes from "Cashel Byron's Profession," was presented the next week at Proctor's Fifth Avenue Theater. Jim's performance as a sketch artist was hailed by the *Clipper.*

> The production was decidedly pleasing, and got plenty of laughs. Mr. Corbett was given a big reception. His jovial, natural manner plainly made an effective impression upon the audience, and his work was keenly enjoyable.[7]

The following week, at another Proctor theater, Jim presented "A Thief in the Night" again. The *Clipper* praised Jim's acting anew. "Mr. Corbett's easy manner and air of absolute sincerity and candor carried him to complete success at once, and the act had merits of its own to recommend it."[8]

What followed was a week in Brooklyn, a return to Proctor's Fifth Avenue, then back to another theater in Brooklyn, culminating in headliner status at Hammerstein's Victoria Theater. Jim was well received at each appearance, with audience response to his performances helping to rebuild his confidence after the Shaw debacle. He seriously considered the continuation of these skits throughout the summer. A calamity of national significance—and one that struck close to Jim's heart—disrupted his plans.

At 5:13 A.M., on April 18, the people of San Francisco were rudely and shockingly awakened by severe earth convulsions, a natural disaster that would come to be regarded as symbolic of the many to follow throughout the new century. During its initial tremors, the earthquake destroyed thousands of houses and buried hundreds of people in their beds. This destruction, however, was overshadowed by the disaster that followed. Wildfires, driven by strong west winds, swept over most of the city. The earthquake had shattered gas lines, exposed electric wires, and upset stoves. In consequence, flames broke out almost immediately in dozens of neighborhoods. The fire department responded to the emergency quickly but when their engines were coupled with hydrants, they found no water pressure. The mains had been ruptured. For two days, the fire roared unchecked across the city.

While Jim was attending to his usual morning exercises, he was informed of the cataclysm. Immediately, he attempted to wire Harry but found that all communication to 'Frisco had been cut off.

The Corbetts had been lucky. Two years before, Joe had sold the old home and stable and moved away from Hayes Street. His new home and that of Harry were both badly damaged, but no one was injured. Catherine and Esther were living in apartments nearby and while their places had suffered damage, they too were physically unharmed. Ironically, the fire that initiated the city-wide conflagration had begun only one short block east of their residences. Luckily, the wind pushed the fire away from their homes. Harry's residence remained sufficiently intact to shelter the entire family until other housing could be found. His current place of business (a liquor store), however, was gutted by the flames.

It was three days before Jim heard from Harry, amid newspaper reports of unprecedented death and destruction sweeping the city. Anticipating an emergency trip west to assist the family, Jim was greatly relieved to learn they were healthy and safe. News of the disaster had dramatically stirred the country to demonstrations of sympathy and charitable donations unparalleled in U.S. history. Millions of dollars poured in to aid the homeless, restore facilities, and begin rebuilding. More than 2,500 people had perished. Property damage amounted to $400 million.

Two days after the event, a benefit performance by New York–based actors was held at the Knickerbocker Theater. It paralleled benefits being held across the U.S. Among the top stars participating was Jim Corbett. Along with his well-practiced monologue, he talked about having been raised in the afflicted city and the fact that his family still lived there. This he bravely revealed prior to hearing from Harry that the Corbetts had survived.

Two weeks after the catastrophe, the major filmmakers—Lubin, Vitograph, and Kleine—were exhibiting moving pictures of a devastated, burnt-out city. Films of an actual event had never traveled so far so fast. Coupled with the almost immediate national coverage in newspapers, these documentary films dramatically heralded the beginning of the rapid dissemination of timely news, an event that revolutionized communications and public perceptions.

When Jim returned to the stage a month later, he appeared on a vaudeville bill, prosaically reciting his monologues. Unfortunately for him, the deal with Proctor had ended when the manager sold his theaters and other assets to the Keith organization, nemesis of the White Rats and their sympathizers. Proctor's had been one of the few remaining circuits in New York not yet under Syndicate control. Moreover, theaters were still dominated by a continuing stream of films documenting "the San Francisco horror." Performers found it very hard to be funny before subdued and somber audiences. Theaters were full, but actors had been "upstaged."

Thanks to his Lambs' Club connections, Jim obtained a short-term contract from Percy Williams, an independent manager with control over a number of local theaters and was able to reintroduce his one-act skits. By early June, most theaters were about to close for the summer and Jim had to begin arranging the next season's bookings. In spite of the current season's mishaps, Jim remained committed to playing in full-length productions; and he sought out backers and managers who might support his interests. He had a strong reputation. What he needed was a vehicle.

The Mittenthal brothers—Harry, Isaac, Aubrey, and Sam—had made millions in the clothing business. The family—six sons and five daughters—had originally come from Germany, opened a business in New York, and moved to Detroit, where they lived for forty years. The four brothers were enamored with the entertainment business and spent much of their time at theaters. This involvement led to their making small investments in vaudeville companies. When these ventures paid handsome dividends, the brothers established a company that underwrote theatrical productions. They were also boxing fans and very familiar with Jim's career. When the two parties met, a marriage of business interests was quickly consummated.

The issue of this association was a melodramatic comedy called "The Burglar and the Lady." The new play opened at the Academy of Music, Scranton, Pennsylvania, on September 3, 1906. It enjoyed immediate success in both Scranton and Wilkes-Barre. But how would it play the sophisticates of Philadelphia?

The first scene takes place in the drawing room of John Harmon (J. Leonard Clark), cashier of the Commercial Bank. Mrs. Moreland, the banker's sister, is the proud owner of a valuable diamond necklace for which the celebrated burglar, Raffles (Jim Corbett) is searching. To this end, he has Cripps (Dore Davidson), one of his associates, secure employment as a butler in the Hermon mansion. On an evening when the family is out to a reception, he allows Raffles to enter by a rear window. They are searching for the necklace when interrupted by the entrance of Jenkins, a detective of the Sherlock Holmes squad. They gag, bind, and conceal him in another room. Raffles then locates the necklace, along with a number of rings, and conceals the necklace in the head of a cane that he carries. The family returns and, finding a robbery has been committed, Mr. Hermon turns the case over to Sherlock Holmes himself (Arthur V. Johnson), who was one of his reception guests. Raffles soon introduces himself as Ned Danvers, the detective, and assures all of them that he has already apprehended the thief. When Holmes recognizes one of the men, he immediately suspects Danvers/Raffles as the actual burglar.

The next night, Raffles and Cripps prepare to rob the bank. After gaining entrance, they are startled by the appearance of Mr. Harmon. Concealing themselves, they see him attempt to crack the safe. Immediately, Raffles steps out to accuse Harmon, empties the safe himself, and sends Cripps away with the money. He notifies police headquarters that a robbery has been committed, and he turns over Harmon as the thief.

For his part, Sherlock Holmes still considers Raffles the robber of the diamond necklace and the bank. He places him under arrest. Yet Raffles proves too shrewd for his captors and makes good his escape. He flees to the house of Norma Gray (Mary Fernier), who loves him and provides him safe haven in her room. While escaping, however, Raffles has been shot through the wrist. A search of Norma's home is made and the Reverend John Banfield (George D. Mockey), who is also in love with Norma, scrutinizes her room and finds Raffles. Confronted by the Reverend, the resourceful Raffles relates an evidently fictitious story of his life and claims to be the brother of the minister. Raffles swears that, if Banfield allows him to escape, he will lead a better life in the future. Yet the Reverend knows too well that, should he do so, Norma would soon follow. Norma discerns this, so she swears that she does not love Raffles, but has given her heart to the Reverend instead. She pleads with Banfield to give Raffles the chance to escape, which he does.

Raffles and Cripps are about to leave, but they miss the last train. Cripps then betrays Raffles to the law, who has followed them in an automobile. Raffles tells Norma to get into the auto and wait for him. An explosion occurs and in the confusion, Raffles escapes in the police car. Raffles intends to recover the necklace, which he has sworn to return to Norma. Cripps, having secretly concealed the necklace, runs away. Raffles tracks him down and, after a physical struggle, recovers the necklace. Banfield forgives and forgets when he discovers that Raffles is actually his own brother. He determines to display fraternal devotion and assists Norma in eloping with the elegant, occasionally honorable thief.

For the first time in his career, Jim played a "bad character," but a charming rogue with redeeming qualities. His performance held audiences from the start. During each of the initial engagements, Jim received considerable applause and, after the third act, was compelled to respond to curtain calls. The audience, not yet satisfied, continued cheering his performance until Jim conceded to making a short speech. This happy result was repeated in Philadelphia, Baltimore, and New York City, where "The Burglar and the Lady" opened at the American Theater, September 24, to SRO crowds. All parties involved were ecstatic over the enormously positive response to the production. The Mittenthals rushed to obtain Jim bookings for the entire season.

Simultaneous with Jim's success in "The Burglar and the Lady" came newspaper articles and columns exclusively devoted to a new, increasingly popular entertainment, moving pictures. Consisting

Jim made a big hit with "The Burglar and the Lady." For the first time, he played a less than perfect character, yet a charming rogue with redeeming qualities. The show ran almost two years to full houses and established Jim as a premier stage actor. (California Historical Society, FN-31468)

primarily of one-reel presentations produced by Edison, Selig, Lubin, and the Vitagraph people, these early films focused on documenting real-life drama—the Galveston Disaster, the Paris Exposition, the Boer War and, more recently, the San Francisco earthquake. Occasionally, a "story" movie of multiple reels would be produced, but the studios firmly believed that audiences would neither be interested in, nor pay attention to, longer films.

Jim was already quite familiar with this business enterprise, having played a starring role in the staged bout with Peter

Courtney filmed in Edison's Black Maria, not to mention the Kinetoscope motion picture of his battle with Fitzsimmons. For the former, Jim had earned nearly $20,000; in the latter, although he gained little money and lost the championship, the national exposure he received served to increase and enhance his reputation. Jim had already experienced the financial and entertainment power of motion pictures; there would come a time when he could make use of their growing popularity.

The "Burglar" tour began in Brooklyn; "big business with James J. Corbett," proclaimed the newspapers. Through November and December, the tour carried Jim and company to towns in New York State, Ohio, and Michigan—twenty stops in forty-one days, with no off-days. Christmas holidays were spent in Chicago, where the *Tribune* labeled the production "exciting" and Jim primarily responsible for its success.

> James J. Corbett did a fine business last week in "The Burglar and the Lady," and was greeted every night by salvos of applause upon his entrance. The play has much of interest in a melodramatic form and the handling of the two well-known characters of Raffles and Sherlock Holmes makes it very interesting for the lover of the exciting. [9]

During January 1907, the company played one-night stands at towns in Illinois, Iowa, and Minnesota. After two "big-business weeks" in St. Paul and Minneapolis, they were stranded for three weeks because bookings had been blocked by the Syndicate, forcing the company to make an unscheduled return to Chicago in early February, where, to everyone's surprise, they enjoyed "capacity business all week."

During much of February and March, however, the tour grew decidedly irregular. From Terre Haute, Indiana, the company jumped to St. Louis; from St. Louis, they traveled to Cleveland, Ohio, then back to Chicago again, their third visit in three months. Amazingly, the show continued to attract full houses. The long march back east included engagements in Louisville, Cincinnati, Pittsburgh, and, finally, Brooklyn, at the end of April, as well as the end of the season. Cincinnati reviews called the show "one of the best Corbett has ever had." Pittsburgh reported that the play "was well received."

When Jim and Vera returned to Bayside after six hectic months on the road, they were happy and thankful for the silence and comforts of home. Since Jim had made no plans to perform during the summer, they looked forward to some quiet time at the beach. But no sooner had Jim shed his stage persona than the Mittenthals called to offer him a contract to tour with "Burglar" the coming season, at a substantial salary increase, of course. Jim no sooner agreed to the new terms than the Mittenthals publicly announced his continued appearance in the play during the '07-'08 season and added enticingly, "to many places he had not yet visited."

During a number of summer benefit performances, Jim had fun playing opposite W.C. Fields, who offered to teach him how to juggle if Jim would teach him how to box, and with Will Rogers, who was unsuccessful in conveying to Jim a mastery of the lasso. Audiences loved their improvisational acts.

At the Polo Grounds in August, a benefit for crippled children saw Jim reenter the ring, as referee for an exhibition between Bob Fitzsimmons and Sailor Burke. He also refereed a match between Jack Johnson, a Negro boxer, who was himself only a year away from winning the heavyweight title, and Joe Lannon, a former sparring partner of John L. Sullivan. In the baseball game that followed, Jim played, along with "Oz's" Fred Stone (in his Scarecrow costume) and other popular performers, among them, George Evans, George Beban, Victor Moore, and George M. Cohan.

Jim's second season with "The Burglar and the Lady" began in Asbury Park, New Jersey, on September 14. Besides relying on a number of new company members, the play had been shortened by fifteen minutes and its scenery reduced in size to compensate for the increased freight charges recently initiated by railroads. Engagements in Providence, Hartford, and Boston preceded the first visit of the season to the New York area. In Brooklyn, the Folly Theater took the occasion to boldly advertise the play as Jim's "best success" and: "...a novelty of exquisite creation, introducing the two greatest heroes of modern times, Ned Danvers (Raffles), the 'Burglar' and Sherlock Holmes, the detective."[10]

The following week, at the American Theater, in New York City:

> The every appearance of Mr. Corbett was the signal for applause, which was always forthcoming. The play was enjoyed by all present, and Mr. Corbett and Rose King played their respective parts well and deserved the applause which they were given.[11]

In spite of these successes, the Mittenthals had difficulty making specific booking arrangements for the show. Apart from the usual problems with the Syndicate, some independent managers refused to engage the show again because it had played at their theaters the previous season. That caused the company to return to New York only three weeks after having appeared there, and again in December. Visits to Baltimore and Washington, D.C., won "packed houses," but stops in Pennsylvania and New York's small towns only "made a good attraction." Nor was the company's morale helped when, after

wrestling with snow storms and train delays in the East, they were informed of a grueling trip to the distant Pacific Coast for the remainder of the season.

During January, 1908, the "Burglar" company played in Pittsburgh, Cincinnati, Chicago, and St. Louis to "immense houses." Though audiences in these cities had seen the play before, they came out to see Jim perform. The *Chicago Tribune's* review mirrored those reported elsewhere. "James J. Corbett has played to splendid business this week, and the big star was heartily greeted on every occasion."[12]

The next day, leaving Chicago behind, the company began a grind of one- and two-night stands, fifteen small towns in three weeks, before reaching the West Coast, having traversed the wilds of North Dakota, Montana, Idaho, and Washington. Their first full-week's stop was to be in San Francisco, whose rapid rebuilding since the earthquake included four new theaters.

Hundreds of people, including the Corbett family, greeted Jim and Vera upon their arrival at the Oakland train station. The ferry trip across the bay proved an occasion for civic gaiety—band music, people singing and dancing, Jim shaking hands with everyone. From the landing dock, crowds followed Jim and Vera to their hotel. Many waited out front to escort him to the Novelty Theater, where "Burglar" would make its first appearance that evening.

Most of the *Chronicle's* review reported the entire social event, the play itself receiving only minor mention.

> Everybody who is or hopes to be a figure in the world of sport was at stageside. Never before did any conquering hero receive a more enthusiastic ovation upon his homecoming than did the star of the night.
>
> James J. Corbett, heavyweight champion-dramatic star of the world appeared before an admiring concourse of old friends,

who marveled over the evolution of the one-time idol of the squared circle into a real, blown-in-the-bottle leading man. [13]

Of the play, "Burglar" was called the "mellowest melodrama that ever regaled the gallery gods." The *Chronicle* also suggested that, even if the play had been supported by such reigning stars as John Drew or Olga Nethersole, they would have fallen victim to little consideration due to Jim's compelling presence. In a speech at the end of the show, Jim told his cheering friends how delighted he was to be with them once again and related some witty anecdotes of his recent travels. In the boxes, the Corbett family applauded loudly and stamped their feet, much to the audience's amusement.

For the next six weeks, the company paid visits to California's small towns, jumped to Salt Lake City and Denver, and gradually made its way back to Kansas City, where the season finally ended. Though the entire tour had been highly successful, the rigors of repeating the show for two seasons had "burnt-out" the actors. Upon completion of the final performance, most of the company immediately headed for the train station to return to New York. Jim and Vera were among them. In total, Jim had played Ned Danvers/Raffles 473 times, in 120 locales. Reaching Bayside, the couple did not venture out of their home for more than a month, sending the maid out for groceries.

When Jim did resurface, at the Fifth Avenue Theater—relaxed, confident, and tanned—it was to present one of his ever-popular monologues.

James J. Corbett, who is a capital entertainer, had some new ones to tell, and signalized his return to New York vaudeville in an auspicious manner. Our theatergoers feel that they know Big Jim pretty well by this time, and they like to show him that they like him.[14]

A month later, Jim played to a Brighton Beach crowd on a vaudeville bill that also featured Eva Tanguay, a saucy, carefree, frizzy-haired blonde, who had already created a reputation for her peculiar delivery and outlandish feathered costumes. Unfortunately, Jim followed her on stage and was faced with an audience still recovering from her eccentric performance. He quickly requested to be put on earlier, so that he could command the audience's full attention. While Jim enjoyed his return to the vaudeville stage, the Tanguay episode reminded him of the inevitable inequities and audience hazards inherent to the vaudeville format. Although touring was exhausting, starring appearances in full-length plays maintained audience focus and admiration.

Harry H. Frazee had begun his theatrical career as treasurer of the Grand Opera House, in Peoria, Illinois. From 1896 to 1902, he did advance work for a number of vaudeville companies. In 1903, he formed a small company of his own and presented three road attractions at popular prices. With the money he earned, Frazee purchased from the Shuberts the rights to a show, "Facing the Music." The previous year, the play had successfully featured Henry E. Dixey at the Garrick Theater in New York. Putting together a touring company, for the vehicle, Frazee sought out Jim to star.

Frazee offered Jim a lucrative, one-year contract to tour the show throughout the Midwest and West. As an added incentive, he promised to open a Chicago saloon, to be called Corbett's, from which Jim would collect royalties. Frazee enjoyed a reputation as an honest producer who backed up his claims and paid salaries on time. What Jim did not know was that, around the Chicago area, Frazee sported a dubious moniker: "king of the one-night stands." Once on the road, Jim quickly found out why.

"Facing the Music" opened August 10, 1908, at Bennett's Theater in Montreal, Canada. "Big houses" attended the engagement. Reviewers called the production "better than Burglar and the Lady," if one could "sit out the first act."

The story, by Charles Henry Darnier, deals with the mistaken identity of two Smith families, one headed by a sporting man, the other by a minister, both of which reside in the same Kensington apartment house. Both men are married to young and beautiful wives who have each been out of the city and, returning unexpectedly, each enter the wrong flat. Complications arise and continue in rapid succession until the finale, when all the resulting confusion is cleared up to the satisfaction of everyone. The play was a typical British farce adapted for American audiences, with just enough humor and sexually suggestive situations to make it attractive without being offensive.

Of Jim and the play, the Montreal reviewer declared:

> We all know that Corbett is not a bad actor, either on the stage or in the ring. Corbett has a congenial role, and his acting was natural and acceptable.
>
> "Facing the Music" was comical enough to keep the audience thoroughly amused. The company which supports Corbett is altogether a very capable one. "Facing the Music" is well worth seeing.

From the beginning, audiences gave Jim hearty applause every night. At the final curtain, he always made a little speech, expressing his pleasure at the opportunity to entertain them.

After a successful week in Chicago, to "immense business"—Frazee had promoted his show heavily—the company "hit the rails." Frazee had put Jim on the western route of the Chicago-Milwaukee and Great Northern Railroads from Minneapolis to Seattle and had booked the

H.H. Frazee was one of Chicago's most flamboyant theatrical promoters. He was also known as the "king of one-night stands." Frazee persuaded Jim to lead a cross-country tour, at an excellent salary. The company quickly discovered they were stopping at every railroad crossing and mining camp throughout the Pacific Northwest. A year of such touring convinced Jim the need for better vaudeville opportunities.

show for every stop along the way. Some towns were only twenty-five miles apart, others were located on spurs just off the main track. Some did not even have a theater in which to perform, saloons or community halls being hastily converted into performance venues. Frequently, actors had to apply make-up on the train and walk to the theater to perform. Many towns in which the company played had never before seen farce comedy, nor did they quite understand elements of the plot.

Between August 30 and October 25, "Facing the Music" stopped at thirty-seven towns. In one three-week period, they played in seventeen. Performers literally lived on the train, entering the town only to perform. Because of the late-autumn season, snow and cold were common inconveniences. Nonetheless, perhaps due to the novelty of the experience, venues were crowded and box-office receipts excellent.

After so murderous a schedule, Jim and the company were delighted to reach Seattle for a week-long engagement. They were able to sleep in a hotel, on comfortable beds, eat at full-service restaurants, and rehearse at fully-equipped theaters. They even had an opportunity to walk around and see the sights. Boredom and stress, which had presented major problems while crossing the country and advanced to very near breaking-point, were now gratefully relieved. An aura of well-earned satisfaction for having survived their ordeal settled over the company.

Week-long engagements in Seattle and Portland attracted "fine houses," and prepared the company for many more weeks of one-night stands. The single remaining exception was a long stop in San Francisco, where Jim was again greeted and treated royally by long-time admirers. By this time, Jim was already exhausted from the seemingly endless tour that Frazee had booked, and he was confronting another four months of the same rigorous routine. As a consequence of this schedule, Jim had grown sluggish, out-of-shape, and overweight. To regain some degree of physical equilibrium, he installed athletic paraphernalia in his train car, began performing daily morning exercises, and invited his colleagues to join him.

After leaving San Francisco, the company played twenty-one towns in California, four in Utah, seven in Colorado, six in Nebraska, seven in South Dakota, and five in Iowa before reaching that comparatively luxurious oasis, Kansas City. In a tribute to their durability and commitment, not one company member had dropped out,

nor had a single day been lost to illness. Part of what buoyed their spirit was the strong support and hearty well-wishes received from audiences at each stop. More than once, when snow or rain delayed the train and the curtain failed to rise on time, audiences remained patiently in the theater while sets were raised and actors prepared themselves for the performance. Such occasions lent the entire event a rare sense of camaraderie and mutual pleasure, shared by both company and audience.

By March, 1909, "Facing the Music" had returned to the Midwest and Chicago, where they "packed the house at every performance." The company now found itself counting down: only six more stops before the season ended. The conclusion of a brutally and punishing tour was in sight. Yet they had all survived, ready and willing to play another season. It was a more than satisfactory professional and personal accomplishment, made even more gratifying by the play's financial triumph.

When the company bade their good-byes to colleagues with whom they had shared seven months of adventure, tears and hugs were mixed with profound appreciation for each member's having contributed essentially to a successful enterprise. Jim, in particular, expressed his sincere gratitude for the company's support and loyalty.

The next day, Jim received a mild surprise, the impact of which was diminished by its being so ludicrous. In the *New York Clipper*, he read that Frazee had announced the purchase of "The Girl Question," another farce drama, for the coming season. James J. Corbett would appear in the leading role.

"I must refuse your kind offer," he cabled Frazee, "as I have other plans for the next season." In truth, Jim had not yet made any future arrangements. One thing was certain, however: he wanted no further part of Frazee's "splendrous" tours.

10. MEN OF COLOR

During the summer of 1909, while Jim was on tour in England, he learned that former heavyweight champion Jim Jeffries had been talked out of retirement to face the current champion Jack Johnson. Jim believed that Jeffries must have been unhinged to have agreed to such a match and, in a cable he sent to his old friend, advised of the dangers he foresaw.

Waiting for Jim when he returned to the States was a long letter from Jeffries, asking for help. "Would you assist in my training for Johnson?" he requested. "I would like your advice." Reluctantly, Jim agreed to help him, but he warned his friend that the odds against beating Johnson were high.

Five years earlier, Jim Jeffries had retired from the ring to his alfalfa farm in Southern California. Unfortunately, he soon returned to his former drinking habit and his once-trim body had ballooned to more than 300 pounds. How could Jeffries be brought into fighting condition, Jim wondered, to compete effectively against such an overpowering opponent as Johnson. The contest was scheduled for July 4, 1910, in Reno, Nevada. Training for the contest would begin in April. In spite of his trepidations, Jim promised his old friend that he would be in his corner.

Jim and Vera had departed for Queen-stown, Ireland, June 30, 1909, on the *Lusitania*, to appear in a full schedule of vaudeville shows during a brief span of eight weeks. On July 17, at the Theatre Royal in Dublin, he opened to a house packed with enthusiastic patrons. From there, he moved to the Royal Hippodrome Theater in Belfast for a week of SRO audiences, everyone seemingly captivated by the ex-champion's monologues of the fight business and celebrity acquaintances. A local reviewer unhesitatingly lauded the actor: "James J. Corbett has been hitting the Irish public and press hard with his entertaining stories." After two highly successful weeks in Ireland, Jim and Vera made their way to London. No other stops were made in Ireland, neither to visit relatives, nor to see the ancestral home.

Billed as star vaudevillian and ex-champion of the world, Jim began his English tour at London's Oxford Theater as part of an all-star show that featured nineteen acts and a moving picture. Unlike the American format, English vaudeville presented more acts on the bill, with each act no longer than ten minutes. Moreover, except for Saturday matinees, performers played only one show a day, a much easier schedule than the usual two-a-days in America's popular houses.

The *Era* reviewer gave an account of

Jim's theatrical return to London, after an absence of fifteen years.

> James J. Corbett, the famous American boxer, arrived in London on Sunday afternoon by train, at St. Pancras at 4:30 PM. There a big reception by a large number of well-known sporting men awaited him, for "Gentleman Jim" is to make his appearance at the Oxford on Monday. Mr. Corbett will not be seen in a boxing sketch or a ball-punching act, but will pose as a story teller, the yarns selected dealing with incidents connected with his travels and his career generally. It will be refreshing to see a great boxer garbed in evening dress, and in well chosen and easy speech demonstrating to the world that the American pugilist is a man of many parts. [1]

After two weeks at the Oxford, Jim appeared for two-week engagements at both the Tivoli and the Metropolitan. Interestingly, all three theaters stood within a short distance of one another. Reports were equally enthusiastic about his performances. From the *Era:*

> James J. Corbett was accorded a most enthusiastic reception. He relied on his powers as a *raconteur* pure and simple, and he tells various stories and anecdotes connected with his career in a delightfully breezy and confidential fashion. [2]

And from *The Stage:*

> James J. Corbett comes here from the Oxford and his opening served to emphasize his popularity and indicate that his success would be renewed.
> He tells many stories connected with his professional career in a natural and breezy fashion, not the least pleasing feature being the complete lack of anything approaching affectation, although all the tales are, naturally, of quite a personal character. [3]

Interspersed with his stage appearances were frequent dinner engagements and speeches given to an assortment of sporting clubs, from which Jim returned with a variety of souvenirs of appreciation. Many of his English admirers "professed surprise at the charm and effectiveness" of his presentations. At one dinner, Jim shared the podium with Arthur Collins, who had been stage manager of the Drury Lane when, fifteen years before, "Gentleman Jack" had played there.

Jim's last performance in England was at Chelsea, as a participant in a benefit cricket match. The following day, he and Vera embarked on the *Lusitania* for their return home. The hurried tour had been both personally rewarding and financially successful, reassuring Jim that his appeal to long-term admirers remained in full force. The year ended with Jim revealing he had signed a contract with William Morris (former actor, now booking agent) for a brief vaudeville tour before committing his full energies "to train Jim Jeffries." The *Clipper* explained:

> Corbett's theatrical tour will be somewhat shortened in order that it may not in any way interfere with his agreement to devote his time to Jeffries for forty days prior to the big fight. During his recent appearances in London and other English cities, Corbett made a tremendous success. [4]

Jim began the short tour at the Fulton Theater, Brooklyn, on January 3, 1910, to a full house anxious to hear about his travels. He also introduced comments about upcoming training plans with Jeffries. Plaudits were frequent.

Engagements in New York City, Newark, and Boston met with the usual SRO successes. As a featured part of his monologue, Jim discussed the Jeffries-Johnson contest, admitting that the battle would be hard, yet confident that "if Jeffries gets into condition, he will give Johnson the same dose that Corbett got from him," a comment that invariably elicited appreciative laughter. Yet when a sports reporter asked if he were really serious about Jeffries's chances to regain the title, Jim replied somewhat evasively: "I am not to be a trainer. I'm simply to help Jeffries acquire speed and skill."

Engagements in Cincinnati and Toronto preceded a return to New York theaters in April, where Jim presented his popular sketch, "A Thief in the Night," to crowded houses. As the *Chronicle* reported, these appearances were to be his last before he joined the Jeffries camp as "advisor." Closing at the Plaza Theater, Jim and Vera boarded a train for the five-day trip to San Francisco and the fateful Jeffries-Johnson championship bout.

Back in 1907, Jim had witnessed a match between Jack Johnson and forty-two-year-old Bob Fitzsimmons. The supposedly ever-dangerous former champion had been unceremoniously dispatched in two rounds. Johnson emerged from the bout recognized as a boxer of great skill, excellent defense, and hard hitting. His greatest asset, however, was his endurance. Never in a hurry, a conservator of strength, he seemed to know exactly when to use his talents to finish off an opponent. He appeared destined to become an outstanding heavyweight boxer. Unfortunately, he was also a Negro. Thus, having won the championship in 1908, Johnson initiated a dark period of racial prejudice and tension that infected both the boxing community and, ultimately, the entire country.

Johnson's victories over Fitzsimmons and another title challenger, Jim Flynn, made him the primary contender for Tommy Burns's crown. Both sportsmen and the press viewed such an encounter as a great story, almost a paradox. An American boxer, a Negro, would meet an undesirable foreigner, a white, in a world's championship contest. At first, boxing observers seemed to care little about the actual outcome. Whoever prevailed, the match would create considerable interest and sell tickets and newspapers.

At this time in U.S. history, however, few supported the idea of racial tolerance. To the contrary, most believed in the superiority—both physical and intellectual—of whites over Negroes. And they argued that, even if Johnson happened to beat Burns, thereby ridding the States of a foreign champion, Johnson would soon lose to a white challenger, thus reaffirming white supremacy.

In a match that took place in Australia, already a hot-bed of anti-Negro feeling, Johnson knocked out Burns in the fourteenth round. The Australian press had already characterized Johnson as "a threatening black menace." Newspapers at the time were not hesitant to describe people they didn't like in the most unflattering terms, often prompting considerable public reaction against them.

After his victory, the press further vilified Johnson for the manner in which he conducted himself, since it was considered unseemly for a Negro to behave like a white winner. They accused him of taunting his defeated opponent, not to mention the press, and portraying himself as superior to whites. To some extent, Australians were correct in their assessment. Johnson did seem to go out of his way to challenge social mores of the day, a predictable result of the many years of gratuitous hostility directed toward him and his race.

The American press quickly picked up the message and it soon became a malignant mantra within the boxing community. By the middle of 1909, pleas to beat Johnson were being directed toward retired Jim Jeffries, America's last great champion. Leading the charge to persuade Jeffries to become the country's "great white hope" were promoter Tex Rickard and reporter/novelists Jack London and Rex Beach.

In 1906, George Lewis "Tex" Rickard owned the preeminent gambling saloon in the small but already notorious town of Goldfield, Nevada. When town fathers debated how to put Goldfield "on the map," Rickard suggested a boxing title match between lightweight contenders Joe Gans and Oscar "Battling" Nelson, which he offered to stage. To gain press attention, Rickard offered an immense purse of $34,000, amazing for the time. In another flamboyant gesture, he stacked the prize-money—34,000 gold dollar pieces—in his saloon window. Rickard then publicized the contest as a grudge match and manipulated the fact that Gans was a Negro to make the bout a battle between races.

Gans beat Nelson in the forty-second round on a foul. Both spectators and the press thoroughly enjoyed the event, if not the outcome, which launched Rickard's career as a flashy promoter. He would later go on to become one of the best-known promoters in boxing history.

By the time Rickard offered to put on the Jeffries-Johnson contest, he had already earned a reputation as a highly successful, if unscrupulous, promoter, one who would stop at nothing to put on a show, as long as it made money.

For their part, the literary lions London and Beach had already revealed their beliefs in white supremacy through their writings. Now they recognized a unique opportunity to focus their opinions on one particular antagonist, Jack Johnson. In league with Rickard, they exploited the race issue, "for the greater good of our society."

At first, Jim Jeffries was reluctant to agree to the match. He turned down initial requests, insisting he was through with the ring. Nonetheless, the combined arguments of Rickard and London, along with pressure from the press and boxing community, finally seduced him. While serv-

ing as referee five years before in Reno, Nevada, Jeffries had reneged on some bets and had been told never to return to the city. To avoid any complications due to this potentially contentious problem, Rickard paid Jeffries's debt, which further obligated the boxer to Rickard.

After all, the press exclaimed, Johnson had continuously and with maliciousness degraded the "exalted realms of boxing." Furthermore, they spitefully revealed, he had broken the rules of society by marrying a white woman. Thus, they argued, Jeffries had a "social and moral responsibility" to beat Johnson and rid the boxing world of its Negro usurper.

Rickard was very pleased with ongoing developments, seeing the bout entirely in light of its potential for his own substantial personal financial gain. For London and Beach, the match and its outcome would be a ringing endorsement for their white supremacy themes, in a social climate already poisoned by its pervasiveness. Soon, the proposed bout moved from the sports pages to the front pages of the national press, and quickly became an issue stained with racial prejudice and mounting anti-Negro hysteria.

When Jim arrived at Jeffries's training camp in Ben Lomond, California, in early May, the place had an almost patriotic fervor about it. Each day, reporters bustled around scrounging material to grab the attention of readers. Rickard frequently dropped in to fan Jeffries's flames, apparently believing he had to remind the challenger of his "social" responsibilities. Both London and Beach were on hand, writing almost daily articles about Jeffries's preparation, coupled with an underlying theme of the possible doom of professional boxing should Johnson win.

Although Jim had fought and befriended a Negro boxer (Peter Jackson) early in his career and had shared the stage with Negro performers in vaudeville and at benefits, he, too, became caught up in the hysteria of the moment. Seemingly to verify which side he was on, the *Chronicle* quoted him as saying, "I want to see a white man win back the heavyweight championship of the world." Thus he began the Herculean task of preparing a grossly out-of-shape Jeffries for the contest.

Jeffries' morning regimen consisted of two hours in the gym performing various exercises, an hour of mat wrestling, and a massage. After lunch, Jeffries did some roadwork, rested, and ended the day sparring some rounds. Enormous effort by Jeffries's trainers—Roger Cornell, Farmer Burns, and De Witt Van Court—to improve the challenger's stamina and help him shed poundage seemed to be working, with no apparent loss in vigor. Both Jim and Joe Choynski, the latter also acting as an advisor, appealed to Jeffries to box more but he ignored their suggestions. Two weeks before the bout, Jim began sparring sessions with Jeffries, to increase his speed and movement. Reports from camp suggested Jeffries was progressing nicely, had lost considerable weight, and resembled his old self in the ring.

In final preparations for the battle, Jeffries moved his training camp to Moana Springs, Nevada. With increased activity taking place in nearby Reno, however, the Jeffries camp took on a carnival air, with reporters, retired boxers, gamblers, and a stream of admirers crowding the grounds. In addition, Rickard had stationed police and Pinkerton men at both camps "to insure a peaceful decorum," another tactic to keep both press and fans excited.

No one seemed to notice that the vast majority of newspaper coverage spoke only of Jeffries. There was so little of Johnson an outsider might easily have wondered whom Jeffries was facing. When it was announced who would second Jeffries in the ring—Jim, Joe Choynski, Farmer Burns, Jack Jeffries,

De Witt Van Court, Bob Armstrong and Tod Bayer—there was no public mention of Johnson's seconds. They were later identified as Sig Hart, Prof. Burns, Doc Furey, Al Kaufman, and the redoubtable Billy Delaney. Ironically, Delaney had been Jim's advisor at the Sullivan match, Bob Fitzsimmons's advisor when he defeated Jim for the title, a previous advisor to Jeffries, and now assisted Johnson.

A week before the bout, confident statements about Jeffries's condition and his chances for victory flowed from numerous "reliable" sources. Jeffries's physician, Dr. Porter, proclaimed "the big fellow is in perfect train." Mike Murphy, a well-regarded trainer, noted that "Jeffries is in perfect condition, trained to the minute." Under questioning by reporters, however, Murphy declined to pick a winner. Sam Langford, a Negro boxer and no friend of the champion, declared, "I hope Jeffries breaks Johnson's jaw in the first round." Photo sessions seemed to have become endless. Most newspaper reporters observed Jeffries to be in "great condition." When asked about Jeffries chances against Johnson, Jim replied, somewhat elliptically, "Johnson has an uncomfortable time ahead." Why wasn't Jim more enthusiastic, they wondered.

Unknown to the public, three days before the contest, panic struck the Jeffries camp. From the moment he awakened that morning, Jeffries had been in a state of nervous collapse. No matter how hard the trainers tried to calm him, nothing seemed to help. It was all Jim could do to prepare Jeffries that day so reporters and photographers would not notice his mental condition.

Jim was particularly dismayed because it was painfully apparent that Jeffries had lost his nerve. He was in mortal fear of facing Johnson. In conversations, Jeffries constantly referred to the amount of money bet on him and his personal responsibilities to the boxing profession. To Jim and the others, it appeared the weight of these concerns had very likely taken its toll on the challenger's confidence. Even before the first bell, they now believed, Jeffries was a beaten man.

Reno was now overcrowded with boxing enthusiasts. Countless fans from the U.S. and foreign countries had all made their way to the Western site to witness what they confidently believed would be a resounding defeat for the insolent Negro. Every hotel and boardinghouse was filled to capacity, as were many private homes opened to guests by enterprising owners. Cot brigades appeared in community halls to care for overflow patrons. Restaurants were jammed day and night and street vendors, offering a wide array of sustenance, prospered. Traffic was so heavy, people found it faster to walk than to ride. Special police had been sent in to guard against anticipated felonies, and a state guard troop was stationed outside of Reno "to cope with any emergency that may arise"—another Rickard invention. Amazingly, though the town was vastly overpopulated and a great deal of drinking took its toll among visitors, there were few arrests and little trouble.

According to Rickard, his arena had been specially constructed so that every seat had a perfect view of the ring. All seats were made of wooden planks. Tiers of benches ascended from a foot above ground at ringside to thirty feet above ground at the rear, the only apparent difference being that the ringside planks were smoothly planed. Seat prices ranged from ten to fifty dollars. Women and the few, brave Negroes in attendance had to sit in sections in the sun; the ring itself and ringside seats were shaded. A considerable number of police were dispersed throughout the crowd. Rickard confidently predicted an attendance of 17,000 and gate receipts of more than $250,000.

The match was slated at forty-five rounds. Scheduled on the country's most venerable day, July 4 (again a Rickard idea), the contest would begin at 2:00 P.M., after the usual introductions. The purse was immense: $101,000, to be divided seventy-five percent to the winner and twenty-five percent to the loser. Tex Rickard selected himself as referee; the esteemed Charley White was chosen as substitute referee. Betting odds at the time of the contest favored Jeffries 10 to 6, although a good deal of money went for Johnson.

Under a cloudless sky, during the hottest part of the day, a crowd of close to 16,000 spectators cheered the national anthem. As the band played "The Star Spangled Banner," someone scrambled over the ropes and ran around the ring waving an American flag. Yet this display of patriotic fervor, along with the ovation they gave Jeffries as he entered the ring, would prove to be the only glorious moments enjoyed by the partisan crowd that afternoon.

To all appearances, Jeffries seemed confident, carefree, and happy as he stood in his corner waiting for the bell. In reality, he was verging on a nervous breakdown, having suffered another anxiety attack in his dressing room. It had continued like this for three days and a frustrated Jim felt powerless for his inability to calm Jeffries. Before the bout, when Jim examined Jeffries gloves, he looked carefully into the boxer's eyes and clearly saw a man in despair. When he did the same with Johnson, he found a man totally confident of victory.

Jim Jeffries fought Jack Johnson only because the promoters and public demanded it, though his emotions had been rubbed raw by worry and fear of letting down the public, invalidating their ambitions. When he entered the ring, he was in a daze and he endured the preliminaries as if he had been doped, a rumor that circulated after the bout but was quickly dispelled when the truth of his condition was later revealed.

Johnson won the bout with systematic ease, giving Jeffries the worst beating of his career. In the fifteenth round, having watched their fighter repeatedly pummeled, knocked down, bloodied, and battered, Jeffries's seconds yelled to stop the bout and rushed into the ring to rescue their fallen man. From the opening bell, Jeffries had been completely outclassed by the champion. It was only due to Johnson's sense of the dramatic and desire to prove his superiority beyond any doubt that the carnage lasted fifteen rounds. Some suggested it was also for the benefit of those financial interests filming moving pictures.

By the third round, everyone in the arena knew Jeffries was beaten; it was only a question of how long Johnson would permit him to remain standing. Actually, Jeffries should have been counted out the first time he fell. The timekeeper carefully tolled off the seconds, but Rickard, unaccustomed to his role, apparently lost the count. He allowed Jeffries to regain his feet; when Jeffries's seconds tried to enter the ring, he waved them back. There followed a second knockdown, which sent Jeffries through the ropes. One eye was shut; blood flowed freely from his mouth and nose. Only Jeffries's courage urged him to stand once again. No strength remained, and Johnson's punishing punches sent him down for the final time.

During the early rounds, Jim had done everything he could to rile Johnson, shouting harsh expletives designed to distract the boxer. His stentorian voice rose above those of other ringside enthusiasts, who were also yelling derogatory remarks. At the beginning of the second round, in line with his plan to irritate Johnson, Jim called out: "He wants to fight a little, Jim. Show him how to do it." To which John-

son retorted, "You bet I do." With that, he proceeded to pepper Jeffries with a flurry of stinging blows that made the wincing challenger retreat. In the sixth, Johnson put his arms around the staggering Jeffries and pushed him across the ring to where Jim was standing. "Where do you want me to put him, Mr. Corbett?" he asked, grinning broadly. Jim had little to say to the champion after that.

Jack London's report of the contest summed it up for the partisan press.

> Once again has Johnson sent down to defeat the chosen representative of the white race. From the opening to the closing round he never ceased his witty sallies, his exchange of repartee with his opponent's seconds and with the spectators. Johnson played, as usual. He played and fought a white man, in a white man's country, before a white man's crowd. And the crowd was a Jeffries crowd. The greatest battle of the century was a monologue delivered to twenty thousand spectators by a smiling Negro who was never in doubt and who was never serious for more than a moment at a time. [5]

Simultaneously awed and overwhelmed by the outcome, the crowd remained well-behaved at the conclusion of the one-sided contest. Jeffries's end came in silence. Only after three minutes, when Jeffries finally regained his feet, did one last cheer mask the depths of disappointment. Spectators retired from the arena quietly and in orderly fashion. Apparently little noticed by the crowd, but observed by the press and moving picture cameras was Johnson's wife, who climbed into the ring to embrace and kiss her husband. For a moment, the white men standing in the ring were stunned, to slack-jawed amazement.

Hundreds of thousands of dollars had been wagered on the bout, with many more losers than winners. George Considine was said to have lost $5,000, as had

Nat Goodwin, the actor. The baseball magnate, Clarence Berry, lost $65,000. A San Francisco businessman, H. J. Strack, reported a loss of $17,000. Jim admitted to losing $5,000 on his friend. Tom Corbett declared that he had handled something like $65,000 in his temporary Reno poolroom, and he estimated that an equal amount had been handled in San Francisco. On the other hand, some members of the boxing community, among them Ed Graney, Charlie Harvey, and Jack Root, made considerable money for having bet on Johnson.

Johnson earned more than $120,000: sixty percent of the purse of $101,000 (at the last minute, Johnson had renegotiated the split from seventy-five/twenty-five to sixty/forty, apparently because he himself was hesitant about the outcome), a bonus of $10,000, and $50,000 for his motion picture rights. Jeffries earned a total of $117,000: forty percent of the purse, a bonus of $10,000, and more than $66,000 for his picture rights. Rickard and his colleagues cleared $120,000, plus another $33,000 for their one-sixth interest in the moving pictures.

Jim remained at Jeffries's side after the match, acting as his spokesman to the press. "I am here solely because Jim lost," he said. "The big fellow takes his defeat much at heart, and we all want to comfort him as much as possible." Shaking his head sorrowfully, he added, "I can't account for his fight. He is sore at himself, too. Poor Jim didn't show the best that was in him." Yet Jim knew the truth of the matter. Out of consideration for a friend, he chose not to reveal it at this time to swarms of reporters hunting for reasons why Jeffries had failed in the ring.

That evening, Jeffries and his entourage left Reno for San Francisco. Jim's carefully laid plans to prevent the crowd from bothering Jeffries proved unnecessary. Few people waited at the station, and

Jeffries retired without incident to his drawing-room car, placed on a siding. Tex Rickard soon joined him and they were reported to have had "quite a talk," the subject of which was never revealed. After Rickard left, Jeffries's departure seemed almost more pitiful than his defeat. Only a week before, he had been greeted by roaring thousands. As the train pulled out, he received but a feeble cheer from the few remaining loyalists.

The next day, pressed by reporters, Joe Choynski refused to disclose the full extent of the debacle, stalling them "until I reach Chicago." Jim, aware that rumors about Jeffries's humiliation were spreading rapidly and included the usual claims of "fight-throwing" and doping, attempted to fashion the true story for the press. He revealed that, three days before the fight, Jeffries had been "in a state of nervous collapse" and, throughout the training period, Jeffries had acted in such a manner as to give his trainers ominous warnings of the bout's outcome.

"Physically, he was all right until three days before the fight," Jim explained. "Then a change came over him, and he seemed to be like a man dazed. All this talk about his being the 'hope of the white race' had got on his nerves."

"All through his training," Jim went on, "he would not listen to advice. Jeffries acted like a man who didn't hear what was being said to him. If he had shown the slightest symptom of aggressiveness, I would have thought there was some hope for him; but he acted as if he was in a stupor."

"I knew how it was going, and I yelled everything I could think of at Johnson, but it was no use," he concluded. "Jeff didn't have a punch that would break an egg."

A few days later, Rickard unashamedly revealed to the press how he had been able to persuade Johnson and Jeffries to sign. It had been, he boasted, a combination of typical Rickard hyperbole and money. He had offered Johnson an extra $10,000 and promised his wife a sealskin coat if her husband would sign a contract. In addition, he had loaned Johnson another $2,500. To secure Jeffries, he had not only paid off Jeffries's Reno betting debt, but also given Jeffries's agent $2,500 as "incentive" to convince the former champion to come out of retirement. It had been only for the press that he had fashioned the contest as a battle between whites and Negroes.

Due primarily to the publicity that pervaded the "moral and social character" of the Jeffries-Johnson bout, reports of Johnson's dramatic victory set off a series of confrontations and riots in many cities across the country, pitched battles in which many Negroes were either beaten up, jailed, or killed. In most cases, accounts were so muddled that it was difficult to determine who had actually initiated the disorders, although newspaper coverage remained highly skewed in favor of white "righteousness." A few street fights occurred in New York, but they were not nearly as unfortunate for Negroes as those in Chicago, Baltimore, Atlanta, and many other Southern cities. Almost immediately, mayors and city councils called for the Jeffries-Johnson moving pictures to be banned, to avoid any agitation that their presentation might create among the populace. Authorities in Chicago, Milwaukee, Cincinnati, Boston, Providence, and Washington, D.C. quickly banned the pictures. In contrast, New York, Philadelphia, and San Francisco refused to interfere with their exhibition. Interestingly, in the cities where the picture was displayed, box office receipts were large and no riots took place. The entire episode, however, prompted the writing of a federal law forbidding the interstate transfer of any fight movies.

Nor did events go well for Johnson. For a proposed victory parade in Chicago, he was refused a police escort. He was not permitted to perform on the stage in Washington, D.C. An Atlanta spokesman publicly declared: "We don't want Johnson down in this part of the country. If he is wise, he will not come to Atlanta." In fact, Johnson's only opportunity to share his victory with admirers came in New York City, where he performed a bag-punching exhibition for three weeks on the vaudeville stage at Hammerstein's Victoria Theater, to full and enthusiastic houses. Less than two years later, his wife committed suicide. He was later indicted under the Mann Act and fled the country for fear of his life, believing that, had he been sentenced to jail, he never would have gotten out alive.

The day following the fight, Jeffries departed for Los Angeles and permanent retirement. Jim and Vera caught a train back to New York, where he had a vaudeville engagement to fulfill. On the same train were Jack Johnson and his wife. No evidence exists that, during the cross-country train ride, the couples ever met.

Not six days after the bout in Reno, Jim took the stage of the American Theater to offer his rendition of the Jeffries-Johnson contest. He attributed Jeffries's defeat to a failure of nerve and the fact that his former manager and trainer, Billy Delaney, had "gone over to the Johnson camp." A number of revealing anecdotes were included.

> I went out to California to box with him, and I put on the gloves the first day, but he couldn't hit me with a handful of rice.
> Mrs. Jeffries told me that the night before the battle she had heard him scuffling and walking about his room, and that he sat up all night, simply worrying.
> I tried to kid Jeffries about Delaney's loss, but he would only mutter, "To think of Delaney being with the nigger instead of me."[6]

Just two weeks after the bout, the Jeffries-Johnson moving pictures were shown at the Alhambra Theater, although New York's Board of Censors had not yet passed on the case. The *Clipper* reported:

A crowd filled the theater on the opening night, and the house will no doubt do big during the engagement. There were few Negroes in the audience, and these took seats in the upper parts of the theater. The pictures were explained by Joe Humphries, the veteran announcer.[7]

After the entire engagement, which continued almost a month, the *Clipper* noted that: "There was no sense of disorder, and the pictures occasioned no glimmer of race riots." During the same three-week period, Jim played to crowded houses, discussing the "inside story" of the now infamous title bout.

The Annual Actors' Fund Field day at the Polo Grounds brought in more than $15,000 and attracted 13,000 people, all of whom were drawn to the event by a host of Broadway's headliners. A parade and band led by George M. Cohan opened the festivities. The Friars and Lew Fields baseball teams followed in procession, along with George Evans's Minstrels, Marie Dressler's chorus girls, Annie Oakley, and the Follies of 1910 company, as well as members of the White Rats, Vaudeville Comedy Club, and the Professional Women's League, featuring the elegantly attired Lillian Russell.

Appearing in blackface for the first time in his career, Jim led the Evans Minstrel troupe. Later in the program, Jim also served as referee for a comic boxing match between Billy Reeves and Bert Williams, the popular Negro song-and-dance man. The show concluded with a group of Negro performers chasing a greased pig and participating in a custard pie-eating contest. Jim's role with Evans Minstrels proved to be the public intro-

duction of his new season's appearance as a "corkonian." The *Clipper* announced his intentions in its next issue.

James J. Corbett in blackface will be the special feature with George Evans's Honey Boy Minstrels, which will open the season of the City Theater, New York, on Saturday, August 13. Mr. Corbett will act as the interlocutor of the show in the first part, and then will tell his story of the recent Reno fight.[8]

Stomping their feet in time with the music as they marched onto the stage, the performers of Evans's Minstrel troupe were greeted by a noisy and boisterous full house. The scenery had drawn applause as soon as the curtains opened, and the electrical effects, which displayed an American flag on the curtain while everyone sang "The Star Spangled Banner," drew loud cheers and more applause. Evans then introduced Jim: "Now, for your pleasure, we have that rising young minstrel..." (brass fanfare)... "James J. Corbett!" Jim came on stage and, after repeated bows to applause, announced the first part of the program.

"Corbett's debut into minstrelsy was an auspicious one," noted the *Clipper*, "and adds another triumph to the man who seems to conquer anything he undertakes." As interlocutor, Corbett talked back to Tambo and Bones in a succession of one-liners that delighted the audience. In one sequence, they discussed the return of Haley's Comet. The end men demanded more proof than merely the interlocutor's say-so for the return of the comet. When Jim declared emphatically that it was indeed returning, Tambo responded, "Yes, but you also told me Mr. Jeff was coming back. How can I take your word?" The crowd howled.

In the second part of the program, Jim talked about his troubles removing the burnt-cork, and gave his insights into the

Jeffries-Johnson contest. The audience was fascinated.

Engagements in Cleveland, Detroit, and Chicago resulted in "packed houses." While in Chicago, Jim entered into the debate about the city's ban on Jeffries-Johnson fight pictures. Chicago's mayor had prohibited them from being shown, but Jim believed they should be made public. Judging by their reactions to his opinions, audiences agreed. A similar episode occurred in Cincinnati when Jim attended a baseball game and was interviewed by the local press.

The fall tour took the company to St. Louis, Denver, back to Omaha and Kansas City, then south to Memphis, Little Rock, and New Orleans for the Christmas holidays. Extra matinees had to be presented to accommodate the overflow crowds in New Orleans, as SRO prevailed and the performers were "warmly welcomed." New Orleans already had the reputation of being an excellent minstrel city.

The early months of 1911 saw the company combining week-long engagements in Washington, D.C., Baltimore, and Brooklyn with one-night stands in the small towns of West Virginia, Virginia, and Pennsylvania. In early March, they returned to the Grand Opera House, New York City, to sizable attendance. By this time, Jim had replaced his monologue on the fight with stories of his travels. Like the Jeffries-Johnson movies, fight stories had become "old business."

April and May usually represented the "dog days" of a tour, full of one-night stands in Massachusetts, New Hampshire, and Maine. The season—196 performances in sixty-four cities—ended in Utica, New York, on May 24. Despite the grueling pace, the tour had been a great success and Jim thoroughly enjoyed his stint in minstrelsy.

Jim and Vera spent the summer volunteering for various children's programs in Bayside. He would often be seen with a group of boys in tow as they attended baseball games at the Polo Grounds. For the first time in many years, he made only one summer appearance, at the Brighton Beach Theater, recounting his minstrel experiences. Negotiating for next season with manager Percy Williams, Jim agreed to carry a small company to perform a number of his playlets in Williams's houses.

Jim's new season opened at Shea's Theater, Buffalo on September 18, where he presented "A Thief in the Night." He played there for two weeks, varying the playlets every few days, before returning to the Bronx Theater, then presenting other engagements close by for the next month. At the New York Theater, Jim, George M. Cohan, Eddie Leonard, George Primrose, and Irving Berlin performed in a testimonial for baseball Manager John McGraw and his New York Giants, who had recently won the World Series. Jim again assumed the role of interlocutor in a minstrel skit.

Jim rationed his appearances now, playing only once every two or three weeks, in nearby cities. Anticipating a welcome change, he wanted to stay in New York for the Christmas and New Year's festivities and rest up for some heavy touring in the coming year.

Early 1912 featured a highly publicized debate between vaudeville managers—prompted by the Keith-Albee organization—and performers, regarding the issue of "curtain calls" and "encores." Managers claimed they wanted to reduce or eliminate such demonstrations of audience approval to speed up the program. Their real reason behind the move was to turn two-a-day shows into three-a-day shows, thereby increasing box-office receipts without having to increase actors' salaries.

Performers balked at the move, correctly noting the inherent loss of salary.

Even more serious, however, was the inhibition of audience participation, so important to an actor's understanding of and rapport with theater patrons. Jim, among others, led the stand against the managers' ploy, introducing the topic in his monologues, which elicited strong audience reactions in favor of actors. Newspapers supported them, as well, placing further pressure against the managers. Within a few weeks, the issue was quietly dropped, at least for the immediate future. Five years later, however, during World War I, the argument would be raised again by theater managers, who suggested that a shortened show would save heating and lighting energy, thereby aiding the war effort. And so would end the colorful history of encores during show performances.

The early part of the year also saw the passing of some boxing icons. Billy Delaney, one of the most talented trainers of the era, though now remembered chiefly for his support of Jack Johnson, died in Oakland, California. Gus Ruhlin, an able contender in the heavyweight ranks, died at his home in Brooklyn. Both had been close friends of Jim's in the past.

Relatively unnoticed by the boxing community was the announcement that John L. Sullivan and Jake Kilrain had begun their farewell tour in vaudeville. With Jeffries's loss to Johnson, it seemed America's boxing enthusiasts had become obsessed by the belief that only a white man should hold a championship and they urgently sought out boxers to fulfill this "noble" desire. For the next several years, a number of men contended for the honor but no one seemed able to capture the mantle of "white hope." Unfortunately, the period became a travesty for the sport that had worked so hard to win national recognition and acceptance. In April, 1915, some five years after Jim Jeffries's loss, the "white hope" crusade finally satisfied its exclusionary beliefs when, in Havana,

Cuba, Jess Willard knocked out an over-the-hill Jack Johnson.

Jim spent the spring of 1912 alternating week-long engagements in Boston, Philadelphia, Milwaukee, and Detroit, with periods at home. Having tired of continuous appearances, he seemed more interested in benefit performances. A Friars dinner honoring Weber & Fields, who had recently reunited after an eight year separation, gathered their former stock-company actors, and, in an unprecedented thirty-day run, amassed the largest box-office receipts in history. At the dinner, Jim gave a short monologue on what it was like following Weber & Fields on a vaudeville bill.

At a Lambs' Club All Star Gambol, Jim refereed a bout between Dave Montgomery, posing as Corbett, and Fred Stone, posing as Jeffries, in which the three rounds were danced to music by Victor Herbert. Also on the bill were acts by William Collier, George M. Cohan, Eddie Foy, Nat Wills, and William and Dustin Farnum. Proceeds of the event benefited orphans of the *Titanic* tragedy.

In June, the Annual Friars' Club Frolic visited Philadelphia and Atlantic City in addition to presenting three performances in New York. The two-part show consisted of a minstrel and olio exhibitions, routines performed by Weber & Fields, Cohan, Collier, Berlin, Lew Dockstater, Louis Mann, and Raymond Hitchcock. Jim played interlocutor in the minstrel portion, and presented a restaurant skit with Collier for the olio, in which they parodied a Weber & Fields sketch. To inaugurate their New York appearances, on the day of the opening performance, the Friars marched down Broadway, with Collier, dressed in a white satin suit and swinging a baton, leading a brass band.

There followed two benefits for the Vaudeville Comedy Club in Atlantic City, at which Jim acted as host and announcer.

A formal grouping of the Friars Club's most important members. The Friars had become the most significant performers' group in New York. Standing, third from the left is Jim Corbett. Sitting, third from left is Will Rogers; fourth from left, Joe Weber. Sitting third from the right is George M. Cohan, head abbott; second from right is Lew Dockstater. The Friars' charitable activities and benefits became well-known throughout the country.

Montgomery & Stone, Van and Schenk, and the irrepressible Eva Tanguay participated in the event, which collected $14,000 for retired actors.

When Jim played an engagement in Boston, however, at the end of August, he caught a cold that hampered his monologues. Very rarely ill, Jim paid little attention to his discomfort. As a result, when he appeared in Philadelphia the following week, he coughed so much through his act that members of the audience were sympathetically calling for him to see a doctor. The illness became so severe that he postponed another week at the same theater and went home to bed.

When his condition deteriorated alarmingly, he was taken to New York City's Jefferson hospital for diagnostic care. Jim was found to be suffering from an acute attack of appendicitis. Immediately, he was operated upon, but the doctors' prognosis was not good. Confined to bed, he was placed under continuous ob-servation as his fever, due to the effects of pneumonia, soared. When it was publicly announced that Jim had been hospitalized, many friends expressed a desire to visit him but, doctors allowed no visitors due to his precarious condition. After one week, throughout which he suffered high fever, the doctors reported they had practically given up hope of saving Jim's life.

What saved him, doctors later claimed, was his exceptional conditioning and his decades-long regimen of drinking twelve glasses of mineral water daily, a habit he had acquired during his early days of training. In another week, the fever receded, though Jim remained very weak. Still, he began making plans to return to the stage, much against Vera's and his doctors' pleas. A visitor to his room found copies of the *Clipper, Dramatic Mirror,* and *Police Gazette* lying on every available surface. Flowers bloomed everywhere. Get-well cards pasted to the wall declared encouragement.

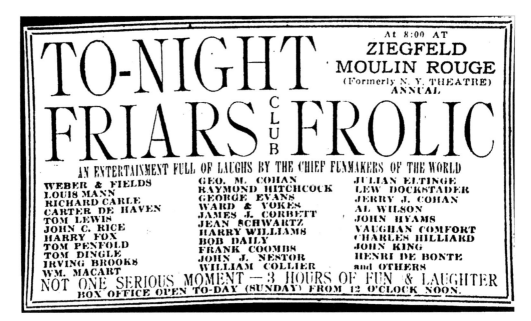

A newspaper announcement for the Annual Friars' Frolic. For three hours audiences saw the best performers offering their specialties, all on a single bill. Much of the material was irreverent, actors taking the opportunity to satirize and parody their colleagues, society, and the notorious Syndicate of theater owners.

Yet, Jim was restless. What seemed to bother him most of all was a self-directed anger at having allowed himself to become ill. What had he done wrong? Neglected exercise? Fallen into the stage lifestyle? Or was he just getting old? Whatever the reasons, Jim resolved to make changes to protect his health. Even as he recuperated in the hospital, he began exercising and bag-punching. By the middle of November, two months from the time he had been reported to be close to death, Jim was back home, admittedly still weak, but improving every day. Eager to return to action, he felt confident enough of his strength to visit the Friars' Club.

James J. Corbett, who was so sick recently that the doctors had given up hope of saving his life, visited the Friars' Club on Monday, and held quite a reception. Jim told the Clipper representative that he would rest for three more weeks and then play the Sullivan-Considine time.[9]

A few weeks later, at a Friars' banquet that Jim attended, a showing of the Corbett-Stone three-round boxing exhibition was reprised for members. At an Actors' Fund benefit the previous summer, Jim and Fred Stone had staged a bout, in proper ring attire, with Dave Montgomery acting as referee. Stone's seconds were all representatives of the boxing profession— Larry Harris, Terry McGovern, and Young Corbett. Jim's seconds were from the theatrical profession—William Courtleigh and John Barrymore. Timekeepers were De Wolf Hopper and George Considine. The ring had been constructed on the stage of the Globe Theater. Spectators consisted of benefit performers and theater patrons.

Stone proved an agile, scrappy opponent and aggressively attacked Jim. Showing a bit of his old form, Jim dropped Stone twice in the first round and once in the second. In the third round, when Stone went down, he displayed his trademark stand-on-the-head routine, then, to the delight of the audience, fell prone with a resounding thud. Jim went to pick him up but, because Stone wiggled comically around the floor, was unable to lift him. The crowd roared their approval.

Jim enjoyed the evening, but the next day suffered a relapse of severe weakness. Doctors demanded that he rest in bed for however long it took for him to regain strength. It would be three months before he reentered a theater. Judging from his condition, some friends feared he might never return.

Sullivan-Considine waited patiently for Jim to recover and when he announced his readiness to perform, they booked him into Denver's Empress Theater, in March, 1913. His monologue consisted of not only various boxing and theater anecdotes, but also some stories about his illness and recovery. Audiences applauded him all the more for sharing his thoughts with them. Jim took a month off before appearing again, this time in Detroit with similar results. Emboldened by his resurgent strength, Jim added engagements in Cincinnati, Indianapolis, and New York to close the season. He expressed pleasure about returning to the stage, but also said he would look for other vehicles that required less touring and offered better working hours.

In June, a White Rats Scamper, a benefit for those members out of work, was held at Weber & Fields's Forty-second Street Theater. The event brought Jim together with George Evans, Al Jolson, Eddie Leonard, and Montgomery & Stone. While in rehearsals, Jim was asked to meet with old friends, the Mittenthal Brothers and Harry Raver, a successful New York businessman, to discuss a new opportunity. Over the past few years, the Mittenthals had enlarged their theatrical business to the point that they were backing shows and managing road companies. Their success had now led them to moving pictures. Raver had recently become interested in public entertainment, particularly moving pictures, and sought to enter this new industry that seemed to promise substantial financial gain. The result of their meeting was quickly announced to the press.

> James J. Corbett, ex-champion pugilist, matinee idol and vaudeville monologist par-excellence, has been engaged by the Mittenthal Bros. to produce and play several of his successful dramatic sketches before the camera. James J., while making his premier in the "movie" field, as far as the sketch thing goes, is no stranger to the cinematograph, as most of our esteemed contemporaries seem to think. Remember those little fistic encounters with "Ruby Robert" and other knights of the padded mitt?[10]

11. MULTI-MEDIA HEADLINER

In 1912, a typical one-reel moving picture was considered nothing more than a twelve-to-fifteen minute turn on a vaudeville bill. However, Adolf Zukor, former fur merchant and now enterprising movie producer, was about to make a decision that would launch a revolution in the moving picture industry. He imported a four-reel picture, "Queen Elizabeth," and advertised it to the public as a "feature" film. Up to that time, moving picture patrons were believed to have little patience and short attention spans. Zukor proved that perception erroneous.

In early 1913, taking advantage of the potential for lengthier moving pictures, George Kleine imported an eight-reel production of "Quo Vadis," proving conclusively that the "feature" movie could occupy an important and profitable niche in popular entertainment. At an unprecedented ticket price of one dollar, "Quo Vadis" ran for twenty-two weeks on Broadway and earned Kleine a substantial profit.

As witnesses to the results of this startling innovation, producers and managers rushed to find stories and reputable actors, so that they too could cash in on the anticipated bonanza. Among this group, the Mittenthal Brothers, had reaped the benefits of Jim's popularity

some years before. Why not tap into his extensive national following again through a moving picture venture? As a precaution, however, they hedged their investment by joining with Harry Raver, a rich clothier, to assist in financing the production. Their timing could not have been more fortuitous.

Not surprisingly, Jim leapt at the opportunity to appear in movies. Though it may have been considered risky at the time, the chance to perform for thousands of people, after only a few weeks' work, for more money than could be made on a months-long vaudeville tour was an enticing proposition. The fact that just one moving picture could achieve these results seemed astounding. Compared to the stage, where performance was always subject to a multitude of variables, from weather conditions to audience reactions, moving pictures "locked in" the best performance an actor could turn out.

The film was shot at two locations: the hilly Palisades at Fort Lee, New Jersey, to simulate a Western locale and a warehouse in Manhattan, set up for interior scenes. For Jim, a day's work consisted of script reading and writing, working out blocking for the scenes to be filmed (cameras were stationary, so all the action had to take place within a confined space), and, finally, the actual shooting of the scene. If all went as scheduled, nine or ten scenes could be filmed in a day. Rarely would a scene be reshot. Interior scenes were handled similarly, though with an even faster schedule, since weather conditions were not a factor. Jim's entire movie was completed in less than two months. In addition, the Mittenthals saw to it that certain episodes were included to mirror Jim's own colorful background, similar to what Brady had done in his production of "Gentleman Jack."

Jim performed his own stunts. He rode a horse well, able to jump on and off the animal with ease. His fight scenes were orchestrated so that opponents would not suffer from his forceful blows. According to reports, there were also a number of scenes where Jim displayed "real daring and bravery."

In one episode, Jim saved a gold mine from destruction by seizing a sputtering bomb and hurling it into a ravine. The bomb was real, and set on a timer; any delay in the action could have been injurious to Jim. In another episode, Jim, at the wheel of a high-powered automobile, raced along a rutted, bumpy road in order to apprehend stagecoach bandits. Over such terrain, handling the auto was difficult and truly dangerous. Since the camera was stationary, the scene had to be shot in segments and spliced together to capture the full-chase effect, requiring many takes. Jim's only mishap during the entire filming was falling off a chair.

When the *Dramatic Mirror* reported that Jim had completed camera work for the movie, they also declared that: "It is a great big production and gives Corbett a chance to show that he is a polished actor as well as one of the world's greatest athletes."[1]

Variety also published a glowing report about Jim's introduction into the picture business.

Considerable of the magnetism which the personality of James J. Corbett exercises over an audience in a theater, particularly in the plays in which he has appeared as a valiant champion of the oppressed, has been successfully transferred to the films in a new five-reel feature, entitled "The Man from the Golden West." The story is one of growing dramatic interest to the patron of the theater who accepts frank melodrama as a necessary factor of the playhouse, and presents its hero in successive situations where he is called upon for the quick exercise of his wits, muscles and daring.[2]

Jim (his movie name), a bank clerk who has come to San Francisco to seek his fortune, lends money to a prospector who plans to deposit his gold in Jim's bank. When the treasure is stolen en route to the bank, Jim, after an exciting chase, manages to catch the robbers, and return the money in time to placate a mob of creditors who, having heard of the robbery, are demanding to withdraw their savings. Back in New York, Jim's business partner brings their Wall Street brokerage firm close to ruin, then forges bonds to cover his losses. During a dinner party arranged to welcome Jim home, his partner kills a detective who had arrived to question him, but Jim, returning to his sweetheart, is mistakenly suspected of the crime. He is arrested and sent to Sing Sing. Jim escapes in the clothes of a servant of his sweetheart's. Later, he proves his innocence by means of a photograph of the eye of the murder victim, revealing in its retina the actual culprit, Jim's dishonest partner.

As early as 1911, theater managers were selling postcards containing actors' photos for the exorbitant price of five cents, the same amount as an admission price. Ballroom dances, which actors were required to attend, were held in major cities so that eager patrons could see and meet their favorite film stars. Simultaneously with promoting personal appearances, producers added credit titles to their films, thereby initiating the first in a long series of elements that advanced the star system.

Soon, moving picture hero contests exploded across the country and actors, much to their delight, found themselves objects of adulation and honor. Observing the trend, a movie critic for the *Pittsburgh Mirror* summed up the movement and astutely prophesied, "Hero worship is something tangible in the moving picture business. The future of the moving picture lies with the player."

When Jim's movie opened in New York theaters, it reflected the new developments brought on by multi-reel features. Enterprising theater managers leased vaudeville houses to present these "long" movies, which, almost immediately, returned good box-office receipts. Newspaper advertising had become so extensive the papers set aside entire pages for movie reviews, ads, and gossip. Personal theater appearances by stars promoting their pictures became routine, at least as long as actors could tolerate the mobs of people seeking autographs.

Both critical and public reaction to "The Man from the Golden West" were excellent, realizing quick profit for the Mittenthal/Raver partnership and providing a considerable exposure and idolization for Jim. The *New York Times* predicted the movie "is bound to go big wherever shown." The film's apparent success convinced Jim that the medium offered a myriad of benefits for him and he publicly expressed a desire to continue in movies. The *Clipper* called him "one of the biggest money winners on the screen," all the more remarkable for the brief time he had appeared in theaters. These days, movies were being released so quickly that a picture would be replaced in a matter of weeks, never to be seen again. As jealous stage critics pointed out, vaudeville still represented a weekly paycheck and con-

tinuous performance, even as the moving picture business worked to overcome their inferiority complex.

Prior to the movie commitment, Jim had agreed to play at a number of F.F. Proctor houses. When he discovered he would be only a third headliner, however, Jim refused the engagement and went instead to Marcus Loew. A contract was quickly negotiated, at close to $2,000 a week and Jim opened his season October 20 at the Francais Theater, Montreal. Ironically, down the street from the Francais, another theater was featuring Jim's movie.

In November, Jim returned to appear in Loew's theaters in New York City. After a month of playing to SRO houses, Jim signed for another short Loew's tour, concerning which the *Clipper* declared:

> Jim Corbett goes back on Loew's time December 29, when he opens a week's stay at the Greeley. The Loews press agent billed him like a circus. Corbett is one of the biggest money winners on the Loew's circuit.[3]

After he closed at the Greeley, the *Times* reported that Jim's engagement had broken all previous records at the theater. They also disclosed that Jim had held "informal sessions" after each show so that he could meet "many of his old admirers," apparently expanding the idea from his movie personal appearances. The following week, Jim repeated the event when he played at the Broadway Theater in Philadelphia. While there, Jim again found himself in competition with his movie, showing only a few blocks away so he decided to make appearances at both venues. The press loved it, and featured the event prominently in their stories.

During the early months of 1914, an amalgam of events set the pace and continued to shape the motion picture business as a viable and exciting enterprise.

Klaw and Erlanger, long the purveyors of stage productions, showed their first multi-reel feature film at the Palace Theater in New York City. The United Booking Office began scheduling movies together with vaudeville acts. Marcus Loew contracted for the distribution of feature films in all his theaters. Adolf Zukor boastfully announced the opening of a moving picture studio in Los Angeles, where "the sun always shines." Not to be outdone, producer Jesse Lasky opened an office in Hollywood, at Selma and Vine Streets. The Louis B. Mayer Company in Boston bought the rights to distribute all Lasky films throughout New England. Many Broadway stars were being enticed to appear in films at such substantial salaries, that they could not refuse.

Having now become both a stage and film star, Jim reaped the benefits of these new practices of popular entertainment. He was singled out as "the highest paid vaudeville star in the East" and was featured with a full-page photo on the front page of the *Clipper*, a decided honor for an actor. When Marcus Loew bought out the Sullivan-Considine circuit, fifty theaters in the Western United States (for five million dollars), Loew offered Jim a full season of work. Loew had started his theatrical career eight years previously, running penny arcades in Cincinnati and New York City. He bought the Royal Theater in New York in 1907, then quickly enlarged his circuit to include twenty-two theaters in the New York area and another twenty-five between New York and Toronto. Loew had recently begun to book and route acts through his own circuit.

Jim had to turn down Loew, if only temporarily, having promised the Lambs' Club to appear in their spring Gambol, which was scheduled to play in eleven cities during May. Included in the Lambs' company were John Phillip Sousa and a band of sixty, Julian Eltinge, Charles Ross, Junie McCree, Corse Payton, and William Collier. Their program consisted of skits parodying "Uncle Tom's Cabin," "Ten Nights in a Barroom," "The Corsican Brothers," and "East Lynne." Jim played everything from a circus barker, to a drunk, and a swashbuckler, with a comic flare that "kept audiences in stitches." The tour netted more than $20,000 for destitute actors.

No sooner had he returned to New York than the *Clipper* revealed that Jim was making "mysterious" visits to the Blanche Studios in Fort Lee to negotiate his appearance in another movie. Under the name U.S. Amusement Corporation, Herbert Blanche had recently formed a new half-million-dollar company to produce and distribute a succession of feature films, derived "from successful Broadway shows, starring well-known actors." Blanche was particularly interested in taking a number of Jim's former hits and turning them into "photodramas." The result of the meetings between Jim and Blanche were "an arrangement where the ex-champion heavyweight fighter of the world is to appear in several big film productions to be launched in the near future." The report continued:

> Mr. Blanche will stage the dramas in collaboration with Mr. Corbett, and "Gentleman Jim" will be surrounded by a cast composed of carefully selected groups of artists, including several members of the companies which appeared in the original stage presentations of the different Corbett plays.[4]

In June, Jim and Vera moved to Fort Lee, where he began studying the scenario for "The Burglar and the Lady," while carpenters and scenic artists built "exact reproductions" of specific locations. One of these, the sewers of Paris, took three weeks to construct. A large tank on top of a platform supplied water to the stage sewer, while a floodgate was so constructed that, when a hole was dug in the wall, the water would burst through with force and sweep everything before it. The scene could only be shot once, so Jim and the camera people had to improvise action depending on how the flood actually occurred.

The story was vaguely similar to that presented in the stage play, with a simplified plot and additional action. When Henry Banfield and his wife separate, each takes one of their sons to raise. The boy reared in poverty by the mother becomes a thief and eventually gains notoriety as the gentleman crook called Raffles. Moving easily in high society, he calls himself Detective Danvers during daylight hours. John, the boy reared in luxury by his father, becomes a clergyman and falls in love with Norma Harmon, the daughter of a wealthy banker. Norma, however, loves Danvers, who, aided by his faithful butler, robs both the Harmon mansion and the bank. Banfield discovers that the burglar is his brother and lets him escape to Paris. After an exciting encounter with the Paris police, Danvers turns himself in and, for Norma's sake, decides to reform.

The Paris sewer scene almost ended production of the movie. When Jim, armed with an iron bar, attempted to batter his way through the wall to escape the police, the floodgate rose prematurely. Hundreds of gallons of water crashed upon him. The iron bar was torn from his grasp and he had to use his hands to tear away the stone wall. Showing "his speed and cleverness," Jim managed to crawl through the hole seconds before the water washed everything away.

Warner Features was distributor of the film, scheduled to be released in November so that Jim could make personal appearances. Almost simultaneously, however, two offers served to alter Jim's original plans.

First, Jim was offered a twenty-week tour on the Pantages circuit, which concentrated its theaters in western Canada and the U.S. Tentatively, he agreed, largely because the tour gave him the opportunity to play an area he had not visited for some years and allowed him to visit San Francisco to see his siblings and their families. The second offer seemed to mesh with his current interests.

H.D. McIntosh was a colorful sportsman and theater impresario in Australia. He managed both boxers and theaters in that country and dominated the entertainment business with his productions. McIntosh was also an ardent admirer of Jim Corbett.

Entertainment in Australia had been greatly depressed due to the war and the loss of stage talent, and McIntosh was seeking ways to boost his business. His U.S. agent contacted Jim regarding a tour of the country, playing the McIntosh theaters, in 1915. And could he help McIntosh promote boxing matches at the same time? Salary would be attractive: $2,000 a week, plus all expenses paid. Moreover, Vera could accompany him. Cables were exchanged to clarify Jim's responsibilities, because they would obviously include more than just performing. McIntosh envisioned Jim speaking at sports clubs, appearing at boxing matches (maybe even to referee a few), and evaluating promising boxers to help build the McIntosh stable. McIntosh appealed to Jim: Would he assist in the sportman's attempt to invigorate a declining and demoralized sports' community?

With no long-term commitments at home, plus the opportunity to visit a country that he had heard good things about from fellow actors, Jim agreed to a sixteen-week tour. He promised to leave for Sydney upon completing his San Francisco engagement in February. McIntosh immediately wired steamship tickets and a contract.

It was Jim's proposed involvement in Australian boxing that really attracted him to the trip. Although he had devoted most of his time to theater in recent years, Jim had never really retired from the boxing scene. Whenever he could find the time, he attended bouts, agreed to interviews by reporters, and counseled boxers. It seemed that Jim could not leave boxing, nor could boxing leave Jim.

In the view of sportsmen throughout the United States, Jim continued to be a national hero, first as a boxing champion and one whose popularity had been greatly enhanced as a stage headliner. Indeed, Jim's public stature seemed to have increased to mythic scale. His theater and film successes and captivating stage persona surely intensified the image. Though some believed that public adulation of the man was out of proportion to his actual boxing achievements, such skeptics were usually dismissed for their lack of generosity. Examining his contributions to the American popular entertainment scene, it was clear that Jim had already reached the status of idol. His name carried great importance, excitement, and promise; it was to be a legacy he would carry throughout his career. And McIntosh was counting on it.

Jim's tour of the Pantages circuit began on November 2, Winnipeg, Ontario. From there, he kept engagements in Edmundton, Calgary, and Victoria, en route to Seattle. At all stops, Jim attracted SRO audiences with his stories of boxing and travel experiences. Visits to Tacoma and Portland preceded Jim's visit to San Francisco. As during previous trips to his hometown, Jim was again feted as a conquering hero.

At the Oakland train station, he and Vera were enthusiastically greeted by hundreds of admirers, including family and Olympic Club members. They escorted him and Vera to the ferry, entertained them with music and speeches while crossing the bay and literally carried them from the dock to the hotel. That evening, the Olympic Club regaled Jim with a large reception, highlighted by speeches of praise and gratitude, some coming from boxers dating back to Jim's instructor days. All through the week, in between family get-togethers, sportsmen's dinners honored Jim.

In the *Chronicle*, Jim was advertised as being "on tour of the world," supported by an all-star cast. Actually, it was the usual mixture of olios filling out a vaudeville bill: a minstrel act, singing and dancing showgirls, a comedy skit, acrobats, a saxaphone-playing sister act, an impersonator, and Keystone comedy films. For the entire program, patrons paid from twenty to thirty cents. Appearing in the city at the same time, in competition to Jim, were Olga Petrova, international actress, in a drama; Sophie Tucker and her jazz band; and Joseph Santley in a musical comedy. At the movies, Marie Dressler and Charles Chaplin appeared in a comedy, "Tillie's Punctured Romance," and Fatty Arbuckle starred in a Sennett film. Although this was a formidable array of popular stars, they did little to diminish Jim's SRO appearances.

Prior to Jim's and Vera's leaving for Australia, the Corbett family gave a reception in their honor. Seven siblings: Catherine, Teresa, Esther, Mary, Frank, Tom, and Joe were in attendance, along with other relatives. Tom was now running the betting parlor, having taken over the business after Harry had died some years earlier. The youngest of the siblings, John, was not mentioned. It would be the last time Jim saw Tom alive.

On February 16, 1915, Jim and Vera departed San Francisco on the steamship *Sonoma* for a three-week voyage to Sydney and a sixteen-week tour of McIntosh theaters. The *Chronicle* noted the embarkation and offered their view of the trip. "Corbett opens early in March. Jim has been billed like a circus, and much is expected of him from a drawing point of view."[5]

Indeed, when Jim and Vera landed in Sydney on the morning of March 9, their arrival inspired a circus-like atmosphere, as enthusiastically reported by a Sydney newspaper.

> Aboard the *S.S. Sonoma* was James J. Corbett, the great past master of the mitt brigade, and one of America's greatest monologue entertainers. A big crowd of sportsmen, headed by H.D. McIntosh, assembled in the afternoon to welcome the great hero of fistic fame, and a magnificent and sumptuous banquet was provided by Mr. McIntosh for the guest and his friends. The Hon. R.D. Meagher, speaker of the Legislative Assembly, occupied the chair with other political and sporting leaders, spoke cheery words of welcome to the famous visitor.[6]

Similar receptions took place wherever he visited. Thanks to intensive press coverage, people on the street recognized Jim and it seemed that they all wished to talk to him, if not just follow him around. Jim remarked that the crowds reminded him of the euphoric days after his defeat of Sullivan. On March 17, Jim opened his vaudeville tour at Her Majesty's Theater, Sydney, beginning a week of full houses.

> James J. Corbett enjoys a world-wide popularity. The personal magnetism of the man is simply irresistible. His great reception nightly is marvelous and he commands the attention of the packed audience while he is telling his interesting stories.[7]

Jim traveled from Sydney, to Melbourne, Adelaide, then back to Sydney, playing three weeks in each city. His engagement in Melbourne was particularly rewarding.

> James J. Corbett was, of course, the biggest attraction of the lot, and the reception he received easily knocked out any previous record at this house. Anyway, the roar of the applause and the cheers from the gallery, stalls, and dress circle which greeted the actor-boxer on his appearance on stage were things to remember. Gentleman Jim has a fine stage presence, and he is also a capital story-teller. He uses his resonant voice easily, and each syllable comes distinctly across the footlights. He recounts various humorous incidents which came under his notice during his long boxing career in the simplest manner, and always without any apparent effort or desire to score on particular points. In this manner he gets directly to the hearts of his audience, and he scarcely allows time for the laughter to subside before he is away on another tack. He rattles along in this way for 15 minutes, recalling scenes and incidents in various parts of the world—from the Bowery, N.Y., to the North Wall railway station, Dublin. He tells of a tremendous "doing" he got in the ring at Frisco and how, when he was being counted out, a man in the gallery shouted, "Hey, Corbett, you're wanted on the telephone." His yarns include incidents which happened in connection with his fight with Jeffries, Fitzsimmons, and other famous boxers, and some of his best ones are in relation to his own father and the anxious time that worthy old gentleman had during the 21 rounds of the fight when the ex-champion met John L. Sullivan. Mr. Corbett's stories are quite refreshing and clean.[8]

In addition to acting, Jim attended sportsmen's receptions and dinners, extolling the benefits and excitement of boxing. At each, he was honored by cheering admirers for his contributions to the sport. Jim also visited a number of training camps with McIntosh, examining and evaluating young boxers. One particularly impressed him, Tom Cowler, a heavyweight whom McIntosh had been promoting as a contender to defeat Jack Johnson. McIntosh had already labeled Cowler the new "white hope" who would regain the heavyweight title. Jim wasn't sure about

Cowler's chances against Johnson, but he agreed to bring the Australian to the States to see if he could become a contender. All that changed when Jess Willard knocked out Jack Johnson in Havana and regained the heavyweight title for "the white race." Jim then talked of grooming Cowler to meet Willard.

Midway through his tour, Jim received an unsettling cable from Frank. On April 16, Tom had unexpectedly died of a heart attack. Since Jim was so far from home, there was no way he could return for his brother's funeral and burial. Because of the time required to return to San Francisco and the nature of his contract with McIntosh, as well as his triumphal conquest of Australian audiences, Jim decided to finish out his engagements "down under."

On the occasion of Tom Corbett's death, Harry B. Smith, *Chronicle* reporter and nationally renowned sports writer, penned a eulogistic column about Tom's accomplishments, as well as those of his illustrious brothers. Like those of other insightful followers of the ring, Smith's observations were further evidence of the passing of boxing's glorious era.

> By the death of Tom Corbett, there has passed away another member of the famous San Francisco family, so thoroughly identified with the sporting history of not only the State, but of the entire country.... James J. Corbett has been naturally enough the leader, for his winning of the heavyweight championship of the world was one of the sensations of his time. Gentleman Jim, always shrewd in realizing the value of printer's ink, has continued to keep himself in the limelight long after his prowess as a ring warrior would have ordinarily passed.... Joe Corbett was no less famous than Jim, although in a different direction. Joe, in those days when the Baltimore Orioles were known the baseball world over, was a leading pitcher of the country.... Harry Corbett, whose death occurred shortly after the fire of 1906, had come to be known in this country as a betting com-

> missioner. He handled wagers, or was the go-between when men cared to bet on one proposition or another.... Tom succeeded to his brother's business. In the capacity of an authority on the fixing of prices, Corbett had come to be known far and wide throughout the United States and even in foreign countries. It is the stock in trade of such a sporting man to have a reputation for honesty. That was the impression which was spread broadcast of Tom Corbett, and it stood him well in hand.
>
> The old state of affairs is passing and it is doubtful whether any one will come up to follow in the footsteps of these San Franciscans.[9]

By the time Jim and Vera returned to San Francisco, on June 24, the Corbett family had already completed their mourning, leaving Jim little to do except pay his respects at Tom's grave. Most family business had already been handled so Jim and Vera departed from the city three days later, on their way back to New York. In their party were Mrs. Snowy Baker, wife of a Sydney sportsman, and Tom Cowler. In retrospect, the entire trip had been filled with a full range of emotions and the Corbetts were looking forward to some quiet time in Bayside.

While at a White Rats benefit the end of July, Jim was approached by William Morris, Marcus Loew, and George M. Cohan, all of them seriously bidding him for the coming season. Since Jim was not interested in returning to the vaudeville grind, he chose to appear in a Cohan-produced drama. "Home Again," the story of a boxer who becomes successful, included in its plot a scene of an actual bout. The play seemed suitable for Jim, although he hadn't played such a role since "Cashel Byron's Profession," nine years before.

At the time, Cohan was churning out various shows cheaply to determine which ones seemed to possess box office appeal. As was his usual routine, Cohan tinkered

Jim's trip to Australia in 1915 was met with great success, both his stage appearances and participation in boxing events. Australians acclaimed Jim for his contributions to the sport, which they believed had saved boxing from oblivion. The trip was interrupted by Tom Corbett's death. From left to right: Vera, Jim, Mrs. Snowy Baker, wife of an Australian impresario, and Tom Cowler, a potential contender against Jess Willard. (San Francisco History Center, San Francisco Public Library)

with the show until he believed it was ready for presentation. As rehearsals continued, Jim became concerned about his role and the many cast changes Cohan made, supposedly to polish the production. First, Cohan changed the name to "Brother Bill"; then he dropped the boxing scene from the script. Jim found himself with a diminished role, one that, he now believed, demeaned his reputation. He and Cohan thrashed out the issues, but both finally agreed to present the show and gauge audience reaction.

"Brother Bill" had its initial performance in Atlantic City, August 30; Cohan planned to perform there one week before moving it to New York. The play received ugly reviews, and Jim's acting was panned. Jim told Cohan he was quitting, but discovered Cohan had decided to close the show anyway. Again they argued and this time they separated in anger. The episode with Cohan soured Jim's feelings about the brash young, impresario, along with his own appetite for any drama appearances, at least for the near future. Although Cohan was the Friars leader and they appeared together in benefits, Jim's dislike for Cohan simmered for some years. Their mutual hostility became clearly evident during the Actors' Equity Strike in 1919, when the imperious Cohan opposed the strikers' action, while Jim stood solidly with his colleagues.

Good old Harry Raver now came to Jim's rescue. Raver had done so well with Jim's first film, he decided to build his own studio and produce his own moving pictures. His second picture, "Cabiria," a multi-reel import, also did well at the box-office and persuaded him to tackle more formidable projects, following the lead of Adolf Zukor and his Famous Players productions. Raver sought out an already well-known story, Augustus Thomas's stage success, "The Other Girl." He boasted of his plan to shoot the photoplay with authentic settings and hire the best filmmakers in the business. As he promised the press: "Not one cent of expense will be spared in any way."

Unquestionably, Raver did hire some of the movies' top production people: Percy Winter, director; W.J. Cagle and William Hartman, producers; Patrick J. McCaffrey, ten years with Lubin, principal cameraman, and Albert K. Greenland, a veteran newsman, in charge of publicity. For inside scenes, Raver leased the Gordon Studios on Staten Island, for its "light," the Pilot Studios in Yonkers, for both interior and exterior scenes, and the Theatre Francaise, one of New York's most ornate playhouses, for "authentic and realistic" backgrounds. Raver also claimed to have interviewed and auditioned more than 200 people to find the fourteen principle characters required for the cast. When Raver selected the protagonist—he had already made up his mind long beforehand—he announced that: "James J. Corbett has been engaged to play the leading role of 'Kid Garvey.'"[10]

In keeping with Raver's picture-making philosophy, "genuine types" were needed. Since an ex-champion pugilist was to play the lead, who better to fill the role than Jim Corbett, an actor who, ironically, had just ignominiously closed a stage production in which he was featured as a boxer. As described by Raver, other characters featured in the movie included: a minister of the Gospel, an anemic society fop, a celebrated health specialist, a judge of the Supreme Court, a vivacious girl of eighteen, a police captain, a butler who considers himself guardian of an entire family, a wealthy banker with a heart of gold, a cook who dabbles in family affairs, a comedic reporter, a music hall dancer, a chauffeur with a speed mania, an intelligent dog, and a cast of hundreds of school children, as well as scores of men and women about town.

Somewhat sarcastically, a reporter asked: "Will this be a burlesque or a serious drama?" To which Raver replied, straight-faced, "Thousands laughed and wept at the stage play. I believe in supplying pleasant surprises as a tonic for the masses. The movie will contain something for everybody." Obviously, Raver wished to take every opportunity to exploit his property.

Shooting began in early October. Raver wanted to have the picture completed for a December release, hoping to take advantage of the Christmas season rush to theaters. Unfortunately, interior shooting required the construction of many sets and delayed the release until the middle of January.

Kid Garvey, an upwardly mobile champion boxer, agrees to teach Reverend Bradford how to box, in exchange for introductions to select members of high society. The Reverend complies by introducing him to Catherine Fulton, Estelle Kittredge, and their wealthy family and friends. In spite of her engagement to Reginald Lumley, Catherine contrives to meet the compelling Garvey at her home, while the rest of her circle attends a vaudeville show headlined by the notorious vamp Myrtle Morrison. Suspicious, Estelle stays behind and eavesdrops on Catherine and Garvey arranging to elope. After locking Catherine in a room, Estelle disguises herself with a veil and takes off in an automobile with an unsuspecting Garvey. In his rush to consummate the bargain, Garvey runs over Reginald, who has fled the theater in horror at the mention of Myrtle's name. Unceremoniously arrested, Garvey is carted off to the police station. Later, at the Fulton's house, identities are revealed and true feelings are exposed. After the Reverend confesses his love for Estelle, and Reginald his for Myrtle, Catherine and Garvey announce their wedding plans. A five-reel film, "The Other Girl" was distributed by States Rights.

Advertising for the movie was both dramatic and extensive. Raver distributed lithographs, window cards, lobby displays, and pamphlets citywide, in conjunction with newspaper ads. "A Strongly Appealing Combination," proclaimed the ads. "A big author (Augustus Thomas); a reliable producer (Harry R. Raver); stars known the country over: James J. Corbett, popular hero actor; Paul Gilmore, matinee idol of many successes; William Muldoon, famed wrestler. This is all offered in the First Raver-Thomas Production, 300 scenes and 400 people, 225 of the scenes are colored."

"The Other Girl" was an immense success, playing for almost two months in New York theaters alone. (It is difficult to determine its success in other cities, although States Rights Distributing kept the picture in circulation through June, an unusually long time for a photoplay.) Jim, of course, appeared at various theaters to promote his film. His appearances were cut short, however, when he and Vera suffered injuries in an automobile accident near their home. Jim had to remain in Bayside almost a month to recuperate.

Raver was not so lucky. He had spent

In a full length photoplay, "The Other Girl," from an old stage play be Augustus Thomas, Jim played "Kid Garvey," an upwardly mobile boxer who aspires to marry a wealthy girl. The movie was an immense success.

so lavishly producing "The Other Girl" that he accrued considerable debt. In spite of the movie's box-office success, Raver proved unable to pay all his bills. Consequently, the Raver Film Corporation went out of business and a chastened Harry Raver retired from motion pictures. To complicate Raver's situation, a threat of censorship had hung over the picture in one of its best potential markets, Chicago. For two months, the local Board of Censorship debated whether "The Other Girl" was fit to be shown to the public, fearing that the prize fight scene "would offend dignified citizens." Unfortunately, too late for Raver, the Board approved the movie and, according to the press, "seemingly enjoyed it as well as any fight fan." Nonetheless, the movie was indeed banned in Maryland, Kansas, and Ohio, states that enforced strong anti-boxing laws.

Healthy again and ready to return to the stage, Jim joined the annual Friars' Frolic tour, scheduled to play fifteen cities during a two-week period in June. Friars' benefits had now grown into major productions featuring the top stage and screen stars of the day, making the show very attractive to the public. It had also gained a reputation for irreverence, satirizing shows, skits, and performers alike in a hilarious, self-deprecating manner. Audiences loved the break with traditional, standardized formats. Actors impersonated their friends, political figures, and typical audiences. Serious dramas were turned into farce comedy. The Friars even presented a travesty of one of their own club dinners.

Characteristically, the Friars' Frolic began with a parade. In New York, it proceeded down Broadway to the New Amsterdam Theater; in other cities, the parade route led from the train station to the theater at which they were to appear.

As in previous years, the Frolic was led by George M. Cohan and William Collier. This year's company included Andrew Mack, Frank Tinney, Neil O'Brien, Lew Dockstater, Nat Goodwin, Irving Berlin, Will Rogers, and James J. Corbett. As usual, the program began with a minstrel presentation, Jim in his now familiar role as interlocutor. In one scene, playing opposite Jim, was comedian Frank Tinney, an accomplished, veteran blackface performer. Their impromptu exchange was so enjoyable that some suggested they team up. An excellent idea, they replied. "We'll consider it."

The remainder of the program consisted of short skits and specialized olios, each performer attempting to gain the most laughs by poking increasingly outrageous fun at colleagues and himself. The finale featured Cohan and Collier performing their version of Shakespeare. Wherever they played, the Friars filled houses. Where else could one get "an uncommon show for the price of a seat." This trip collected more than $65,000 for the Actors' Fund.

That summer, a number of Long Island residents, who also happened to be popular stage performers, formed a charity-oriented social and entertainment group of their own, calling themselves "The Lights" (Long Island Good Hearted Thespians). Breaking with prevailing rules for such organizations, the club admitted women as equal members. Victor Moore was elected president. Jim, one of the founders, was elected to the Board of Directors. At the dedication of their new clubhouse in Freeport, Long Island, many of the members provided entertainment. Charter members included: Wilton Lackaye, Frank Tinney, Max Figman, Will Rogers, Nat Goodwin, Julian Eltinge, Charles E. Evans, Gertrude Hoffman, Sophie Tucker, Harry Von Tilzer, and Julius Witmark. Initially, the organization put on benefits and athletic events for children's charities. When the war began, they devoted most of their time to performing at army camps and war bond rallies.

At the "Lights'" inaugural performance, a featured two-act again paired Jim and Frank Tinney. Attired in a tuxedo, tall, commanding, dignified, Jim epitomized elegant masculinity. The elfin Tinney, short and thin, seemed all the less prepossessing for his shabby clothes and blackface. The physical contrast alone was both startling and humorous. This was Jim's initiation to a comedy two-act as the straight man; he loved the role, as did the audience. A running gag was Tinney's poking fun at Corbett's boxing feats, which he continually referred to, in exaggerated Negro dialect, as "de feats."

Purported to have been one of the funniest men on the stage, Frank Tinney was born in 1878 at Philadelphia's Naval Hospital, his father an officer in the U.S. Navy. A talented youngster who liked music, Tinney learned to play a number of instruments, which led to various orchestral assignments. When he began to strike up conversations with the orchestra conductor, all the while continuing to play his instrument, much to the amusement of musicians and audiences alike, his comedy career began. Joining a summer show in Atlantic City when he was twenty, Tinney became a blackface comic in minstrels. During the early days of the Syndicate, Tinney was banned from their theaters, and thus relegated to "pickup" shows in the Midwest. Discovered by independent agent Max Hart while playing in Milwaukee, Tinney made his way to Hammerstein's in New York as a featured blackface comic, both in minstrels and as a solo act. He also appeared in the 1910 and 1913 Ziegfeld Follies.

Tinney was a funny man both on and off the stage. He was also a daredevil. One story told of his riding in a train's observation car, hanging onto the handrail so that his body rocketed along parallel to the roadbed. A notoriously frugal man, Tinney was said to have invented the joke about the Scotsman who trimmed his nails so short he was unable to pick up the dinner check, at which moment Tinney would display his own shortened nails to the audience. Tinney and Al Jolson had a years-long feud, begun when both played blackface in minstrels. Once, when both were headlining at rival Chicago theaters, a noisy fire engine passed Tinney's venue in the middle of his act, to the obvious distraction of the audience. "I'll bet Al Jolson's driving it," he quipped. The patrons howled.

A month after their initial get-together, Tinney and Corbett performed so successfully at another "Lights" benefit that they agreed to team up. The act would have to wait, however, because both had other commitments to begin the new season, Tinney in a musical comedy, Jim in the Midwest on the Orpheum vaudeville circuit. The tour had all the trappings of success, however, White Rats action soon intruded on Jim's season.

After years of dormancy, a resurgent White Rats group, newly vitalized by aggressive leadership and an influx of money, threatened theater managers with rolling strikes if the actors were not granted immediate raises in salary. In fact, even before managers were able to respond to the threat, the Rats called a strike for October 5 in selected Eastern cities. Jim was to open in Chicago, October 4, to play a week's engagement at the McVicker's Theater. At the last minute, likely due to increasing management pressure, the Rats delayed the strike until October 24. Jim's appearance at the McVicker's generated capacity audiences, obviously unconcerned about any possible theater shutdowns. "James J. Corbett tells the same good gags he used when last seen here, but they all went over splendidly. His footlight personality is superb."[11]

By the time Jim reached Grand Rapids, however, Rats leaders had issued a statement demanding their full rights. The Vaudeville Managers Association (an amalgam of former Syndicate managers) retaliated by declaring that, if the actors struck, the V.M.A. would book no Rats members after October 31. The White Rats backed off again and delayed their walkout, but managers followed through their own threat and barred all Rats performers. Jim's act was abruptly terminated and he had to return to New York, not at all pleased by the events, nor the way in which Rats leadership had handled strike procedures. Other actors felt the same and although they were members, refused to follow their leaders' edicts, seeking work where and how they could.

When the White Rats appealed to the American Federation of Labor for support, Samuel Gompers, the A.F.L. leader, refused them. He wanted no trouble with theater managers at this time and believed the Rats' threat of a strike to be misguided. Still, many actors found themselves out of work. Some members sought other engagements; even non-members found their scheduled routes collapsing, or in a state of disarray.

Jim was lucky enough to obtain bookings in Atlanta, Memphis, and New Orleans in December, but he seriously considered resigning from the White Rats, because he believed the actions of the leaders to be detrimental to the very people they professed to protect. In the end, no strike took place, nor did actors achieve any financial gains. If anything, the episode badly eroded White Rats membership and loyalty, almost destroying the organization.

When Jim and Vera returned to Bayside after spending the Christmas holidays in New Orleans, they were shocked to find that their house had been robbed, completely stripped of Jim's boxing and theater memorabilia. Disturbed and outraged, they reported the break-in to police, whose subsequent investigations, unfortunately, netted almost nothing. None of the stolen materials were recovered, nor is there any record of their ever having surfaced. Many of the items taken reflected Jim's early days with the Olympic Club, including the material his mother had so proudly and carefully preserved, as well as the beginning of his stage career with Brady.

By January, 1917, troubles caused by the White Rats disruption seemed to have abated. Theater bookings returned to normal, albeit still under the control of the Vaudeville Managers Association. The Rats' management team seemed to have been thwarted in their attempt to disrupt theater operations among V.M.A. members. Nonetheless, even though membership and money had dwindled, they were not yet finished.

Jim performed at two New York theaters, with the usual good results. At the Fifth Avenue Theater, he "cleaned up." At the Colonial Theater, heading a bill that included Chic Sale and Blossom Seeley, Jim attracted substantial applause "both coming and going off." Yet, no sooner was he settling in back on the vaudeville stage than White Rats/V.M.A. hostilities broke out again. This time, the struggle would prove even more spiteful than before.

Harry Montford, White Rats president, ordered performers to strike in Boston, Chicago, St. Louis, and Kansas City, which effectively closed down most theaters in these cities. Theater managers reported having only two or three acts available to fill a bill. In retaliation, the V.M.A. declared that no performers who participated in the strike could hope for future bookings on their circuits. Montford responded to the threat by issuing a statement: "If nothing happens within the next three weeks, I will call a general strike across the country." In the meantime, Montford again solicited support from the A.F.L. Surprisingly, he now received it, although the assistance did not include money. Rats action floundered, however, in Chicago where actors refused to strike. In other cities, theater managers replaced vaudeville acts with movies and "news reels," gaining increased attention as the country drew closer to war. When the White Rats asked stage hands for support, the actors were refused, undermining their efforts. Still, sporadic strikes kept many performers off the stage and patrons out of theaters. Jim obtained a week's work at the Riverside Theater, New York, in March, sharing the bill with Gertrude Hoffman and Mrs. Vernon Castle. During these uncertain times, it was not surprising to see multiple headliners on the same bill.

At the same time that long-suppressed belligerence was emerging in the entertainment world, international hostilities were rapidly propelling the country toward a declaration of war. The White Rats had effectively closed houses in Boston and incited police action against them. On April 6, however, when the U.S. declared war on Germany, the entire entertainment landscape was altered overnight.

Patriotic fervor quickly swept the country. White Rats' labor actions were immediately deflated. Moreover, the organization was discovered to be greatly in debt, led there by Montford and his colleagues. Theaters not only survived, but emerged from the battle with increased attendance. Newsreels became the preferred movie format, and "The Star Spangled Banner" now began every show. Most performers put aside their differences with managers to volunteer for war bonds benefits and military camp shows, the first of which took place April 15 at the Hippodrome Theater. John Phillip Sousa and his band played patriotic music; a bill con-

sisting of George M. Cohan, Sam Bernard, Leon Errol, Irving Berlin, and Jim Corbett entertained. With the advent of war, it appeared that popular entertainment had regained focus and stability, however artificially.

Only days prior to the beginning of the war, Jim had been approached by King Features Syndicate, a newspaper group that featured well-known celebrities who offered their inside views of the field they represented—another effect of the star system. The corporation had already persuaded Lillian Russell to write articles about beauty and Manager John McGraw of the New York Giants to share his views on baseball. Working for King Features meant newspaper exposure across the country. It required only brief negotiations for Jim to agree to a year-long contract, at more than $20,000. He was to prepare daily articles on fitness and the "inside" of sports. In fact, Jim did not do the actual writing; that was accomplished by a group of writers working for King Features. He did, however, suggest topics and personally answer all questions sent in. Within a short time, so many letters were received that most of Jim's columns were solely devoted to answering reader's questions. The "Corbett Service," as King Features called it, began its run April 2 and became an immediate hit among both readers and sportsmen.

Letters and telegrams from sports figures flooded in, congratulating King Features and Jim for the partnership. Irving S. Cobb, himself one of the country's most esteemed sports writers, labeled reader reaction to Jim "the most extraordinary tribute ever paid to a sporting authority." Other sports luminaries, among them Charles Chomiskey, Clark Griffith, Connie Mack, and Christy Mathewson, seconded Cobb's comments. King Features acknowledged they had made the decision to feature Jim to "clinch attention" and exploit his reputation as a knowledgeable and respected sports hero; their sole goal, to increase newspaper circulation. While the "Corbett Service" may have achieved King's intent, the war clouded results. All newspapers now showed increased circulation, as readers avidly devoured news of this country's military activities.

For his part, Jim quickly discovered that daily articles demanded considerable attention, and he found the effort difficult, particularly when he was touring. As the year went on, his participation in preparing articles declined. Since he had less to do with them, his interest declined as well.

Whether due to his nationwide popularity—enhanced by a newspaper by-line—or to the widespread perception of him as an outstanding athlete and physical specimen, Jim was asked by Secretary of War Newton Baker to chair the War Department Committee on Athletic Instruction. The job required visiting camps, inaugurating athletic programs, and speaking to the troops about health and conditioning. Evidence suggests that Jim did indeed visit camps early in the war, but when on tour, he was unable to fulfill the job's responsibilities. It appears the assignment was primarily designed to enhance the government's public relations, yet, it also contributed to Jim's public image and fame.

The next few months were occupied with benefits and camp visits on behalf of the war effort. Both the Friars and Lambs clubs put on shows to collect money. A week-long Actor's Fund benefit generated more than $110,000. A National Vaudeville Artists show collected $60,000. Jim appeared in all of these shows, either presenting his monologue or appearing as interlocutor in a minstrel skit. In addition, at the N.V.A. benefit, Jim and Frank Tinney reprised their two-act routine, much to the pleasure of fellow actors and theater patrons. The *Clipper* singled out and

praised their act with a provocative comment. "Frank Tinney and James J. Corbett proved to be such an entertaining duo that it is to be regretted the two-a-day houses cannot see their work together."[12]

Regretted, indeed.

When the "Lights" announced a two-week benefit tour, prominent on the bill were Tinney and Corbett. The short tour began at the Astor Theater, New York, and visited Far Rockaway, Bay Shore, Patchogue, Long Beach, and Freeport. Originally, the company had planned to travel by boat, but bad weather forced them into a convoy of automobiles, covered with banners proclaiming who they were and what they were doing. Included in this company were Eddie Foy, Houdini, McIntyre & Heath, Victor Moore, and the new comedy team of Tinney and Corbett. The tour raised more than $8,000 for the war effort.

By the fall of 1917, the entertainment business, particularly vaudeville, had been hard hit by the war. Close to 5,000 actors had been called to military service, badly depleting the ranks of available performers. Railroad restrictions imposed by the government severely limited touring companies. Theaters were obliged to start shows earlier and end them sooner to save fuel. Tuesday closings and electric lighting restrictions on Broadway dimmed the street for the duration. Congress passed a Theater War Tax, with ten percent of every ticket sold going to the government. Meanwhile, "German" comedians quickly dropped their suddenly suspect costumes, makeup, and dialect to appear as non-ethnic comics. A situation problematic for most young actors was a boon for older ones, they were the only available performers to fill bills and were wooed with excellent salaries. The duo of Tinney and Corbett had no problems finding work. And their new partnership was soon abetted by an argument between Tinney and J.J. Shubert.

FRANK
TINNEY.

JAMES J. CORBETT.

A newspaper caricature of the vaudeville comedy team of Corbett and Tinney. The juxtaposition of starkly contrasting appearances and behaviors added to the hilarity of their act. Jim's straight-man role was singled out as the funniest in the business.

Tinney had signed a contract with the Shubert organization to appear in a show being produced by J.J. Shubert. When the autocratic J.J. discovered that Tinney was about to perform with the "Lights," he forbade him to appear with the group. Tin-ney refused Shubert's command and dared him to break their contract, which made no mention of benefit performances. The Shubert revue, "Doing Our Bit," was being promoted as a production designed to en-tertain the troops, but in fact, it simply used a patriotic theme to attract patrons at a time when anything not overtly patriotic received little attention.

When the Shuberts noticed the positive reactions to Tinney and Corbett, they offered them a headliner slot in the company. For $1,750 a week each, the duo accepted. The company also boasted other stars, such as Ed Wynn, Herman Timberg, Charles Judels, and the Duncan Sisters, along with lesser seasoned vaudeville acts. The revue was to open at the Winter Garden and play indefinitely, that is, until the Shuberts noticed a decline in box-office receipts, at which time, the company would be moved.

"Doing Our Bit" opened at the Shubert Theater in New Haven, Connecticut, October 10. After a week to smooth out the show, the company began their Winter Garden run. First night reactions were recorded by the *New York Times* critic.

> There is a big, patriotic inspiration behind "Doing Our Bit" which, in the opinion of a first-night audience that packed the Winter Garden to capacity Thursday, is the best, biggest, most dazzling, spectacular, snappiest, funniest and successful show ever produced at the world's greatest musical playhouse. From the time that the curtain went up to the finale of the last act one surprise followed another, and every scene seemed to be more wonderful than the preceding one.[13]

Sigmund Romberg and Herman Timberg collaborated on the music, while J.C. Huffmann staged the production. There were two acts and seventeen scenes, with twenty-eight musical numbers. Practically no plot existed, but patrons of revues cared less whether the plot thickened or evaporated altogether, as long as there was plenty of action and fun.

The *Telegraph* called the production "spectacular, gorgeous and replete with melody." The *Journal* went even further in its praise.

More gorgeously gowned than any of its predecessors and abounding with good music and wonderful dances by the best drilled chorus, "Doing Our Bit" was welcomed by a most appreciative audience last night.[14]

Among the headliners on stage, Tinney and Corbett were singled out as "being the funniest things in the gala show." That Jim poked fun at his boxing exploits as an unassuming foil for Tinney amused audiences all the more.

The *Telegraph* tagged Jim as a versatile actor who "contributed as much as any one factor to the comedy of last night's performance." The *Journal* lauded his performance by pointing out "the manner in which Corbett carried the thing through that proved his ability as an actor." Jim may not have been the premier star of the show, but he received first-rate recognition for his acting.

Indeed, the team of Tinney and Corbett scored so well that they found themselves featured in newspaper articles recounting how they had created their routines. Tinney talked about composing the show on his typewriter each day. "When we get back for the evening performance, we'll talk it over and select the material." Jim spoke animatedly about his partner. "To me, Tinney is the funniest man in the world. His humor is natural and spontaneous. You never know what he is going to do or say at any performance. Sometimes he follows his lines, but oftener he doesn't. We make things up from there."

"All Corbett has to do is throw me a line," explained Tinney, "and I try to come back with a funny retort. It grows from there."

"The boy is a genuine genius," Jim lauded.

In response to further questioning, Jim admitted to being "a happy man" in this production. The fact that the show was stationed in New York and "we've come to dread the fall and winter, because that meant the road, may be a selfish reason," he admitted, "but Mrs. Corbett and I simply aren't fit for hard travel anymore."

"Doing Our Bit" played at the Winter Garden for seventeen weeks (until the middle of February, 1918) to full houses and continuous accolades for its performers. Yet when Ed Wynn was pulled out by the Shuberts to appear in another production, it was time to move. Montreal was the first stop, for three weeks, followed by week-long engagements in Baltimore

and Washington, D.C., in all of which venues they could have played longer except for the fact that the theaters had already been booked for other Shubert shows.

The final engagement—or so the company was told—was at the Chestnut Street Opera House in Philadelphia, opening the last week in March. Newspapers called the show "one of the real hits of the New York season," and the crowds agreed. Box office receipts were so profitable, the Shuberts decided to extend the production's life. Two days before "Doing Our Bit" was scheduled to close, J.J. Shubert announced to the company, by wire, that they had been booked into Chicago for an extended stay. No one in the company was pleased. Some wanted a rest; others had already made arrangements for another booking. Still, it meant additional work.

The company opened at the Palace Music Hall, Chicago, on May 15, at a time when other theaters were about to close for the summer. The war had had a depressing effect on Chicago audiences, and the Shuberts believed the already successful show would reap financial benefits for them. They were more than correct in the assessment. "Doing Our Bit" played ten shows a week for seven weeks, finally closing at the end of June. Overall, the show had been performed 256 times and was regarded the runaway hit of the 1917-1918 season.

Later that summer, as Jim was making plans to return to vaudeville in the fall,

Poster for the Shubert-produced patriotic salute to the war effort, "Doing Our Bit," a typical Shubert revue, with the requisite connection to the war. Corbett and Tinney played their now-famous routines. The show ran for more than twenty-nine weeks.

preferably with Frank Tinney, a highly contagious and virulent strain of influenza began to ravage military camps in the East and Southeast. Labeled the "Spanish Flu," it quickly spread across the country. By September, it had surged beyond epidemic proportion and accounted for tens of thousands of deaths. Since no one knew what effect the epidemic might have on potential audiences, theater bookings were temporarily frozen. Tinney and Corbett found themselves out of work.

The closure of all places of public assembly—stores, beaches, schools, churches, athletic events, and theaters—was ordered by local authorities in most towns and cities. In many places, the epidemic hit so hard that theater audiences were almost non-existent. Only in New York did most theaters remain open. It was later revealed that powerful theater owners had "paid off" local politicians.

Of course, closures throughout the country caused confusion among touring managers and booking agents so many acts and productions were summarily abandoned. By early October, nearly all theaters in the country had been closed or were operating on reduced schedules. Everyone in the entertainment business agreed that salvaging the new season would be the most "Herculean job" the industry had ever undertaken.

All the while, Jim sat at home, increasingly concerned about his inability to sign up with any circuit, even for future engagements. While relieved that he and Vera had themselves not fallen ill, Jim was anxious to get back on stage.

12. A MAN FOR
ALL OCCASIONS

Upon his arrival in Los Angeles in 1919, Jim was met at the train station by none other than Carl "Pops" Laemmle, boss of Universal Pictures. Laemmle was there to make certain Jim would be greeted in accordance with his headliner status, then personally escorted to Universal City. The ride to the studio grounds proved both picturesque and dusty.

Bumping and bouncing on a rutted dirt road over the Cahuenga Pass in the Hollywood Mountains, Jim observed a few widely scattered dwellings, a gypsy camp, and pleasantly wooded landscapes. Once over the rise, however, he came upon a seemingly endless tract of high, white walls, within which, Laemmle related proudly, were two sound stages, offices, dressing rooms, a water reservoir, a hospital, two restaurants, shops, mills, garages, even a school.

Jim's initial impression was that the entire layout, surrounded by the forbidding walls, resembled a prison, that was, until he noticed the splendid fountain splashing languidly just beyond ornate iron gates. Moreover, he observed, there were more people trying to enter the compound than leave.

Laemmle squired Jim into the com-missary for lunch, and Jim was immediately struck by a kaleidoscope of colors and a cacophony of sound. The King of Siam ate pork and beans, while, next to him, a Hawaiian hula dancer daintily sipped her soup. An Indian brave had set aside bow and arrow to attack a platter of corned beef and cabbage. A beautiful girl in bridal regalia ordered a New York steak rare, with all the trimmings. A group of people dressed as American colonists entered carrying farm implements. Jim's introduction to big-time movie-making in California was indeed a dazzling display of diverse excitements.

Universal Pictures was the brainchild of Carl "Pops" Laemmle. After building a successful theater business in Chicago during the early days of moving pictures, securing material from independent and small-time filmmakers, Laemmle determined to become a movie producer, thereby supplying product directly to his own exchanges. In 1909, having rented production space in New York, he produced a one-reel drama, "Hiawatha." It bore the name of his new enterprise, Independent Motion Picture Company, nicknamed IMP, both lovingly and hatefully, depending on how one perceived

Laemmle's operation. His aggressive tactics quickly put him in competition with the already established producers. Over the next few years, as he built the Universal Pictures empire, Laemmle demonstrated his business acumen by buying (some said stealing) the services of "the Biograph girl," Mary Pickford, and her family, as well as those of director Thomas Ince.

In 1912, Laemmle incorporated his IMP production interests into Universal Pictures. Two years later, he conceived the idea of constructing his own studio lot. For $165,000, he bought 230 acres of land in the San Fernando Valley, then some ten miles beyond the Los Angeles city limits. Ground for the studio was broken in October, 1914 and it was completed five months later. By the time Jim arrived at Universal City, Laemmle's company was one of the commanding motion picture studios in the country.

By early November, 1918, as the flu epidemic receded, theaters in the East had reopened. Chicago theaters were about to be reopened. Only the West Coast still suffered through the deadly plague. New York theaters had resumed their regular schedules. Euphoria soon swept the country when, a few weeks later, the armistice was signed by Germany, thus ending the slaughter of World War I. The public flooded theaters as fast as their doors could be opened.

When Jim discovered that Frank Tinney had been made a captain in the Army, in charge of staging shows for the returning soldiers, he persuaded fellow Friar Jack Wilson to team with him. Obtaining bookings was no problem; they began the partnership at the Riverside Theater, New York, December 21. The *Clipper* complimented their initial efforts.

They depended entirely on the give and take of a seemingly impromptu conversational offering for their laughs, and the naturalness of this procedure made for real spontaneity in the response evoked in the audience.[1]

The *Dramatic Mirror* praised them even more.

The two constitute a wonderful new team of entertainers in vaudeville. Proof of Corbett's adaptability to the stage has been forthcoming quite regularly in past years, and Wilson's recognized drag with the devotees of the two-a-day is founded on methods that made him "surefire."[2]

Whether Jim found the relationship with Wilson unsuitable, or the movie offer from Universal appeared a more lucrative opportunity cannot be pinpointed. In any case, Corbett and Wilson parted after only two weeks and it was announced that "Jim would leave for Universal City, California, December 30." He had been signed by Universal Pictures to star in an eighteen-episode serial, "The Midnight Man," at a reported $2,000 per episode.

For nationwide theater audiences eager to view adventure thrillers, the movies' equivalent of an original stage melodrama, studios discovered that serials met the market. Patrons sympathized with the heroine, cheered for the hero, and hissed the villain, just as their grandparents had done fifty years before.

By 1915, almost all movie production companies had at least one serial, sometimes two or three, playing at any given time. The serial was a bonafide moneymaker. In fact, serials had become the "dessert" of the movie business, providing excellent financial returns that offset the high costs of producing and distributing multi-reel films featuring major stars.

The year Jim came to California, 1919, was a particularly big one for serials, aided to a considerable degree by the end of the war, and studios' decisions to increase investment in these reliably popular productions. Employing well-known personalities, Universal had already produced a number of serials that generated good box-office. Laemmle sought to exploit Corbett's long-time hero status, lending the value of his fame to the theater marquee. Some at Universal, however, were not entirely taken with the idea. After all, Corbett was fifty-three years old and had not boxed professionally for sixteen years. Could he come across on screen as a death-defying, athletic hero, as did younger men in similar roles? Laemmle, who was already familiar with Jim's stage persona and previous screen appearances, saw no problem hiring him.

When the *Dramatic Mirror* heard of Universal Pictures' selection, they lauded the decision, adding to the news a little hyperbole of their own.

> Mr. Corbett's entrance into films will undoubtedly find favor with many thousands of personal friends and followers in all parts of the world, for "Gentleman Jim" has personally appeared in every country in the world.[3]

When shooting for the serial began, Jim quickly dispelled the notion that he was "too old" for serials. He performed all of his own stunts, which, in the first episode alone, included leaping from a motorcycle onto a moving train, fighting with "tramps" in a boxcar, and being thrown backwards over a bridge into water. In short, he gamely performed physical feats that put younger men to shame. When reporters asked Jim how he felt about his new acting role, he replied with a smile, "I really like it." Reporters came away assured that Jim would prosper.

The studio planned to complete all eighteen episodes by June—three episodes a month for six months—intending to release the film for summer viewing. Unfortunately, travel to various location sites and director James Horne's illness delayed completion nearly a month. Although Jim worked every day, he and Vera still enjoyed some leisure time with filmmaking colleagues.

A suite of rooms had been prepared for them at the Los Angeles Athletic Club. A

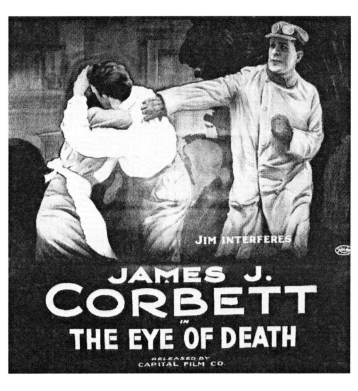

Universal Pictures enticed Jim to appear in a multi-episode serial in 1919. The result was an eighteen-chapter serial called "The Midnight Man," this lobby card promoting Chapter Fourteen. Shooting the film took six months, and in spite of a lucrative offer to continue making serials, Jim chose to return to vaudeville.

limousine took Jim to and from Universal City each day. Evenings were spent at Jack Doyle's bar, where filmplayers met on Tuesdays and Fridays to see prizefights in the adjoining arena. Jim and Vera often stopped at Levy's Cafe for ice cream and the Orpheum Theater for vaudeville. Both the Lambs and the Friars had branches in Los Angeles, and Jim frequently attended club dinners and benefits. He and Douglas Fairbanks played in a charity baseball game on behalf of the Salvation Army. In an exhibition game between the Chicago Cubs and their Los Angeles farm team, Jim umpired. Reporting on the game, the *Los Angeles Times* noted, tongue-in-cheek, "not a single pop bottle was hurled at him, and not one 'boo' was uttered in the bleachers or grand stand." During their entire stay in Los Angeles, Jim and Vera received regal treatment.

The final episode of "The Midnight Man" was shot in the nearby mountains the last week in June. Immediately after the final take, Jim and Vera left for New York, with a brief stop in Toledo, Ohio, to view the Dempsey-Willard heavyweight championship bout.

Jim joined "old timers" Benny Leonard, Battling Nelson, Jack McAuliffe, and Philadelphia Jack O'Brien as informed spectators. The highly-touted match was the first major boxing event since the war had ended and reflected the country's attempt to forget the gruesome conflict and the thousands of casualties it had generated. Hope abounded that a new era of boxing was about to be initiated: an arena designed to hold an unprecedented 97,000 people; 400 reporters from around the globe churning out thousands of words daily for their constituents; chartered trains sponsored by the New York Central and Pennsylvania Railroads bringing enthusiasts to the site in luxury, and, thanks to the increasing enlightenment of high-profile promoter Tex Rickard, the many

hundreds of women who attended were treated to their own commodious section.

Male enthusiasts, however, did not yet enjoy the benefits of the new era, not as far as comfort was concerned. Raw pine benches, replete with knots and splinters, were made even more uncomfortable by the sticky pine sap elicited by soaring summer temperatures.

Dempsey knocked Willard down seven times in the first round. He then proceeded to pound his opponent mercilessly for two more. Willard was unable to answer the bell for the fourth, and Dempsey was crowned the new heavyweight champion.

Jim could not help but notice many similarities between himself and Dempsey, the most telling of which was spectators' embrace of the new champion as a potential national hero. The press noticed too. Sportswriters and other journalists immediately proceeded to build a mythos around the "The Manassa Mauler" to satisfy the star-starved public. That would soon mean personal, theater, and movie appearances for the "young, pleasing, affable" man. Knowing well the kind of life Dempsey would face every day from this point on, Jim expressed to the champion his hope that he could handle the challenge of celebrity as well as he handled opponents in the ring.

Jim arrived back in New York just as the Actors' Equity Association presented their demands to theater managers and producers. After the White Rats demise, the A.E.A. had taken over representing performers and had recently obtained official affiliation from Samuel Gompers' American Federation of Labor. This powerful alliance resulted in a stampede of new members eager to join Actors' Equity and greatly increased the organization's operating income.

Jim was all too familiar with the actor-manager conflict, which dated back to the early 1900s when he had vigorously supported the White Rats. Following the war, the nationwide flu epidemic had temporarily delayed the predictable confrontation between entertainment management and labor; however, it resurfaced in early 1919, while Jim was in Los Angeles. He had heard reports and rumors through his colleagues at the Lambs and Friars but remained unaware of how enflamed the situation had actually become.

When George M. Cohan announced that he would establish a rival, non-union performers group, in support of managers, Jim was one of the first to denounce him for deserting his fellow actors, many of whom had been Cohan's club colleagues and supporters. Under intense pressure, Cohan was forced to resign from the Friars' Club.

Unhappy with the managers' stalling tactics, the A.E.A. called for an actors' strike, to begin August 7. Immediately, many theaters went dark. Touring companies stopped work wherever they happened to be. Production was halted on the coming season's new shows. Managers were stunned by the concerted action and its negative impact on their business.

To gain sympathy and public attention for their cause, the A.E.A. sponsored a parade down Broadway, to good effect. Benefits held at various theaters netted thousands of dollars and served to unite both actors and theater patrons against the oppressive managers. Jim participated in all these events. In addition, he organized a number of boxing exhibitions at Madison Square Garden to collect funds for out-of-work actors.

By the third week of the strike, the managers' losses in gross receipts had risen to more than $245,000 a week and they began to show signs of panic. The managers quickly called for a meeting with actors to discuss a settlement. Representa-

tives of the opposing groups met across the bargaining table on August 31. One of those speaking for management was William A. Brady, now one of the most powerful stage and movie producers in the country.

During the ensuing debate, Brady made a number of derogatory comments about actors' abilities, character, and commitment. From his seat in the audience, Jim rose to challenge Brady's remarks. Jim pointedly rebutted his one-time manager, jabbing effectively at his self-serving argument. Jim accused Brady personally, as well as his colleagues, of manipulating actors for excessive financial gain and deliberately abusing actors' rights. Brady's face flushed red. He pounded the desk with his fist and rose to his feet defiantly. Jim took a step forward, as if to meet Brady's foolhardy physical challenge. A sudden silence pervaded the room. Seated next to Brady, A.H. Woods grabbed his arm firmly and pushed Brady back into his chair. The immediate confrontation was defused, but Jim and Brady never spoke to one another again. Had Vera been in the audience, she would have been exceedingly proud of her husband.

A new contract was negotiated, with managers agreeing to the actors' demands. Within a few days, theaters reopened and actors were back at work. At least, most of them were.

Although one of the provisions of the new contract stated that managers could not blacklist any Equity actor, a number on the frontlines of the battle, like Eddie Foy, Marie Dressler, and Jim Corbett, all of them highly visible opponents of management, found it suddenly difficult to obtain work. Dressler opted to go into the movies. Foy remained out of work for more than eight months. For four months, Jim was unable to negotiate a booking. Had not his serial been playing in theaters during this period, Jim would have earned no money. Universal Pictures came to his rescue again.

Initially, Universal had wanted to sign Jim for another serial. Jim refused. Next, they offered him a feature, "Kentucky Jim," a vehicle that was an adaptation of "Pals," Jim's early stage success. Because the role reprised his old boxing productions, Jim again refused the offer. They finally came to an agreement on a drama called "The Prince of Avenue A." Jim was to arrive in Los Angeles immediately to begin shooting the film.

Cast as the son of political leader, Patrick O'Conner, Jim played Barry O'-Conner, labeled "The Prince of Avenue A" for his foppish demeanor. The O'Conners are supporting William Tomkins for mayor. When Tomkins' daughter, Mary, throws Barry out of a party at the Tomkins house, Barry's father is enraged. Candidate Tomkins, fearful of losing O'Conners's support in the election, insists that Mary invite Barry to the district ball. At the gala, when Tomkins' rival in the election insults Mary, Barry comes to her rescue, convincingly demonstrating his manly boxing skills. Mary realizes the appeal of Barry's true self, and they fall in love. The movie was completed in less than two months and released February 23, 1920, to theaters across the country.

The *Dramatic Mirror* review was complimentary, yet subtly alluded to Jim's age.

> The "Prince of Avenue A" is a photoplay that the fans will claim as being truly entertaining in every way. It contains action, pathos, and plenty of humor of the Irish flavor. The story is constructed around the peculiarities of the Irish people in their New York settlements that existed some years ago—in the days of horse cars.... Corbett is the same genial "Gentleman Jim" of former years. He contributes an unctuous humor and a most agreeable personality to the character of the Irishman of Avenue A.[4]

Variety believed that Jim remained an attractive star.

> Gentleman Jim still packs a punch and didn't fake it. In fact, he goes well in pictures. Exhibitors should test his pulling power, and unless all signs are wrong, they'll yell for more.[5]

Upon his return to New York, Jim began a renewed search for a vaudeville partner. He could not have found a better comedian than Billy B. Van, a stage veteran whose improvisational business gained him a reputation as one of the funniest people on the vaudeville stage.

Van (William Webster Vandergrift) was born in Pittstown, Pennsylvania, in 1868. At age fifteen, he began his stage career in the chorus of the California Minstrels. Settling in New York, he appeared in a succession of farce-comedy, minstrel, and variety companies until the middle 1890s. Then he gained widespread attention as "Patsy," playing comedy skits opposite various women performers, some of whom came to be numbered among his wives. During the 1900s, Van was featured comedian in a string of hit stage plays, among them, "The Dream Girl," "The Errand Boy," "Little Nemo," "Words and Music," and "The Rainbow Girl." He had recently separated from Dan Ferguson and was, likewise, seeking a new partner.

The team of Van and Corbett made their debut at a Friars' Frolic late in March and were applauded by their compatriots for more than a minute. A week later, the *Clipper* reported that Van and Corbett were to open at the Colonial Theater, New York, April 20. Reviews of their act were outstanding.

> Billy B. Van and Jim Corbett could draw a big crowd to a theater through their names alone, but, in addition to that, they have turned out one of the cleverest, and, without a doubt, funniest two-man talk acts to

be seen. As a comedian, Van is a scream, and Corbett is a splendid "straight."

No audience is going to be disappointed after seeing Van and Corbett.[6]

Since they had launched the partnership late in the theater season, continuous playing dates were hard to schedule. Many theaters were closing for the summer, and those remaining open had already booked acts. After appearing together at a number of benefits, Van and Corbett were hired to play in John Murray Anderson's continuing musical revue, "What's In a Name." The duo was unaware, however,

that the show was losing money and Anderson was feuding with the producers. Moreover, Anderson was slated to begin production of the "Greenwich Village Follies," which would demand his entire attention. "What's In a Name" appeared to be terminal. Indeed, it closed the last week in June, with a reported loss of more than $90,000 to producers. Van and Corbett had played in the show for six weeks; apparently, they were never paid in full for their work.

They obtained an engagement at the Riverside Theater, the week of July 17.

Billy B. Van and James J. Corbett headlined the bill, and did just what a headline act is supposed to do, that is, draw strong at the box office and make good on stage. The act was a laugh from start to finish and finished with big applause and encores innumerable.[7]

Billy B. Van was one of the most amusing men on the vaudeville stage. The team of Van and Corbett quickly became headliners and frequent visitors to the Palace Theater stage. Jim regarded moments in this partnership as the best and funniest times he ever had on the stage.

The following week, at the famous Palace Theater, the duo repeated their success. "Van is a great comedian, there is no doubt of that, and Corbett's work as 'straight' could hardly be improved upon."[8]

Van was preparing to leave for England to appear in a new version of "The Rainbow Girl," and he persuaded the producers to sign Jim, as well. Unfortunately, theater problems in Europe, prompted by a recession and rising production costs, aborted the trip. Redirecting their efforts to find a season's booking on one of the vaudeville circuits, Van and Corbett discovered that U.S. theater companies faced similar financial problems. Not only had hot weather reduced patronage, but managers saw audiences as reluctant to visit theaters because of the uncertain economy. The years immediately following the end of the war had brought prosperity to Broadway. Now, by contrast, postwar inflation and the cost of living were having their affect on theater attendance.

It was presidential season, as well, and Senator Warren G. Harding was making a strong effort to gain support from the acting profession. In September, the Actors' Republican League was formed, with Frank Bacon as president and Henry E. Dixey, executive secretary. Chief among the organization's members were Al Jolson, Lillian Russell, and Lew Fields. For these wealthy star performers, Harding was the preferred candidate of big business, tax reduction, and law and order.

In opposition, the Cox-Roosevelt Theatrical League was formed by Captain Frank Tinney. To plan fund-raisers, benefits, and campaign appearances, an executive committee was formed, comprised of Ed Wynn, Lew Dockstater, Pat Rooney, Eddie Leonard, and James J. Corbett. These actors were more concerned with the slump in theater business, brought on by the financial downturn, rising production costs, the onset of Prohibition and, ironically, the growth of motion pictures. They spent the next two months working for the Democratic candidate. Van and Corbett performances were temporarily shelved.[9]

Harding's election as president did nothing to improve theater business. If anything, it hastened the changes taking place in the entertainment industry, which were determined by purging the "old" for the "new," whatever that was perceived to be. Musical theater was ridding itself of the excesses of production now and featured a more intimate and sophisticated ambiance. The "jazz age" had been launched and its best composers were erudite musicians. In contrast to the stage, movies offered a revelation in elaborate production values, visual techniques, and star power. Vaudeville appeared to be losing its hold in New York, although it remained the people's entertainment west of Newark.

Jim was clearly cognizant of these industry changes. Luckily for him, making movies the past few years had compensated for erratic vaudeville touring, and teaming with Frank Tinney and Billy Van offered him new acting opportunities. At this time, popular theater business was in decline. Without a partner, Jim could only return to monologues if he wished to remain in vaudeville and monologue artists were losing their audience. He also saw his national hero status being overshadowed by others taking full advantage of vastly improved media outlets and professional merchandisers. Maybe it was time to retrench, to more closely evaluate his career alternatives.

After seeing no mention of Jim in the press for some months, admirers were surprised to read that he had applied for, and received, a judge's license from the New York State boxing commission to officiate bouts at Starlight Park, a new venue, in the Bronx. Twice weekly, throughout the fall and winter, Jim worked the matches and, in addition, supplied comments to reporters regarding the careers of new boxers appearing at the arena. No question, Jim said, he felt comfortable in the job. Indeed, he readily admitted that it offered neither the excitement of the stage, nor the gratification of audience laughter and applause. Still, while many of his colleagues were standing in long lines outside of booking offices, Jim was earning a weekly check.

Jim's comfort was short-lived, however, when, in the middle of January, 1921, Starlight Park went into bankruptcy and

Jim is featured in his new role as boxing judge in Brooklyn. He did a good job and made great copy, but the club's bankruptcy aborted a potentially lucrative position for him.

closed its doors. Nor did it avail Jim to recognize that Broadway shows were closing, movie moguls claimed their industry was in a slump, and politicians bemoaned the signs of recession. At a Friars' Club dinner one evening, Jim and his friends were discussing the bleak outlook when Billy Van came in, looking expressly for Jim.

"Let's team up again," he suggested. "I think we can find some playing time." Grasping arms, the duo danced their way out of the dining room to encouraging cheers from their colleagues.

Van and Corbett opened at the Royal Theater, New York, on February 23, to a full house eager to see the duo perform again. It was the beginning of a four-month tour, one that quickly returned them to headliner status on the vaudeville circuit, in spite of the generally poor theater business nationwide.

The press singled out two jokes that garnered extensive laughter from audiences. Van tells Corbett he possesses a lot of jokes and, to prove it, pulls out a stack of index cards of varied colors. The white cards contain jokes for old maids, the pink ones for close friends; the green ones, Irish jokes, and one red card that contains, Van claims, the joke of the act. He gets no chance to tell it though, no matter how often he attempts to, because he is continually interrupted by a straight-faced Corbett. Each time, the audience was sent howling by Van's frustrated antics. The comic pair ended their routine with a quick give-and-take.

Corbett: I ate today.
Van: That's nothing. I sixteenth today.
Corbett: What do you mean, sixteenth?
Van: Ate twice.

Billy B. Van and James J. Corbett got a big hand when they marched on and with the aid of their red card and Billy's mannerisms kept the patrons giggling and chuckling throughout the time they frolicked. Van never missed a trick and at times had them roaring while Corbett worked well in the comedy feeding process.[10]

Successive weeks in New York at the Palace, Hamilton, Jefferson, and Colonial theaters kept the team in headlines and assured full houses at the same time that newspapers decried "the worst theater slump in years.

After a week in Washington, D.C., where the press reported they were "one of the few real comedy acts in vaudeville," Van and Corbett returned to the Palace to SRO audiences. They spent three more successful weeks at New York theaters before "hitting the road." Co-starring with them at two of the theaters were Eddie Foy and Family and the Four Marx Brothers. Also on the bill was a child comedy duo, Elizabeth Kennedy and Milton Berle. However, after being threatened by crusading prigs of the Gerry Society because the talented youngsters were underage, they had to withdraw.

Theater business continued its decline throughout the spring. Chicago theaters reported lingering poor attendance. Road conditions were bad. Broadway houses showed films instead of vaudeville, and the idea was quickly picked up by theaters in other cities. To raise money for out-of-work vaudeville artists, the N.V.A. (National Vaudeville Artists) staged a gigantic fifty-act, two-theater benefit at the end of May. Limited to three minutes, each act played at both theaters. Popular theaters' most renowned performers appeared, including George M. Cohan, Ed

Wynn, Al Jolson, Lillian Russell, Eddie Foy, and Van and Corbett. More than $100,000 was collected.

A month later, the Friars' Club put on an All-Star Jamboree of its own, again for the benefit of unemployed actors. The first part was minstrel, with Jim serving as interlocutor. Tambo and Bones were played by Frank Tinney and William Collier. In the skit, Corbett claims he is an actor, to which Collier replies that he is as good a fighter as Corbett is an actor. Corbett then insists he is a better fighter. "Well, then," exclaims Collier, "I must be a better actor." Jumping up and down, the pint-sized Tinney continually attempts to interrupt Corbett and Collier but is constantly shoved aside, to the delight of the audience. The *Clipper* reported both performers and audience "had great fun," and more than $20,000 was collected.

Appearing to defy all talk of bad touring business, the following week, Van and Corbett played in Pittsburgh, then went on to engagements in Cleveland and Baltimore. Vaudeville houses were closing all around them, but "good business prevailed" at their venues. The situation finally caught up with them, however, when they returned to New York to find nearly all of the top vaudeville houses temporarily closed.

In order to survive, theater managers predicted they would have to make drastic cuts for the coming season: reducing the size of orchestras, cutting admission prices, and, to the A.E.A.'s dismay, lowering performers' salaries. Yet little argument ensued, since everyone acknowledged that the entertainment business was in the doldrums. Of particular interest to Jim was a *Clipper* article describing the difficulty athletes were having as actors. In an attempt to leverage his unparalleled baseball reputation, Babe Ruth failed as a drawing card. Touring the Pantages circuit, Jack Dempsey was reported to be near a nervous breakdown and fighting hard to have his contract annulled.

Van and Corbett were about to sign a contract to play the Orpheum circuit when they were offered roles in an upcoming International Film Company production to be distributed by Cosmopolitan (Paramount Pictures). Given the choice, they agreed to spend a month working in a film before embarking on their tour; it was good money, at a time when theater attendance was problematic.

"The Beauty Shop" had been a relatively successful 1914 musical comedy, written by Channing Pollack and Rennold Wolf and starring Raymond Hitchcock. Revised for filming, the story told of Dr. Arbutus Budd (Hitchcock, reprising his stage role), a New York beauty specialist, who, in spite of doing good business, is pursued by creditors. Under false pretenses, he obtains the noble crest of a forgotten baron of Bolognia and uses it as a trademark on bottles of beauty lotion. When the crest is recognized, Sobini (Van) and Panatella (Corbett) are commissioned to bring back the "baron" to Bolognia. Expecting to inherit a fortune, Dr. Budd takes his attorney, Phil Briggs (Laurance Wheat), and his ward, Anna (Diana Allen), with him. His only legacy, however, proves to be a duel with Maldonado (Montagu Love), a notorious villain and excellent marksman. At the same time, Cremo Panatella (Louise Fazenda), an ugly girl, falls in love with him. He gives her some beauty preparations, which she applies and is unable to remove. Budd attempts to flee with Cola (Marion Fairbanks), a dancer with whom he has fallen in love, but is captured. He removes the paste from Cremo's face, and she is discovered to be strikingly beautiful. The duel is canceled, and they all sail to America. The film was directed by Edward Dillon, the sets designed by Joseph Urban.

Van and Corbett played small, humorous parts, Jim wearing a wig and heavy mustache. *Variety* declared about Jim: "It doesn't present him in a favorable light; and in acting what Corbett does here will never be held for or against him." The entire review of the film was uncomplimentary.

> Labored is the whole sum of this comedy effort.... Everyone in the feature tries so hard to be funny. The labored effort ruins the effect, with the result remaining that if the names of this picture can not be played up for business, there won't be much business.[11]

After their brief, apparently unsatisfactory, movie-making interlude, Van and Corbett were quite happy to return to the boards. Amidst headlines claiming that more than 5,000 actors were idle as a result of the nation-wide recession, the duo opened their vaudeville tour at the Majestic Theater, Chicago, on September 25. For the remainder of 1921, they had engagements in Indianapolis, St. Louis, Milwaukee, Detroit, Toledo, Kansas City, Chicago, St. Louis (a return at Christmas), and Memphis, for the New Year's celebration. Finally, by the end of the year, theater business seemed to be improving as the overall economy stabilized. Although the *Clipper* reported that fifty percent of the new shows failed, they also observed that "big names and $1.00 top shows were getting all the road money." Van and Corbett could readily verify the report.

The duo began 1922 in New Orleans to "packed houses." Long jumps between engagements had become quite common during the period and Van and Corbett were not spared the inconvenience. They had to travel from New Orleans to Sioux City, Iowa, their initial engagement on the Orpheum circuit, in less than forty-eight hours. They made the opening at the Orpheum in Sioux City, but had to don their costumes and makeup as the train pulled into the station, then run directly to the theater.

Off all the operating circuits in the country, the Orpheum was the only one making money, due to its roster of headliners and well-spaced theater locations, making for more efficient routing. Their headliners included: Houdini, Pat Rooney, Eddie Foy and Family, Blossom Seeley, the Four Marx Brothers, Gallagher & Shean, and Victor Moore. Their theaters were lined up from Minneapolis-St. Paul, across Canada to the West Coast, and from Vancouver south to Los Angeles.

Late March heralded the arrival of Van and Corbett to San Francisco for a two-week engagement. As always, Jim was met by a large contingent of admirers who accompanied him to his hotel from the train station. Many remained in the hotel lobby to accompany him and Van to the theater. In spite of fine weather, two capacity audiences on Sunday were on hand to welcome the duo to the Orpheum stage. The *Chronicle* predicted: "Corbett was accorded a rousing reception and his extreme popularity in this, his home, should prove an exceptional draw during his two weeks' engagement."[12]

On Monday night, 400 members of the Olympic Club appeared at the theater to pay tribute to their "fellow clubman." The Olympians all wore white hats and were so seated that their hats formed a huge letter "O." After the performance, Jim and club members enjoyed a gala, late-evening supper, jovial with speeches and toasts.

When Van and Corbett opened their second week, Jim stopped the show to introduce each of his family, sitting in the boxes; they all received long rounds of applause. At the end of the performance, he had them all come on stage with him. The duo easily filled the house the remainder of their appearance.

Their Los Angeles visit proved more difficult. On a bill with a number of lesser acts, Van and Corbett had to fully extend themselves to awaken somnolent audiences. A juggling act was nervous and messed up several feats; a comedian couldn't get the audience to laugh at his jokes for the first three minutes of his act; a jazz dance team left patrons uninspired. By the time Van and Corbett appeared on stage, the key second-to-last act, the crowd seemed to be "sitting on their hands." Even the "red card" joke elicited little laughter. However, when Van remarked he was a splinter hunter for a barefoot dancer, the audience loosened up and gave the team a healthy reception.

While in Los Angeles, Jim cut a number of phonograph records for a company expounding the virtues of physical culture. The result of these efforts is unknown.

Stops in Denver and Chicago were made on the way back to New York. The Denver engagement was well-received, but Chicago was merely a reprise of their previous visit in September, and the fact that their act played "stale" was expressed in mediocre attendance.

Both the *Clipper* and *Dramatic Mirror* echoed the grumbling attributed to theater managers and producers about theaters' "worst season in history."

Supposedly, more than $1.5 million had been lost. Out of 184 plays and companies, only 23 had been successes. Van and Corbett were included among the successful performers. Yet, as the 1921-1922 season limped into theater history, the death of Lillian Russell seemed to emphasize the end of a musical theater era renowned for its opulent styles, splendid shows, and glamorous performers.

President Harding declared three days of national mourning for Russell. A memorial service was held for her at the Hippodrome Theater, New York, the service attracting more than 4,000 people, many of whom were members of the theatrical community. Jim and Vera attended. A few days later, another memorial ceremony was held at the Palace Theater. There, Russell was eulogized by many of her colleagues, including Jim, who presented a short monologue about Russell's years of strong support for fellow performers. Generally, speakers agreed that the musical stage was in transition, but what it might or should become, no one could suggest. It would be another two years before the refreshing waters of mu-

sical theater would begin to flow freely again, with an abundance of glamorous, colorful, tuneful, audience-riveting productions.

The Keith circuit hired Van and Corbett to play a four-week tour of Eastern cities, since they had not been seen there for almost a year. Reviews of their past touring triumphs were generously plastered across each city. New joke material had been added, a fact noted in the reviews.

> Billy Van is funnier than ever and Jim Corbett is more effective than he ever was as a straight man. A lot of new lines have been injected, all of which are screams. A gag at the finish, in which Van whispers in Corbett's ear that Ford is out front, resulted in a yell when Corbett started to apologize to Ford, saying that if he was out front he must excuse him for calling the attention of the audience to him. Then suddenly turning to Van, he asked, "How do you know he's out front?" Van replied, "I saw his car in front of the theater."[13]

Vera and Jim enjoying an intimate moment at home. Vera was said to be a good pianist. Jim's singing never appeared in any of his vaudeville appearances, although his colorful monologues enchanted audiences for years. (San Francisco History Center, San Francisco Public Library)

Jim and Vera retired to Bayside for a quiet summer. Meanwhile, the team was offered a thirty-two week route on the Keith circuit and both were leaning toward signing the contract. The upcoming season looked more promising, as reports of increased business arrived from many theatrical quarters. Vaudeville remained the "bread-and-butter" of the business, and top-performing headliners were in short supply. A bidding war between the Keith and Orpheum circuits for the duo's services sparked negotiations. In the meantime, feeling confident about the new season,

Billy and Jim rehearsed new material. In the end, they chose the Keith circuit, at $1,500 a week each.

Simultaneously with the announcement that Van and Corbett had signed with Keith for the 22-23 season, they opened their tour at Keith's Atlantic City, in a comedy skit entitled "The Eighteenth Amendment," a travesty on prohibition and its dour adherents. When they appeared at the Palace Theater the following week, the *Clipper* remarked about the duo's compatibility, a personal and professional rapport that had ensured them two years of continued stage successes.

> Few comedians are lucky enough to get a straight man of Corbett's caliber; and darn few straight men are lucky enough to get a comedian of Van's type. Their comedy flows along like the proverbial brook and with no apparent effort.[14]

Included in the Palace program were a duo piano act, a dancing revue, a bicycle riding exhibition, burlesque comedy, Mrs. Sidney Drew, presenting a dramatic reading, and a newsreel. (An observer would note that the composition of vaudeville acts had remained largely unchanged the past few decades.) Listed in the program notes were the other headliners featured on this season's Keith circuit: Ona Munson, Joe Laurie, Van & Schenk, the Great Blackstone, Mae West, Sophie Tucker, and Eddie Foy and Family.

For the next sixteen weeks, Van and Corbett toured the East and Midwest to crowded houses, including a rewarding two weeks in Chicago. Though audiences were quite familiar with their act, the *Tribune* declared that "fans could not get enough of it." On the bill with them for one week was Sophie Tucker. Deliberately, the acts often invaded one another's time on stage and they engaged in some comic improvisational business, much to the audience's delight. Tucker kidded Jim about his "old" boxing adventures, and Jim likened her to Jeffries before he began training to face Jack Johnson.

Van and Corbett ended 1922 performing in Memphis and New Orleans during the holiday season, just as they had the previous year. While there, Van completely surprised Jim when he indicated a desire to retire to a home he had recently purchased in Newport, New Hampshire. They had two more months on the road to work out their plans, but Jim knew well that, when Van made up his mind, little could be done to change it. With little choice in the matter, Jim began to search for a new partner.

Fittingly, Billy and Jim played their final engagement at the Palace Theater, at the end of February 1923. Much was said in the press about the partnership, lauded as one of the most successful in recent vaudeville history. At the end of their act each performance, crowds cheered the team. At the last evening's performance, the show was stopped to present them plaques from the Friars' Club, in honor of their entertainment contributions. Flowers overflowed the stage. Billy and Jim gave short speeches of thanks. Then, instead of simply walking off the stage, they stepped into the aisles, shaking hands with patrons as they passed through the theater. Applause continued for many minutes after their departure, the crowd hoping they would reappear one more time.

Actually, the pair performed two more times: at a banquet given them by the Friars' Club and at a Sunday night concert appearance at the New Amsterdam Theater with Paul Whiteman and his orchestra. In sum, Van and Corbett had appeared in sixty cities and performed more than 600 times, over an almost three-year period. A few weeks later, Jim announced that he would team with comedian Jack Norton and continue in vaudeville.

Mortimer J. Norton was born in Brooklyn in 1887. He began his stage career in local cabarets and perfected an act portraying a drunk. Norton, who never took a drink, did so well that managers were unwilling to cast him in any other role. His comic persona lent itself well to Jim's straight role, and their performances were quickly embraced by audiences. In stark contrast to Jim's elegant evening attire, Norton wore the rumpled clothes of an alcoholic who never seemed ashamed of his condition. Some years later, Norton played cameo roles in many movies, having become the films' quintessential drunk.

Corbett and Norton played their first engagement in April, at the New Amsterdam Theater, in an actors' benefit. Sitting in the audience was Flo Zeigfeld, who had been spending a great deal of time at the theater, preparing for a summer version of his Follies, scheduled to open in June. Ziegfeld was so impressed with the Corbett-Norton act, he offered to sign them up for the summer, to which they readily agreed. It could not have been a more fortuitous way to introduce the new team to theater audiences.

Featured in this version of the Follies were Eddie Cantor, Ann Pennington, Fanny Brice, and Paul Whiteman's orchestra. Corbett and Norton appeared in Act Two, scene four, in a skit entitled "The Society Break-Down." A drunken Norton dares Corbett to hit him in an effort to unhinge his society front. Each time Corbett attempts to punch Norton, his drunken antics cause Corbett to miss. Corbett grows increasingly exasperated and throws even more punches. Each time, Norton falls without being touched, and Corbett believes he has hurt him. Norton gets up and taunts Corbett, who tries yet again to land a blow. Again, Norton falls without being hit and Corbett walks away baffled.

Jim also appeared briefly in an Act Two, scene ten, skit, "Amateur Night," with Fanny Brice, Ann Pennington, and Bert Wheeler. The skit takes place twenty years previously, at Miner's Eighth Avenue Theater, where weekly tryouts are being held to discover new vaudeville talent. When Jim enters for his turn, the announcer, in an aside, looks the man over and mutters, "Now we'll suffer." Jim gives his name and tells the announcer that "reciting is my specialty," to which the observers respond with a rousing "Ho, hum." Haltingly, Jim begins his recitation, replete with pronunciation mistakes, parodying his characteristically slick monologue delivery.

If I could paint, I'd paint a lily white,
And painting I'd paint you.
Your hair with all the color of the night
Your cheeks with all the blush of roses hue,
If I could paint.

The announcer chases Jim off the stage, declaring, "You should be ashamed of yourself, you big bum. Why don't you take up boxing." While the audience laughed at Jim's self-effacing travesty, it was an undistinguished cameo. In contrast, the skit with Norton was considered one of the highlights of the show. Their engagement ran until the middle of September.

On October 1, Corbett and Norton opened their vaudeville tour at Proctor's Theater, Albany, New York. *Variety* reported on their success.

They were breaking in the act here, and are a riot. It is the best vaudeville turn Corbett has ever had. Corbett and Billy Van teamed up well, but Corbett and Norton pair up so great it would be hard to obtain a better partner for the ex-champion. Their verbal passages are clever and witty, and they bring the act to an end with a "slow motion picture" travesty that is a scream. Corbett and Norton are in for the Big Town.[15]

A month later, Corbett and Norton introduced themselves at the Palace Theater, to SRO crowds. A full page ad in *Variety* heralded their appearance and the *Times* called them "winners." For the remainder of the year, they toured the Keith circuit throughout the East and Midwest, then jumped to the Pacific Coast for holiday season engagements. *Variety* reported them to be one of the highest grossing acts in the business.

While Jim and Jack were playing in Los Angeles, Harry Rapf, a producer for Warner Brothers Pictures, offered Jim a small role in a film about to go into production. "It will take only one week of your time," he promised. Thus, Jim agreed to appear in another film, "Broadway After Dark," playing a cameo role, as himself, along with Fred Stone, Raymond Hitchcock, old friend Frank Tinney, Irene Castle, and Paul Whiteman, all of whom appeared as tenants in a theatrical boarding house frequented by the hero, Adolphe Menjou, and his girl friend, played by Norma Shearer. Actually, Rapf had overestimated Jim's time to shoot the scene; within three days, he and Norton were on their way to Salt Lake City, to continue their tour. The movie was released May, 1924. It achieved a moderate success, but few paid any attention to the cameo players. Like the other celebrated performers, Jim was included solely to exploit his name on behalf of the movie.

Even before Jim returned to New York, he and Norton agreed to an extended tour on the Orpheum circuit beginning in April, 1924, at salaries of $1,750 a week each. They would have only a two-week rest between assignments, finishing the Keith stint at the Palace Theater the last week in March. While Jim would have enjoyed a longer time at home, these days an actor did not turn down such a plum. The tour promised him and Norton a year of continuous performance.

During Jim's "vacation," he took part in the Friars' annual benefit, held at the Metropolitan Opera House. An overflow crowd greeted a succession of stars for almost five hours of entertainment. Jim played interlocutor in the minstrel sketch. Also appearing on the bill were Eddie Cantor, Joe Laurie, Louis Calhern, George Gershwin, and Victor Herbert. George M. Cohan was the emcee. (He had recently been forgiven for his behavior during the A.E.A. strike, and had returned to his leadership position with the Friars.) For the first time at a Friars' Frolic, the "gentler sex" were also featured, headed by Fannie Brice, Jeanne Eagels, Ann Harding, and Florence Moore. The Frolic collected more than $20,000 for the Actors' Fund.

On April 21, Corbett and Norton opened at the Orpheum Theater, Sioux City, Iowa.

> James J. Corbett and Jack Norton held down the next-to-closing spot with ease. It is a rough comedy turn, with Corbett as a physical instructor and Norton the pupil. The dialogue that follows is humorous, with Norton taking several falls, always for good laughs.[16]

After five excellent weeks in the Midwest, the duo made a long jump to San Francisco in June for a two-week engagement. "The ovations were tumultuous," reported the *Chronicle*.

> The reception that Jim received never has been equaled by anyone. That Gentleman Jim (Corbett's pet name nearly now forgotten) was a California product and made good in whatever he undertook from the ring to the stage held the State of California for Corbett as though he had it in his vest pocket.[17]

Not surprising, then, that Corbett and Norton played three weeks in Los Angeles and another week in San Francisco before returning East. They ended the Orpheum tour in Kansas City in late September. On their trip back to New York, the Keith booking agent caught up with them in Chicago to obtain signatures on contracts for the following season. Jim also held an unplanned meeting there with a representative from the *Saturday Evening Post*.

Within a matter of days, *Variety* revealed that Jim had signed a contract and received an advance of $10,000 from the *Post* for the story of his life, "to be written by himself," the magazine proudly announced. Actually, Jim's so-called autobiography was written by Robert Gordon Anderson. The writer trailed Jim on tour for more than three months to obtain the necessary "first-hand" data. The first episode appeared in the *Post* October 11, and the biography ran in serial form through the middle of November. The story dealt primarily with Jim's career as a boxer, but also made reference to selected theatrical experiences. The *Post* also said the story would be published in book form by Doubleday, Page and Company in 1925.

The announcement brought Jim more offers for work than he could handle. One movie studio offered him a starring role. Another sought him to make a tour of theaters, giving lectures and relating anecdotes, along with presenting films of famous knockouts, for a salary of $1,750 a week. A producer offered Jim $400 a lecture, with a guarantee of four a week and all expenses, if he would speak on the history of boxing. Meanwhile, the Keith people waited impatiently for his decision, holding off on booking time. Vera suggested this might be a good time for Jim to retire.

At the moment, Jim wasn't sure what he wanted to do, they all seemed to be excellent opportunities. When *Variety* revealed that the Keith organization was initiating an extensive program to present famous personalities as vaudeville attractions, so as to promote their bills, and had included Jim in their list of desired headliners, his mind was made up.

13. ANYTHING FOR THE MONEY

For the first time in many years, Jim and Vera spent his birthday—the 58th—at home. They held a quiet celebration, with a simple birthday cake (sans candles), and gifts from a coterie of invited friends. Long-time friend Eddie Foy and current partner Jack Norton led the singing of "Happy Birthday." The affair produced some nostalgic moments, as well.

Surrounding Jim at this party were friends near his own age, some even older. All were veterans of popular entertainment who had begun their careers in the 1880s or 1890s. Having experienced every imaginable theater condition, all testified to the wear-and-tear of long years of performance. Yet they all seemed satisfied with their accomplishments, if somewhat confounded about the reasons for their fortunate status. As popular as actors happened to be, they never failed to marvel at their success.

The past year, Jim had often been kidded about his longevity in the business. While always intended as a compliment, such jocularity was nevertheless a direct reflection of his age. When Vera suggested that Jim consider retiring, he had to agree that the last few years had been tough. In fact, he had likely worked harder in recent years than ever before and for less remuneration. Indeed, the changing forces in popular entertainment were continuing to divert attention (and attendance) away from the vaudeville stage. Jim was surely aware of it, as were his colleagues. Together, they represented most of the few remaining veterans who had so cheerfully and diligently participated in the growth and development of the "people's theater."

After World War I, vaudeville's decline began when America's social climate softened from vigorous to sentimental. The post-war era introduced beautified theater bills with the concomitant restriction or total loss of specialized artists with unique talents. Popular music exemplified this change, with the replacement of coon songs by romantic ballads. At the same time, larger and more ornate theaters tended to usurp the intimacy of performance, particularly for the comedian, who, to do his best, had to be in close touch with the audience. Many of the new theaters were so opulent that they actually detracted from the performance itself.

The speed of vaudeville's decline increased after the war and the effects of the 1921-1922 economic recession saw the emergence of highly competitive entertainments: movies (full length, star-studded, fantasy-driven, thrilling epics); radio (promoted as "free entertainment"); and glossy magazines, whose editorial policies were contrived to reflect current life styles. Combined, these new forces quickly became formidable. Indeed, they were all but unbeatable opponents with whom vaudeville could no longer compete.

When, in the middle 1920s, popular theater's arbiters refused to stay in touch with the cultural changes taking place around them, even vaudeville's strongest supporters acknowledged that its end was near. Vaudeville's place on the popular stage was being taken over by musical theater, presenting the most creative, tuneful, and colorful productions ever yet seen. Many vaudeville stars, sensitive to these changes, quickly turned to these new acting opportunities.

When E.A. Albee instituted five-a-day shows to bolster his circuit, it was a last desperate attempt to attract audiences. Instead, it proved to be theatrical suicide, an excess that devoured actors and audiences alike. Not surprisingly, the result made everyone tire of vaudeville more quickly. With finality, The Great Depression buried what remained of the once vivacious vaudeville organism.

Beginning his theater career as an intermission entertainer (boxing exhibitions), Jim had astutely altered his act to suit changing audience tastes. Upon reaching the status of national hero, he played the lead in melodramas that featured his boxing acumen. When interest in melodramas declined, he switched to dramatic comedy. When that form no longer fit his image, he returned to vaudeville as a compelling monologist.

When monologues lost their appeal, Jim, ever alert, sought to team with accomplished comedians, which helped to maintain his headliner status into the middle 1920s, at the same time that vaudeville itself was being assailed by other attractions. During his long career, Jim had become a uniquely versatile performer, having made good in—indeed, scaled the heights of—boxing and popular theater, both of which he had done much to legitimize as entertainments.

At this point in his career, however, Jim found few opportunities to explore. He was too old for serials. In feature movies, he had been replaced by high-profile Hollywood stars. Stage musicals featured performers who could sing and dance, and others who were bonafide comedians. Only vaudeville remained and that medium had become dominated by prettified acts and movies. By the middle 1920s, every vaudeville bill ended with a film.

When Jim and his friends evaluated the situation, they clearly recognized the profession's shortcomings. Some expressed relief that they were near the end of their careers. Still, some were frightened about how they would comfortably manage the remainder of their lives. Many feared what life might bring once they stopped performing. Jim struggled similarly. No doubt that is why he chose to remain in vaudeville, to eke out what income he could in the twilight years of his career.

Some old boxing friends had given him an idea, one he could possibly translate onto the stage. He could no longer box, but he could readily infuse the boxing theme into his act. By exploiting the activity that had first brought him to public attention, and by injecting fisticuffs into the formula, Jim convinced himself he had the opportunity to, frankly, extend his career and, at the same time, command a reasonably good salary.

When Jim discussed this idea with Norton, Jack was delighted with the possibilities. His trademark drunk role lent itself very well to a boxing-oriented skit. They quickly began work on the new routine, but decided not to introduce it until it had been sufficiently rehearsed; after all, a missed cue could be quite dangerous. Moreover, the realism of the skit had to be properly developed for audiences, to ensure their acceptance and generate the appropriate laughter. Nevertheless, in a pensive moment, Jim wondered whether the audience would embrace his return to boxing, albeit on the stage.

Corbett and Norton opened their new season at the State-Lake Theater, Chicago, on October 1, 1924, in their old act. Unfortunately, after a succession of good houses, Norton sprained his ankle and they had to leave the bill for an entire week. A tour of Southern cities met with enthusiastic audiences and much applause, but most theaters failed to fill to capacity. One had only to walk downtown streets and see long lines in front of movie houses to know where entertainment patrons were spending their time and money.

A return to Chicago, to fulfill their previous engagement, attracted good crowds, but this time the duo had to share headliner status with Cissie Loftus and Marjorie Rambeau. Still, *Variety* singled them out as "the outstanding laughing turn of the bill." While in Chicago, Jim was badgered anew about touring the lecture circuit; again, however, he turned it down, since the financial guarantee was well below what he was earning in vaudeville.

The duo returned to New York the middle of January 1925, to play the last seven weeks of their tour at theaters in and around Manhattan. *Variety* not only reviewed the now-familiar act, but also engaged in a bit of analysis, the topic being Jim's image and longevity in the business.

> Holding himself in the publicity and theatrical spotlight as no other former champion of the ring ever did or has done, James J. Corbett repeatedly appears somewhere before the footlights, backed up by his most agreeable presence, an assurance that must have come to him naturally and an abundance of good nature that doesn't object to a little raillery pointed at him.

It's the same with Mr. Corbett as a public character which he has remained likewise, and in the same measure with his stage popularity. Acknowledged an authority on sports, the same James J. is forever in the prints, as a writer or commentator or the interviewed. This latter edge he always has maintained has been a big asset to his stage career. The latest feat of Corbett, possibly no less in this day than his other accomplishments in other days was a serial in the Saturday Evening Post.[1]

Of Corbett and Norton's act, called "Taking the Air," *Variety* reported:

> It isn't difficult to believe the act has never stopped writing itself since starting. It's of quips, cross-fire, retorts and some slapstick. It's a pleasant turn. That combination with what goes with it—a noted personage and excellent comedian—make Corbett and Norton well worthwhile.[2]

No sooner had the duo concluded their short season, than it was announced that, after a brief rest of two weeks, Jim would enter the lecture business. Interviewed by *Variety* regarding this unexpected change of venue, Jim quipped: "It is with sincere regrets I leave the stage, though that is one profession from which I go out on my feet."

Lee Keedick, the route manager, told the press of Jim's lecture tour: four weeks of lectures, two to a city, in fourteen cities, concentrated in the Midwest. Corbett, Keedick said, will call his speech "Muscles and Morals."

Jim opened in Detroit, March 11, at the General Motors Corporation. This was followed by a talk before students of the Cass Technical High School and their parents. The Detroit newspaper declared that "on both occasions Gentleman Jim scored as definite a knockout as ever he did in the prize ring or on the stage."

Similar reactions followed Jim wherever he lectured. Interestingly, all of the talks were in front of business or school groups. Near the end of his tour, however, Jim refused additional bookings, citing fatigue and a desire to return home.

Three months later, *Variety* revealed that "Corbett and Norton are reteaming." Jack Norton, who was then appearing in Earl Carroll's "Vanities," retired from the cast to join Jim. The article also stated that Jim had had a successful lecture tour and planned a return to that circuit because he was "in demand." Why, then, the return to vaudeville?

The answer, simply, was money. Though more exhausting, Jim could earn as much in one week of vaudeville as he could in three weeks of lectures. The availability of a long touring contract also played an influential role in Jim's decision, although his salary had again declined, to $1,250 a week.

Corbett and Norton opened at the Capitol Theater, Chicago, August 15, performing their new boxing skit. Jim had no need to worry about audience reactions to the incorporation of boxing into his act. They responded so strongly that an encore for the entire act was demanded. The duo repeated it, with the same result. Unfortunately, since managers had generally forbidden encores in subsequent shows, Jim and Jack had to turn down requests to encore their act, a disappointment for performers and audience alike.

However, unexpectedly, Corbett and Norton parted a month later, amiably it was said, Norton for a skit in the latest Ziegfeld Follies, Jim to seek another partner to complete the Keith circuit tour. There was no inkling what might have caused the separation.

A week later, Jim joined with comedian Bobby Barry, a three-decades veteran of dramatic comedy and vaudeville. Born in 1886, Barry first appeared on the stage at age five with his father, in Barry and Fay farce-comedies. As a teen, his acting

in "Hogan's Alley" attracted George M. Cohan, who then featured Barry in "Foxy Grandpa." In 1905, Barry appeared in the Cohan shows, "Little Johnny Jones" and "The Governor's Sons." After a year performing vaudeville in Australia, he played the Columbia circuit in minstrel and vaudeville roles. Barry had recently lost a partner due to an automobile accident.

The new team opened at the Rialto Theater, Amsterdam, New York, on September 28. They performed a typical two-act routine, with Barry in blackface, similar to Corbett and Tinney's act several years previously. The audience, however, demanded they perform the boxing act and in a matter of days, the skit was reintroduced, Barry duplicating Norton's role. Response to the act was so superb that Keith decided to keep the team in New York through November.

When they began the road trip, Keith requested that the pair increase their performances, from two per day to three. All circuits were attempting, in this manner, to attract larger audiences, again, at the expense of actors. Citing their contractual agreement, Barry and Corbett refused. Not surprisingly, tension between the parties surfaced due to the disagreement. Through indirect sources, Jim discovered that Keith planned not to resign them for next season.

Stops throughout the Midwest finally landed them in Pittsburgh during the Christmas holidays, where they played to amazingly full houses. While there, Jim spent some time with the local sporting crowd and even refereed a bout. Back in New York in early January, the new team made their first appearance at the Palace Theater. *Variety* declared that Jim "disclosed the best and fastest act he had had in twenty years," and:

> Bobby Barry gave him tireless and punchy comedy support. There is some comedy

boxing, a feature Corbett had eliminated for many years. A drop suddenly appearing out of a blackout, with twinkling stars to indicate what his uppercut did to Barry, was a wow and a novelty. Gent Jim had to speech it off.[3]

However, in the same review, *Variety* bemoaned the Palace's lack of attendance. "Attendance didn't live up to the name and form of the fast-disappearing two-a-day's castle of topmost eminence."

For the next eight weeks, Corbett and Barry played the New York area to satisfactory, if not SRO, success. At the conclusion of their final week, the *Times* reported: "a good comedy show with Corbett and Barry with a different line of laughing gas, a fine combination for next to close anywhere."[4]

Such accolades made the road visits profitable, though they were playing Pennsylvania's small towns and their final engagement of the season was in Norfolk, Virginia. No sooner did the pair get home than they proudly announced signing a full season's contract to play the Pantages circuit, at $1,500 a week each, a princely sum for vaudeville headliners in those days.

Understandably weary after another exhausting season—he and his partners had taken to the boards more than 350 times in twenty-nine cities—Jim stayed home and rested for the whole summer. When they celebrated his sixtieth birthday, Vera again suggested that he consider retirement.

Corbett and Barry, employing the same skit (with a few new jokes), opened at the Pantages Theater, Toronto, on September 6, the beginning of a thirty-six week tour. After Toronto, they played engagements in the Midwest and northern states, making stops from Milwaukee to Vancouver, British Columbia. Engagements south along the Pacific coast to San Diego preceded a return to New York.

The duo played San Francisco during the holidays, which afforded Jim the opportunity to celebrate Christmas with the family and many old boxing colleagues. As always in San Francisco, his shows attracted SRO audiences and usually required a speech at the conclusion of each performance. A note of nostalgia: Jim and Vera visited the site on Hayes Street where the old Corbett homestead had recently been demolished.

Unlike previous years, however, Corbett and Barry found themselves back in New York, without a contract for the coming '27-'28 season. They anxiously awaited a call. Jim received one, but it was not for vaudeville.

Would he be interested in writing on the September 22 Dempsey-Tunney heavyweight championship match, the Hearst rep inquired? And would he like to start by covering the July 21 non-title Dempsey-Sharkey bout? For a fee of $5,000, Jim embraced both assignments with relish.

The Dempsey-Sharkey bout was to be held at Yankee Stadium, billed as a Tex Rickard-promoted "comeback" for Dempsey. The boxer was now thirty-one, had not fought in three years, and no longer seemed confident of his ring capabilities. Rickard was adept at convincing boxers to come out of retirement (Jeffries vs. Johnson) and the purse he dangled in front of Dempsey persuaded the boxer to take on Sharkey. Jim's initial impression of Dempsey was quite positive, commenting that he "seemed to be a fighting man" but he tempered his opinion by suggesting that age often did unexpected things to one's will.

Dempsey began training at the White Sulphur Springs Hotel and, within a few weeks, was reported to be rounding into "top shape." Three weeks before the match, however, misfortune dealt a blow to the Dempsey camp.

Jim celebrated his sixtieth birthday at home. He looked forty-five, according to observers, and playfully challenged younger friends to a "few rounds in the ring." (San Francisco History Center, San Francisco Public Library)

worked himself back into adequate shape in time to face Sharkey.

Although outpointed by his opponent in the early going, Dempsey won by a knockout in seven rounds. Sharkey grew cocky after winning the first few rounds and elected to challenge his opponent directly, exactly what Dempsey wanted. Dempsey easily outpunched him for the victory. Seventy-five thousand people attended the bout, and gate receipts amounted to more than one million dollars. Envisioning a multimillion dollar gate, Rickard immediately announced the staging of a second Dempsey-Tunney championship match.

Jim seems to have done reasonably well with his newspaper reports, but was apparently not up to Hearst expectations. They wanted his by-line, not his writing. Another writer would be assigned do his articles for Dempsey-Tunney; he would not, the publishers hoped, be offended. Quickly, Jim solved Hearst's dilemma and likely his own, as well.

Dempsey was informed that his older brother and sister-in-law were dead. Evidently due to a quarrel, the boxer's brother had shot his wife, then put the gun to his own head. Dempsey was required to identify the bodies. Upon his return to camp, the boxer plunged into a deep depression, unable to continue training. There immediately arose some question as to whether the match should be postponed. Jim knew full well what Dempsey was experiencing. In fact, comments to friends suggested that Jim was reliving the anguish he had suffered after his parents died.

Miraculously, likely as a result of Rickard's persuasive powers, Dempsey

In conjunction with the Friars' Club and the Pennsylvania Railroad, the "James J. Corbett Special" was marketed especially to New York's boxing and theatrical community. Jim would act as host and program director, as well as prepare a series of articles on his observations and experiences during the entire trip. (Another Hearst reporter, Gene Fowler, covered the Dempsey camp, while continuing to use Jim's by-line.)

In a day, all available berths on the train were sold out. The "Special" was advertised to be all-stag, but not quite. Jim stashed Vera in his drawing rooms, getting her on board the train while workmen loaded other cars. Supposedly, no one knew that Vera was aboard, though she appeared in the women's section for the match at Soldier's Field, Chicago, and attended a baseball game during the Pittsburgh stopover.

The exclusive Pullman train carried two diners, a club car, and an observation car with radio and phone attachments. Reporters planned to broadcast from Jim's train immediately after the match, by means of its long-distance wire connection to New York.

The passengers included theater, newspaper, and sporting men, all of whom planned to live on the train. Ringside seats were included in the cost, said to total $250. The round trip would take three days. Arriving in Chicago the afternoon of the bout, the train would depart directly after the bout for its return to New York. A number of well-known people, headed by comedian and film star Harold Lloyd, requested permission to hitch their own private cars onto the "Corbett Special."

A month before the bout, excitement was already at high pitch. Tickets were selling fast. In early September, Rickard publicly boasted of a $3 million gate. Collected from almost 105,000 people, the actual take proved to be $2.6 million, still a record for a sporting event. That the bout captured the attention of the entire country could be seen in headlines and features in newspapers and magazines. Boxing seemed to have been embraced as America's number one leisure-time entertainment among both men and women, at least for the time being. Comparing purses and gate receipts generated by his own matches, Jim could only shake his head in wonder at the sport's changes in twenty-five years.

When Tunney arrived in Chicago, he received a Lindbergh-like greeting. Still, Dempsey was the center of attention and he bested Tunney's reception. Yet, underneath it all, Dempsey was edgy; weighing heavily on his mind were his wife's unstable mental condition and his brother's recent suicide. Add to that the typical press-generated charges and rumors that always seemed to precede a title bout. Supposedly, three days before the bout, Dempsey had sent a letter accusing Tunney of helping to fix their first meeting. Who had actually written the letter was open to question. Not surprisingly, rumors of a new fix surfaced. Rickard loved the controversy; rumors plus accusations equaled money.

Tunney beat Dempsey in what historians called "The Battle of the Long Count." Among the rules agreed upon before the bout was one stating that, in the event of a knockdown, the boxer scoring it should retire to the farthest neutral corner. When Dempsey knocked Tunney down in the seventh round, he refused, or forgot, to obey the rule. The referee delayed the count until Dempsey complied, giving Tunney additional seconds to recover. The next round, Tunney retaliated, dropping Dempsey. He then proceeded to outpoint his opponent for a decision.

Dempsey's championship boxing career had come to an end, though he made a good deal of money on subsequent bouts and exhibitions. As had Jim's before him, Dempsey's popularity seemed to increase, even though he had been defeated.

Variety, following events aboard the "Corbett Special," hailed the outing as "a never-to-be-forgotten spectacle. The trip aboard the 'James J. Corbett Special' train from New York to Chicago and back was one of the most pleasurable journeys a bunch of good fellows could ever expect to make."[5]

Entirely stag (with the exception of Vera). Never an argument. A million laughs. That's the kind of trip it was, *Variety* reported. On board the "Corbett Special" were such luminaries as Messrs. William Morris, both Sr. and Jr., comic actor Roscoe "Fatty" Arbuckle, theater financier Felix Isman, and many members of New York's social and political elite. "Just a bunch out for a good time," declared *Variety*.

In the observation car, Jim sat telling stories the entire trip. Much of the cross fire dealt with his earlier ring experiences. When he was informed by an enthusiast that Jeffries had never hit him in the twenty-third round, Jim replied, "Well, they told me he hit me." Another commented on a telegram sent to him while he was in the hospital some years before: "Hear they opened you up and found one of Jeffries's gloves inside." To which Jim answered, "Yes, and there was a horseshoe in it."

A practical joke on the return trip took everyone in. One of the passenger's brothers posed as a detective seeking a man supposedly mixed up in the Sacco-Vanzetti case. As each man reboarded the train in Pittsburgh, he was stopped, asked to prove his identity, and questioned. The travel agent, Fred Block, whispered to everyone not to tip-off Jim, who pretended to be deeply hurt that his party had come under such suspicion. Actually, it was Jim who had framed the whole joke.

One negative note: Jim had arranged for fight tickets with Rickard. He found later that seventy-five too many had been purchased. Despite his enormous take, Rickard refused to make a refund. When *Variety* learned of the transaction, they sided with Jim. "The refund was hardly clubby towards a man like Corbett, who did more to bring boxing into repute than any heavyweight up to the present day."[6]

On November 17, at Loew's Boulevard Theater, New York City, Corbett and Barry began their belated 27-28 vaudeville season, presenting last year's boxing skit. There was no reason to change, audi-

ences now wanted to see only the widely popular routine. The duo played New York-area theaters to the end of the year, to good houses.

Starting the new year, Corbett and Barry faced nineteen more weeks of continuous two-a-day performances on the road. They first visited Southern cities (Atlanta, Birmingham, Memphis, New Orleans, and Houston), then, cities in the Midwest (Columbus, Detroit, Cleveland, and Pittsburgh), and finally, Eastern cities (Buffalo, Toronto, Montreal, and Boston), ending the tour where they had started, in New York. They had played every theater on the Loew's circuit.

As an incentive to build business, Marcus Loew initiated a contest among his theater managers to reward the man who could bring in the largest box-office for Corbett-Barry appearances. First, the Atlanta manager held the lead. The Detroit manager replaced him by getting Jim to write sports columns for the local newspaper. The State Theater, in New York won the contest by presenting the duo along with Ruby Keeler and her tap dancers. Corbett and Barry ended their season at Loew's Metropolitan Theater, Brooklyn, to SRO audiences. No one but they knew it would be their last engagement together. Barry had been signed by Keith to appear in a skit; Jim had been quietly discussing a non-theatrical venture with investors.

A month later, Jim revealed he was planning to open a "health farm" at Wappingers Falls, New York, near Poughkeepsie. It was to be designed for "those men who wished to remain in condition." Jim would direct daily exercises and consult on menus and leisure-time activities. Up to fifty men could be accommodated at one time. While no further details of the venture were uncovered, the business seems to have survived the summer, closing in September for lack of customers.

Corbett and Barry performing their familiar boxing routine. Jim attempted to teach Barry how to box. Barry kidded Jim about the amount of time he spent on the floor after a bout.

Jim then attempted to reunite with Barry, whose vaudeville skit had flopped, and it appeared they might be able to contract for another season. At the time, however, vaudeville circuit managers were struggling against a new form of competition—talking pictures. Signings were delayed because many managers were grappling with the expense of wiring their theaters for sound. If they decided to upgrade, the choice would hold up resumption of the new season. Audiences, however, were clamoring for talkies. Of the 200 vaudeville houses ready to open, only fifty did. Most others delayed, to gird themselves for the talking picture onslaught. The delay left many available acts without venues. Jim could afford to wait a while for theaters to solve

their problems, but Barry could not. He signed with R-K-O.

In the meantime, to earn him some additional money, Jim's familiar profile and endorsement appeared in popular magazines on behalf of Barbasol shaving cream. "Popular faces are shaved with Barbasol," headlined the ad.

For the man who wants to keep on friendly terms with his face—I recommend Barbasol. It's fast, sidesteps all the old shaving troubles, while making the whiskers come clean. I'm a Barbasol rooter every morning when I shave, and all day, too.

(signed) Jas. J. Corbett

Unfortunately, the close-up photo of Jim proved less than complimentary. It revealed thinning hair, lines etched deep across his forehead, bags under his eyes, and "crow's feet" at the corners. Jim looked old.

In early 1929, Jim announced to *Variety* that he and Neil O'Brien had joined forces for vaudeville. Their opening would be delayed, however, because Jim was again leading a special excursion to Miami, Florida, for the Sharkey-Stribling battle. This time, included in the entourage was a large company of Friars who planned to put on a benefit performance in the fight city. The entire trip was going to be an all-star bash, they said, rocking Miami as never before.

"The James J. Corbett Friars Sports Special" departed from Penn Station for one full week of festivities. The train party consisted of 125 people, all of whom planned to live and dine on the train. Unlike the previous stag trip, cars in the rear were reserved for those who were accompanied by their wives. Working with Jim were Jack Dempsey and Fred Block, the agent who had assisted in the Dempsey-Tunney trip. Dempsey had been hurriedly called upon to help promote the bout when Rickard unexpectedly died from an appendix operation.

Jim would not only act as host, but also participate in the Friars Frolic, scheduled to be presented at the Olympia Theater on the eve of the bout. William Morris, Jr., was in charge of the show. Dempsey and William Collier would emcee the show, with headliners like W.C. Fields, Bugs Baer, Lou Holtz, Harry Hershfield, and Jim.

Sharkey gained the decision over Stribling, but it was the Friars' activities that engendered all the attention. Upon their arrival in Miami, the Town Kiltie Band led the troupe to city hall, where the mayor presented Jim the key to the city. They then marched on to their hotel. (It had been decided that, with so many wives in the entourage, a hotel would be more comfortable than train berths.) The next day, the Friars visited the race track. Although the main race was dubbed the "Friars Purse," few made money. That evening, they all attended the dog track, with similar results.

It was SRO at the theater, the admission scale topping fifty dollars. More than $22,000 was collected for charity. The show began with fifty Friars, all in monastery garb, singing the club song. Highlights of the show were Lou Holtz, in a comedy guitar number, and Jim and Jack Dempsey in their version of a comedy two-act.

"Would you mind answering a personal question?" Dempsey asked.

"Of course not," Jim replied.

"Well," queried Jack, "how did it feel when Jeffries knocked you out?"

"Jack, how did you feel when Firpo was leveling you?"

They both indicated that things looked black, to which the audience howled. Ted Lewis and his band entertained. Then, with only fifteen minutes of rehearsal, Louise Groody, the only girl in the show, went over smartly.

Following the bout, a number of night club evenings ensued, at which the Friars not only attended, but also played impromptu shows. *Variety* summed up the excursion as "one of the best they had seen." "The Frolicking Friars returned from Miami Sunday, aboard the James J. Corbett special train, ending the most satisfactory and enjoyable excursion in the history of the club."[7]

As briefly mentioned in the article, Jim and Jack had come across so well on stage that they were asked to repeat the performance at the next Friars Frolic in New York, which they promised to do. Prior to that event, Jim was selected to host the American Health Sports Carnival, at the Grand Central Palace. Along with his emcee duties, Jim offered a short monologue on what it was like to be a defeated champion.

> Once, after coming out of a theater, shortly after the battle when Fitzsimmons put me out, I heard two little boys discussing me, my fight, and my solar plexus. "It's on the left side," said one little fellow. "Go on," the other contradicted. "It's on the right." When they saw me they asked me what side the solar plexus was on. I explained that the solar plexus was neither on the left or right side, but in the middle. "What does he know about it!" yelled the youngster who had championed the right side. "He was asleep when it all happened."[8]

The Friars Frolic, at the Metropolitan Opera House, featured an all-star cast of actors, song writers, and dancers. John Philip Sousa led the orchestra. Songwriters Bert Kalmar, Harry Ruby, Irving Caesar, and Morrie Ryskind parodied one another's songs. Clayton, Jackson, and Durante put on a funny skit. Rudy Vallee sang. Maurice Chevalier did likewise. Also appearing were Lou Holtz, Jack Haley, Phil Baker, Fanny

Brice, Louis Mann, and Adolf Zukor in a walk-on.

Then Dempsey and Corbett came on, repeating their Miami act, with some added jokes, compliments of Bugs Baer. The new topic concerned Dempsey's fight with Tunney. Jack declared he would never fight again, even for a million. Jim replied he would return to the ring for half that dough and would fight anybody. Jack retorted there would be a line around the theater taking Jim up on his offer. The show closed with a special honor to New York City Mayor Jimmy Walker, who wanted to know why so many actors were content to play four shows a day, but would vote only once.

Again, Corbett and Dempsey were so well received that they were signed for a four-week engagement at the Balaban & Katz picture houses in Chicago, at a reported $8,750 a week. The act was promoted as the first time two ex-champions would appear together for a purse, outside of the ring. Theaters were crowded with spectators eager to see the two celebrities together, but their act proved mediocre, disappointing the crowd. The *Tribune* wondered why Jim had combined with a partner who was unable to "crack a joke."

Jim's rehearsals with Neil O'Brien were again interrupted, this time by a Fox Films request for him to play a small role in a talking film revue, "Happy Days." In the first years of sound pictures, the musical revue was the preferred vehicle. All other studios had already produced their versions. This was Fox's second attempt; their first had turned out poorly. With all the new sound movies, quality sound reproduction was difficult to achieve. Actors appeared to be shouting (they probably were) or they spoke too slowly and distinctly. In some scenes, it was hard to hear the dialogue at all. Camera work was static, filming the stage head-on, with little movement or panning.

Typical of stage revues, there was almost no plot. Everybody who was anybody in vaudeville was included in the cast: Charles E. Evans, William Collier, George Jessel, Will Rogers, Walter Catlett (who also staged all the acts), Ann Pennington, and Jim Corbett. They supported the stars of the movie, Janet Gaynor, Charles Farrell, Victor McLaglen, Edmund Lowe, and Warner Baxter.

The first routine in the movie was a minstrel show, with all the performers in blackface. Jim repeated his familiar role as interlocutor, with Catlett and Collier as end men. The movie was released in September, 1929, but its New York premier did not take place until March, 1930.

Finally, on July 13, Corbett and O'Brien opened their Keith circuit vaudeville tour at the Keith Theater, in Syracuse, New York. O'Brien appeared in blackface and shabby clothes (as had Frank Tinney); Jim was elegantly attired in a tuxedo. The skit consisted of each man attempting to outshine the other by bragging about past accomplishments. The more they tried to best one another, the more ridiculous (and funny) the routine became. The local newspaper described the act as "the only substantial comedy act on the bill."

The tour got rolling with a succession of engagements in the Midwest, then, at the end of September, a jump to the Pacific Coast and San Francisco. For the first time in Jim's theatrical career, family members were the only ones to meet him and Vera at the train station. When Corbett and O'Brien appeared at the Orpheum Theater, crowds were good but the houses were not sold out. Newspaper coverage of their act was minimal, all theatrical reporting pushed aside by coverage of the country's impending economic crisis. The decade's prosperity was about to come to an abrupt, unruly, and cataclysmic end.

During the exuberant 1920s, the U.S. economy had soared to spectacular heights, spurred by a succession of Republican presidents who espoused policies favorable to big business. Because the manufacturing segment of the economy prospered—in contrast to agriculture and labor—the public invested heavily in corporate stocks, providing companies with additional capital to further expand. The more money that was invested, the higher went stock values. This led to widespread speculation, which soon pushed stocks well beyond their actual value and promoted extensive buying on margin. In late October, a decline in stocks began. Since so many investors were overextended, panic selling soon followed, drastically lowering stock prices and dragging many into financial ruin. The Great Depression had begun, although its real impact on the general public would not be felt until early 1930.

The first signs of economic turbulence appeared in August and September, 1929, and theater managers bemoaned the new season's slow start. Attendance at all shows was down. Even movies were suffering the downturn, though they remained hard at work promoting sound. Terminally ill, vaudeville continued to manifest the symptoms of incipient mortality. What Jim had experienced in the Midwest and was witnessing in San Francisco were clear indications, he observed, of vaudeville's increasingly rapid and irreversible decline.

Jim and Neil were playing San Diego on the day of the stock market crash. Because of the time difference, news of the crash reached the city early in the morning, soon enough to appear in newspaper headlines. When the afternoon show opened, the theater was nearly empty. It was no better in the evening. In fact, theater attendance across the country was so dismal that some circuit managers halted tours for a week to monitor the situation.

Jim and Neil were stalled in San Diego almost two weeks before traveling to Denver, on their way back to New York.

Theater managers were scrambling to pump up their bills, in the hopes of maintaining attendance. While in Kansas City, the duo was informed that their upcoming engagement in New York during the Christmas holidays was going to be "enhanced" by the addition of Jack Dempsey. Would Jim be willing to include Dempsey in his act, just as he and Dempsey had done in Chicago? Actually, Jim had little choice but to agree to the request.

Variety succinctly sized up the Corbett-O'Brien-Dempsey engagement.

> The Riverside as viewed by Christmas matinees would have been playing to echoes without the influence of Corbett and Dempsey as headliners. Even then, they couldn't fill more than half the main floor seats.[9]

Jim and Neil performed their usual "bragging" skit. Dempsey was then introduced. Jim embraced him and jokingly told the audience that Dempsey was and always would be just a big kid. To complete Dempsey's walk-on role, the ex-champions engaged in some good-natured mutual belittling, each kidding the other about how it felt to be "knocked goofy." Sadly, *Variety* noted with no little sarcasm, "this was the bill's best bit of entertainment."

The Corbett's Christmas party was not a cheerful gathering. There was no question that theater, particularly vaudeville, was headed for hard times. Evaluating their recent experiences, Jim and Neil agreed their act had become old and, since they had contracted for three more months of engagements—including eight weeks in the New York area—changes had to be made.

Early in January, *Variety* listed their new act, but when it appeared, many old admirers were struck by its similarity to previous Corbett two-acts.

> James J. Corbett and Neil O'Brien have a new act with a load of comedy chatter, It is good in spots but can stand considerable jacking up. Corbett has been with divers partners. His latest is from minstrelsy, retaining the under cork character in the present skit. Jim's popularity more than anything else will have to be depended upon to put them over as is.[10]

In an obvious attempt to hedge their concerns, Jim and Neil placed a big ad in *Variety* declaring, "We are interested in the talkies." They attracted no immediate takers.

Their early 1930 appearances in New York ranged from good—"having pleased by their presence and incited giggles by their puns"—to average—"slim laughter through the turn, and only fair hand." In half-filled theaters, one could hear all the echoes. At about the same time, a series of feature articles in New York newspapers delineated vaudeville's demise: the death of routes; no long-term contracts; thus, no more work. As far as vaudeville was concerned, actors believed, "the future had little in store for them." Many said they were leaving show business entirely.

Jim and Neil made their final appearance together on April 1, at the Capitol Theater, Trenton, New Jersey. They took the boards on an inauspicious bill, played to light audiences. "Corbett and O'Brien floated along on inverted comedy about politics and economy, with Corbett's rep the mainstay of the turn."[11]

At the end of their final act, Jim and Neil sat in a deathly quiet dressing room. Vaudeville was indeed dead, they agreed. Or maybe, Jim mused privately, he was dead in vaudeville.

Fally Markus, a long-time theatrical booking agent, was now spending all his time getting non-acting jobs for his clients. "Actors are brighter than the average applicant," he proudly declared, "besides shrewder, and the personal appearance of most gives a decided advantage." Markus continued: "Youngest of the actors are especially suited." He strategically omitted his opinion on old-timers.

For a number of headliners, including Jim and Neil, The Vitaphone Company came to the rescue. Joe E. Brown, Vivienne Segal, Rudy Vallee, and Eddie Foy, Jr. had recently appeared in Vitaphone talking shorts, which seemed to offer the actors entree to other films or stage productions. Jim and Neil signed to reprise their vaud act on the talking screen.

The short begins with Jim, in a monologue, telling the story of the two boys arguing about the solar plexus punch. He then admits to having returned to the fight game by managing boxers. Enter O'Brien, employing a Negro dialect, looking for a boxing manager. Jim refuses to acknowledge him as a competent boxer. He makes pointed reference to O'Brien's incompetence in the ring and his frequent knockdowns. The skit ends with Jim bragging about the number of times his own picture has appeared on the front pages of newspapers. O'Brien claims he can remember only one, a photo of Jim sprawled flat on the canvas. The entire act seemed out-of-date, forced and clumsy.

Shortly afterwards, Jim was featured in another Vitaphone short, entitled "At the Round Table," with De Wolf Hopper and newspapermen Damon Runyon and Mark Hellinger. The skit opens in Corbett's gym, where he is overseeing girls in their exercises. Hopper drops in to tell Jim that a newspaper man wants to see him at the club.

The next scene takes place at a round table, in what appears to be the Friars' Club. Four men are seated for lunch when a newspaperman from Pittsburgh enters, asking to see Corbett. He claims to know

Corbett, Runyon, and Hellinger, but the men seated at the table insist they are not the ones he knows. A comic explanation, a laugh; and Hellinger is presented the check.

Sime, from *Variety*, gave it a guarded review. "A short to display the celebs featured in it. No story, just a skeleton of a frame. Good novelty anywhere with publicity possible because of personages." It was also Jim's last appearance in films.

On completion of the Vitaphone short, Jim complained of recurrent stomach aches and he admitted to having lost vitality.

EPILOGUE

A dark, ominous layer of clouds rolled over Manhattan on the morning of November 28, 1930. The *New York Times* forecast heavy snow by evening, a prediction that signaled companies to send their workers home early. An equally somber atmosphere engulfed a meeting being held on the second floor of 1674 Broadway, the austere offices of the American Federation of Labor. In a cigar smoke-filled room, four men sat at a table, each of them holding a single sheet of paper. They were examining the charter of the White Rats, who had been members of the A.F.L. since 1919.

After thirty years of valiant battling for the rights of and benefits due to popular theater performers, the White Rats organization, by these four signatures applied to its charter, was declared summarily and officially dead. Prior to this gathering, more than fifty veterans of the Rats, a group that included such longtime headliners as Fred Stone (one of the Rats original eight founders), De Wolf Hopper, Ed Wynn, Eddie Cantor, and Jim Corbett, had voted unanimously to disband the organization. They cited a continuous decline in membership and dues as the reasons for the dissolution. In reality, however, it was vaudeville's own demise that terminated the venerable union. As a

final gesture, Harry Montford, Rats past-president, released an emotionally-charged statement to the press explaining the performers' decision.

> Vaudeville, as the White Rats knew it, is no more. When the class performers passed out of existence, it meant our doom. The position of the entire situation finally became so serious we all appreciated it was practically useless to continue. We have worked for the actors for thirty years. We have been kicked around, abused, vilified, threatened, sued, and called everything under the sun by managers. The Actors Equity is the only house of refuge left for the browbeaten actor. It is the last stand of talent and brains against money force.[1]

Everyone nodded in agreement. The gloomy occasion was the final chapter in a long series of events that had pronounced the end of vaudeville's glorious reign. At the conclusion of the meeting, old friends and colleagues shook hands and hugged each other warmly, said quiet good-byes, and sadly left the building, painfully cognizant that they had been unwilling participants in the burial of an honorable part of their own careers.

Riding home on the subway, Jim mused on the many White Rats adventures with which he had been involved over the years. He acknowledged that the end of the Rats likely spelled the end of his own career. Maybe it was finally time to retire. Vera would be glad to hear him admit the possibility.

As he was exiting the subway at the Bayside station, climbing the long flight of stairs, Jim was seized by a sharp pain in his chest, a grip so strong that it momentarily paralyzed the left side of his body. Gasping for breath, he slumped against the station's tiled wall, "waiting for death," he told friends afterward, yet he called for no assistance. Jostling crowds hurried past, paying scant attention to the stricken man, who seemed only a bit tired. Within a few minutes, Jim had mustered enough strength to ascend from the subway. At street level, he hailed a taxi to get safely home.

The following day, Jim and Vera visited the family physician, Dr. G. Willard Dickie. After a thorough examination, Jim was told he was suffering from a heart condition. While not serious, the illness nevertheless called for certain restrictions on his activities. Jim issued a bulletin to the press, telling of his malady and assuring his admirers he would address the issue head on, just as he had addressed every issue in his life. "I want everyone to know," he declared, "that Jim Corbett can take care of himself." Under questioning by reporters, Jim admitted to having been alarmed by the episode in the subway.

For the next few months, Jim was rarely seen in public, appearing only at boxing matches, where he was continually badgered by journalists curious about the state of his health. In June, 1931, however, his appearance at the annual Friars' Frolic, in an acting role, suggested to everyone that Jim had apparently recovered from his ailment.

It was a typical Friars' extravaganza, an opportunity for the audience to see all of theater's premier entertainers on one stage, doing what they did best. Emceed

by George M. Cohan, the program began with a salute to composers—Irving Berlin, George Gershwin, Gus Edwards, Harry Warren, and Harry Ruby—who played and sang their own compositions. Maurice Chevalier unexpectedly appeared and imitated Rudy Vallee, and Al Jolson. Chevalier's French-accented interpretations brought down the house. Then followed a series of olios, brief turns by Joe Frisco, Phil Baker, Jack Benny, Joe Laurie, Jr., and George Jessel, each performing his own stage specialties. The minstrel part, which satirized a Cohan musical, featured Jim as interlocutor, with Bert Wheeler and Charles King as endmen. The afterpiece, a parody of college boys, called "The New Dean," was led by Willie and Eugene Howard, Lou Holtz, and Jim Corbett. William Collier closed the show by reminiscing about a quarter century of Friars' Frolics and the demise of vaudeville, admitting that some of this year's participants had appeared in nearly all of the annual events.

During the summer, Jim's trips to the Friars' clubrooms and to boxing matches were frequent. Ever ready to comment about the boxers he observed, Jim was often quoted in the press. One match in particular garnered press attention, because it caused Jim to question a referee's behavior. During a fight at which Jim was present, the referee had cautioned the boxers to "stop talking." Jim took some offense at the referee's admonition: "Now what right has a referee to say that?" he questioned. "I never heard of such a thing. That is part of boxing, and always had been." Judging from his frequent public appearances, everyone assumed that Jim had fully recovered his health.

In September, Jim's strong voice was heard over local radio stations. He had been hired to appear in a series of fifteen-minute programs, sponsored by Mail Pouch tobacco (ironic since Jim had been forbidden to smoke by his doctor). The programs were all health-related, with Jim discussing how to eat and how to exercise healthfully. "I'm not a pro or a scientist when it comes down to actual food and exercise values," he related, "but I'll tell you all I know from experience." Twenty-six interviews were completed, to be aired only once on each radio station. Jim received $5,000 for the job.[2]

Jim's radio lectures included, along with diet tips, recommendations on hiking, care of the teeth, and periodic physical examinations. The use of tobacco received no mention in his speeches. Revealing his own level of activity after reaching sixty, he concluded, "at present, it is a simple mode of life."

The same day the radio programs were reviewed by *Variety*, in the gossip section, it was reported that Jim had entered the hospital for observation. "Something wrong with his interior," was the rumor. While Jim's heart condition seemed to have improved, his periodic abdominal pains required attention.

To Jim, as to the press, Dr. Dickie reported that his patient had experienced a flare-up of the heart condition. Privately, to Vera, he revealed a far more serious illness: Jim was suffering from liver cancer, and it was uncertain how long he had to live. Together, Dr. Dickie and Vera agreed never to reveal the actual illness to Jim. Of necessity, Jim's activities were again curtailed; and he rarely made trips into Manhattan. Instead, a steady round of friends visited Jim, bringing with them all the latest gossip and rumors. For news of the day, Jim avidly read New York's daily papers.

In early 1932, Jim returned to the hospital, apparently for another evaluation. Dr. Dickie's latest press release said that Jim had checked out OK. In reality, the cancer had metastasized. Jim had been losing weight and was getting progressively weaker.

A month later, unable to hide the effects of her husband's illness any longer, Vera told the press that Jim was "seriously, but not critically ill." Yet everyone knew what that meant. Newspapers immediately initiated a "death watch" on Jim, releasing weekly reports with whatever information they could obtain, publishing even rumors. Reading about himself in the papers must surely have affected Jim, providing him insight into his condition, yet he said nothing of these stories and their implications. Still, friends continued to offer him solace and reassurance. Jim now passed each day listening to baseball games, reading the newspapers, and visiting with intimates. According to visitors, Jim never revealed any personal feelings about his obviously failing health.

Jim had to be assisted to his chair at the Corbett's annual Christmas party. Though thin and weak, he continued to dress in his customary dapper fashion, wearing a long, black, silk robe, white silk ascot, and gray suede spats over polished black shoes. The party was pleasant but subdued. The determined conviviality was interrupted only once, a stark reminder to guests of Jim's tenuous hold on life. Jim turned to Vera, took her hand, and, in a half-whisper, said: "When it comes my turn, darling, I will die happy if you are there to hold me." A few days later, however, Jim seemed to rally, expressing optimism about the future.

In January 1933, even though so infirm he was unable to feed himself, Jim refused to enter the hospital. He was now restricted to bed, his loss of weight (from 180 to 140 pounds) having severely weakened him. Nonetheless, he seemed to rally when friends visited. Old family friends John and Denny Kelleher arrived from Boston to assist Vera, to handle the seventy-five to eighty telephone calls and dozens of letters Jim received each day. John circulated daily reports of Jim's

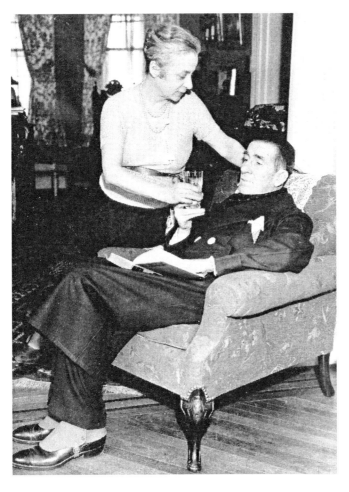

By March 1932, Jim had been confined to home, under Vera's care. Everyone seemed to be aware Jim was dying, and it is likely he recognized it as well. Friends and colleagues visited Jim nearly every day to share the day's entertainment gossip. (San Francisco History Center, San Francisco Public Library)

struggling in vain to speak to those gathered around him. Finally, with great effort, he turned to Vera and whispered, "You're still there, dear, aren't you?" Hovering at his bedside, she touched his arm in reply.

"Of course, Jim."

"Kiss me, darling," he murmured.

As he sought her comfort, Vera leaned over to embrace him. She took Jim in her arms and kissed him with tender passion. He lapsed into unconsciousness, from which he never emerged.

Jim died at 1:30 P.M. Besides Vera and the Kelleher brothers, an old Bayside associate of Jim's, John Smollen, was at his bedside. The priest was immediately called to deliver the last rites of the church. The ever-alert press notified Dr. Dickie of Jim's death, and he rushed over to the Corbett home. At 2:00 P.M., the doctor verified Jim's death. He immediately issued a statement to the press.

condition to the press and to friends who called.

Abruptly, although to no one's surprise, Jim's condition turned critical. He fell into a coma, with intermittent periods of consciousness. When awake, he suffered considerable pain, at which times Dr. Dickie would administer a sedative, returning Jim to a deep sleep. The local parish priest was called to give Jim his last communion.

On the morning of February 18, 1933, Jim awoke from a drug-induced sleep,

James J. Corbett died at 1:30 P.M. at his home in Bayside after a lingering illness, resulting from carcinoma (cancer) of the liver with metastasis (spread of the disease) in adjacent organs. His unusual reserve of vitality was amazing to all. His persistent determination to fight to the end was only overcome by the seriousness of the disease.[3]

In press interviews, the doctor went on to reveal the facts of Jim's long illness. "The fact that he was suffering from cancer was kept a secret from the sick man," Dr. Dickie explained. "No one was allowed to know it because it might get into the newspapers, and he read the newspapers regularly. The only reason we said he was suffering from a heart ailment was because we did not want him to know he had something different."

In concealing it from Jim, the physician had in mind a remark Jim was said to have made to friends at the beginning of his illness: "If I thought I had cancer instead of heart disease, I believe I would shoot myself."

Surviving Jim, besides Vera, were brother Joe and three sisters, Mrs. J.A. McInerney of San Francisco, and Miss Esther Corbett and Mrs. J.A. Boyd, both of San Carlos, California. Factors of distance and time prevented them from attending the funeral mass and burial services.

Hundreds of people came to view Jim's body, both at home and at the funeral parlor. Thousands of telegrams and letters flooded the Corbett house.

Funeral services were held two days later at St. Malachy's Roman Catholic Church, on Forty-ninth Street, just off Broadway. The Reverend John Hayes, a parish priest from Sacred Heart Church, Bayside, and frequent visitor to the Corbett home during Jim's last days, celebrated a high requiem mass.

The press estimated that more than 4,000 people attended Jim's funeral services. Some one hundred celebrities were named honorary pallbearers. They included boxing luminaries Gene Tunney, Jack Dempsey, Joe Humphries (official Madison Square Garden announcer), and William Muldoon (of the New York Athletic Commission), Jack Sharkey, and old friend Jim Jeffries. Among theater people were Gene Buck, Charles Dillingham, Harry Hershfield, George M. Cohan, William Collier, Fred Stone, and De Wolf Hopper.

Newspaper sportswriters included Ring Lardner, Damon Runyon, Paul Gallico, and Grantland Rice. Among political and civic leaders in attendance, the most notable were James A. Farley, President Roosevelt's chief of staff, Judge Harry McDevitt, former New York City mayor, governor, and presidential candidate Alfred E. Smith, and former Gotham mayor Jimmy Walker.

Upon hearing of Jim's death, the entire town of Bayside went into mourning, for Jim had been as popular among his neighbors as with his friends of boxing and theater days.

A long procession followed Jim's hearse to Cypress Hills Cemetery, where he received a brief but formal burial ceremony. Jim had chosen Cypress Hills so that Vera, who was not Catholic, could ultimately lie next to him. The casket was placed in an ornate mausoleum that Jim had previously purchased.

A month later, Jim's will was filed in Queens County Surrogate Court. In approximately one hundred words, Jim left his entire estate—estimated at close to $100,000 (more than a million by current standards)—to Vera, who was also named sole executrix. The will, witnessed by sisters Catherine and Mary, was dated October 20, 1903.

Vera revealed that Jim's life savings had been converted into gold certificates, on the advice of a banker friend, shortly before the stock market crash. Vera turned in all the certificates to the government and paid the inheritance tax on them, as well. "He left enough cash to keep me comfortable as long as I live," she stated with proud affection. "He left me independent for all my days."

As if having held back until Jim died, when people spoke fondly of him now, nearly all of them freely employed the moniker "Gentleman Jim," by which he is familiarly known to this day.

Vera continued to live at the Corbett home until she died on September 10, 1959. She was buried next to Jim. During her later years, Vera participated in various local civic activities. She often entertained at home and, in nostalgic moments, spoke lavishly and lovingly of her adventures with Jim.

Nine years after his death, Warner Bros. began production of the movie "Gentleman Jim," based very loosely on the early portions of Jim's book, "The Roar of the Crowd." When the movie was finally released, it contained little that was true to Jim's life. Errol Flynn reluctantly portrayed the title role. He didn't like the part and often delayed shooting of the film. Extensive script rewrites reflected the many letters, meetings, and litigations required to smooth out rights issues, the use of specific place names, and the substitution of actual events.

In the end, Vera received $18,000 for rights to the book. Jim's ghost writer, Robert Gordon Anderson, got $2,000, only after he brought a suit against the studio because they had neglected to recognize his copyright. Aged, angry, and senile, Joe Choynski got $1,000 to keep his mouth shut. Joe Corbett, the last surviving member of the famed Corbett clan, thought the movie a travesty.

The movie resulted in two radio adaptations: one by the Screen Guild Theater in 1944; the second by Theater of Romance in 1946. Erroll Flynn played Jim in both shows.[4]

To honor Jim, Bayside changed the street name on which the Corbett home was located to Corbett Road. Streets in San Francisco and Reno were named after Jim, as well. In October, 1971, thirty-eight years after Jim's death, the Bayside Historical Society dedicated a plaque in his honor in the front yard of the old Corbett home. It read:

James J. Corbett
1866   1933
World's Heavyweight
Boxing Champion
1892   1897
Beloved Resident
of Bayside
who resided at
221-04 Corbett Road
1902   1933

At various of Jim's anniversaries, members of the Bayside Historical Society visit the Corbett mausoleum to pay their respects. Jim's boxing accomplishments continue to be related with appreciation, but the genuine man and equally remarkable aspects of his famed career have passed out of mind, as do those of most one-time public idols.

Although Jim's death had been expected for many weeks, news of the actual event brought countless tributes from the boxing and theatrical communities. Accolades for Jim's pugilistic prowess came from Jim Jeffries, Jess Willard, Tom Sharkey, Gene Tunney, and Max Schmeling—even Jack Johnson—all of whom recognized him as "the father of scientific boxing" and "the man who elevated boxing to legitimate status." Testimonials from England, Ireland, Germany, France, and Australia all hailed Jim as the "man who blazed the trail for the boxing profession."

W.O. McGeehan, renowned sports writer for the *New York Tribune*, summed up the press's feelings about Jim, the boxer.

With the death of James J. Corbett another figure of the romantic era of the American prize ring passes into the twilight of the modern demigods. In the romantic days of the prize ring there was little in the game except romance. But the demigods of the game lived on romance. Corbett never railed over the big purses they paid later. He had lived. Corbett made the greatest of ring dramas and revolutionized ring customs and ring ideals.[5]

With solemnity and deep respect, on behalf of theater colleagues, George M. Cohan hailed Jim's contributions to the entertainment world.

No man has ever had more warm and loyal friends in New York than this tall, slender, blue-eyed former heavyweight champion, one of the most popular members of the Friars and Lambs Clubs. Corbett was not only the best boxer who ever acted, but probably the best actor who ever boxed. He always had real thespian ability.[6]

Jim Corbett revolutionized boxing, changing it from brawling to an art. He changed the public role of champion, as well, dressing like a gentleman, behaving like a college graduate, and greeting the world with a smile instead of a scowl. Bringing a sense of decency to boxing, Jim attracted a better class of spectator and, doing so, helped legitimize the sport in our society.

Jim invested this appealing grace in popular theater, and the results were similar. Starting in 1892, he embarked on a theatrical career that was astounding for its success and variety. During the late 1890s, he was the highest paid actor on the popular stage. Jim helped pioneer vaudeville, bringing to it the same kind of legitimacy and hero worship as he had brought to boxing.

Jim's long-term success in popular entertainment was due to his ability to convince audiences of his down-to-earth humanity. He came across as a courteous, unassuming, self-effacing man, one with a profound talent for making and keeping friends. He was friendly to everyone, a pal, a member of the family, a stranger on the street. "How's the folks?" his usual greeting, touched everyone he encountered.

Jim had a vibrant sense of humor and acute intuition with regard to the value of a joke. He was willing to do anything to produce a laugh, even—indeed especially—if the joke happened to be on him. Audiences loved him all the more for it.

Present at the creation of film heroes, Jim personified the role of fearless adventurer. The compelling personality he transmitted over the footlights came across strongly on the silver screen, with equal success.

For all entertainment idols in our culture, no matter the era, age is the greatest adversary. When, inevitably, they slip from public view, they become ephemeral characters. It is then that their authentic lives, as interpreted by later, distant observers, are made the subjects of self-serving myths, fantasies, preconceptions, and fabrications. Like those of many of America's legendary headliners, Jim's authentic story tells of an individual's triumph over obstacles, emerging from the rigors of a tough childhood to enjoy the well-earned rewards of a conquering hero, a faithful rendition of the classic American Dream. Let us accept these colorful lives at face value, for their unrefined naturalness, endearing simplicity, and good, old-fashioned nostalgia.

As James J. Corbett proved to all the world, with talent, commitment, and courage (and a little luck of the Irish), dreams do come true.

PERFORMANCE CHRONOLOGY

1884

James J. Corbett's first amateur boxing encounter with Billy Welsh, Ariel Rowing Club's middleweight champion. Spring

1884–85

Many boxing exhibitions with members of the Olympic Club including Watson (Corbett's instructor), Kenealy, McCord, Requa, McCarthy, and a return match with Billy Welsh. Exhibition with Jack Dempsey, the "Nonpariel." In November, Corbett wins the heavyweight trophy at an Olympic Club tournament

1886

Exhibitions at Olympic Club including Mathews, Watson, McCarthy.

No. 1 professional bout: Corbett (fighting under the name of Jim Dillon), vs. Duncan McDonald, July 13, 1886, Salt Lake City, Utah; six rounds; draw

1887

Exhibitions at Olympic Club including P.T. Goodloe, Tom Johnson. Corbett given job teaching boxing two days a week at the Golden Gate Athletic Club. Exhibition at Olympic Club: Corbett vs. Jack Burke, August 28, 1887, eight rounds, no decision

1888

Watson resigns as Olympic Club boxing instructor. Corbett appointed instructor. Corbett exhibitions against Kenealy and Frank Glover (two rounds at testimonial for Tom Cleary)

1889

Corbett exhibition against Rich McCord (two rounds at benefit for Joe McAuliffe)

Corbett vs. Joe Choynski, May 30, 1889, in barn near Fairfax, California, four rounds, no decision

Corbett vs. Joe Choynski, June 5, 1889, on barge near Benetia, California, twenty-seven rounds, Corbett winner

Exhibition: Corbett and Joe Choynski, July 15, 1889, four rounds, no decision (benefit for Choynski)

Corbett exhibition against John Donaldson, four rounds, no decision

December 21, 1889, Corbett resigns instructor position at Olympic Club to face Dave Campbell

No. 2 professional bout: Corbett vs. Dave Campbell, December 28, 1889, Portland, Oregon; ten rounds; draw

1890

No. 3 professional bout: Corbett vs. Jake Kilrain, February 17, 1890, New Orleans, Louisiana; six rounds; Corbett winner

March: Corbett rehired as boxing instructor by Olympic Club

Exhibition: Corbett vs. Dominick McCaffrey, April 14, 1890, New York Athletic Club, New York; four rounds; Corbett declared winner

September: Corbett resigns instructor position at Olympic Club

1891

January 31, 1891, Corbett and John Donaldson, boxing exhibitions. Parson Davies Vaudeville Company, Eighth Street Theater, New York (between act interludes), one week

February 6, 1891, Corbett and John Donaldson, boxing exhibitions. Parson Davies Vaudeville Company, Hyde & Behman's Theater, Brooklyn, New York; one week

February 16, 1891, Corbett and John Donalson, boxing exhibitions. Parson Davies Vaudeville Company, Olympic Theater (one week); Madison Street Opera House (one week), Chicago, Illinois

No. 4 professional bout: Corbett vs. Peter Jackson, May 21, 1891, California Athletic Club, San Francisco, California; sixty-one rounds; draw

June 26, 1891, exhibition: Corbett and John L. Sullivan, Bush Street Theater, San Francisco; three rounds (Sullivan appearing in melodrama "Honest Hearts and Willing Hands" at theater)

August 13, 1891; "After Dark," Taylor's Opera House, Trenton, New Jersey, Corbett sparring with Jim Daly, three rounds, as interlude between acts. After three weeks, sparring act is inserted into third act concert hall scene; 15 weeks, 18 cities

1892

January 1 to March 26, 1892, "After Dark", on tour; 12 weeks, 12 cities

February 16, 1892, three boxer exhibition, New York: Corbett and Bill Spillings, one round, Corbett and Bob Coffey, one round, Corbett and Joe Lannon, three rounds. Corbett declared winner of all bouts

April 9, 1892, exhibition: Corbett and Mike Donovan, New York Athletic Club, New York, two rounds, no decision (Donovan's annual benefit)

June 3, 1892, "Sport McAllister," Opera House, Canton, Ohio, Corbett and Daly sparred in performance; one night, June 6, 1892; "Sport McAllister," Bijou Theater, New York; Corbett and Daly in speaking and sparring roles; one week

No. 5 professional bout: Corbett vs. John L. Sullivan, September 7, 1892, New Orleans, Louisiana; twenty-one rounds; Corbett wins heavyweight championship

James J. Corbett in "Gentleman Jack," opened October 3, 1892, Temple Opera House, Elizabeth, New Jersey; on tour; 13 weeks, 15 cities

1893

January 1 to April 15, 1893, "Gentleman Jack"; on tour; 15 weeks, 21 cities

James J. Corbett in "Gentleman Jack," opened June 10, 1893, Haymarket Theater, Chicago, Illinois, two weeks (in conjunction with Chicago World's Fair)

July 2 to July 29, 1893, James J. Corbett in boxing exhibitions at Chicago World's Fair (Midway Plaisance) as part of small vaudeville company; two-a-days

August 24, 1893, "Gentleman Jack," Opera House, Newberg, New York; one week

1894

No. 6 professional bout: Corbett vs. Charley Mitchell, January 25, 1894, Jacksonville, Florida; three rounds, Corbett winner

"Gentleman Jack," opened January 29, 1894, Boston Theater, Boston, Massachusetts; on tour; 10 weeks, 10 cities

"Gentleman Jack" tour of England, Ireland, and France, April 21 to August 6, 1894

"Gentleman Jack," opened August 14, 1894, Opera House, Asbury Park, New Jersey; on tour; 13 weeks, 18 cities

September 7, 1894, Corbett vs. Peter Courtney, Edison Kinetoscope film; six rounds, Corbett winner (planned outcome)

1895

January 1 to May 4, "Gentleman Jack," on tour; 18 weeks, 28 cities

November 4, 1895, exhibition: Corbett and Steve O'Donnell, spar three rounds between acts of "The White Squadron", Lyceum Theater, Memphis, Tennessee

James J. Corbett in "A Naval Cadet," opened November 25, 1895, Lynn Theater, Lynn, Massachusetts; on tour; 4 weeks, 4 cities

1896

January 1 to May 2, "A Naval Cadet," on tour; 17 weeks, 31 cities

No. 7 professional bout: Corbett vs. Tom Sharkey, June 24, 1896, San Francisco, California; four rounds; draw

"A Naval Cadet," opened October 17, 1896, Glen Falls Theater, Glen Falls, New York; on tour; 9 weeks, 11 cities

1897

January 1 to February 12, 1897, "A Naval Cadet," on tour; 5 weeks, 5 cities

No. 8 professional bout: Corbett vs. Bob Fitzsimmons, March 17, 1897, Reno, Nevada; 14 rounds, Fitzsimmons wins heavyweight championship

April 12, 1897, Corbett and John McVey spar between the acts of "The Man-O-War Man," National Theater, Philadelphia, Pennsylvania, one week

April 19 to May 23, 1897, "A Naval Cadet," on tour; 4 weeks, 4 cities

"A Naval Cadet," opened October 4, 1897, Columbus Theater, New York; on tour; 11 weeks, 11 cities

1898

January 1 to January 29, 1898, "A Naval Cadet," on tour; 4 weeks, 3 cities

James J. Corbett in "The Adventurer," opened January 31, 1898, Grand Opera House, Peoria, Illinois; on tour; 5 weeks, 9 cities

"A Naval Cadet," opened March 7, 1898, Maguire Opera House, Butte, Montana; on tour; 9 weeks, 12 cities

No. 9 professional bout: Corbett vs. Tom Sharkey, November 22, 1898, New York; 9 rounds; Sharkey winner (McVey, Corbett second, jumped into ring stopping bout)

1899

Summer: opening of Corbett's Bar and Poolroom, Thirty-fourth Street and Broadway, New York

James J. Corbett in revue, "Around New York in 80 Minutes," opened November 11, 1899, Koster & Bial's Music Hall, New York; 6 weeks, on tour one week

1900

January 1 to February 3, 1900, "Around New York in 80 Minutes," on tour; 4 weeks, 4 cities

No. 10 professional bout: Corbett vs. Jim Jeffries, May 11, 1900, Coney Island, New York; 23 rounds, Jeffries winner

No. 11 professional bout: Corbett vs. Kid McCoy, August 30, 1900, New York; five rounds, Corbett winner

1901

White Rats benefit performances in February

James J. Corbett, headliner, White Rats Vaudeville, opened March 3, 1901, Columbia Theater, Washington, D.C., on tour; 7 weeks, 3 cities

1902

March 30, 1902, Actor's Home benefit, New York, James J. Corbett, headliner

April 26, 1902, Lamb's Gambol, New York, James J. Corbett, headliner

Vaudeville, James J. Corbett, headliner (monologues), opened July 14, 1902, Morrison's Theater, Rockaway Beach, New York; on tour; 3 weeks, 3 cities

"The Empire Show," vaudeville, James J. Corbett (monologues), opened September 28, 1902, Davidson Theater, Milwaukee, Wisconsin; on tour; 13 weeks, 12 cities

1903

January 1 to April 4, "The Empire Show," on tour; 13 weeks, 13 cities

Vaudeville, James J. Corbett, headliner (monologues), opened April 27, 1903, Proctor's 125th Street Theater, New York, on tour; 4 weeks, 3 cities

August 1-2, 1903, James J. Corbett and Nance O'Neill in Shakespeare's "As You Like It," Sutro Heights Park, San Francisco, California

No. 12 professional bout: Corbett vs. Jim Jeffries, August 14, 1903, San Francisco, California; ten rounds, Jeffries winner

Vaudeville, James J. Corbett, headliner (monologues), opened August 31, 1903, Highlands Theater, St. Louis, Missouri, on tour; 9 weeks, 8 cities

1904

January 25 to June 25, 1904, vaudeville, James J. Corbett, headliner (monologues), on tour; 12 weeks, 12 cities

James J. Corbett in "Pals," opened September 12, 1904, Proctor's Fifth Avenue Theater, New York, on tour; 13 weeks, 15 cities

1905

January 1 to April 15, 1905, "Pals," on tour; 15 weeks, 16 cities

April 17 to November 6, 1905, periodic vaudeville appearances on Proctor's circuit; on tour; 9 weeks, 6 cities

1906

James J. Corbett in "Cashel Byron's Profession," opened January 1, 1906, Hyperion Theater, New Haven, Connecticut, on tour; 6 weeks, 4 cities

Vaudeville, James J. Corbett, headliner (monologues), opened March 5, 1906, Proctor's 58th Street Theater, New York, (Proctor's circuit); on tour; 11 weeks, 4 cities

James J. Corbett in "The Burglar and the Lady," opened September 3, 1906, Opera House, Scranton, Pennsylvania, on tour; 16 weeks, 33 cities

1907

January 1 to April 27, 1907, "The Burglar and the Lady," on tour; 17 weeks, 22 cities

Vaudeville, James J. Corbett, headliner (monologues), opened May 20, 1907, Chestnut Street Opera House, Philadelphia, Pennsylvania; on tour, periodic appearances; 7 weeks, 6 cities

September 14 to December 31, 1907, "The Burglar and the Lady," on tour; 15 weeks, 23 cities

1908

January 1 to May 23, 1908, "The Burglar and the Lady," on tour; 20 weeks, 43 cities

Vaudeville, James J. Corbett, headliner (monologues), opened June 22, 1908, Fifth Avenue Theater, New York, on tour; 4 weeks, 2 cities

James J. Corbett in "Facing the Music," opened August 10, 1908, Bennett's Theater, Montreal, Canada; on tour; 20 weeks, 74 cities

1909

January 1 to April 18, 1909, "Facing the Music," on tour; 15 weeks, 48 cities

Vaudeville, James J. Corbett, headliner (monologues), opened May 3, 1909, Alhambra Theater, New York, on tour; 6 weeks, 4 cities

Vaudeville tour of England and Ireland; headliner, monologues; July 10 to September 18, 1909

1910

Vaudeville, James J. Corbett, headliner (monologues), opened January 3, 1910, Fulton Theater, Brooklyn, New York, on tour; 10 weeks, 6 cities; (William Morris circuit)

Advisor/consultant to Jim Jeffries in match with Jack Johnson, April to July, 1910

Vaudeville, James J. Corbett, headliner (monologues), opened July 10, 1910, American Roof Garden, New York, 3 weeks

James J. Corbett in George Evans' Honey Boy Minstrels; interlocutor and monologist; opened August 13, 1910, City Theater, New York, on tour; 20 weeks, 20 cities

1911

January 1 to May 24, 1911, George Evans' Honey Boy Minstrels, on tour; 21 weeks, 44 cities

Vaudeville, James J. Corbett, headliner (monologues), opened June 26, 1911, Brighton Beach Music Hall, Brighton Beach, New York; one week

Vaudeville, James J. Corbett and Company, opened September 11, 1911, Temple Theater, Hamilton, Canada, on tour; 7 weeks, 6 cities

1912

January 1 to March 30, 1912, James J. Corbett and Company, on tour; 13 weeks, 8 cities

Summer filled with Friar's Frolic tour, three cities, Lamb's Gambol tour of two cities, and Vaudeville Club benefits in two cities

Vaudeville, James J. Corbett and Company, opened July 1, 1912, Palisades Park, New Jersey, on tour; 6 weeks, 4 cities; tour terminated because of acute appendicitis and pneumonia

1913

Vaudeville, James J. Corbett, headliner (monologues), opened March 24, 1913, Empress Theater, Denver, Colorado, on tour with periodic appearances for two months; 4 weeks, 4 cities

James J. Corbett in production of movie "The Man From the Golden West"

Vaudeville, James J. Corbett, headliner (monologues), opened September 1, 1913, East End Theater, Memphis, Tennessee, on tour with periodic appearances for three months; 5 weeks, 5 cities

1914

Vaudeville, James J. Corbett, headliner (monologues), opened January 5, 1914, Broadway Theater, Philadelphia, Pennsylvania, on tour; 11 weeks, 3 cities (Loew's circuit)

Lamb's Gambol, opened May 22, 1914, on tour; 11 cities in 10 days

James J. Corbett in production of movie "The Burglar and the Lady"

Vaudeville, James J. Corbett, headliner (monologues), September 17, 1914, Orpheum Theater, Clinton, Iowa; 2 days; October 11, 1914, Orpheum Theater, Peoria, Illinois; 3 days

Vaudeville, James J. Corbett, headliner (monologues), opened November 2, 1914, Pantages Theater, Winnipeg, Canada, on tour; 8 weeks, 6 cities (Pantages circuit)

1915

January 1 to January 30, 1915, vaudeville, on tour; 4 weeks, 3 cities

Vaudeville tour of Australia, headliner (monologues), February 16 to June 26, 1915

James J, Corbett in "Brother Bill", a George M. Cohan production, opened August 30, 1915, Opera House, Atlantic City, New Jersey; 2 weeks

James J. Corbett in production of movie "The Other Girl"

1916

Friar's Frolic tour, opened May 27, 1916; 15 cities, 3 weeks

Lamb's Gambol tour, opened July 12, 1916; 2 cities, 2 weeks

"Lights" benefit tour, opened August 9, 1916; 6 cities, 3 weeks

Vaudeville, James J. Corbett, headliner (monologues), opened October 4, 1916, McVicker's Theater, Chicago, Illinois, on tour; 12 weeks, 7 cities (U.B.O. circuit)

1917

January 1 to January 31, 1917, vaudeville, on tour; 4 weeks, 1 city

White Rats strike, February through April

Vaudeville, James J. Corbett, headliner (monologues), opened May 2, 1917, Orpheum Theater, Brooklyn, New York, on tour; 9 weeks, 4 cities

Lamb's Gambol, June 17, 1917, Corbett and Tinney comedy duo

"Lights" benefit tour, opened July 29, 1917; 8 cities, 2 weeks

July through September, series of shows at military camps, Corbett and Tinney

Corbett and Tinney in "Doing Our Bit," Shubert production, opened October 17, 1917, Winter Garden, New York; 10 weeks

1918

January 1 to May 15, 1918, "Doing Our Bit,"

Winter Garden, New York, 5 weeks; Shubert Theater, Montreal, Canada, 3 weeks; Shubert Theater, Baltimore, Maryland, 1 week; Shubert Theater, Washington, D.C., 2 weeks; Chestnut Street Opera House, Philadelphia, Pennsylvania, 4 weeks; Palace Music Hall, Chicago, Illinois, 7 weeks

Corbett and Wilson, vaudeville, opened December 21, 1918, Colonial Theater, New York; 2 weeks

1919

James J. Corbett in production of Universal Pictures 18-episode serial, "The Midnight Man" (January to July)

Actors' Equity Strike, August 6, 1919; strike ends September 7, 1919

1920

James J. Corbett in production of Universal Pictures "The Prince of Avenue A"

Van and Corbett, vaudeville, opened April 21, 1920, Colonial Theater, New York, on tour; 11 weeks, 6 cities

September to November, Corbett works on Harding presidential campaign

October 13, 1920, Corbett obtains judge's license to officiate at boxing bouts; works weekly bouts at Starlight Park, Bronx, New York through remainder of year

1921

January 1 to January 19, 1921, Corbett as boxing judge; venue goes bankrupt

Van and Corbett, vaudeville, opened February 9, 1921, Hamilton Theater, New York, on tour; 12 weeks, 5 cities (Keith circuit)

Van and Corbett, vaudeville, opened August 3, 1921, Rockaway Beach, New York, on tour; 13 weeks, 12 cities (Keith circuit)

Van and Corbett in production of movie "The Beauty Shop" (cameo roles)

1922

January 1 to May 31, 1922, Van and Corbett, vaudeville, on tour; 18 weeks, 17 cities (Orpheum circuit)

Van and Corbett, vaudeville, opened June 21, 1922, Keith's Theater, Washington, D.C., on tour; 3 weeks, 3 cities

July: James J. Corbett makes a series of phonograph records for a physical culture company

Van and Corbett, vaudeville, opened August 23, 1922, Opera House, Atlantic City, New Jersey, on tour; 17 weeks, 15 cities (Keith circuit)

1923

January 1 to March 21, 1923, Van and Corbett, vaudeville, on tour; 11 weeks, 9 cities (Keith circuit)

June to August: James J. Corbett in "Ziegfeld Follies," comedy routine with Jack Norton, and monologue

Corbett and Norton, vaudeville, opened October 1, 1923, Keith's Theater, Albany, New York, on tour; 5 weeks, 5 cities

1924

James J. Corbett in production of movie "Broadway After Dark" (cameo role)

Corbett and Norton, vaudeville, opened April 21, 1924, Orpheum Theater, Sioux City, Iowa, on tour; 26 weeks, 22 cities (Orpheum circuit)

1925

January 1 to February 25, 1925, Corbett and Norton, vaudeville, on tour; 7 weeks, 4 cities

James J. Corbett lecture tour, opened March 11, 1925, General Motors Company, Detroit, Michigan, on tour; 8 cities, 4 weeks

Corbett and Norton, vaudeville, opened August 15, 1925, Capitol Theater, Chicago, Illinois, on tour; 4 weeks, 2 cities (Corbett and Norton separate)

Corbett and Barry, vaudeville, opened September 23, 1925, Rialto Theater, Amsterdam, New York, on tour; 7 weeks, 7 cities (Keith circuit)

1926

January 1 to May 17, 1926, Corbett and Barry, vaudeville, on tour; 20 weeks, 19 cities (Keith circuit)

Corbett and Barry, vaudeville, opened September 1, 1926, Pantages Theater, Toronto, Canada, on tour; 16 weeks, 16 cities (Pantages circuit)

1927

January 1 to June 12, 1927, Corbett and Barry, vaudeville, on tour; 15 weeks, 13 cities (Pantages circuit)

Corbett Special Train to Tunney/Dempsey bout, Chicago, Illinois, September 22, 1927; 5 days

Corbett and Barry, vaudeville, opened November 17, 1927, Boulevard Theater, New York, on tour; 6 weeks, 3 cities (Loew's circuit)

1928

January 1 to May 13, 1928, Corbett and Barry, vaudeville, on tour; 19 weeks, 17 cities (Loew's circuit)

August-September: James J. Corbett "health farm," Wappingers Falls, New York

September-November: James J. Corbett testimonial ads for Barbisol shaving cream in various magazines

1929

Corbett Special Train to Sharkey/Stribling bout, Miami, Florida, February 24 to March 3, 1929, in conjunction with Friar's Frolic

James J. Corbett promoting American Health Sports Carnival, Grand Central Palace, New York, May 18-25, 1929

Friar's Frolic, May 20, 1929, Corbett and Dempsey comedy duo

Corbett and Dempsey, vaudeville, opened May 28, 1929, Balaban & Katz Theaters, Chicago, Illinois; 4 weeks

James J. Corbett in production of movie "Happy Days" (cameo role)

Corbett and O'Brien, vaudeville, opened July 13, 1929, Keith's Theater, Syracuse, New York, on tour; 20 weeks, 18 cities (Keith circuit)

1930

January 1 to April 1, 1930, Corbett and O'Brien, vaudeville, on tour; 15 weeks, 9 cities (Keith circuit)

June: Vitaphone short with Neil O'Brien, comedy dialogue

October: Vitaphone short, "At the Round Table"

1931

Friar's Frolic, June 21, 1931, James J. Corbett as interlocutor (Corbett's last public appearance)

September: 26 fifteen minute radio interviews on health and physical well-being, sponsored by Mail Pouch Tobacco

1932

June: James J. Corbett, author of "Health Hints for Amateur Athletes," published by Department of Health (ghost-written)

CHAPTER NOTES

1. Hard Road to Respectability

1. Mormon Library, Salt Lake City, Utah; South Mayo (Ireland) Family Research Center

2. Asbury, *The Barbary Coast.*

3. *Ibid.*

4. Burchell, *The San Francisco Irish, 1848–1880.*

5. San Francisco Directory, 1856 to 1900.

6. W.M. Kramer & M.B. Stern, "San Francisco's Fighting Jew," *California Historical Quarterly*, 53, No. 4, Winter, 1974.

2. Escapades In and Out of the Ring

1. The History of the Olympic Club, San Francisco.

2. Corbett, *The Roar of the Crowd,* p. 18.

3. *The History of the Olympic Club.*

4. *San Francisco Chronicle,* Aug. 25, 1885.

5. *Ibid.,* July 20, 1886.

6. *Ibid.,* Jan. 27, 1887.

7. *Ibid.,* March 10, 1887.

8. *Ibid.,* Aug. 8, 1887.

9. *Ibid.,* Aug. 15, 1887.

10. Kramer & Stern, "San Francisco's Fighting Jew."

11. *San Francisco Chronicle,* Feb. 13, 1888.

12. *Ibid.,* March 26, 1888.

13. *Ibid.,* April 23, 1888.

14. *Ibid.,* May 21, 1888.

15. *Ibid.,* July 9, 1888.

16. *Ibid.,* April 29, 1889.

17. *Ibid.,* June 6, 1889.

18. *Ibid.,* June 10, 1889.

19. *Ibid.,* July 22, 1889.

20. *Ibid.,* Oct. 21, 1889.

21. *New York Clipper,* Jan. 11, 1890.

3. The Road to Sullivan

1. *San Francisco Chronicle,* April 17, 1890.

2. *Ibid.,* March 3, 1890.

3. *New York Clipper,* April 12, 1890.

4. *San Francisco Chronicle,* March 31, 1890.

5. *New York Clipper,* April 19, 1890.

6. *New York Times,* April 19, 1890.

7. *San Francisco Chronicle,* April 12, 1890.

8. *Ibid.,* Dec. 30, 1890.

9. *New York Clipper,* Jan. 31, 1891.

10. *Ibid.,* Feb. 28, 1891.

11. *San Francisco Chronicle,* April 13, 1891.

12. *Ibid.,* May 14, 1891.

13. The *New York Clipper* offers a detailed description of the entire bout, round by round. Additional "color" details can be found in the *San Francisco Chronicle,* May 22, 1891.

14. *San Francisco Chronicle,* May 25, 1891.

15. *Ibid.,* June 25, 1891.

16. *Ibid.,* June 27, 1891.

17. Brady's life is colorfully reprised in his two biographies, *The Fighting Man,* published in 1916, and *Showman,* published in 1937. Dates and specific episodes mentioned by Brady involving Jim Corbett have to be regarded with caution.

18. *New York Clipper,* Aug. 15, 1891.

19. *Ibid.,* Aug. 22, 1891.

20. *Ibid.,* Oct. 17, 1891.

21. *Ibid.,* Jan. 2, 1892.

4. *Fight of the Century*

1. *New York Clipper,* March 12, 1892.
2. *San Francisco Chronicle,* Aug. 29, 1892.
3. *New York Clipper,* Sept. 3, 1892.
4. *New York Herald,* Sept. 3, 1892.
5. The account of the Corbett-Sullivan championship bout was collated from reports in the *New York Times, Chicago Tribune, San Francisco Chronicle,* and *New York Clipper.*
6. *New York Times,* Sept. 8, 1892.
7. *San Francisco Chronicle,* Sept. 8, 1892.
8. *New York Clipper,* Sept. 17, 1892.

5. *The Irresolute Champion*

1. *New York Clipper,* Nov. 26, 1892.
2. *Ibid.,* Nov. 12, 1892.
3. *Ibid.,* Dec. 10, 1892.
4. *Boston Globe,* Dec. 10, 1892.
5. *New York Clipper,* June 24, 1893.
6. *Ibid.,* Nov. 11, 1893.
7. *Ibid.,* Nov. 25, 1893.
8. *San Francisco Chronicle,* Jan. 25, 1894.
9. *New York Clipper,* Feb. 3, 1894.
10. *The Era,* April 14, 1894.
11. *New York Clipper,* May 26, 1894.
12. *The Era,* June 16, 1894.
13. See: Musser, *Edison Motion Pictures, 1890–1900,* for a detailed discussion of the film's production.
14. *New York Clipper,* Sept. 15, 1894.
15. *Ibid.,* Sept. 15, 1894.

6. *Trial and Tribulation*

1. An excellent biography of Dan Stuart and his boxing promotional career can be found in Miletich, *Dan Stuart's Fistic Carnival.*
2. *New York Clipper,* Nov. 30, 1895.
3. *Ibid.,* Dec. 14, 1895.
4. *Ibid.,* March 7, 1896.
5. *Ibid.,* April 4, 1896.
6. *San Francisco Chronicle,* June 25, 1896.
7. *Ibid.,* Aug. 25, 1896.
8. *New York Clipper,* Oct. 31, 1896.
9. *Chicago Tribune,* March 2, 1897.
10. *Ibid.,* March 8, 1897.
11. *Ibid.,* March 11, 1897.
12. *Ibid.,* March 15, 1897.
13. *San Francisco Chronicle,* March 19, 1897.
14. *New York Clipper,* April 24, 1897.

15. *Ibid.,* Oct. 4, 1897.
16. *Ibid.,* Oct., 23, 1897.
17. *Ibid.,* Feb. 12, 1898.
18. *Ibid.,* April 2, 1898.
19. *San Francisco Chronicle,* March 29, 1898.

7. *On the Edge*

1. *San Francisco Chronicle,* Aug. 17, 1898.
2. *New York Clipper,* Nov. 11, 1899.
3. *Ibid.,* Nov. 18, 1899.
4. *San Francisco Chronicle,* May 8, 1900.
5. *Ibid.,* May 9, 1900.
6. *Ibid.,* May 12, 1900.
7. *New York Times,* May 13, 1900.
8. *San Francisco Chronicle,* May 13, 1900.
9. *Ibid.,* Sept. 16, 1900.
10. *Ibid.,* Sept. 15, 1900.
11. *Ibid.,* Sept. 20, 1900.
12. *Ibid.,* Sept. 24, 1900.

8. *Knock Down, Knock Out*

1. For the story of the White Rats see: Golden, *My Lady Vaudeville and Her White Rats.*
2. *New York Clipper,* March 9, 1901.
3. *Ibid.,* March 16, 1901.
4. *San Francisco Chronicle,* Nov. 16, 1901.
5. *Chicago Tribune,* Oct. 6, 1901.
6. *Ibid.,* Oct. 10, 1901.
7. Examples of Jim's monologues can be found in various joke books, like Case, *Vaudeville Wit,* and Newton, *Some Vaudeville Monologues.*
8. *New York Clipper,* Jan. 24, 1903.
9. *Ibid.,* April 4, 1903.
10. *San Francisco Chronicle,* May 10, 1903.
11. *Ibid.,* Aug. 15, 1903.
12. *Ibid.,* Aug. 15, 1903.

9. *Tour de Force*

1. *New York Clipper,* Oct. 8, 1904.
2. *Chicago Tribune,* Nov. 26, 1904.
3. *New York Clipper,* Feb. 18, 1905.
4. *New York Times,* April 15, 1905.
5. *New York Clipper,* April 22, 1905.
6. *New York Times,* Jan. 9, 1906.
7. *New York Clipper,* March 17, 1906.
8. *Ibid.,* March 24, 1906.
9. *Chicago Tribune,* Jan. 12, 1907.

10. *New York Herald,* Oct. 8, 1907.
11. *New York Clipper,* Oct. 19, 1907.
12. *Chicago Tribune,* Jan. 27, 1908.
13. *San Francisco Chronicle,* March 30, 1908.
14. *New York Clipper,* June 27, 1908.

10. Men of Color

1. *The Era,* July 31, 1909.
2. *Ibid.,* Aug. 2, 1909.
3. *The Stage,* Aug. 26, 1909.
4. *New York Clipper,* Dec. 25, 1909.
5. *San Francisco Chronicle,* July 5, 1910.
6. *New York Herald,* July 11, 1910.
7. *New York Clipper,* July 23, 1910.
8. *Ibid.,* Aug. 13, 1910.
9. *Ibid.,* Nov. 23, 1912.
10. *Ibid.,* June 21, 1913.

11. Multi-Media Headliner

1. *New York Dramatic Mirror,* Sept. 20, 1913.
2. *Variety,* Aug. 8, 1913.
3. *New York Clipper,* Dec. 27, 1913.
4. *Ibid.,* May 16, 1914.
5. *San Francisco Chronicle,* Feb. 16, 1915.
6. *New York Clipper* Sydney, Australia, correspondent, March 9, 1915.
7. *Ibid.,* May 22, 1915.
8. *Ibid.,* June 12, 1915.
9. *San Francisco Chronicle,* June 25, 1915.
10. *New York Clipper,* Oct. 30, 1915.
11. *Ibid.,* Oct. 7, 1916.
12. *Ibid.,* June 6, 1917.
13. *New York Times,* Oct. 18, 1917.
14. *New York Journal,* Oct. 18, 1917.

12. A Man for All Occasions

1. *New York Clipper,* Dec. 21, 1918.
2. *New York Dramatic Mirror,* Dec. 21, 1918.

3. *Ibid.,* Jan. 4, 1919.
4. *Ibid.,* Feb. 28, 1920.
5. *Variety,* Feb. 27, 1920.
6. *New York Clipper,* April 21, 1920.
7. *Ibid.,* July 17, 1920.
8. *Ibid.,* July 24, 1920.
9. *Dramatic Mirror,* Sept. 25, 1920.
10. *New York Clipper,* March 2, 1921.
11. *Variety,* March 12, 1922.
12. *San Francisco Chronicle,* April 7, 1922.
13. *New York Clipper,* July 12, 1922.
14. *Ibid.,* Aug. 30, 1922.
15. *Variety,* Oct. 4, 1922.
16. *Ibid.,* April 25, 1924.
17. *San Francisco Chronicle,* June 10, 1924.

13. Anything for the Money

1. *Variety,* Jan. 7, 1925.
2. *Ibid.,* Jan. 7, 1925.
3. *Ibid.,* Jan. 6, 1926.
4. *New York Times,* March 23, 1926.
5. *Variety,* Sept. 28, 1927.
6. *Ibid.,* Sept. 28, 1927.
7. *Ibid.,* March 6, 1929.
8. *Ibid.,* May 20, 1929.
9. *Ibid.,* Dec. 25, 1929.
10. *Ibid.,* Jan. 8, 1930.
11. *Ibid.,* April 2, 1930.

Epilogue

1. *Variety,* Dec. 10, 1930.
2. *Ibid.,* Sept. 8, 1931.
3. *Brooklyn Daily Eagle,* Feb. 19, 1933.
4. University of Southern California Cinema-Television Library: Warner Bros. Archives
5. *New York Herald Tribune,* Feb. 19, 1933.
6. *Boston Globe,* Feb. 26, 1933.

BIBLIOGRAPHY

Archives, Collections, Libraries

American Motion Picture Arts and Sciences
Archdiocese of San Francisco, Chancery
  Archives
Bayside Historical Society
Bayside Public Library
California Historical Society
Friar's Club
International Boxing Hall of Fame
Institute of the American Musical
Lamb's Club
Library of Congress-Film Division
Mormon Library, Salt Lake City, Utah
Museum of the City of New York
Nevada State Library and Archives
New York City Vital Statistics Department
New York Public Library at Lincoln Center,
  Billy Rose Theater Collection
Olympic Club, San Francisco
San Francisco Directory
San Francisco Public Library—History Center
Shubert Archive
Sutro Library, San Francisco
University of California, Los Angeles,
  Microfilm Library
University of Southern California, Cinema-
  Television Library
University of Southern California, Special
  Collections
Vitaphone Project

Periodicals, Newspapers, Miscellaneous Publications

Dramatic News, 1890 to 1910

Dramatic Review, 1900–1914
National Police Gazette, 1885–1930
New York Clipper, 1888 to 1923
New York Dramatic Mirror, 1890 to 1922
San Francisco Chronicle 1884–1911
Variety, 1906 to 1933

SELECTED ISSUES FROM:

Billboard
Green Book
Literary Digest
Motion Pictures
Photoplay
Ring
Saturday Evening Post
Stage
Theater

SELECTED NEWSPAPER ARTICLES, 1886 TO 1933, FROM:

Alta California
Bayside Times
Boston Globe
Chicago Tribune
The Era (London)
The Illustrated Sporting and Dramatic News
  (London)
Los Angeles Times
Miami Herald
Milwaukee Sentinel
New York Herald
New York Times
New York World
San Francisco Chronicle
San Francisco Examiner
The Vaudeville News

Books

Asbury, Herbert. *The Barbary Coast.* New York: Knopf, 1933.

Brady, William A. *Showman.* New York: Dutton, 1937.

———. *The Fighting Man.* Indianapolis: Bobbs-Merrill, 1916.

Burchell, R.A. *The San Francisco Irish. 1848–1880,* Berkeley: University of California Press, 1979.

Case, C.B., (ed.) *Vaudeville Wit.* Chicago: Shrewesbury, 1917.

Corbett, J.J. *How to Build Muscle.* 1931.

———. *Jabs.* New York: R.K. Fox Athletic Library, 1907.

———. *The Roar of the Crowd.* Garden City: Garden City Publishing Co. 1925.

———. *Scientific Boxing.* New York: R.K. Fox Athletic Library, 1905.

———. (edited by Frederic A. Felton). *My Life and My Fights.* 1910.

DeFord, Miriam Allen. *They Were San Franciscans.* Caldwell, Ida.: Caxton, 1941.

Doherty, William J. *In the Days of the Giants.* London: G.C. Harrap, 1931.

Durant, J. *The Heavyweight Champions.* New York: Hastings House, 1973 (revised edition).

Fields, A. *Eddie Foy.* Jefferson, N.C.: McFarland, 1999.

———. *Lillian Russell.* Jefferson, N.C.: McFarland, 1999.

Fleischer, Nat. "*Gentleman Jim*": *The Life Story of James J. Corbett.* New York: Ring Magazine, 1942.

———. *The Heavyweight Championship: An Informal History of Heavyweight Boxing from 1719 to the Present Day.* New York: Putnam, 1949.

———, and Sam André. *An Illustrated History of Boxing.* Secaucus, N.J.: Citadel, 1997 (revised edition).

Fox, R.K. *Life and Battles of James J. Corbett: Champion of the World.* New York: National Police Gazette, 1894.

Gilbert, D. *American Vaudeville: Its Life and Times.* New York: Whittlesey House, 1940.

Golden, G.F. *My Lady Vaudeville and Her White Rats.* New York: The Board of Directors of the White Rats of America, 1909.

Gorn, E.J. *The Manly Art: Bare Knuckle Prize Fighting in America.* Ithaca: Cornell University Press, 1986.

Guttman, A. *From Ritual to Record: The Nature of Modern Sports.* New York: Columbia University Press, 1978.

Harding, William Edgar. *The Life and Battles of James J. Corbett.* New York: R. K. Fox, 1892.

The History of the Olympic Club. San Francisco: Art Publishing Co., 1893.

Hoff, S. *Gentleman Jim and the Great John L.* New York: Coward, McCann & Geohegan, 1977.

Isenberg, M.T. *John L. Sullivan and his America.* Urbana: University of Illinois Press, 1988.

Johnson, A. *Ten and Out.* New York: Ives Washburn, 1927.

Kelly, H.P. (ed.). *Gems of Irish Wit and Humor.* New York: Geo. Sully & Co., 1906.

Lahue, K.C. *Continued Next Week: A History of the Moving Picture Serial.* Norman: University of Oklahoma Press, 1964.

Lurie, C.N. *Make 'Em Laugh.* New York: Putnam, 1927.

Miletich, L.N. *Dan Stuart's Fistic Carnival.* College Station: Texas A & M University Press, 1994.

Mrozek, D.J. *Sport and American Mentality, 1880–1910,* Knoxville: University of Tennessee Press, 1983.

Musser, C. *Edison Motion Pictures, 1890–1900: An Annotated Filmography,* Washington, D.C.: Smithsonian Institution Press, 1997.

Myler, P. *Gentleman Jim Corbett: The Truth Behind a Boxing Legend.* London: Robson Books, 1998.

Newton, H.L. *Some Vaudeville Monologues.* Chicago: T.S. Denison, 1917.

O'Brien, R. *This Is San Francisco.* New York: Norse, 1948.

The Ring Record Book. Nat Fleischer edition, New York: Ring Book Shop, 1960.

Roberts, R. *Jack Dempsey, The Manassa Mauler.* New York: Grove, 1979.

———. *Papa Jack: Jack Johnson and the Era of White Hopes.* New York: Free Press, 1983.

Sammons, J.T. *Beyond the Ring: The Role of Boxing in American Society.* Urbana: University of Illinois Press, 1988.

Somers, D. *The Rise of Sports in New Orleans 1850–1900.* Baton Rouge: Louisiana State University Press, 1972.

Spehr, P.C. *The Movies Begin: Making Movies in New Jersey 1887–1920.* Newark: Newark Museum, 1993.

Van Court, DeWitt C. *The Making of Champions in California*. Los Angeles: Premier Printing Co., 1926.

Van Every, E. *Sins of New York As "Exposed" by the Police Gazette*. New York: Frederich A. Stokes, 1930.

Articles and Essays

Adams, W.H. "New Orleans as the National Center of Boxing." *Louisiana Historical Quarterly* 39 (1956).

Corbett, Mrs. J.J. "How My Husband Whipped the Great John L." Auction catalog, 1945.

Collins, N. "History of Corbett." *Ring*, February 1930.

"Corbett to Tunney on 'How to Win the Mob.'" *Literary Digest*, January 14, 1928.

Davids, L.R. "Jim Corbett Playing First Base." *Baseball Research Journal*, 1983.

"The D'Artagnan of the Prize Ring." *Literary Digest*, March 4, 1933.

Earl, P.I. "The Fight of the Century." *Nevada* 57, no. 2 (March/April 1997).

Friscia, J.T. "The Man Who Beat John L."

Kramer, W.M., and N.B. Stern. "San Fran-cisco's Fighting Jew." *California Historical Quarterly* 53, no. 4 (Winter 1974).

Naughton, W.W. "James J. Corbett." *The Blue Book of Sports*.

O'Brien, R. *Riptides*: "Gentleman Jim and the County Surveyor." *San Francisco Chronicle*, February 16, 1948.

_____. *Riptides*: "The Squaring of Gentleman Jim." *San Francisco Chronicle*, March 10, 1948.

_____. *Riptides*: "Gentleman Jim Pens a Note." *San Francisco Chronicle*, July 29, 1949.

_____. *Riptides*: "Gentleman Jim, Actor of the Century." *San Francisco Chronicle*, August 18, 1950.

_____. Riptides: "Mrs. Corbett Looks Back." *San Francisco Chronicle*, April 21, 1952.

Sequeira, J. "Le Preux Chevalier of the Winged 'O.'" *Olympian*, December 1960.

Sher, J. "Gentleman Jim, The Man Who Licked John L." *Sport*.

Streible, D. "A History of the Boxing Film 1894–1915." *Film History* 3, no. 3 (1989).

Weston, S. "James J. Corbett: Bringing Science and Sophistication to the Sport." *World Boxing*, October 1990.

Woods, A. "James J. Corbett: Theatrical Star." *Journal of Sport History* 3, no. 20, 1976.

INDEX

251